How real is the
DIVINE
REVELATION?

J.U. CHOWDHURY

CONTENTS

This is a research oriented analysis and discussion on religion that claims to have originated in the heavens! The trustworthiness of this claim has been investigated logically against scientific backdrop with reference to some Hadiths and selected verses from the Quran.

PREFACE

Religion is a sensitive subject and most people have a tendency to avoid discussing it in public as it relates to a number of embarrassing questions! It is a fact that a great majority of mankind still believe in religion! They practice religion because their ancestors humbly did the same! People all over the world get automatically integrated into religious subjugation passed on from generation to generation accepting it as a way of life! This is how propagation of various forms of religions and dogmatic ideologies continued to dominate over mankind from the very early days of civilization! In the past questions have been raised by a handful of our ancestors who had doubts about the existence of heavenly creatures and their impact on humans but others took existence of heavenly deities for guaranteed and had accepted all creations around them not only as a proof but also as an answer to their questions and queries! Their intellectual development did not reach to that level so as to think of a creation without a creator! What the Prophets or the Popes said on genesis was taken seriously! Progress of dogmas and doctrines overtook science and civilization in the race and as a result various ideologies with different views had been able to brainwash a great majority the mankind! Legitimacy of these faiths and doctrines need to be evaluated against a scientific perspective! Science and religion cannot stay together as that will be highly detrimental to the mankind! It is also not possible for the mankind to come to terms with two contradictory discipline that are loaded with conflicting concepts and contents widely opposed to one another! The world has a significant number of people who still believe that the God brings the sun from the east to the west during the day and returns it to the west at night! I may remind the readers that I am not a physicist, yet I would like to give you a brief history of the present state of research into the creation of the cosmos being pursued by the scientific community worldwide! If we trace back the roots of the creation in scientific terms, eventually we have to end up at the elementary particle or the so-called "God Particle"! Even if we take it for guaranteed that the God has created the tiny elementary particle, question still remains to be resolved as to who created the "Biggest Particle"; the God? Of what particle God himself is made of? If the God has a creator, then who is the creator of that creator?

This is an open ended question with no answer in sight! Do we really need a creator? Is the creator indispensable to life? Do other creatures worry about their creators as humans do? After nearly fourteen billion years, since the Big Bang, science has been able to come up with something that partially answers our question about the beginning of the creation of the universe! Out of four fundamental forces, scientists had tough time explaining the gravitational force! In the late seventeenth century, for the first time Newton was able to explain in a rational manner why the apples fall down on earth and not going towards the sky! Though the "Fall of Apple" was scientifically accepted but the story of the "Fall of Adam" still remains foggy! John Milton, a compatriot as well as a contemporary of Newton, took a different stand to make people believe that the God took only "Six Days" to create everything! But the "Creation" strategy is so complex that even after fourteen billion years, we, the best of all creatures, have not been able to find what particle we are made of! The mankind is still searching for that very "Equation" which will be able to explain and unify all forces of the universe! Newton explained how all planets of the solar system including the earth are tied to the sun and move around it due to its gravitational force! In most cases his idea worked well until the discovery of General Theory of Relativity by Albert Einstein in 1915! He dismissed the theory on gravitational force developed by Newton! His ground-breaking discovery of the "Theory of General Relativity" and a new dimensional concept called the "Space-Time" provided better explanation why the planets and other heavenly bodies rotate around bigger objects in the space maintaining a bond between them! He visualized the Space-Time as a spider-web made of very thin fabrics! The spider makes the web to catch its victims for survival but the God, like a weaver, made his web extending from the earth to the heaven to catch the Godless people to fill the hell! Many physicists, including Einstein, insisted that the space is not flat, as previously thought, but wrapped or curved! Whereas Allah, the Lord of the Seven Heavens and the author of the Quran says that he "Spread Out" the earth and then "Affixed" mountains on it so that it does not move or shake! Every matter in the universe is on the move and nothing is flat. Gravity of the bigger objects make smaller objects revolve around it! Even the stars of the galaxies revolve once in millions of years around the supermassive Black Hole located at the center of the galaxy! Theory of relativity has gone through many tests and trials and proved to be real for scientific applications such as GPS! However, its application is limited to bigger objects like Galaxies, Stars, Planets etc.! Another theory developed by other physicists known as "Quantum Theory" or "Quantum Mechanics" works well on miniature objects like Atoms, Protons, Neutron and other subatomic particles! This Quantum Mechanics also suggests that the space is filled with many "Quantum Fields" which are the real building blocks of the universe! All scientists including Einstein were looking for a theory that could be called 'Theory of Everything" to unify and explain all four forces of nature! They are desperately trying to find that magic elementary particle to explain its role in the creation of everything of the cosmos! The Relativity theory and the Quantum theory together cannot solve the puzzle of the creation! So the scientists also need a "God Equation" which might again involve a more complex mathematical nightmare! Thousands of scientists joined hands to carry out an experiment at LHC! The experiment resulted in the discovery of a particle known as "Higgs Boson" often referred to as "God Particle"! There appeared another confusion about "Higgs Boson" as some physicists say that there may be more than one of them! But this is not the end of the story! The "Standard Model" or the "Periodic Model" needs more particles to be found! Present LHC is incapable of producing such particles. Some scientists hope that upgrading the LHC might solve the problem! Yet the quest for the ultimate particle, like the "Quest for the Holy grail" may not come to an end so soon! Then comes the so-called "Super Symmetry" which suggests that every particle has a "Super Partner"! It seems that we may have to build a collider as powerful as the "Big Bang"! Out in the space, there may be still many more particles waiting to be discovered since no one knows the exact number of particles created after the Big Bang! So far many potential hypothesis emerged and out of all "String Theory" is the one that has been able to draw attention as a likely solution to the puzzle but not without inherent shortfall! Yet a community of scientists believe that this theory has the potential to come up with a solution that they are looking for! String vibrations appear to have more capabilities to generate particles with more variants! In less than hundred years ago it was established beyond doubt that our universe is expanding every moment with an accelerated speed! This discovery has put an end to the old idea of a "Stationary State" of the universe! What causing the universe to expand so rapidly? Is there a "Creator" out in the space either pushing or pulling the universe to expand to the End? But where is the end? Some scientists believe in the "No boundary Condition" of the cosmos! Allah claims he has planted a "Lot-Tree" at the outermost boundary of the heaven beyond which nothing can pass! So far most of the scientists, save a few, have been focusing only on the aftermath of the "Big Bang"! What went before the "Big Bang"? What was all around that "Singularity" which exploded releasing immeasurable amount of energy? Was it an absolutely empty space around the Singularity? Many physicists think that the expansion of the universe is being caused by the so-called dark energy that alone accounts for 68% of the total energy of the universe but no one knows how it was created! Another claim suggests that the universe is made of more than ninety percent of dark matters which are not visible as they do not reflect light! There may be a probable relation between the dark energy and the dark matter! It is not entirely unlikely that before the Big Bang, the universe was already filled with a "Quantum Field" due to some mysterious force or energy? The initial Inflation caused by the Big Bang may have a connection with the dark energy which is causing the expansion of the universe to accelerate! This expansion may not come to a halt until the universe itself is swallowed by an extra-ordinary super massive Black Hole with its massive force of gravitation many times stronger than that of the dark energy! The other scenario suggests that the expansion may ultimately convert all matters of the universe back into energy leaving it in a state of super coolness! The probable transformation of dark energy into dark matter or vice versa deserves in depth scientific investigation considering the ground breaking equation of Einstein (E=MC squared) This is necessary because some of the scientists believe dark energy as the fifth fundamental force! As of now no scientific evidence is available to describe how the void looked like before the "Big Bang"! What the computer model suggests is also not an empty space! Can we not hypothesize a scenario, assuming that the vacuum around the "Singularity", before the Big Bang, was already filled with dark energy? Why the tiny particle of the "Singularity" exploded fourteen billion years ago and why not before or after? May be that was time when the "Singularity" could not hold itself together in one piece due to a mysterious force! How and where God existed if nothing existed before creation? No sooner the massive explosion of the Big Bang occurred, it may have begun pushing the dark energy with its massive inflation paving the way for the creation of the Space-Time since that explosion is also assumed to be the beginning of Time! Immensely powerful waves created by the Big Bang encountered no opposing force rather it was amplified many times by the repulsive force of the dark energy resulting in the continuous expansion of the universe! If it is found to be true, as per Quantum Theory", that the universe was already filled with "Fields" of invisible forces, which might have aided the expansion of the universe creating waves of outward motions in all directions! This process may have continued for hundreds of millions of years and by the time all celestial bodies like Galaxies, Stars, Planets, Black Holes, etc. began to form in different size and shapes! Albert Einstein introduced a "Cosmological Constant" in order to explain the expansion of the Space-Time which he later described as one of his greatest mistakes! After his death many scientists have accepted it as a far-sighted thinking into the mystery of the expansion of the universe! After the expansion began, initial temperature of millions of millions of degrees dropped to a level that facilitated the creation of various celestial bodies! Due to gravitational force, large objects began to collide with one another releasing particles of different kinds having diverse characteristics in terms of mass, color, flavor and electrical charges! How do we get the vibrations of the "Strings" that the "String Theory" predicts? According to this theory different vibrations of the strings create different subatomic particles! Besides the dark Energy, the acceleration to the expansion of the universe may have been augmented by incessant gravitational waves created by the collisions of the billions of massive Black Holes in all the galaxies in space! Creation of large objects like galaxies, stars, Black Holes etc. is a continuous process and frequency of collision between them is also on the rise! So these gigantic waves, created mostly by the collision of the large Black Holes, travel in a circular motion and add to the ones preceding them and accumulatively provide more acceleration to the ultimate wave that pushes the boundaries of the universe to a point of no return! Game of mighty gravitational forces is responsible for the continuous destruction and creation of matters all over the cosmos! We also cannot forget that the cosmological "Arrow of Time" is pointing outward in the direction of expansion! Convergence of the universe into another Singularity, called the "Big Crunch", may not happen as predicted! We know when a particle comes into contact with an anti-particle, they evaporate leaving only the energy! Existence of anti-matter is a reality and every particle has its counterpart with opposite charge. Death of our universe might happen at any point of time if it comes into contact with a universe made of anti-matter! The consequence is easily understood! Over the last few hundred years, the world has seen hundreds of physicists coming up with many hypothesis on the creation of the universe! Emerging ideas often do not supplement one another as the scientists are not Gods! This helps the terrorist reinforce their propaganda against science and humanity! Since they view the "Creation" as a matter of God and as such humans have no right to fiddle with it! However, either way the mankind is not going to see a happy ending of their doom! The "Creator" is busy preparing for the resurrection of the mankind of this mini planet while the scientists are looking for Multiverse or the Parallel universe! Allah says Islam is the only religion he has chosen for the whole of mankind! The Sun, the Moon and the planet Earth are the three celestial bodies that are closely linked to Islamic rituals. Allah, as the Master of the Creation, wants the entire mankind to follow the religion of his own choosing and to materialize this simple objective he has created an endless universe filled with billions of trillions of galaxies, stars, planets, black holes etc.! This hugely disproportionate creation of matters itself puts a question mark on the existence of Allah and his claim of being the "Creator"! How does the so-called "Anthropic Principle" fit into God's scheme? How and where the "Resurrection" or the "Day of Judgment" will take place in this ever-expanding universe? Let us wait and see what JWST (James wave space telescope) brings to light from the past and compare with what has been said by the prophets, priests and popes since the beginning of the dogmatism!

INTRODUCTION

This work is purely a personal endeavor undertaken to express my own views and observations on religion against a scientific perspective! In my view it is completely possible to lead a life on earth disowning any religious obligations or disregarding all divine interventions that have no relevance to human existence! It is rather the dogmatic interference in our life that takes away liberty and freedom! We cannot blame our ancestors for being loyal to the unseen! What about those living in the civilized world? Could anyone, since the dawn of civilization, present the slightest testimony in favor of the existence of a "Creator"? By all means this is an unfeasible task! Ghosts and Gods both exist only in imagination! Enormous fictions and fantasies have been told and retold about Gods and Ghosts ever since the humans came into being! What about Gods? Do they live in heavens hiding in Dark Matter! Civilized world has not seen a single ghost in reality! Since the inception, mankind has gone through millions of catastrophic debacles! Did anyone of those Gods intervene when devastations play havoc on humanity? "It is darkest before the dawn", but I feel that the darkness is over; there will be a stirring of fresh life, a kindling of new desires! Let "The Gods descend from Olympus and live once more amongst men" so that we don`t have to ascend to the "Seventh Heaven" to look for the "Creator"! In the absence of science, divine faiths and forces filled the vacuum! It was easy to mislead men with miracles! The entire humanity is ashamed of past and present immoral activities of the papal regime in their holy enclaves! Cruel atrocities in the name of some assumed divine beings have been rampant across the globe! Nothing of that sort could dent the reputation of the scientific community! After the renaissance we have found Galileo, Newton, Einstein, Darwin, Hawking and others who carried the torch of science to cultivate civilization; illuminate the humanity! Has the world seen arrival of another Moses, Jesus or prophet Muhammad? Why the so-called divine revelations stopped after the seventh century? Because the dark days of deception disappeared as soon as the sun of science appeared over the horizon!

Why and how humans are here on this planet is still an issue globally debated by the scientists and philosophers! The "Anthropic Principle" is still a matter of contention! The best gift of evolution was that it enabled humans to walk on two legs emanating from their four-footed ancestors! Whether we are direct descendent of Apes or Adam has gone under scrutiny after the discovery of the three and a half feet fossil of "Lucy" in Africa! Since then we have attained, on an average, a height of six feet through evolution! We do not know the height of Eve but that of Adam was 90ft; claims Allah, the "Creator"! For reasons best known to him, Allah decided to reduce our height gradually from ninety feet down to around six! Apparently Charles Darwin and many of the modern scientists have viewed evolution as the only natural process that has resulted in the evolution of humans and other creatures on earth! Can any of the spiritual leaders deny the scientific facts that life begun on earth from tiny microbes and thru transformation of single to multicellular bacteria? On the other hand religious scholars and believers claim earnestly that the life was created by some "Creator" living in the heaven! The Quran says that Adam was created by Allah in his own "Image" by his "Two Hands"! Adam, the first man was miraculously created and obviously he began to walk upon landing on earth! This was Allah's special favor to father of mankind! But his offspring cannot walk immediately after being born save the animal's! The most popular divine story that mesmerized all mankind about their origin is the Adam-Eve saga! Surprisingly they have no more stories to tell about the origin of life of other creatures on earth except that Allah sent eight pairs, two pairs each of four species of animals namely Sheep, Camels, Goats and Oxen! These contrasting views on creation, based on information drawn from science and scriptures, have divided the mankind and since then the religions and the realities remained entangled into continuous conflicts and confrontations! Though the evolution of life on earth took millions of years and that process is more realistic than the story which tells us that fall of a pair of man and woman from heaven initiated the procreation! The Lord's plan had an inherent fault in it! The creation of Satan was a mistake! To sum up his plan in a nutshell; the "Creator" created Adam and Eve and dropped them on his farmland to create generations after generations so that he could rule over them as the absolute "King" to implement his doctrine of Monotheism without any opposition from any rival! After death he will resurrect all to judge them for their deeds on earth and accordingly they will either be punished or rewarded on the "Day of

Judgment"! Under these rigid terms and conditions set by the "King", only a handful of men might qualify for a place in paradise and the rest would be shouting aloud from the hell; "Burning, burning, burning! Burning with the living dead! O Lord, pluck me out but the Lord wouldn't listen!

With the gradual development of brains, humans switched from menial to mental activities! Though intellectually retarded on a large scale, yet they formed groups and cults to celebrate social events for entertainments and thanks-giving for the "Benevolent" living above their heads in the heavens! Our ancestors after going through a long process of evolution attained a unique physical stature different from the rest of the creatures! Despite the lengthy transformation process of evolution, humans have retained more than ninety eight percent similarities to their four-footed ancestors in terms of DNA! This scientific fact is enough to highlight our real identity whether we are the offspring of Adam or Apes! Despite the discovery of this revolutionary fact, many people of scriptures are still not convinced! Addiction to religion is more dangerous than addiction to drug! A difference between man and apes of less than two percent in terms of DNA has helped humans to grow a sense of superiority over all other creatures and made them feel that they are not made to be "Gone with the wind"! But the old notion, that there must be "Someone" over their head who may have "Created" them and as such he has exclusive rights to "Discipline" them, lingered in their thought process! Later they invented the idea of dogmatism to feel that they are not abandoned like the roaming animals and grew a sense of pride for being able to dominate over the beasts! So, the "One" who is "Overseeing" their actions from the sky deserves to be worshipped! In that darkness of time they were naturally amazed by the vast sky blooming with stars! People were misled into believing that a star can be used as a missile to hit the devils on earth! It was the "Creator", not the asteroids, who misguided them! As a matter of fact what has instilled the "Existence" of a powerful "Creator" as an absolute "Truth" in the minds of those ancients is the complex relationship between the "Stationary" earth and the revolving sun and moon around it! Cycle of events repeating precisely round the year, involving these three heavenly bodies, further cemented the existence of deities! What never came to their thinking, until the scientific discovery of Nicholas Copernicus in early fifteenth century, that the earth is round and revolving around the sun like other planets of the solar system! That was a period when every aspects of administration, governance, all disciplines of knowledge including the science, religion, philosophy, astronomy etc. were in the hands of the priests! They claimed that their right to rule over man stemmed from the ultimate "King" of the Heaven! For many centuries, these priests enjoyed their absolute right to rule over the loyal subjects undisputedly! His doubt on the existence of an unseen "Creator" may have inspired young Shelley, still a freshman, to write a Pamphlet entitled "The necessity of Atheism"! In the primal stages most people who lived in caves under the open sky viewed everything around them as the "Home" with a sky as its canopy created by an unseen power! The "Power" that never speaks! Coleridge, switching from poetic pantheism to religious orthodoxy, wrote; "And we did speak only to break; The silence of the sea"! He could not break the silence of the "Creator God"! Thunders, thought to be the voice of the God, threatened and terrified the people and poets alike! Fresh ideas, constructive attributes and scientific innovations, evolved out of enlightened human knowledge, helped mankind come out of darkness! What about that comes from the merciful "Creator"? Are the blessings coming from him always constructive; without detrimental impacts on life? The rain that comes from above to save life also kills life! Calamities coming from heaven have destroyed the climate of trust on the "Creator"! As every particle has an anti-particle, so it is not unlikely that the Lord has an Anti-Lord! Think of water against fire, rain against drought, light against darkness, creation against destruction, life against death, heaven against hell, angels against devils, mercy against curse, vice against virtues, war against peace! Creator's actions contrast sharply with his promises! Then what makes the "Creator" different from the "Created"? Only the invisibility? What about the truth and transparency? The "Creator" who has no creator is taking away all the benefits of doubt! His threats and temptations are yet to be understood by his creatures!

"IN THE NAME OF ALLAH, THE MOST GRACIOUS, THE MOST MERCIFUL"; this is the meaning of the first verse of the Quran and by virtue of being born in an orthodox Muslim family, I am also obliged to begin writing this book in the name of Allah! All Muslims are obliged to utter this verse before they intend to do anything! Allah also began writing the Quran "In the name of Allah" since he is not "Created", he does not have to dedicate his work in the name of his "Creator"! Unfortunately this first verse itself has given birth to the first controversy regarding the so-called revelation! Allah also claims that this first verse, because of its extraordinary significance, is preserved in the "Mother Book" of the Quran held with him at his Throne over Seven heavens! No Islamic scholars can say for sure that this first verse of the Quran was revealed first! The verses of the Quran are neither revealed nor compiled in chronological order! Allah, the "Time Creator" had taken long twenty three years to reveal the Quran in stages, yet Prophet Muhammad and his close associates could not maintain chronological discipline of the revelation! So, how can we believe that the Lord has finished creation of the earth and the heavens only in "Six Days"? With regard to revelation, collection, composition and compilation, the history of the Quran is a total mess! Did the "Revelations" really come from the "Time-Creator"? Allah is very much fond of appreciations! He has ninety nine names and each one of them denotes his multiple qualities! According to the defenders of Islam, the most appropriate name of Allah is "RABB" and English language has no equivalent word for this as such they have chosen to use the word "Lord"! The word "RABB" means "The one and the only Lord for all the universe; its Creator, Owner, Organizer, Provider, Master, Planner, Sustainer, Cherisher and Giver of security"! To make a Confession as a Muslim, one has to say: "I TESTIFY THAT THE CREATOR OF ALL THE UNIVERSE INCLUDING THE STARS, THE PLANETS, THE SUN, THE MOON, THE HEAVENS, THE EARTH WITH ALL ITS KNOWN AND UNKNOWN FORMS OF LIFE, IS ALLAH"! In the words of "Confession" the Galaxies and Black Holes should have been included! There is no mention of any planets of our solar system in the entire Quran except the earth! To Allah, the Sun and the Stars have separate meanings since the Sun is so "Big" that he cannot use it as missile to hit the Devils!

Awakening of consciousness among our ancestors did happen even in that darkness of time! In other part of the contemporary world echoed a wonderful realism of a rational mind when Muhammad was still alive and preaching messages he claims to have received from Allah! A thane of King Edwin, in the year 627 A.D. while addressing the king, said; "IT SEEMS TO ME, O KING, THAT THIS PRESENT LIFE OF MAN, IN COMPARISON WITH THAT WHICH IS UNKNOWN TO US, IS AS IF YOU SAT AT THE BANQUET TABLE IN THE WINTER TIME, WITH YOUR CHIEFS AND YOUR MEN AROUND YOU, AND A FIRE BURNED, AND THE HALL WAS WARM, WHILE OUTSIDE IT RAINED AND SNOWED AND STORMED, THERE CAME A SPARROW AND SWIFTLY FLEW THROUGH ONE

DOOR, AND IT FLEW THROUGH THE HALL. IT CAME IN THROUGH ONE DOOR, AND IT FLEW OUT THROUGH THE OTHER. NOW, SO LONG AS HE IS INSIDE, HE IS NOT CUFFED BY THE WINTWR'S STORM, BUT THAT IS FOR ONLY A MOMENT, THE TWINKLING OF AN EYE, AND AT ONCE AGAIN HE GOES FROM WINTER BACK INTO WINTER. SO THIS LIFE OF MEN APPEARS BUT FOR A MOMENT. WHAT WENT BEFORE IT OR WHAT COMES AFETR IT, WE DO NOT KNOW. THEREFORE IF THIS NEW TEACHING BRINGS ANYTHING MORE CERTAIN OR FITTING, IT DESEVES TO BE FOLLOWED". So, we know nothing about our past and future but the present; which is "Only a Moment" but we got to take the momentous decision! New teaching that brings anything more certain or fitting deserves to be followed! At least we can learn from the new teaching of science that the Stars cannot be used as missiles to hit the devils by any divine or un-divine entity!

The ancient thinkers and writers freely borrowed from religions but cautiously refrained from crossing the "Red Line" so as to avoid being killed! Copernicus was afraid of the Papal regime to publish his views that the sun is at the center of our solar system! We also know what happened to Galileo! For the sake of truth, with an open mind, I have candidly tried to explain my point of view on religion, revelation and their relevance to creation, citing some tidbits from science and literature. Please don't get me wrong; you don't have to agree on everything I said in this book. Accepting resentment and disagreement graciously is key to achieving peace and tranquility.

DISCUSSION ON SELECTED VERSES FROM THE QURAN

The Quran contains 114 surah or chapters. Each chapter is composed of different number of verses. Some chapter contains hundreds of verses while some have only three to four verses. Chapter # 1 has only seven short verses while the chapter next to it has 286 verses! These chapters are divided into two groups; one group is called "MADANI" as because they were probably recorded or scripted in Medina! And those scripted in Mecca are called "MAKKI"! Interesting to note that only one or two Arabic alphabets can form a verse that are called the "Miracles" of the Quran and only Allah, the "Author" knows their meanings! The Quran as a whole is also defined as a "Miracle" from Allah to Prophet Muhammad! The Quran is often termed as the "Light" and a "Plain Statement"! Quran has a "Mother Book" also known as "Book of Decree" held with Allah at his palace in space! All verses of the Quran are said to have been derived from that Mother Book! The Quran is a medium size book of around three hundred (300) pages that Allah took twenty three (23) years to reveal through Gabriel, an winged angel created from light! The first chapter of the Quran comes with the title "Al-FATIHA" which has seven verses in it. Islamic scholars claim that this is the first complete chapter revealed! But they also say that Allah revealed some discrete verses before this Surah! Muhammad describes surah "AL-FATIHA" as the greatest surah in the Quran and says no other revealed books contain a "Surah" of this significance. Whoever does not recite "AL-FATIHA" in his prayer, his prayer will be invalid! Whoever attends five obligatory prayers, will have to recite this surah nearly fifty times a day! Imagine the ordeal of being a Muslim when Allah ordained his believers to go to mosque fifty times a day! Muhammad is said have brought the number down to five during his space mission after a lot of arguments with Allah on the advice of prophet Moses whom he met at the Sixth of the Seven Heavens! This surah is also regarded as an "Antidote" against all kinds of diseases! Muhammad suffered from prolong diseases, before his death at the age of 63, despite having such a powerful antidote at his disposal! Probably it proved to be ineffective! So, futility of the Allah's revealed verses begun with the prophet himself!

Verse-1, Ch-1: "IN THE NAME OF ALLAH, THE MOST GRACIOUS, THE MOST MERCIFUL"! This is the first verse of the Quran! What motivated Allah to write a book in his own name is a matter of concern for those who are not familiar with this kind of writing skill! Doubts creep into Quran right from its first verse as a book of religion and more so when it is claimed to have been written and revealed by Allah; the Lord and the creator of the universe! The meaning of the first verse itself is a clear evidence that someone deeply devoted to Allah began writing this book with these words of appreciations for his "Creator"! For instance, If Albert Einstein had written a book beginning with; "IN THE NAME OF ALBERT EINSTEIN, THE MOST FAMOUS, THE MOST LEARNED SCIENTIST", how would the readers react? The very first sentence of his book would have damaged his reputation not only as an author but also as a scientist! Another point of discord is that many Islamic scholars believe the first verse of the Quran actually belongs to another chapter called "AN-NAML"! This first verse of the Quran is also preserved in the "Book of Decree" held with Allah! Another peculiar aspect of the Quran is that all of its chapters begin "In the name of Allah, the most gracious, the most merciful" except one! The exception has happened with chapter # 9! Why? All-Knower Allah knows better! Prof. M.M. AZAMI of U.K. Islamic academy has brought to light an interesting fact about composition of the Quran saying; "The prophet used to instruct the scribes about the placement of different verses as they were revealed"! If so, then why the controversy started right from the first verse itself? Did Muhammad live until the compilation of the Book? What was the state of the manuscript when Muhammad died? All sorts of maneuvering that took place about the collection and compilation of the manuscript, since the death of Muhammad until the reign of UTHMAN, were incoherent as well as incomprehensive! All stories related to compilation were aimed at proving that the Quran was written by none but Allah! But the Arab Pagans always believed that the Quran was fabricated by Muhammad and his associates!

Verse-4, Ch-1: "THE ONLY OWNER AND ONLY RULING JUDGE OF THE DAY OF RECOMPENSE AND RESURRECTION". In fact the Quran has more than hundred verses linked to the Day of Resurrection giving good tidings to the believers and threatening disbelievers with dire consequences. I think it will not be irrelevant to give a short account of the Day as stated in the Quran: It will be a "Day of Destruction" and the end of the world. An angel named ISRAFEEL is entrusted with the task of blowing a horn to mark the beginning of the destruction. The blowing of the horn will take place on a Friday! Why Friday? ABU HURAIRAH, an authority on Hadiths, quotes Muhammad as saying; "THE BEST DAY ON WHICH THE SUN RISES IS FRIDAY; ON FRIDAY ADAM WAS CREATED, ON IT HE WAS ADMITTED INTO HEAVEN, ON IT HE WAS CAST OUT OF IT, AND THE HOUR WILL ARRIVE ONLY ON FRIDAY!". So Allah had chosen Friday since he considered it as the best day to create Adam; the first human being created by his "Both Hands"! According to science we cannot have Friday all over the entire planet simultaneously because of the relative position of the earth and the sun in our solar system! Adam was created in paradise, supposed to be situated over seven heavens! How does it have any relation with our weekdays on earth? Does the Lord follow the same calendar in the heavens as we do on earth? However, Allah Says: "I am AD-DAHR" or "I am the creator of time"! Being the "Time Creator" he may have a different concept of time! These weekdays are totally meaningless even in the neighboring planets of our solar system! Who invented these weekdays before the creation of Adam? What "Truths" and "Facts" do we get from the "Revelation"? One thing we cannot forget that Allah is almighty and claims that he is able to do everything at his will! Believing in Allah and his actions unquestionably is mandatory in Islam!

Verse-7, Ch-1: "THE WAY OF THOSE WHOM YOU HAVE BESTOWED YOUR GRACE, NOT OF THOSE WHO EARNED YOUR ANGER (JEWS AND CHRISTIANS)". Allah bestows grace only on the followers of Muhammad and he is displeased with the Jews and the Christians because they went astray! So all the messengers of Allah sent to the people of scriptures failed to bring them to the right path! Explaining this verse, the translators narrate a story that happened between Muhammad and a companion of his named ZAID BIN AMR about refusing to eat meat of an animal which was not slaughtered in Allah's name and this happened long before the Revelations! So, it is evident that Muhammad had his undisputed loyalty for Allah long before he was appointed a messenger and prophet! No other scriptures that came before had this name (Allah) mentioned in them! All sponsors of divine faiths conceived the idea of the existence of creator in their own world of imagination with a simple logic; since there is a creation, there has to be a "Creator" as well! They not only invented their creators but also named them differently in their own way and painted their pictures in many mysterious methodology! That is why the pictures and descriptions of ALLAH, GOD, ISHWAR, VAGHWAN etc. are dissimilar in their respective books of religions! A frequently asked question is who created Allah or God? The commonly conceived answer is; "Creator" is self–created. If an immensely powerful God or Allah can be created without a creator, why a bacteria needs a creator? Another event that happened to Muhammad's life, fifteen years before the revelation, was his first marriage to a wealthy Arab lady named KHADIJA when she was forty and Muhammad was only twenty five! Did Allah bestow his grace on their marriage? Islamic Sharia Law demands that some verses from the Quran must be recited during marriage ceremony to give the marital bond an Islamic legal status. Since the verses are said to have been revealed after fifteen years of his first marriage, so, what was read out to legalize his marriage with KHADIJA? Could that be called a Halal (Lawful) marriage? All of his marriages were abnormal and inconsistent to his personality and reputation as a Prophet. He married more than dozens of women aged between seven to seventy. AISHA was only six or seven when he married her. This minor girl was the daughter of Muhammad`s dearest friend ABU BAKR, the second caliph who succeeded him. How on earth the last and the best Prophet of Islam, who was entrusted to enlighten the mankind, could succumb to such a worst decision as to marry an underage girl? Did he not find a better option to look after a minor? Even a man of ordinary intellect would have adopted this little girl as his own daughter to provide her with all the love and protection she deserved. Surely this was not a graceful way! Dr. M. H. DURRANI, a Pakistani Islamic scholar defended the prophet by saying that he wanted to honor and cement his friendship with ABU BAKR through this marriage! What a noble example of friendship Muhammad has set for the mankind! May I ask what Dr. DURRANI would have done in such situation? Love is blind but not as blind as the Faith. Muhammad also married a widow; an old woman of seventy for the reason that she was one of the early converts to Islam. Mohammad set the example of polygamy among his followers and that is why polygamy is rampant in Islamic world specially among the Arabs. Slavery, another flop of his time, was wide-spread and having sex with the slave girls was not considered a crime when possessed by one's so-called "Right Hand"! MUTAH is another means of legalizing sex in an Islamic way! This is known as temporary marriage that may last for few hours to few days or weeks! This is another form of sexual slavery which is still practiced by some Muslim communities mostly in the Middle East! This is "THE WAY OF THOSE" who have earned the "Grace" of Allah, the Lord of judgment! And those who have earned his "Anger" have taken a different path!

Verse-1, Ch-2: "ALIF-LAM-MIM"! These are three alphabets of Arabic language and they form a complete verse! There are instances where a single Arabic alphabet is considered a verse in the Quran! This is one of the weird features of divine composition! The translators provided an explanation saying; "THESE LETTERS ARE ONE OF THE MIRACLES OF THE QURAN AND NONE BUT ALLAH ALONE KNOWS THEIR MEANINGS"! These translators are also professors of an Islamic university! May I ask how they explain these miracles to their students? Do they not ask questions? Muhammad, the messenger, was also in the dark about the meaning of these words! What Allah demands is nothing but unquestioning obedience! If the Quran is meant for the mankind, then why Allah kept these meanings within himself? Muhammad should have rejected these miracles as they are meaningless to the mankind! Muhammad's dilemma as a messenger was that he often took meteors for missiles coming from Allah! Galileo accepted, under papal pressure, to come to a conclusion that it is beyond men to understand the "Acts of God" and they cannot define boundaries of the dominion of the almighty! Yet Galileo won the war; popish hegemony is now history! Omniscient Allah's miracles are also beyond human's "Limited" knowledge and as such they are totally irrelevant to mankind! Papal days are gone and boundaries of man's knowledge is now defying limits! Mankind's domain of intellectual faculties expanding, keeping pace with the expansion of the universe! No reader would really understand Shakespeare without the Glossary of terms and terminology he used! But Allah's "Miracles" and the "Revelations" shall continue to remain beyond human understanding until the "Resurrection"! His miracles are as mysterious as his "Existence"! The Lord being invisible himself had chosen to send his messages for the mankind also through an invisible angel! Was that the best communication means available to him?

Verse-2, Ch-2: "THIS IS THE BOOK (THE QURAN) WHEREOF THERE IS NO DOUBT, A GUIDANCE TO THOSE WHO ARE PIOUS BELIEVERS OF ISLAMIC MONOTHEISM WHO FEAR ALLAH MUCH AND LOVE ALLAH MUCH". The Arab pagans were the first to express doubt on the Quran! However, this verse has cleared our misunderstanding about the Quran: Its messages are not meant for the entire mankind! Whereof there is no doubt that it is the book, a "Guidance" to those who are pious believers of Islamic monotheism! The Quran is a "Light", yet the believers do not find the right path to paradise! They are splintered into numerous groups! Some devotees visit mosques day and night seeking blessings from Allah! Others run after Mullah and get radicalized, killing friends and foes alike! In the name of Allah they are divided into SHIA, SUNNI, WAHABY etc.! Many of the devotees go round the KABAH at Mecca which, according to Islamic science, is located parallel to the "Throne" of Allah over Seven Heavens! Most of the terror groups, like the Taliban, the ISIS, the AL-QUIDA, AL-SHABAB are more interested to grasp power to rule over man on this earth than going to paradise! The Kings in the Muslim world regularly defy Allah's orders (Verse 118:3) to stay in power! Doing something out of love and doing something out of fear are quite different in tone and texture! The fanatics love Allah more than their loved ones! To them Killing is the most viable option to demonstrate their love for Allah! Prophet Muhammad also demanded similar love from his followers saying if they do not love him more than their fathers, children and the mankind, their faith will be invalid! How many of the world's population of seven billions honestly "Love" and "Fear" the Lord? Allah demands unquestioning love and loyalty in return for the life he has given to all humans! Rest of the creatures are born free! Let the mankind wait for the second coming of Jesus who, according to Muhammad, would rule the world for a period of only forty years by the Law of the Quran! He might have to "Revoke" Bible!

Verses-4 & 5, Ch-2: "AND WHO BELIEVE IN (THE QURAN AND SUNNAH) REVEALED TO YOU (MUHAMMAD) AND IN THAT WHICH WAS SENT BEFORE (TORAH AND GOSPEL) AND BELIEVE WITH CERTAINTY IN THE HERAFTER, (RESURRECTION, RECOMPENSE, HELL AND PARADISE) ARE ON TRUE GUIDANCE FROM THEIR LORD AND THEY ARE THE SUCCESSFUL"! So, what makes a man religiously successful, as per the conditions set in the above verses, is the one who believes in the revelations of Quran, Gospel or Torah and also have trust in the Hereafter, Resurrection, Hell and Paradise! It is a glad tiding from the Lord (Allah) to the people of scriptures! Above verses clearly acknowledge that the Torah and the Gospel are also revealed books like the Quran and assure all followers of those books that they "ARE ON TRUE GUIDENCE FROM THEIR LORD AND THEY ARE THE SUCCESSFUL".

Dr. M.T. AL-HILALI of Medina Islamic University Says; "He is the All-Mighty, Omnipotent. He sent his messengers and prophets to guide humanity towards monotheism"! The Christians and the Jews also follow monotheism but not "Islamic monotheism"! They have their own version of monotheism! The ambiguity regarding the revelation began with the creation of Adam! Islam claims that he was the first Muslim prophet! According to Dr. MANEH HAMMAD AL-JOHANI of Saudi Arabia; "Willing submission to God" is the essence of Islam which was "Revealed" to Adam and he passed that on to his offspring! But the truth of the matter is that Adam first submitted himself to the "Will of the Satan"! The messages revealed to Muhammad was applicable to all mankind and Jinn! Who is the father of Jinn? Who passed Allah's messages on to the Jinn? Another Islamic scholar from the same country Dr. ABDULLAH AL-KAHTANY says, "Allah has implanted his own religion (Islam) in innate, with which all humans are equipped"! Why then Allah kept sending prophets and messengers? The translators of this English version of the Quran gave very clear answer to this question saying, "Ever since the people innovated the dogma of SHIRK (joining others in worship along with Allah) Allah had been sending prophets and messengers to his devotees. As the divine revelation has stopped after the death of prophet Muhammad and it will not resume except at the time of the descent of Jesus"! First of all, the "Essence" of Islam was revealed to Adam and then Allah implanted religion of Islamic monotheism in innate with which all humans are equipped and lastly it is claimed that Allah began revelations only when people innovated other dogmas of their own liking! And with the death of Muhammad Allah stopped revelation and it will resume once again with the arrival of Jesus! Prophet Muhammad himself testified that Jesus would rule the mankind by the Law of the Quran! Why should he then require new revelation? Can anyone with sane mindset find coherence in the above statements made by those Islamic scholars about revelations? It is evident from the above verses that it was Allah who first began "The Battle of the Books" by sending books of revelations off and on, dividing mankind into believers and non-believers like the "Bees" and the "Spiders" in the battle between the Ancients against the Moderns! Though Jonathon Swift had no intention to highlight religious tension between the Catholics and the Protestants, yet he deserves thanks for his satirical intentions! The faithful want to suck heavenly honey in paradise as promised by a vast network of religions but the faithless people want to break away from that sticky "Web"! Prophet Muhammad demanded that the Christians and the Jews must recognize him as messenger of Allah to avoid being dwellers of hellfire! Why is it so important that Muhammad be recognized as the messenger of Allah? What about others? Were they not sent by Allah? It is to be noted that the words within the brackets in the above verses are not part of the revelation! The All-Mighty has not "Abrogated" these verses for bestowing blessings to the followers of Torah and Gospel and calling them as "Successful"! What is surprising is that Allah contradicts his own statement: "Truly, the religion with Allah is Islam" (V. 19:3)

Verse-6, Ch-2: "VERILY, THOSE WHO DISBELIEVE, IT IS THE SAME TO THEM WHETHER YOU (MUHAMMAD) WARN THEM OR DO NOT WARN THEM, THEY WILL NOT BELIEVE"! This is the thirteenth verse out of more than six thousand verses of the Quran! Allah has quickly realized that the revelation and the selection of Muhammad as the messenger for mankind is not going well! Allah might have spoken these words out of frustration! Can we lay our trust in the Lord who claims to have sent messengers for all nations and Muhammad for all of mankind and Jinn (A creation created by Allah from fire)? Prophet Muhammad died at the age of 63 leaving huge number of disbelievers to wait until Jesus's second coming for converting them to Islam! If Allah was so sure that the disbelievers would not believe despite being warned by Muhammad, then what was the need for sending so many prophets and messengers with divine revelations? This disposition of the "Creator" regarding his own creation makes his existence not only doubtful but turns it into a misconception! When Allah realized that the reality on ground was not going well as expected, he decided to end Muhammad's life untimely! Muhammad got depressed and disheartened for his failures as the only messenger for whole of mankind! He could not mobilize opinion of the mankind in his favor! In this respect Jesus did well! He could bring larger chunk of the mankind under his fold to form the largest religion; the Christianity! Under the new plan Allah would send Jesus as a Muslim prophet with a new set of revelations to rule over the world for a period of forty years only! If Jesus comes as a Muslim Prophet this time, he is likely to be "Crucified" by the Christians themselves and God may not be able to raise him to heaven leaving an imposter on the rood! What if Jesus fails to accomplish his mission to rule the world by the Law of the Quran? Lay the blame on Satan as he might still be alive and active to mislead Jesus into committing another "Original Sin"!

Verse-7, Ch-2: "ALLAH HAS SET A SEAL ON THEIR HEARTS AND ON THEIR HEARING AND ON THEIR EYES THERE IS A COVERING". So, Allah himself has sealed most important organs of the disbelievers! Could anyone be regarded as "Enemy" whose hearts, hearing and eyes are out of order by the grace of the Lord? In that situation how can a prophet preach his messages of Islamic monotheism amongst people whose vital organs are dysfunctional? This kind of revelations are not expected of a merciful "Creator"! Allah has promised to handover records of deeds to the disbelievers on the Day of Judgment to read for themselves what they did in this life on earth! So, at least on the Day of Judgment, functions of their senses will be restored in order to facilitate them to see and read their records! It is by all means a good decision! Every criminal has the right to see what charges have been brought against him! Will the Judge allow the criminals to defend themselves by alleging that they were misguided by the devils? Not a chance! Allah knowingly granted Satan a respite to mislead humans until resurrection keeping his hearts, eyes and hearing in good conditions! What would be the fate of the Satan on the Day of Judgment? Will he be resurrected? Probably not, since death will not touch him like humans! If Jesus on his arrival finds most people with impaired hearts, hearings and visions, will it be possible for him to convert them to Islamic monotheism? They will be deprived of accepting Allah's guidance! Specially he will face steep resistance from the Jews and the Christians! In his first mission he was "Crucified" by the Jews and this time the Protestants may be reluctant but the Roman Catholics are not going to show any mercy on him! Allah may kindly bring back all senses of the disbelievers to functional state since a level-playing field is essential for a fair trial! As for the mankind, there is still "A COVERING ON THEIR EYES" which needs to be removed to see the "Truth"!

Verse-10, Ch-2: "IN THEIR HEARTS IS A DISEASE (OF DOUBT AND HYPOCRISY) AND ALLAH HAS INCREASED THEIR DISEASE". Allah has indeed increased the disease of doubt and hypocrisy in the hearts of the mankind first by revealing his messages through an unseen angel and then by unleashing Satan to mislead Adam and his offspring! General expectation was that Allah would decrease the "Disease" to facilitate cultivation of his Islamic monotheism in the hearts of those hypocrites! But his actions have increased "Doubts" on his own sagaciousness! Allah's plan of action to induce entire mankind into Islamic monotheism has failed because of strategic failures! Doubt in the hearts of so-called hypocrites persisted ever since Allah kept sending messages to Muhammad and it multiplied when revealed verses began to make landfall on the shores of the sea of men! All those revelations have created more and more doubts and diseases in the hearts of the men as they were not revealed in a transparent manner! For more than six hundred years, since Jesus's "First" arrival and the rise of Muhammad as a messenger for mankind, Allah remained silent on revelations! After that long period of silence he realized that mistakes have been made and the mankind deserves a new set of revelation abrogating all those sent before! And this is how "ALLAH HAS INCREASED THEIR DISEASE"! Even the ordinary Arab Pagans were not convinced of the process of revelation! With the death of Muhammad, Allah terminated all forms of revelations! Later, somehow Allah changed his mind and decided to send Jesus on earth again! He also promised to restart revelation once again with the arrival of Jesus! He wants all disbelievers to convert to Islam and accept Islamic monotheism only dismissing all other forms of monotheism! Since Allah has already infected their hearts with doubts and diseases, the number of hesitant hypocrites might increase many folds making it real hard for Jesus to convert all of them to Islam!

Verse-15, Ch-2: "ALLAH MOCKS AT THEM AND GIVES THEM INCREASE IN THEIR WRONG DOING TO WANDER BLINDLY". Is this not a misfortune for the mankind to have a "Creator" who mocks at his own creation? What a debacle has fallen on the Lord of the universe; letting loose his loveliest creation do wrong and wander blindly? Interestingly, the fact of the matter is that it is mostly the believers in Allah who are wandering blindly forming terror groups to commit crimes against humanity in the name of Islam to introduce Islamic rule of law across the world and to ensure a pompous life in the world hereafter! "A Book in his hand, and a great burden upon his back", the pilgrim asks; what shall I do? Yet he begins his perilous journey to the Heavenly Gates! He doesn't want to wander blindly, lest his Lord mocks at him! Allah "GIVES THEM INCREASE IN THEIR WRONG DOING"! But what the mankind has been witnessing for long is the "Increase" in senseless killing of innocent people across the world by religiously intoxicated killer groups in the name of Allah! They are inspired by the divine verses to undertake such brutal misadventures! One may escape a wildfire in this world but no chance to escape hellfire! Moreover, who can resist the temptations of an eternal life amidst "HURS"; irresistible beauties Allah has especially created for the pious dwellers of paradise! Those insane killers are fully convinced that they have found the "Straight Path" to paradise! As for mocking; I cannot imagine it as an attribution of the "Creator"! By mocking his creation, the Lord of the Universe has downgraded his stature from the sublime to the ridiculous! Besides mocking, Allah also curses disbelievers! It is claimed that Allah has ninety nine names which signify his qualities in superlative degree but mocking and cursing surely disqualify him as the "Best of the Judges"! Everything has a dark side! Even a super moon cannot hide its dark side! Mocking is a business of those who make false prophecies! Who would like to worship a mocker or a curser?

Verse-18, Ch-2: "THEY ARE DEAF, DUMB, AND BLIND, SO THEY RETURN NOT TO THE RIGHT PATH". I feel obliged to repeat a Hadith (BUKHARI, Vol. 3, #335) time and again in which Allah promised to keep Muhammad alive until all of mankind return to "Straight" path and say in one voice; "THERE IS NO GOD EXCEPT ALLAH! Whereas Muhammad said goodbye to this life leaving most of the mankind "DEAF, DUMB, AND BLIND"! To verify the truth about this Hadith and the promises Allah made, the readers may have to travel back to history to see under what circumstances Muhammad left the mankind before his death! Does his legacy justify his position as a messenger for mankind? Did Allah keep his promises as was made in the above Hadith? The idea, to instill an ideology among "Deaf, Dumb and Blind", makes no sense at all! If we look back on a few verses just quoted above, it will not be difficult to visualize the pitch-black darkness that the humanity has gone through! And that darkness acted as a smooth platform for myths and miracles to spread far and wide! In between more than eight hundred years elapsed when the European Renaissance emerged as an enlightenment for the humanity! A stirring of fresh life with new desires saw the dawn aglow in Italy and Germany! Though it had assumed a religious character in Germany but Italy accepted some of the pagan influences including nudity as an artistic form! After the Renaissance, a naked woman wrought in bronze was placed upon the tomb of the Pope! We all are born naked and will be "Resurrected" naked, including Muhammad, on the Day of Resurrection, says Allah! Nudity is natural; neither Allah nor God sent thunderbolts to demolish that naked statue of the woman! Thomas More said, "God has given them life that they may live...How can we find more pleasure in seeing a dog run after a hare then in seeing a dog run after another dog"? Who is pursuing the "Right" path? Body of the "DEAF, DUMB AND BLIND" is now glorified: "Beauty is Truth, Truth Beauty"!

Verse-22, Ch-2: "WHO HAS MADE THE EARTH A RESTING PLACE FOR YOU, AND THE SKY AS A CANOPY, AND SENT DOWN WATER FROM THE SKY AND BROUGHT FORTH THEREWITH FRUITS AS A PROVISION FOR YOU. THEN DO NOT SET UP RIVALS TO ALLAH". The "Creator" is selfish, not selfless! He gave us an Earth with a Canopy over it, he sends Rain to grow Fruits as a Provision but not without condition: "DO NOT SET UP RIVALS TO ALLAH"! The "Resting Place" is so small and its canopy is so huge that one can hardly believe it has been planned by an intelligent architect! Does the rain come from the sky? Whether the earth is a place for "Rest" or "Unrest" is debatable as it is always going through a kind of turbulence caused by the Tug of War between two lives; one is temporary and the other is eternal! Only an ignorant may call this earth a "Resting Place"! The sky does not listen to draught-stricken people! Millions of lands turn into deserts for lack of rains! Man and animal get together to join the "Great Migration" for survival! Only the fittest survives! The mankind lose faith in the "One and Only" and, out of frustration, set up rivals! Unfortunately, the rivals to Allah are also not better in any way! On the contrary, heavy flooding does the same damage as the drought! A Hadith (Al-BUKHARI, Vol. 6, #4) attached to this verse states that when Muhammad was asked to name the greatest "Sin" in consideration with Allah, he replied; "THAT YOU SET UP A RIVAL UNTO ALLAH THOUGH HE ALONE CREATED YOU"! This "Sin" is even greater than the "Original Sin"! AR-RAD, the angel appointed by Allah to drive the clouds is not doing his job judiciously! Many Muslims in the Islamic world gather for a "Rain-Prayer", known as "ISTISQA", invoking Allah for rain during draught! In Saudi Arabia it is held by a royal decree from the monarch! Allah often ignores call of the King! The Fisher King is dead! He must be brought back to life for regeneration on the dry "Waste Land"; the "Resting Place"!

Verse-23, Ch-2: "IF YOU (ARAB PAGANS, JEWS AND CHRISTIANS) ARE IN DOUBT CONCERNING THE QURAN, THEN PRODUCE A CHAPTER OF THE LIKE THEREOF". The "Creator" is autocratic not only as the Lord but also as an "Author"! He doesn`t want any other gods to be worshipped besides him and accordingly he does not want a partner to him who can be compared as an author as good as himself! Allah has thrown a challenge to the disbelievers to produce a "Surah" like one of those in the Quran! But he has not mentioned the size of the surah he wants them to write; as the one that has 286 verses or the one that has only 3 sentences? There are many books of religion on this earth that were not revealed from the sky but composed by the sons of the soil! Allah has taken twenty three years to reveal his "Book" thru an angel and must have taken twenty three thousand years to "Write" it! Allah will never accept anything written by his "Enemies" as better than what he has written in the Quran! We cannot imagine Shakespeare, the greatest of English poet and playwright, challenging his readers to write an "Act" or an "Episode" better than those he wrote in his plays! Because that would have surely over-shadowed his superiority and genuineness as a poet or playwright! It is only the inferiority complex that leads someone to this kind of challenge or confrontation! But the "Author" of the Quran and the "Creator of the Earth and the "Seven Heavens" did not feel as such when challenging the disbelievers to produce a "Surah" like the one in his "Book of Miracle"! Writing a surah, as the one in the Quran, is not a rocket science! The challenge reflects a child-like behavior! Instead Allah should have challenged his adversaries (Arab Pagans, the Jews and the Christians) to produce an "Earth" like the one he has created in "Two days"! This verse is one of the instances that testifies the real identity of the "Author" of the Quran! The "DOUBT CONCERNING THE QURAN" is not as grave as the doubt concerning its "Author"! The reality behind the revelation is being revealed!

Verse-24, Ch-2: "BUT IF YOU DO IT NOT, AND YOU CAN NEVER DO IT, THEN FEAR THE FIRE WHOSE FUEL IS MAN AND STONES, PREPARED FOR THE DISBELIEVERS". What is the point challenging those who "CAN NEVER DO IT"? Above verses unambiguously express the doubts that persisted regarding the divine revelations of the Quran since its inception! Doubts and confusions have attained universality because of shallow evidences produced in favor of the authenticity of the Revelations! There are occasions, when Muhammad was in trouble with social as well as marital issues, Allah immediately sent verses from heaven for his rescue! Is this trustworthy? The translators have not explained how and why Allah wants to use "Man and Stones" as fuel for hellfire! How did "Stones" angered Allah? Trillions of stars burning in the space need no "Man" or "Stones" as fuel! As part of mandatory Hajj ritual, the pilgrims throw stones at a concrete monument of Satan but Allah wants to use stones as fuel for fire! Allah is said to have created "Stars" to use them as "Missiles" to hit the devils! This is analogous to using an ICBM to kill a mosquito! To express their solidarity with Allah, the pilgrims show their disgust by throwing small pieces of stone at the statue of Satan during

Hajj since the "Missiles" are beyond their reach! Allah granted "Respite" to Satan for misleading Adam and his offspring and now he wants pilgrims to throw stones at him! Either it was ordained by the Lord or the Satan had deliberately shown disrespect to his "Creator"! Allah has prepared fire for the disbelievers in case they fail to produce a "Surah" but he has not mentioned the reward if they succeed! A challenger should chose an adversary more or less equally equipped like him! Otherwise there would be no valid reason to celebrate the victory since defeating a weaker adversary brings no glory! An impartial review of Allah's personality, as depicted in the Quran as a divine "Creator", falls far short of expectations! The Lord as the author of the "Book", has projected himself very poorly!

Verse-25, Ch-2: "AND GIVE GLAD TIDINGS TO THOSE WHO BELIEVE AND DO RIGHTEOUS GOOD DEEDS THAT FOR THEM WILL BE GARDENS UNDER WHICH RIVERS FLOW (PARADISE), AND THEY SHALL HAVE THEREIN PURIFIED MATES OR WIVES"! So far dozens of verses occurred in the Quran which say Allah has made "GARDENS UNDER WHICH RIVERS FLOW"! Is it mandatory that all gardens in paradise have to be built on the rivers? A Hadith (Al- BUKHARI, Vol. 4,#468) adds more to this verse saying; "THESE PURIFIED MATES OR WIVES WILL HAVE NO MENSES, STOOLS OR URINE! The words "Mates" and "Wives" are not interchangeable! They have separate meanings and applications! As these ladies will drink heavenly water, milk, honey and wine with fruits, there must be some means to dispose of the waste! "HURS" are created free of menses as they are created "Not from the offspring of Adam"! What about their "Husbands"? Would they be relieved from passing stools and urine as well? The best way would have been if Allah could devise a survival strategy for them so that they could live without food and drinks! What is conspicuously missing is the absence of similar provision for the pious women in paradise! Don`t they deserve "PURIFIED MATES OR HUSBANDS"? Though "The Father of heaven sends death to summon every creature to come and give account of their lives in this world" but he has "Glad tidings only for those who believe" in him! The "God of Life and Death" is also the "Lord of Wine and Women"! He has a lot to give as a way of temptations! Following the examples set by the Lord, men in this world buy favor from influential people using the same technique; wine and woman as baits! An act of God is not bound by ethics or morality! The clouds that bring rain and thunders come and go but those that hide the truth take time to vanish! Allah or the Lord is also a WALI (Protector):

O Lord! Protect us from those who are fighting to get "PURIFIED MATES AND WIVES" in Paradise in return for the 'RIGHTOUS GOOD DEEDS" on earth!

Verse-27, Ch-2: "THOSE WHO BREAK ALLA`S COVENANT AFTER RATIFYING IT, ARE THE LOSERS"! When did man sign a deed or covenant with Allah? Is it possible for humans to strike a deal of any kind with the "Creator"? Who did ratify the deal? Did Allah make any kind of covenant with humankinds before creating them? Did the mankind consent to Allah`s concept of creation cramped with conditions? It is Allah who has created mankind unilaterally; without consensus! The "Creator" is an absolute dictator! It is said that during Renaissance "The clergy were obliged to find some method of teaching and explaining to the ignorant masses the doctrinal truths of religion"! Did the Church find the doctrinal truths? What did they do to Galileo? Rather, to attract the masses, they began staging drama in the Churches "Combining Instruction with Amusement"! In fact most of the faiths have adopted this policy of combining religious activities with amusing cultural performances save the Islam! In Islam all amusements are preserved in the cold-storage of the paradise! All forms of entertainment including dancing, singing, acting etc. are forbidden in Islam! But Islam embodies a lot of covered options for sexual gratifications! Besides believers, the prophets and messengers have taken full advantage of that liberalism! In terms of entertainment, sex is given the highest priority in paradise! On earth, even the use of gold is forbidden for man! None can wear silk! Islam is a way of self-mortifications and as such it has very few real devoted Muslims among the believers who spontaneously observe its rituals with enthusiasm! Among the creatures, it is only the humans who are under sever obligations to acknowledge existence of creators! If they find none, yet they have to invent one as if life is unthinkable without a creator! Every religion has a road-map to paradise and that poses the biggest problem to the mankind! Humans are on a cross road facing a dilemmatic situation to choose the right path to take! We are not born-free but innately burdened with religious obligations!

Verse-29, Ch-2: "HE IT IS WHO CREATED FOR YOU ALL THAT IS ON EARTH. THEN HE ROSE OVER TOWARDS THE HEAVEN AND MADE THEM SEVEN HEAVENS". General view among humans is that the heavens were created before the earth but Allah did the opposite! Allah also created the sky as the "Canopy" for the earth! Allah creates everything in "Due Measurements" but in this case, the size of the canopy seems immensely larger than the "Resting Place"! Allah has never explained why he created trillions of galaxies! Surprisingly his attention is focused only on this tiny planet to implement his chosen doctrine of Islamic monotheism! He "Created for you all that is on Earth" including virus, bacteria, insects, mosquitoes etc. to bestow a dictionary of diseases upon the mankind so that none can live a life in good health! But why he sent Dinosaurs ahead of Adam is not clear since he does nothing without "Purpose"! The "Seven Heavens" has no place in the astronomical vocabulary but it is analogous to Ptolemy's cosmological model of second century AD. This model, later proved to be incorrect, contained five planets, the moon and the sun covered by an outer space filled with stars. The Quran was scripted five hundred years later. These five planets including the moon and the sun may have been referred to in the Quran as "Seven Heavens"! Allah, after creating the earth, rose over to Heavens, but how? The translators said, "In a manner suitable to his majesty" and this ambiguous information has been repeated in more than ten verses! But the "Manner" how Muhammad rose over to "Seven Heavens" riding an animal has been clearly described! Sometimes Allah comes down to first heaven, especially on the "Day of Arafat"! Surely he gets disappointed seeing a very small fraction of mankind present at Arafat! So it was rightly said, sometimes the "Gods descend from Olympus"! After going through all these stuffs you may be introspective and say, "Tired with all these, for restful death I cry"! Not to be! Even the best of messengers was not allowed a restful death while departing the "Resting Place"!

Verse-30, Ch-2: "VERILY, I AM GOING TO PLACE GENERATION AFTER GENERATION OF MANKIND ON EARTH". Why on earth the "Creator" is going to place generation after generation only on this earth? Can we take it for guaranteed that he has not placed any generation on any other planet of the universe? Is this the only planet in the entire cosmos that Allah has chosen to generate intelligent creatures? The assurance could put many scientists at rest who are busy round the clock looking for extra-terrestrial civilizations! The angels disagreed with Allah on his proposed plan to send generation after generation citing good reasons that the mankind "WILL MAKE MISCHIEF THEREIN AND SHED BLOOD WHILE WE GLORIFY YOU WITH PRAISES AND THANKS AND SANCTIFY YOU". The angels had a point, yet rejecting their arguments Allah said; "I KNOW THAT WHICH YOU DO NOT KNOW"! At the end of the day angel's predictions came true! Allah got himself into trouble by creating the mankind, most of whom turned out to be ingrate! The brotherly bloodshed began almost immediately; Adam's two sons, Cane and Abel fought a dual over marriage! Yet Allah pledges to place "Generation after Generation" on earth until he gets one of his own liking! The bad beginning; a blood feud over women between bothers, signaled a dark future of the mankind! Was it irreversible? To quote Dr. ABDULLAH AL-KAHTANI who said in his book "The Original Sin" that "Mankind stands an innate religion (Islam) inseparable from human nature"! This statement does not hold good since an innate religion would never require so many prophets and scriptures to be established! All creatures are equipped with innate qualities to communicate with each other; move from place to place; devise unique living strategy; adapt to new climatic conditions and continue procreation as a matter of necessity! Did they need prophets, messengers or scriptures to lead their lives? Who misled humanity into disintegration? Those who believe in the Adam-Eve saga cannot escape their responsibility!

Verse-36, Ch-2: "THEN THE SATAN MADE THEM SLIP THEREFROM (PARADISE), AND GOT THEM OUT FROM THAT IN WHICH THEY WERE. WE SAID, GET YOU DOWN, ALL, WITH ENMITY BETWEN YOURSELVES. ON EARTH WILL BE A DWELLING PLACE FOR YOU AND AN ENJOYMENT FOR A TIME"! Nay! In fact it is Allah, not Satan, who "MADE THEM SLIP FROM PARADISE"! As the Lord claims that nothing in this universe can happen without his "Will"! He is the absolute "KING" of his Kingdom"! What Allah did was to get them down to live on this earth with enmity and the results became evident almost immediately between two sons of Adam! What the Angels predicted in the previous verse proved to be right and Allah got it all wrong! Satan was made the scapegoat! Why on earth Allah planted that tree of the forbidden fruits in paradise? How Satan entered into paradise? Since Allah decided to send generations after generations on earth, he needed a pair of man and woman to kick-start the procreation of mankind to implement his scheme! This is more like buying a pair of chickens to raise them into millions! Similarly the Lord planned the "Fall of Adam and Eve" to initiate the creation of man! But why he cooked up a story of forbidden fruits? Was it not possible for Allah to send them un-sinned? Biblical version of the story also blames the Satan and his associates for the expulsion! These three religions, namely Judaism, Christianity and Islam originated from the same source with almost similar concept and contents! They are also identical and instrumental in creating confusion about Crucifixion, Creator and the Creation! What about other forms of life? Did the creator send a pair of male and female for each one of those billion of species! This is a cooked-up story with a lot of holes in it! Allah wished Adam and Eve well, saying; "Earth will be a dwelling place for you and an enjoyment for a time"! On the contrary their offspring are living their life with an unending enmity! Then the Lord sends Satan to turn the "Resting Place" into a "Pandemonium"!

Verse-37, Ch-2: "THEN ADAM RECEIVED FROM HIS LORD WORDS AND HIS LORD PARDONED HIM". Adam was pardoned by his Lord when he pleaded guilty and begged for his mercy saying; (Verse-23 of Chapter-7) "OUR LORD! WE HAVE WRONGED OURSELVES. IF YOU FORGIVE US NOT, AND BESTOW US NOT UPON US YOUR MERCY, WE SHALL CERTAINLY BE OF THE LOSERS". Adam is said to have pleaded guilty in chapter seven scripted at Mecca while the Lord already pardoned him in chapter two scripted at Medina? Why the pardon came before confession? The "Glad Tiding of Pardon" preceded the "Plea for Mercy"! In between exists a gap of more than two hundred verses! This is also an example how the Quran was compiled and in addition to this, it does put the authorship of the Quran in question! lastly it unfolds the truth that the so-called Revelation did not happen in an orderly manner! Despite being pardoned, why Adam still feels ashamed and unfit to intercede with Allah on behalf of his offspring on the Day of Resurrection? Why Adam, the "Father" of mankind and the "First" prophet of Islam is now residing in the "Lowest" heaven, farthest from Allah? According to a Hadith (AL-BUKHARI, Vol. 6, #3) all succeeding prophets starting from Noah, Abraham, Moses and Jesus decline to undertake the right to intercede with Allah and finally it goes to Muhammad! By all accounts the right to intercede with Allah should have gone to Adam! This is also an example of preferential treatment meted out to Muhammad by all Islamic scholars including the Hadith writers in order to give him the highest honor and raise him to the stature of a God! All efforts have been made by the majority of the Islamic Gurus to install Muhammad as the center of gravity around which all believers in Islam should revolve! Though Allah said Muhammad is like any other messenger, yet it is mandatory not only for every Muslim but also for the Jews and Christians to recognize Muhammad as the last messenger of Allah! Otherwise they will be deprived of an entry into paradise!

Verse-62, Ch-2: "VERILY! THOSE WHO BELIEVE AND THOSE WHO ARE JEWS AND CHRISTIANS, AND SABIANS, WHOEVER BELIEVE IN ALLAH AND THE LAST DAY AND DOES RIGHTEOUS GOOD DEEDS SHALL HAVE THEIR REWARD WITH THEIR LORD, ON THEM SHALL BE NO FEAR, NONE SHALL THEY GRIEVE". This verse may surprise some readers and it deserves to be read time and again! It seems to me that the tone of the Quran is suddenly changed! More surprising is the fact that this verse has neither been omitted or deleted by the "Author" himself but "Abrogated" by some Islamic theologian as the content of the verse goes contrary to what the Quran has been saying all along! A number of verses of the Quran unambiguously state that the Jews, the Christians and the "SABIANS" have nothing to fear or grieve about their rewards from the Lords if they believe in Allah, the "Last Day" and do "Righteous Deeds"! The SABIANS are a nation of the past who lived in Iraq and had a scripture known as "AZ-ZABUR"! Believing in the messages of Muhammad is not mentioned as a precondition for them! Surprisingly the same message is also repeated in verse-69 of Chapter-5! Here the translators have trickily mentioned believing in the messages of Muhammad as a condition within the bracket which, of course, is not a part of the original text. An attached footnote warns that this verse and verse (V. 69, Ch-5) "Should not be misinterpreted by readers" because IBN ABBAS, an Islamic scholar claims in his book "TAFSIR AL-TABARI" that the provisions of these verses have been abrogated! What spiritual authority did IBN ABBAS possess to abrogate verses sent by the Lord of the Heaven? Is there any statement from Allah about these abrogation? If Allah is not to be blamed for this double mistakes, then some human being should take the blame! The best way for Muhammad would have been to get clarifications about these verses from Allah when he visited him in the heaven! What in the end might prove that these verses have not come down from the sky! Throughout the Quran, translators have included their own remarks and opinions in the brackets in-between the original texts! The aim may have been to keep the Quran on track to avoid clash and conflicts between Allah`s verses and the sayings of Muhammad! However, they have failed to mitigate the suspicions on the Quran and its "Author"! Translators have also mentioned that whatever is said regarding the Jews, the Christians and the SABIANS in these verses (V. 62, Ch-2 & V. 69, Ch-5) have been abrogated by another verse (Verse-85, Ch-3) Which says, "AND WHOEVER SEEKS A RELIGION OTHER THAN ISLAM, IT

WILL NOT BE ACCEPTED OF HIM"! This verse also fails to include any statement from Allah or the "Author" about the abrogation of other two verses! In fact they should have been omitted all-together! Also to be noted that mistakes made in chapter two and five are being abrogated by a Hadith in reference to a verse from chapter three that says nothing about abrogation! This abrogation is neither logical nor chronological! So it is apparent that all-Knowing Allah does make mistakes! But in this respect Allah has repeated his mistakes! Every verse of the Quran is said to have come from Allah through an angel who delivered these verses to prophet Mohammad verbally and Mohammad narrated them to a group of scribes. Why a mistake of this magnitude, which is totally opposed to the very fundamental objective (i.e. to establish Islamic monotheism) could not be detected at any stages of this long chain of transmission? What is the truth? Is Allah the real "Author" of the Quran? Does Allah exist? There are more questions than answers! The Chinese way of glorifying their ancestors, instead of divine deities, is a much better option! Tracing of the ancestral roots might extend to the generation of monkeys and apes who possess more than 98 percent of DNA similar to those of humans! Yet the mankind blindly follow the hero of "The pilgrim's progress" carrying burdens of sins, leaving the City of Destruction to find the City of God!

Verse-79, Ch-2: "THEN WOE TO THOSE WHO WRITE THE BOOK WITH THEIR OWN HANDS AND THEN SAY THIS IS FROM ALLAH". This verse expresses the real sentiment of the Pagans, Jews, Christians and others about those who have written the Quran with their own hands and said this is from Allah! The Lord of the heaven did not allow every nation to have a poet like Dante to write the "Divine Comedy" but he kept sending "Divine Revelations" to messengers who were not able to write or read the messages themselves! When Muhammad and his partners were in the lime-light, some people took advantage of it and began writing verses similar to those of the Quran to steal the show! None of the prophets including Muhammad had formal education! How could anyone ascertain what is from Allah and what is from those who "WRITE THE BOOK WITH THEIR OWN HANDS"? Right from the inception, people were fearful of an entity living in the sky! Muhammad and associates took advantage of that prevailing fear and attributed Quran's authorship to that unseen deity! Criticism of the Quran with respect to its authenticity begun right from the day of revelations. Replying to western critics Dr. M. UMAR CHAPRA, a research advisor based in Jeddah says; "ONE WOULD

EXPECT THAT IN THE INTEREST OF PROMOTING INTERNATIONAL HARMONY AND PREVENTING THE CONFLICT OF CIVILIZATION FROM TAKING PLACE, THE WESTERN ORIENTALISTS WOULD NOT ATTACK OTHER PEOPLE'S RELIGIOUS BELIEFS AND PRACTICES"! Islamic scholars should read the Quran with an impartial mindset to see many verses Allah himself has "Authored" attacking other people's beliefs! Allah mocks at them; curses them to death! Taking lessons from those verses, followers of Muhammad are making mockery of the harmony and civilizations every day killing thousands of innocent men mercilessly in the name of Jihad waged by Allah! Is this the teaching of Islam? Yes, it is! Because Allah justifies Jihad! Why not say; "WOE TO THOSE WHO KILL IN THE NAME OF ALLAH"!

Verse-96, Ch-2 says "AND VERILY, YOU WILL FIND THEM (THE JEWS) THE GREEDIEST OF MANKIND FOR LIFE AND EVEN GREEDIER THAN THOSE WHO ASCRIBE PARTNERS TO ALLAH". The Lord created man with innate religion of Islam! So, it was Moses, one of Allah's most trusted prophets, who turned the Jews into "The Greediest of Mankind"! Probably for this reason Lord sent Jesus to the people of Israel but they rejected him outright as fake messenger and the rest is history! Shakespeare must have read the Quran and got inspiration from these verses to write his famous play "The Merchant of Venice"! Shylocks are everywhere! They know no religion! Greediness is also one of the innate attributes with which humans are born! A generalization of this kind, about the Jews from the "Author" of the Quran, testifies how he hates a nation of his own making! "The greediest of mankind" are also the works of the "Finest of the Creators"! Being greedier for life on earth is a much better choice than being greedier for a life in the hereafter! Allah wants to stay alone all along! Let us suppose that there is only "One" creator who created "One" universe, and then he selected "One" Galaxy to create "One" solar system in it with "One" sun at its center! From that system he created "One" planet with "One" moon going round it! When the time was right he decided to create "One" male and "One" female to create "One" mankind to implement "One" religion on them! His "Oneness" and "Singularity" remained as solid as rock for billions of years! But it started to fall apart when he began sending numerous prophets and messengers one after another with revelations of various kinds! Every generation of mankind invented their own brand of creators in their own way! The confusion about creation has a long history and will continue to repeat itself until the End! Einstein, who belonged to the "Greediest of Mankind" politely refused to be president of the Jewish nation because he considered an "Equation" serves the humanity better than the politics! His is also not the last "Equation"!

Verse-116, Ch-2: "AND THEY (THE JEWS, CHRISTIANS AND PAGANS) SAY ALLAH HAS BEGOTTEN A SON"! To dismiss this claim, the translators quoted a Hadith (Al-BUKHARI, Vol. 6, #9) in which IBN ABBAS quotes Muhammad and then Muhammad quotes Allah as saying, "THE SON OF ADAM TELLS LIES AGAINST ME THOUGH HE HAS NO RIGHT TO DO SO, AND HE ABUSES ME THOUGH HE HAS NO RIGHT TO DO SO. AS FOR HIS TELLING LIES AGAINST ME HE CLAIMS THAT I CANNOT RE-CREATE HIM AS I CREATED HIM BEFORE, AND AS FOR HIS ABUSING ME, IT IS HIS STATEMENT THAT I HAVE A SON. NO! GLORIFIED BE ME! I AM FAR FROM TAKING A WIFE OR A SON". Please note the number of references, namely; BUKHARI, IBN ABBAS, MUHAMMAD and ALLAH! This Quran is so puzzling that one has to follow a jig jag tunnel to figure out who said what! If it is the sayings of Allah, it should have been included directly in the Quran as a revealed verse! Why Muhammad has become a spokesperson for Allah? The Christians firmly believe that Jesus is the "Son of God" and not just "Son of Mary"! They are comforted with the assurance that the Messiah shall return "To reward his faithful, and receive them into bliss"! Allah says, the son of Adam tells lies! What an irony of fate! Adam, whom Allah created by his "Both Hands", has fathered a host of liars! Who is to blame? Even Adam, the "Father" of the mankind began his maiden voyage after committing the "Sin"! Allah has "TWO HANDS", yet he is not a man! He is "Far from taking a wife or a son" yet he is not a male! Allah is in real dilemma: Satan is relentlessly misleading humans and the son of Adam is telling lies against him! The misunderstanding about the God and the Son of God would not have surfaced if the Lord had followed identical method of creation for all the prophets! Mary's story of giving birth to Jesus has put Allah's own existence in doubt! Muhammad's visit to space lacks trustworthiness as it begun when he was "IN A STATE MIDWAY BETWEEN SLEEP AND WAKEFULNESS", "Like a patient etherized upon a table"!

Verse-117, Ch-2: "THE ORIGINATOR OF THE HEAVENS AND THE EARTH, WHEN HE DECREES A MATTER, HE ONLY SAYS TO IT "BE" AND IT IS". Scientists say that our universe was created about fourteen billion years ago! The solar system, including the planet earth, came into existence approximately nine billion years after that! Whereas the Lord took only "Six Days" to create the earth and the heaven! He took "Four Days" to create "Sustenance" for the earth! His one day is equal to a "Thousand" years of world standard time but later, without assigning any reason, he changed that to "Fifty Thousand" years! He also claims to be the "Creator of Time"! In this verse Allah claims that he can create anything just by uttering a word "Be"! Human consciousness and intellect are under severe stress to find credibility between the words and actions of the self-styled "Creator"! Light takes about one hundred thousand years to travel from one end of the galaxy to the other! So far the scientists have discovered billions of galaxies in the space! Now think about the whole universe in which we live! Neither any scientific measurements, nor even our imagination is able to grasp the vastness of the universe! No end, no boundary in sight! Then comes into play the possibility of the existence of multiverse! We have to wait until we find a "Warm Hole" to prove that! Probably our world, compared to a universe, is just a molecule of water in the Pacific! Now think of the universe and its "Creator", if it has one, to make a comparative assessment between his skill and his genius as the "Author" of the Quran! Only then a human being will be able to assess or guess who wrote these confusing and conflicting verses! It is a universally accepted fact that there has to be a realistic balance between the intellectual faculty of the "Creator" and his charismatic "Creation"! Can we expect a heavenly deity to draw a painting as good as the "Last Supper"? Can the Lord do it only by uttering the word "Be"! When do we expect to get out of the religious whirlpool? Are we not consciously sinking into the "Black Hole"?

Verse-155, Ch-2: "AND CERTAINLY, WE SHALL TEST YOU WITH SOMETHING OF FEAR, HUNGER, LOSS OF WEALTH, LIVES AND FRUITS, BUT GIVE GLAD TIDINGS TO THE PATIENT"! Those who will pass these tests, will they be relieved of the trial on the Day of judgment? Should they be resurrected naked to wait for the verdict of the Judge? Fear of death, disease and destruction is part and parcel of our everyday life! "Hunger" haunts us every moment! "Loss of Wealth, Lives and Fruits" regularly reminds mankind of the fallacies of the faiths! All creatures including the humans have learnt to live with these kind of calamities since the dawn of life on earth! Could the mankind pass a single day on earth without the devastation of one kind or the other? Allah is able to make the matter worse, terrible, painful and sad! Allah calls this earth a "Resting Place"! We are restlessly struggling to live our life here on earth to have an eternal peace and prosperity hereafter! I know not why words of Webster echoed suspicion; "My soul, like to a ship in a dark storm, is driven I know not whither"! Adam, the "Father" of mankind was also "Tested" by Satan with "Forbidden Fruits" though he failed the test! No doubt fruits are a great source of vitamins, we can patiently wait to have them in paradise; so tells the "Glad Tidings"! Allah's "Test" testifies how terrible a life he has bestowed upon us! We, the mankind, never signed a treaty with Allah to take such a terrible test in this life! Testing with tortures, torments, threats and temptations is doomed to fail to tantalize the tormented! Recall what Francis Bacon said regarding the nature; "Man, the servant and interpreter of nature, can understand so much and so much only as he has observed in fact or in thought, of the course of the Nature, beyond them he neither knows anything nor can do anything"! We are engaged in a constant struggle with nature for survival! On the other hand the whole spectrum of theology is based on speculations! Whatever lies beyond us, we neither know anything nor can we do anything about it!

Verse-161, Ch-2: "VERILY, THOSE WHO DISBELIEVE, AND DIE WHILE THEY ARE DISBELIEVERS, IT IS THEY ON WHOM IS THE CURSE OF ALLAH, AND OF THE ANGELS AND OF MANKIND, COMBINED". Let there be "Curse" on the disbelievers from Allah alone but why the angels and the mankind should join Allah in cursing them? Is Allah not sufficient as a curser? The funny side of this verse is that the disbelievers, who are destined to be "Cursed" by Allah form the lion part of the mankind and Allah is asking that mankind to curse itself! True believers are a small minority of the mankind! Allah will have to depend heavily on the angels to form the "Cult of Cursers"! Angels are often seen as the symbols of goodness but Allah now using them as cursers! Should the mankind sympathize with a cursing creator? How on earth the "Merciful Creator" turns merciless to curse his own creation? The Lord of the universe believes in the principle of intimidation! He thinks temptations will make paradise more attractive! Similarly threats will generate fear, so that people will be scared of the eternal life inside the inferno where, according to Allah death shall never come as an escape! The angels should have no right to curse disbelievers as they fail to refrain devils from misleading the humans! The Lord repeatedly said that for the protection of all human beings, he has detailed angels, one for each! But the result is a total disappointment! Disbelievers are on the increase! According to original plan, the Lord made the Heaven larger than the Hell! But now, in view of the new realties, he may have to reverse his decision! Allah claims to have created the earth and the heaven alone, why he needs partners to curse the disbelievers? Combined curses may outweigh his mercies! It may be recalled that Allah has kept ninety nine percent (99%) of the total mercy with him! Only one (1%) percent he has kindly bestowed upon all creatures including humans! Is not Allah the "Best of Judges"? He allocated the mercies in "Due Measures", isn't it?

Verse-178, Ch-2: "O YOU WHO BELIEVE! AL-QISAS (THE LAW OF EQUALITY IN PUNISHMENT) IS PRESCRIBED FOR YOU IN CASE OF MURDER; THE FREE FOR FREE, THE SLAVE FOR THE SLAVE, AND THE FEMALE FOR THE FEMALE. BUT IF THE KILLER IS FORGIVEN BY THE BROTHER OR THE RELATIVES OF THE KILLED AGAINST BLOOD-MONEY, THEN ADHERING TO IT WITH FAIRNESS IN MAKING PAYMENTS TO THE HEIR. THIS IS AN ALLEVIATION AND MERCY FROM YOUR LORD". Indeed, this is an "Alleviation and Mercy from the Lord" to the killers! How this "Law of Equality" was applied to the first killer of the mankind? Who did forgive Cane? He should have been killed by Adam under the provision "Free for Free" since no blood-money was paid to him! Adam, the first Muslim prophet was in the horns of a dilemma! He was the father of both the killer and the Killed! Moreover Adam was penniless when he landed on earth from paradise! Allah's "Law of Equality" measures life with money on the scale of justice! When a murder takes place, it vanishes life. So, this blood-money should better be called "Life-Money"! This provision of blood-money might have embolden the Crown Prince to undertake brutal killing of his critique, a globally known journalist! How much of money to be paid for a life? When it comes to Allah, even an earth full of gold will not be accepted by him as ransom to pardon a disbeliever on the "Day of Judgment! What is even more surprising in this verse is that Allah has acknowledged the existence of slavery and he did not reveal any verse asking Muhammad to abolish slavery! After reading the Quran what is crystal-clear is that it lays more emphasis on preserving the faith than humanity! Islam treats a disbeliever like an animal! Islamic scholars claim that Muhammad did free some slaves! The hard fact is that Muhammad allowed others to have sex with slaves if possessed by their so-called "Right Hands"! Allah, the "Creator", has kept the question unresolved whether the religion is for man or man for the religion!

Verse-190, Ch-2: "AND FIGHT IN THE WAY OF ALLAH THOSE WHO FIGHT YOU BUT TRANSGRESS NOT THE LIMIT". Incitement to fight man against man bears no hallmark of a divine Lord! It rather displays hatred; a human nature of taking revenge on enemies! Who is going to set the "Limit" of transgression and where does it stop? Who would set the limits for TALIBAN, ISIS, AL-QUIDA and others with similar motives operating around the globe? Ask ten different Islamic Gurus, each one will come up with ten different interpretations of the "Limit" set by one Allah! Muhammad is quoted to have said in a Hadith (AL-BUKHARI, Vol. 4 # 41) that "AL-JIHAD (HOLY FIGHTING) IN ALLAH'S CAUSE, WITH FULL FORCE OF NUMBERS AND WEAPONRY, IS GIVEN THE UTMOST IMPORTANCE IN ISLAM AND IS ONE OF THE PILLARS ON WHICH IT STANDS. BY JIHAD ISLAM IS ESTABLISHED. BY ABANDONING JIHAD ISLAM IS DESTROYED AND THE MUSLIMS FALL INTO AN INFERIOR POSITION, THEIR HONOR IS LOST, THEIR LANDS ARE STOLEN, THEIR RULE AND AUTHORITY VANISH"! Please note the difference between the Verse and the Hadith in terms of their tone and temperament! Volumes of hadiths written by a number of groups have amplified the Islam, the religion of Allah, by more than hundred times in their own perspective! They all agree on radicalizing the Islam as it failed to register popular support from the mankind! Jihad is an all-out war to be fought "With full force of numbers and weaponry" against the non-Muslims! Those who have made friends with the Christians and the Jews, disobeying Allah's commandments feel relatively safe! At the last moment, Jesus, as ordained by Allah, might become the Commander-in-Chief of the "Holy War" only to surrender to the opponents with utmost humiliation! Damage done by Muhammad and his predecessors is irreparable! The Muslims as a whole might get a respectable position in the committee of nations only by abandoning all forms of Jihad and pursuing a policy of humanity and brotherhood! A life in the "Light" is much better than the one in the "Dark"!

Verse-193. Ch-2 Says; "AND FIGHT THEM UNTIL THERE IS NO FITNAH (DISBELIEF AND WORSHIPPING OF OTHERS ALONG WITH ALLAH)". To eliminate "FITNAH", Allah and his followers will have to eliminate more than five billions of the seven billions human beings! In this verse, the word "FITNAH" deserves our keen attention more than the rest of the words! Though it's meaning is given in the bracket but, according to glossary of the Quran, it stands for "Trials, persecution, confusion in the religion, conflicts and strife among the Muslims" and surprisingly Islam embodies all of these ingredients! It is said that every Arabic word has a wealth of meanings and this word "FITNAH" is an example of that claim! Allah and Muhammad together brought the dire message for the entire mankind that they have no right to live in this world unless they believe in Islamic monotheism! Some anti-Semites believe the Jews have no right to exist! But Allah's messages warn all mankind, save the Muslims, to face annihilation for being disobedient to him! Besides the fanatics, a great majority of Muslims believe that one day the whole of humanity will turn to Islam to make Allah's dream come true! Many terror groups engaged in the fighting are funded by forces hiding in "BURQAH" located around the place where the message of Jihad landed from the sky! The "Liquid Gold", "Delicious Dollars" and "Man in Arms" make up a triangle that is more dangerous to mankind than the "Golden Triangle"! Harmony among humans has been shattered by Allah's call to Muslims not to trust the Christians, Jews and Pagans! At dawn Allah invites believers to attend prayers at the mosque with the "Pious" who fight against humanity! Coincidently "A bell rings, who is up early, to call others to go to Church" to join in prayers with the clerics and the cardinals in whose hands young children are sexually molested! In the Church "Holy Father" delivers Godly Sermon while the "Holy-Child" sings the choir! In the Mosques or in the Church, they all dance to the tune of the same "Divine Composer"!

Verse-213, Ch-2: "MANKIND WERE ONE COMMUNITY AND ALLAH SENT PROPHETS WITH GLAD TIDINGS AND WARNINGS, AND WITH THEM HE SENT DOWN THE SCRIPTURE IN TRUTH TO JUDGE BETWEEN PEOPLE IN MATTERS WHEREIN THEY DIFFERED". So, the prophets who came with "THE SCRIPTURES IN TRUTH" truly divided the mankind that was hitherto united! None of those prophets had the capacity to keep the mankind united as one community! Man are created to be tested, tried and then tormented if found guilty of being ungodly and to be rewarded if found submissive to the will of the sublime! We are not created to live a life but to live a religion that sets a chain of parameters around life and we are not supposed to break the rules of the Lord! Allah, the "King" of the universe created the mankind that was

"One Community" once upon a time! How can we believe that an "All-Knowing" creator has failed to perceive the end result of his grandest scheme? The messengers, who brought the "Glade Tidings", "Warnings" and "Scriptures in Truth" for the mankind, created more divisions than before! Before his death Muhammad predicted that his community would be divided into 73 factions! It will be interesting to watch the dilemma of Muhammad and Jesus on the Day of Judgment! The divide between Shia and Sunny; Catholics and Protestants may still remain even after Resurrection! The All-Mighty also says that he can create and destroy generations after generations with no regrets! As a result, people differ in every matters of religion and resort to fight to ascertain real color of the "Truth" sent down from the sky in various scriptures! They have learnt to question the very existence of God, dismissing the idea that the universe was created by a "Creator"! Existence of Gods and Ghosts has always been a great puzzle for the mankind! No prophet could command love and loyalty of the entire mankind! The Lord promised to send his "Son" back to earth again! Good luck to him! Jesus deserves to be raised as he is believed to have raised Lazarus from the dead!

Verse-219, Ch-2: "THEY ASK YOU (O MUHAMMAD) CONCERNING ALCOHOLIC DRINKS AND GAMBLING. SAY; IN THEM IS A GREAT SIN, AND SOME BENEFITS FOR MEN, BUT SIN OF THEM IS GREATER THAN THEIR BENEFIT". It is quite interesting to note that Allah has found "Some Benefits" for men in alcoholic drinks and gambling! Man in millions, believers and non-believers alike, flock to Las Vegas probably to receive "Some Benefits" ignoring the consequences of a "Greater Sin"! Mohammad is quoted to have given a very interesting information in a Hadith (AL-BUKHARI, Vol. 7, #483) that says; "BEFORE THE DOOMS DAY ILLEGAL SEXUAL INTERCOURSE AND ALCOHOLIC DRINKING WILL INCREASE AND AS A RESULT MEN WILL DECREASE AND WOMEN WILL INCREASE SO MUCH SO THAT FOR EVERY FIFTY WOMEN THERE WILL BE ONLY ONE MAN TO LOOK AFTER THEM!" This is going to be an alarming situation indeed! Man to woman ratio will drastically change to an unprecedented level that "There will be only one man to look after (?) fifty women"! This reminds me of a special species of rats who keep mating until death! If a male has to "Look after" fifty females, his consequences will be like that of those rats! One can easily visualize a large group of women chasing a man for sex or whatever! This is more like a usual scene often seen in the streets during mating season when many sex-hungry dogs run after a bitch to receive her favor! As the Dooms day draws near, the mankind is going to face a reverse situation in which group of female would be seen chasing a male! The men to women ratio, more or less has been naturally stable! Even the Lord began his creation of man with only one pair of male and female i.e. Adam and Eve! Cane and Abel were born with twin sisters, maintaining a balance between male and female so that they find no problem for marriage! It seems that as the dooms day draws near, the "Creator" will lose his control over male female ratio! Even Muhammad, the best of all messengers, had great trouble maintaining conjugal harmony with only a dozen of wives! The Lord under the "Doctrine of Necessity" allowed Cane and Abel to marry their twin sisters! Now it is forbidden! However, Cleopatra, the Egyptian Queen is said to have married her brothers due to "Royal Necessity"! How illegal sex and alcoholic drinking is going to adversely affect the age-old gender ratio has not been explained by Muhammad! Excessive use of sex and alcohol may really affect fertility of men but why gender ratio, which is determined by X,Y combination of chromosome that comes from the sexual discharge (Allah calls it "Despised Water") of both male and female? X+Y combination of chromosome produces male while X+X produces female! So, as per the above Hadith of Muhammad, illegal sex and drinking will have an adverse effect on the chromosome combination in favor of females before Dooms Day! Such reduction in the number of males might also adversely affect Allah's Jihad against the disbelievers! This 1:50 ratio between males and females is going to bring marriage, as a social institution, to a breaking point! Love will be lost forever in that chaotic gender imparity! However, it is not an immediate concern for humanity since the sun has enough fuel to survive for at least another five hundred million years! As such the Dooms Day is still far-off, if Allah decides otherwise! Will it not be fascinating to watch a world having women fifty times more than the men? But the learned translators stated that "Provision of this verse concerning alcoholic drinks and gambling has been abrogated by the verse 90 of chapter 5 which says, "Intoxicants and gambling are an abomination of Satan's handiwork"! So what? Allah created Satan for that purpose! This mistake was detected after 633 verses recorded! Who will abrogate the Hadith of Muhammad regarding male-female ratio? It stands as it is! All verses of the Quran that have been "Abrogated" were also part of the Revelation! Why these verses have been abrogated by his followers without divine authority? Who is intoxicated? Who is "Gambling" with our lives on earth?

Verse-252, Ch-2: "THESE ARE THE VERSES OF ALLAH, WE RECITE THEM TO YOU (MUHAMMAD) IN TRUTH, AND SURELY, YOU ARE ONE OF THE MESSENGERS"! If we look closely at the contents of this verse, I hope all will agree that this verse should have been placed in the beginning of the Quran! Why Allah decides at this stage (i.e. the 259th verse of the Quran) to assure Muhammad that he is surely a messenger and that these verses are real and not fake? It is also demeaning for prophet Muhammad when Allah terms him as "One of the Messengers"! He is supposed to be the "Best" and the "Unique" among all messengers which is evident from the Hadith (AL-BUKHARI, Vol. 1, # 331) in which Muhammad claims that Allah bestowed upon him five special things that were not given to any other messengers before him! He states them in his own words: (a) ALLAH MADE ME VICTORIOUS BY FRIGHTENING MY ENEMIES, (b) THE EARTH HAS BEEN MADE FOR ME (AND FOR MY FOLLOWERS) FOR PRAYING, (c) THE WAR BOOTY HAS BEEN MADE LAWFUL FOR ME. (d) I HAVE BEEN GIVEN THE RIGHT OF INTERCESSION ON THE DAY OF RESURRECTION and (e) ALL PREVIOUS PROPHETS WERE SENT TO THEIR RESPECTIVE NATIONS ONLY BUT I HAVE BEEN SENT FOR THE WHOLE OF MANKIND"! In addition to these Allah also honored him by forgiving his past and future sins; revealed many verses from heavens to resolve conjugal problems between him and his wives; gave him the magical power to split the moon; assured him of the highest place in paradise; made a special house for him in paradise called "MAQAM MAHMUD"; he would be the first to be resurrected and last but not least Muhammad was the only prophet to have paid a visit to Allah and saw the paradise in his lifetime! I hope, no Islamic scholar would dispute the special favors Allah bestowed upon prophet Muhammad which I have mentioned above! After assuring him of so many special favors, yet Allah asks Muhammad to say to his followers that; "I AM NOT THE FIRST MESSENGER, NOR DO I KNOW WHAT WILL BE DONE WITH ME OR WITH YOU" (V. 9 of Ch-46)! Can we still continue to believe in Muhammad and his "Creator"? What is not yet clear is the whereabouts of Muhammad after his death! Is he still in his grave? This question arises as all prominent prophets are alive and well, living at different heavens of the Seven Heavens allocated to them by Allah and Muhammad had called on w them during his space mission! So we may safely assume that he is not in any of the Seven Heavens? Why Muhammad was not raised to heaven like Jesus? Because of his unique position as a messenger, he should have been given a place in one of the Seven Heavens or he could be taken directly to his specially-built home "MAQAM MAHMUD" in paradise! It is said that Muhammad would be resurrected from the cracking ground like all other human beings! The five special favors Allah bestowed upon prophet Muhammad may now be discussed one by one! Did Allah help Muhammad in all the wars he fought? Did he win all of those wars? The answer is NO! What was the end results of the Battle of UHUD? The second favor is an absurd claim! Has the Lord of the universe made the earth as a place of worship only for Muhammad and his followers? So, the followers of other religions have no right to worship on this planet? The third favor is about legalizing war booty for him by Allah! Looting properties of the defeated was considered a "Right" of the victorious in ancient era long before the advent of Islam. "Might is right" was the order of the day! Though in the modern era this kind of looting by force was mostly done by the Imperial powers or occupiers! What Muhammad did was a continuation of that ancient trend! The fourth favor is about the right to intercede with Allah! He gets it when Adam, Noah and others reject the offer! As usual Muhammad claims that he is the only messenger who has been sent for the whole of mankind! His short span of life does not support this claim. What about Adam? Was he not sent as the "Father" of the whole of mankind? Muhammad himself stated that Jesus is coming again as a messenger to rule over the whole of mankind! So his claim is not undisputed!

Verse-256, Ch-2: "THERE IS NO COMPULSION IN RELIGION. VERILY, THE RIGHT PATH HAS BECOME DISTINCT FROM THE WRONG PATH. WHOEVER DISBELIVES IN *TAGHUT* AND BELIEVES IN ALLAH, THEN HE HAS GRASPED THE MOST TRUSTWORTHY HANDHOLD THAT WILL NEVER BREAK"! This may be true for all religions save the Islam. As Allah himself said, "BY JIHAD ISLAM IS ESTABLISHED" and Jihad justifies killing of the disbelievers! Please take note of the word "TAGHUT"! According to the Islamic experts it covers a wide range of meanings. It means anything worshipped other than the real God (Allah). It includes all false deities such as Satan, devils, idols, sun, stones, stars, angels, human beings, saints, graves, rulers, leaders, false judge etc.! Why Muslim nations have enacted blasphemy laws? Because it is compulsory for a Muslim to worship Allah alone and according to Muhammad, setting a partner to Allah is the gravest of all "Sins"! Even killing one's own son for sharing food is not as grave a "Sin" as worshipping any other "God" besides Allah! It is also compulsory for the believers to attend five congregational prayers everyday which was fifty before the ascent of Muhammad to the space! This is beyond our conviction how the Lord, supposed to be the best of judges, could make fifty congregational prayers compulsory for his believers! The most important compulsion is that a believer will not be considered a "Muslim" unless he believes in Muhammad as the messenger of Allah! Muhammad stands firm between the worshippers and Allah as the first stumbling block! Believing in Muhammad is a "Compulsion" as mandatory as believing in Allah! Besides many "Miracles", the Quran also concedes of having "Unclear" and "Abrogated" verses with contradictory statements! "NO COMPULSION IN RELIGION" does not apply to Islam in reality! Why does Islam allow killing of those people who worship their own deities! Out of so many who is the "Real Lord"? Is God essential for life?

Verse-257, Ch-2: "ALLAH IS THE WALI (PROTECTOR) OF THOSE WHO BELIEVE, HE BRINGS THEM OUT FROM DARKNESS INTO LIGHT BUT AS FOR THOSE WHO DISBELIEVE, THEIR SUPPORTERS AND HELPERS ARE FALSE DEITIES, THEY BRING THEM OUT FROM LIGHT INTO DARKNESS". Look at the plight of the Palestinians to vindicate the above verse of the Quran! As a matter of fact the reality on ground is exactly opposite to what has been stated in the above verse! In this "Resting Place" it is the believers in Allah who are less protected; vulnerable to attacks from the "People of the Scriptures"! If Allah is unable to protect them on earth, how can they build their trust on his words! Numerous prophets, including Muhammad, had come and gone with the wind but the darkness still persists over the creation and the "Creator"! The tunnel is utterly zigzag with no light in sight! No prophet could leave behind an enlightened mankind! Passage to paradise is perilous and murky; leading the pilgrims out of light into darkness, darker than the Dark Matters! Believers are killing believers while the "WALI" (protector) is watching helplessly from the heaven! Allah's protection is so fragile that even the mosques, known as the "House of Allah", are not immune to bloodshed! Those who fought with Muhammad in the battles died in thousands unprotected! For how long Allah would lay the blame on Satan? Muslim rulers of the Middle East seek protection from mighty Christian rulers; the disbelievers! Though Allah promised to bring them out from darkness into light, yet they are not out of the woods! All religions combined, pushed the humans to a crossroad that they can no longer decide confidently which road to take and which God to choose from! Does a "Creator" really exist? Could he protect his believers? It is the invisible virus, not angel, that brings the clear message for the mankind! Do we ever expect to find a "Creator" out of its many variants? It is the truth that shall bring us out from darkness into light!

Verse-258, Ch-2: "VERILY ALLAH BRINGS THE SUN FROM THE EAST, THEN BRING IT YOU FROM THE WEST"! These words are spoken by Prophet Abraham when a dispute arose between him and a disbeliever! The Quran has declared time and again that "ALLAH IS ABLE TO DO ALL THINGS"! If Muhammad could split the moon, why can't Allah bring the sun from the east to the west? Abraham challenges the disbeliever to bring the sun from the west to the east? On the Dooms Day Allah will order the sun to rise from the west! Probably the "Day of Judgment" will happen on Venus where the sun rises in the west! All living being on this earth know from time immemorial that sun rises in the east and sets in the west because we are used to believing in what meets the eye! Even the famous Greek philosopher Aristotle (340 B.C.} and astronomer Ptolemy (2nd A.D.} believed in a cosmological order in which the Earth was presumed to be stationary at the center of the cosmos and the sun, the moon and other planets revolved around it! The Christian Churches also accepted this model as it coincided with their Biblical belief! After more than a decade Nicholas Copernicus and other scientists came up with the idea that the earth is not stationary rather it revolves around the sun and also rotates on its axis and as a result we see the sun rising in the East and setting in the West. Allah, the creator of the universe and his prophets cannot think of a rotating Earth as they have affixed mountains on its surface lest it should move! These misleading Revelation from the heaven misguided not only the ordinary people but also confused many intellectuals of the period! "Big Brains" of the time considered it a duty to defend the God! The papal repression that Galileo had gone through created lots of fear among scientists and free thinkers! One could hardly speak of what he believed! Law of Blasphemy has always been used to neutralize the disbelievers! Allah claims that every day he brings the sun from the east to the west and then brings it back to the east from the west! This is not science but an "Act of God"!

Verse-286, Ch-2: "ALLAH BURDENS NOT A PERSON BEYOND HIS SCOPE". "LAY NOT ON US A BURDEN LIKE THAT WHICH YOU DID LAY ON THOSE BEFORE US (JEWS AND CHRISTIANS). PUT NOT ON US A BURDEN GREATER THAN WE HAVE STRENGTH TO BEAR!" So, the believers themselves testify that Allah did lay a burden on the Jews and the Christians heavier than they had strength to bear! This unbearable burden may have back fired and as a result they turned against Allah! No "Creator" should over-burden his "Slaves" lest they lose their faith in him before reaching the destination; the Paradise! This misery increased "Burden of Sins" on the back of the pilgrims who at the end failed to reach the "City of God"! Leave aside the people of scripture; what happened to the believers in Islam? Allah ordained fifty obligatory prayers for them! Going to mosques, fifty times a day to attend prayers, was not considered a "Burden" by the Lord! Luckily Allah sent Gabriel to take Muhammad to heaven riding on a horse-like animal and there, on the advice of Moses and other prophets, he managed to get it reduced to five times a day! Oh, what a relief! It is really hard to believe that an All-Knowing Allah could lay such an unbearable burden on his creatures! Visiting mosques fifty times a day would make their life a hell! When would they eat and shit? Why did Allah ask prophet Abraham to sacrifice his minor son in the dream? Was it within his scope as a loving father to kill his dearest son? My experience, by virtue of being born to a Muslim family, tells me that the Islam is the most burdensome, boring and controversial religion compared to any other faiths of its kind! Mentally an Islamic life is nothing better than a bird locked in the cage! Free thinking, free speech, free movement or in short freedom of life is totally restricted! It keeps its believers "Chained" both mentally and psychologically round the clock! All aspects of life and liberty are restrained and controlled! Islam comes your way every moment! Every step in life is obstructed by numerous Islamic do's and don'ts. Locally invented Islamic customs create even more problems than those revealed from the sky! In the eyes of Islam, every form of entertainment such as singing, dancing, acting are a "Sin", and therefore those are strictly forbidden! Even wearing silk is a "Sin" because it is exclusively preserved for paradise! Tens of thousands of HADITHS, FATWAS, VERSES, along with their multi-faced interpretations will keep you on the run from early morning to late at night! Whether you are in wash-rooms or in bed-rooms, you have quite a number of verses to recite! Some selected verses of the Quran, if recited, promise different kinds of benefits like ailment from diseases, security of food, peace of mind, prosperity in life and many more! The reality is completely different! No disease is ever cured even after reciting the entire Quran from its beginning to the end! Many believers in Islam wear what is known as "TABIZ" to get rid of diseases which is actually prepared by writing some verses of the Quran on a piece of paper and then folding into a metal case so that it can be wrapped around neck, arms or waist! Large number of Muslims across the world still believe in this kind of futile superstitious practices! Surprisingly the Muslims in general don't blame Allah for the ineffectiveness of these verses! In this regard a Hadith (AL-BUKHARI, VOL. 5, #345) quotes Muhammad as saying; "Whoever recites the last two verses of surah AL-BAQARA at night, that is SUFFICIENT for him"! The word "Sufficient" has not been sufficiently explained! Even the recitation of the whole Quran has no effect on disease or disasters! One might ask how the Muslims lead their life? The answer is, ninety nine percent of the Muslims all around the world follow a life style which is a mixture of both Islamic and un-Islamic culture! Muslims, going to mosques, don`t mind going to movies, bars or even brothels! This is obvious for a human being to lessen his burden bestowed on him by an unseen entity! Islam allows beheading; stoning to death! It asks its believers to forgo this life for the sake of one in the eternity!

Verse-19, Ch-3: "TRULY, THE RELIGION WITH ALLAH IS ISLAM. THOSE WHO WERE GIVEN THE SCRIPTURES (JEWS ANS CHRISTIANS) DID NOT DIFFER EXCEPT (OUT OF MUTUAL JEALOUSY) AFTER KNOWLEDGE HAD COME TO THEM. AND WHOEVER DISBELIEVES IN THE PROOFS, EVIDENCES, VERSES, SIGNS, REVELATIONS etc. OF ALLAH, THEN SURELY, ALLAH IS SWIFT IN CALLING TO ACCOUNT"! The first sentence of this verse means to say that "Islam" is the only religion acceptable to Allah! This is a diplomatic way of avoiding a direct question! What is Allah's religion? Does Allah practice any religion? Is Allah a Muslim? Islamic scholars are of the opinion that Allah has no gender, no children! But Allah often expressed his intent not to have offspring as such he did not take any wife! Probably he does not practice any religion since he is not "Created" by any "Creator" to impose a religion upon him! Does Allah have a physical shape with a soul in it? But Allah surely has "Hands" since he claimed to have created Adam by his "Both Hands"! People of the scriptures not only ignored the "Knowledge" but also disbelieved in all of the proofs and evidences of Allah! Dr. AL-KAHTANY, an eminent Islamic scholar from Saudi Arabia claims in a book that "EVERY NEW

BORN CHILD IS BORN ON THE INNATE NATURE; ISLAM"! Then his parents change him into Judaism, Christianity etc.! If so why did he give scriptures to the Jews and Christians? Which angel brought the revelations to them? Why did he send Moses and Jesus to the people of Israel? Out of jealousy and personal ambition, Muhammad and his associates emerged to discredit Judaism and the Christianity! Gabriel, who is said to have brought the verses from the heaven, was himself invisible despite being made of "Light"! Doubts over revelations kept all proofs beyond visibility! Why the revelation has to begin in the darkness of a cave? "PROOFS, EVIDENCES, VERSES, SIGNS AND REVELATION" have failed to convince a great majority of mankind, as such they have overwhelmingly rejected Islam; the only religion acceptable to Allah!

Verse-54, Ch-3: "AND THEY (DISBELIEVERS) PLOTTED TO KILL JESUS AND ALLAH PLOTTED TOO. AND ALLAH IS THE BEST OF THOSE WHO PLOT". Allah is definitely a better "Plotter" but not a better "Planner" than the disbelievers! The Jews thought they had "Crucified" Jesus but Allah made a better plot to deceive them and "Raised" Jesus, the "Son of Mary", unto him! What the Jews Crucified was a "Dummy" of Jesus! Remember, Allah also sent Gabriel, in the disguise of a man, to Mother Mary to conceive Jesus in her womb! May I remind you again that "ALLAH IS ABLE TO DO ALL THINGS AT HIS WILL"! So, the creator is claiming superiority over his own creations not only as a "Creator" but also as a Plotter! Does it sound rational? What is the end result of Allah's plot? A creator's credibility is undoubtedly destroyed when he has to plot against the "Created"! How many of the mankind do believe that Jesus was raised by Allah unto him? Like the revelation and the resurrection, crucifixion is another apple of discord that divided the mankind to a point of no return! To establish supremacy of one faith over other, Allah has shattered the prospect of peaceful co-existence of mankind! The story about raising Jesus to heaven and then sending him again on earth before resurrection has not sold fairly! Who was the person crucified instead of Jesus? Dr. MANEH HAMMAD AL-JOHANI, an Islamic scholar admits; "The Quran does not elaborate on this point nor does it give any answer to this question. The interpreters of the Quran have suggested a few names. But all these are individual gausses not supported by the Quran or the sayings of prophet Muhammad"! So what's in a name? He also adds something about Jesus' coming back to earth again; "The second coming is not clearly mentioned in the Quran but supported by sayings of prophet Muhammad"! This is of no concern whether the Crucifixion has really taken place or not, but it has definitely taken roots in the hearts of the Jews, the Christians and the Muslims to generate hatred against one other!

Verse-55, Ch-3: "AND WHEN ALLAH SAID; O JESUS! I WILL TAKE YOU AND RAISE YOU TO MYSELF AND CLEAR YOU OF THE FORGED STATEMENT (THAT JESUS IS ALLAH'S SON)". When did Jesus feel ashamed of that "Forged Statement"? Does Jesus need to be cleared of that? The Christians do not think so! Whatever Allah had to say to Muhammad, he did so through Gabriel! Jesus came to this world more than six hundred years before Muhammad! Did Allah send Gabriel or any other angel to Jesus to say that he intends to "Raise" him unto himself? Is there a verse of this kind in the Gospel? It is said that the Bible has a verse which forecasted arrival of Muhammad to replace Jesus! After hundreds of years Allah felt it necessary to disown Jesus as his son! How and in what manner Allah raised Jesus to heaven is not known but Muhammad was flown to heavens on a donkey-like animal, called "BORAK" during night and returned back to earth before dawn! Difficult to digest? Well, "ALLAH IS ABLE TO DO ALL THINGS"! What makes this verse more interesting is the information given in a related Hadith (AL-BUKHARI, Vol. 4, #654) in which prophet Muhammad, swearing upon Allah, says; "THE SON OF MARY WILL SHORTLY DESCEND AMONGST THE MUSLIMS AND WILL JUDGE MANKIND JUSTLY BY THE LAW OF THE QURAN AND NOT BY THE LAW OF THE GOSPEL!" Then who deserves to be regarded as the last Prophet? When Muhammad, the best of the Prophets, failed to unite Judaism, Christianity and Islam, how Jesus is going to implement the law of the Quran over a fragmented mankind? Allah has stopped revelation with the death of Muhammad but he is likely to resume it once again with the arrival of Jesus! How the Christians would react to see the "Son of God" converted to Islam abandoning their religion and the Bible? Paradise is not yet lost; Christians say, when Messiah returns; "Then the earth shall all be paradise, far happier place Than this of Eden"! Believe it or not, Islamic narrative claims that on his second term Jesus will rule this world for forty years to turn this earth into a Muslim world!

Verse-59, Ch-3: "VERILY, THE LIKENESS OF JESUS BEFORE ALLAH IS THE LIKENESS OF ADAM. HE CREATED HIM FROM DUST, THEN SAID TO HIM "BE" AND HE WAS". This verse informs us that the likeness of both Adam and Jesus is same before Allah! We know of no striking resemblance or likeness between Adam and Jesus! They were created by two different methods of creation! Adam was created in the heaven and then kicked out of paradise for committing sins! Father or mother, Adam had none though he himself is regarded as the "Father" of mankind! Jesus was born to Mary in a stable! Lucky indeed he was for having had at least a mother but no one including Allah accepted responsibility of having fathered him! Gabriel, who came to Mary disguised as a man, is also not given the credit of being father of Jesus! Jesus was given the miraculous ability to talk and was appointed a prophet with scripture while still in his cradle! Probably Adam was also able to talk right after his creation as he was not born but created soon after the word "Be" was pronounced by Allah! Jesus is also ordained to come back to earth for a second term! In fact Adam should have the chance to come again on earth so that he could amend the mistakes he made as a beginner! Adam is lodged in the lowest of the seven heavens whereas Jesus is in the second! Jesus was "Crucified" and Adam was not! Adam is often dubbed as the first "Muslim" prophet and Jesus a Christian! The Quran said Adam was thirty meters in height whereas the Rude shows Jesus having an average stature of a normal human being! Adam had Eve as his wife and raised his children whereas Jesus had none of those! There are more dissimilarities than similarities between Adam and Jesus! Physically they stand wide apart and spiritually belong to two different ideology! Only "God" knows what kind of likeness Allah found between them? Allah has a kind of weakness for Jesus! Muhammad says he is the closest to Jesus as brother since all prophets are born of the same "Father"!

Verse-71, Ch-3: "O PEOPLE OF THE SCRIPTURE (JEWS AND CHRISTIANS): WHY DO YOU MIX TRUTH WITH FALSEHOOD AND CONCEAL THE TRUTH WHILE YOU KNOW". In this verse Allah accuses Jews and Christians of mixing facts with falsehood in order to conceal the truth! The "TRUTH", as the Quran claims, is that there are some verses in their scriptures (Torah and Gospel) which have forecasted arrival of Muhammad as the last messenger of God but they rejected this claim outright! With respect to this verse an eye-catching story is narrated in a Hadith (AL-BUKHARI, Vol. 4 #814} which says: A Christian after converting to Islam used to write revelations for Muhammad. Later he reverted to Christianity alleging that "MUHAMMAD KNOWS NOTHING BUT WHAT I HAVE WRITTEN FOR HIM." Then Allah cursed him to die but his body was thrown out by the grave three times after each burial and finally it was left unburied as the ground refused to accept the body anymore! But the people who buried the body complained that "THIS IS AN ACT OF MUHAMMAD AND HIS COMPANIONS. THEY DUG THE GRAVE OF OUR COMPANION AND TOOK HIS BODY OUTSIDE IT, FOR HE HAD RUN AWAY FROM THEM"! The Whistleblower had to pay the ultimate price! Muhammad and his companions did not want the secrets behind the revelation be leaked to the public, because that would invalidate the authenticity of the Quran as a "Divine Book"! So, they killed that guy saying; "ALLAH CAUSED HIM TO DIE"! There is not a single instance in the recorded history of mankind that a body has been thrown out by the grave after burial! This brief story has unfolded the truth about the so-called revelations! All stories and events linked to revelation appear similar to fairy tales cooked up craftily by all those involved in it! The bridge between the earth and the heaven, built by prophet Muhammad and his associates, is the weakest link in the chain of so-called revelations! All forms of divinities have devastated the humanity; divided the mankind as bitter adversaries against one other!

Verse-79, Ch-3: "IT IS NOT POSSIBLE FOR ANY HUMAN BEING, TO WHOM ALLAH HAS GIVEN A BOOK AND PROPHETHOOD TO SAY TO THE PEOPLE; BE MY WORSHIPPERS RATHER THAN ALLAH'S"! Was it not possible for All-knowing Allah to know in advance that followers of Jesus would regard him as a "God" if the "Scripture" was given to prophet in his infancy? Whether the Christians worship the "Son of God" or the God or both is also a matter of contention! Miraculous conception of Jesus by Mary; the ridiculous way of baby Jesus defending his mother against adultery; his claim of being a Prophet with scripture while still in the cradle have generated a God-like character of Jesus in the minds of his followers! For all of these, Allah should bear the responsibility! Prophet Muhammad claimed that no Muslim will have his faith complete unless he or she believes him as the messenger of Allah! So, believing in Allah is as mandatory as believing in Muhammad as his messenger! Only believing in Allah doesn't make you a Muslim! Has he not raised himself to the stature of a God? He is quoted to have said; (AL-BUKHARI, Vol. 4 #654) "DO NOT EXAGGERATE IN PRAISING ME, FOR I AM ONLY A SLAVE OF ALLAH, THE CHRISTIANS OVER PRAISED JESUS TILL THEY TOOK HIM AS A GOD BESIDES ALLAH". Muhammad is a "Slave of Allah"! A believer must believe in Allah and his "Slave" as well! Though Muhammad denies being God but he acted like one! Believing in Muhammad as the

"Recipient" of messages is as mandatory as believing in Allah as the "Sender"! Muhammad stands as a barrier between Allah and mankind! None can reach Allah bypassing Muhammad! He even asked his followers to "Love" him more than their fathers and children! All Muslims must treat Muhammad's wives as their "Mothers"! Dr. M.H. DURRANI, an Islamic scholar claims; "THE HOLY PROPHET BEING VERY CLOSE TO THE ALMIGHTY, LEARNT ALL THOSE ATTRIBUTES"! Whereas Adam being created in his own "Image" by his "Both Hands", could not learn those "Attributes" of Allah!

Verse-91, Ch-3: "VERILY, THOSE WHO DISBELIEVED, AND DIED WHILE THEY WERE DISBELIEVERS, THE EARTH (WHOLE) FULL OF GOLD WILL NOT BE ACCEPTED FROM ANYONE OF THEM EVEN IF THEY OFFERED IT AS A RANSOM". The religion with Allah is Islam and under Islamic Law a killer may be pardoned if he pays "Blood-Money" to the victim's family but an "EARTH FULL OF GOLD" will not be accepted by Allah as ransom to pardon a disbeliever from eternal torments in hell! Which of the disbelievers will be in a position to offer Allah a ransom on the "Day of Resurrection"? According to a Hadith (AL-BUKHARI Vol. 8 #546) Allah will refuse to accept the ransom from the disbeliever and would say to him; "YOU WERE ASKED FOR SOMETHING EASIER THAN THAT (to join none in prayer with Allah but you refused)"! So, tit for tat! Disbeliever refused to accept Islam and Allah refuses to accept ransom! But the Verse and the Hadith have again reminded us that gold is a precious metal not only in this life but also in the life hereafter! This earth has very small amount of gold which may not be one trillionth of its weight! An earth full of gold as ransom, even as an example, is too little to please the Lord of the heaven! This verse is another example of immaturity of the "Author" of the Quran! Citing examples is not unusual practice but those examples must have a realistic relation with the actual subject matter! How can the "Creator" of the Earth and the Heaven asks for Ransom like a "Kidnapper"? None of the disbelievers after resurrection will be in a position to offer such a huge ransom to the "Best of Judges" on the "Day of Judgment"! Satan plotted against Allah and successfully ousted Adam and Eve from paradise; an unforgiveable crime! Yet to the astonishment of all, Satan has been able to obtain "Respite" from Allah until resurrection without paying a single penny as ransom! Satan, a creation of Allah, has outwitted his "Creator"!

Verse-103, Ch-3: "AND HOLD FAST, ALL OF YOU TOGETHER, TO THE ROPE (QURAN) OF ALLAH, AND BE NOT DIVIDED AMONG YOURSELF". Unfortunately the "Rope" has many weak links from the start to the finish! How fast the believers hold the "Rope" together is evident from the words of the messenger himself! A hadith (AL-TIRMIDHI) quotes Muhammad as saying; "THE JEWS AND CHRISTIANS WERE DIVIDED INTO SEVENTY ONE (71) OR SEVENTY TWO (72) RELIGIOUS SECTS, AND THIS NATION (Muslims) WILL BE DIVIDED INTO SEVENTY THREE (73) RELIGIOUS SECTS, ALL IN HELL, EXCEPT ONE, AND THAT ONE IS THE ONE ON WHICH I AND MY COMPANIONS ARE TODAY"! Muhammad, the best among the prophets, has drawn a very bleak picture of the religious reality of his period! This assessment reflects his own failures as the only messenger for mankind! Jesus on his second arrival would be highly disappointed to see the fragmented mankind; almost dilapidated to the verge of extinction! According to Muhammad, Jesus would be arriving at a time when Fifty women would be running after a Man! The number of man will reduce to an alarming situation that the "Rope" will break itself into pieces leaving the believers scattered! All verses and words of the Quran are open to various interpretations and each interpretation creates a new group! "All in Hell" is a severe warning for the Muslims! Out of seventy three Sects, the one with Muhammad shall be admitted into paradise! In verse 9 of chapter 46 prophet Muhammad, the most-loved messenger, was asked by his Lord to say to his followers; "I AM NOT THE FIRST MESENGER, NOR DO I KNOW WHAT WILL BE DONE WITH ME OR WITH YOU"! As par the Hadith quoted above, only Muhammad and his companions who are with him "Today" will be admitted into paradise and the rest of the mankind will find themselves in Hell unless they "Hold fast to the Rope (Quran) of Allah"! This is why Allah created tens of trillions of "Twinkle, Twinkle Little Stars" so that he might use them as "Hell"!

Verse-118, Ch-3: "O YOU WHO BELIEVE! TAKE NOT AS ADVISORS, FRIENDS, PROTECTORS THOSE OUTSIDE YOUR RELIGION (PAGANS, JEWS, CHRISTIANS) SINCE THEY WILL NOT FAIL TO DO THEIR BEST TO CORRUPT YOU. THEY DESIRE TO HARM YOU SEVERLY. HATRED HAS ALREADY APPEARED FROM THEIR MOUTHS, BUT WHAT THEIR BREASTS CONCEAL IS FAR WORSE"! Allah in verse 6 of chapter 109 asks Muhammad to say to the disbelievers; "TO YOU BE

YOUR RELIGION, AND TO ME MY RELIGION"! Verse 256 of chapter 2 says; "THERE IS NO COMPULSION IN RELIGION" and in this verse Allah is asking his devotees not to make friends with disbelievers nor take them as advisors or protectors since "HATRED HAS ALREADY APPEARED FROM THEIR MOUTHS"! Allah reiterates his position in the Quran as the WALI (protector) of the believers but they have very little trust in his assurances! Taking lessons from the helpless Palestinians, other Muslim nations of the believers are seeking security and protection from the disbelievers! Guardians of Islam, including the "Custodian of the two Holy mosques" openly defy these verses of the Quran by making friends with the forbidden people! Does it not constitute a defiance of the Quran and its "Author"? Is this not blasphemy? So, it is Allah who is preventing mankind to live in harmony? Do they deserve to be custodians of those holy mosques if they themselves defy Allah's verses? Some of the Muslim monarchies have even made friends with the Jewish state! They have realized that there is no sense in what these verses say considering the geo-political realities! The Christian leaders are not only acting as de-facto custodians but also as the protectors, advisors and friends of the many Islamic nations! The Jews and the Christians are enemies of Allah! What about the Palestinians? Why Allah is not helping them? Gaza has become the worst example of a burning "Hell"! Yet, raising from the rubbles they shout "ALLAH-HU-AKBAR"! Neither a Revelation nor a response is forthcoming from Allah, the "Protector"!

Verse-125, Ch-3: "YES, IF YOU HOLD ON TO PATIENCE AND PIETY, THE ENEMY COMES RUSHING AT YOU, YOUR LORD WILL HELP YOU WITH FIVE THOUSANDS ANGELS HAVING MARKS OF DISTINCTION". In the battle of BADR (V. 3:124) Muhammad said to his fellow fighters: "IS IT NOT ENOUGH FOR YOU THAT YOUR LORD (ALLAH) SHOULD HELP YOU WITH THREE THOUSAND ANGELS SENT DOWN"? But if the they hold on to patience and piety and the enemy comes rushing at them, Allah might consider sending "Five Thousand Angels" having marks of distinction! The Palestinians holding on to their patients and piety for more than half a century, yet Allah has not considered sending any "Angels with marks of distinction"! It is claimed that every day seventy thousands Angels assemble at Allah's palace lovated over seven heavens to offer their prayers! It is really unthinkable that Allah made Muhammad and his soldiers accept defeat at the battle of UHUD, one of the great battles in the history of Islam! Allah then laid the blame on Satan alleging that he instigated the Muslim soldiers to flee the battle field! Does history repeat itself? How long Allah wants Palestinians to hold their patience and piety in the fight against the Jews? Are the Palestinians not pious believers? More than half a century of bloodshed has seen no help coming forth from the ALLA-HU-AKBAR! He is yet to send his elite forces of angels, having marks of distinction, to fight for the Palestinians against the Jews! The enemies still come rushing! Jihadists across the world are relentlessly busy fighting to establish rule of Allah! Since the dawn of ancient civilization many Muslim nations fought wars against enemies of Allah to establish their faith, culture and tradition but a lasting victory never came to them! The merciful "Creator" stood a silent spectator during Holocaust! He was happy to see his bitter enemies, the Jews, being dragged into gas chamber! Allah wants to use Man as 'Fuel' for Hellfire and Hitler did the same for his inferno! Flames of burning hearts rose unto Heaven with a big question mark on its back!

Verse-138, Ch-3: "THE QURAN IS A PLAIN STATEMENT FOR MANKIND, A GUIDANCE AND INSTRUCTION TO THOSE WHO ARE PIOUS". Well said! What are the "Plain Meanings" of verses that are composed of a few Arabic alphabets such as "ALIF, LAM, MIM"? What about the letter called "NUN"? This single letter itself is a verse of the Quran! The so-called "PLAIN STATEMENT" says that these alphabets are "Miracles" of the Quran and their meaning is only known to Allah, the "Author"! About thirty chapters of the Quran begins with these "Miracles"! How these "Miracles" will act as "Guidance" to bring the mankind out of darkness into light and show them the straight path to paradise? Besides "miracles", the Quran also contains "Unclear", "Abrogated", "Entirely Unclear" verses, not to mention those that are contradictory and inconsistent! These "Miracles" are meaningless and irrelevant to the mankind! The Lord claims he does not do anything without purpose! What purpose do these "Miracles" serve for the human being? Though Allah intended this Quran for the entire mankind, but the reality on ground suggests otherwise! The Muslims as a whole have not taken this plain statement seriously as guidance and instruction for themselves! Leave aside the ordinary Muslims, even the Muslim Kings and the Rulers have openly defied "GUIDANCE AND INSTRUCTION" given in verse 118 of surah 3 of the Quran! Probably Quran is the only revealed book of religion that has received unprecedented criticism worldwide! Un-trustworthy stories related to its revelation to compilation, involving no less than hundreds of people, have rendered the Quran into a book of contention right from its inception! It has failed to register spiritual recognition as a charter of magnanimity from peace-loving mankind because of its advocacy for violent Jihad and total disregards to humanity! Most dangerous agenda of Islam is that it does not recognize other people's right to practice their own faiths! Allah claims to have "revealed" the Quran as a "Plain statement" for the mankind but only for those who are "Pious"!

Verse-144, Ch-3: "MOHAMMAD IS NO MORE THAN A MESSENGER, AND INDEED MANY MESSENGERS HAVE PASSED AWAY BEFORE HIM" This statement of Allah is a complete reversal of what Muhammad unequivocally claimed about himself in the Quran and Hadiths! The most unique of all the special features that prophet Muhammad claims is that he is the only messenger who has been sent for the "whole of mankind" and the rest came for their respective nations only! No incumbent messenger was taken to space to meet with Allah except Muhammad! None of the messengers, except Muhammad, was given the magical power to split the Moon! No messenger but Muhammad claimed that the Earth has been "Created" only for him and his followers to worship Allah! No messenger before Muhammad was given so many options to marry! No other messenger was promised to be given the highest place in the paradise! It was only Muhammad for whom a special palace has been made, called "MAQAM MAHMUD"! Muhammad will be the first to be resurrected and will have the right to intercede with Allah on behalf of the mankind! Muhammad is the only messenger who wanted his followers to love him more than their fathers and children! He is the one who said that no Muslim will have his faith complete unless he be accepted as the messenger of Allah! We cannot rule out the possibility that Muhammad's companions and the scribes were divided into two camps, one praising him more than he deserved and the other spoke of him as he was! Allah branded Muhammad as "NO MORE THAN A MESSENGER" but his followers raised him to the stature of no less than a God! Like the quest for the "Holy Grail", man's quest for the "City of God" is also a venture on a perilous voyage! Besides the burden of sins, questions and queries shall make the journey as perilous as it could be! Hump-backed pilgrims who yielded to temptations are terrified! Finish line is yet to be seen! Last mile is the longest! Hold your breath and wait for the angel to blow his Trumpet!

Verse-145, Ch-3: "AND NO PERSON CAN EVER DIE EXCEPT BY ALLAH'S LEAVE AND AT AN APPOINTED TERM". What about those who commit suicide? Do they do it by Allah's leave? A baby dies in his mother's lap also by Allah's leave since no person can ever die by himself! Allah also says that the dwellers of paradise will live life and those in the Hell will live death eternally! Allah called the Jews the "Greediest People" and as such Shakespeare painted Shylock! They are also the bitter enemies to Allah, Muhammad and Islam! To the Christians; they are the killers of the "Son of God" as they "Crucified" him against the will of the "Creator"! lastly, the ultimate "Curse" fell upon them from heaven and Hitler did the rest! Sixty Million of them became victims of the Holocaust; burnt to ashes in the gas chamber as if the Hell came down on earth! No one could escape the "Inferno"! Allah and Hitler both acted against their common enemy! Now I come to the point to draw your attention to the verse above where Allah says; "NO PERSON CAN EVER DIE EXCEPT BY ALLAH'S LEAVE"! Hitler's Holocaust is one of the many debacles that took tens of thousands of innocent lives! Did they die by Allah's leave? So it was also by Allah's leave that Cane killed Abel at "an appointed term"! If some Islamic scholar is asked to explain this plain verse, he might discover a wealth of meaning behind it so as to defend Allah, Muhammad and Islam and lastly he will come up with a conclusion that the real meaning of the verse is "Beyond" human knowledge! We have no reason to blame Muhammad why he was not able to compile the Quran and complete his mission in his lifetime! He died leaving behind the "Revelation" scattered all over the place! Why? Because Allah did not extend the "Appointed Term" for the "Messenger of Mankind" although he promised to keep him alive until the "Crooked mankind" became "Straight"! The only exception is Jesus! Allah "Raised" him alive so as to send him again on earth to revamp failed mission of Muhammad with renewed resolve and "Revelation"!

Verse-155, Ch-3: 'THOSE OF YOU WHO TURNED BACK ON THE DAY OF THE BATTLE OF *UHUD*, IT WAS SATAN WHO CAUSED THEM TO BACKSLIDE AND RUN AWAY FROM THE BATTLEFIELD BECAUSE OF SOME SINS THEY HAD EARNED". Right in the beginning of this "Divine" drama, Satan instigated Adam to eat the forbidden fruits in paradise and now in the battle of UHUD he has caused Allah's soldiers to backslide and run away from the war field! For every failure, Allah uses Satan as a scapegoat! Between these two adversaries, Satan looks smarter than Allah!? This Battle of UHUD took place near Medina between the disbelievers and the believers with the prophet himself leading from the front! Muhammad claimed that Allah always made him victorious in the war field by frightening the enemies and sending army of angels to fight for him! What happened in the battle of UHUD? Who is to blame for the humiliating defeat Allah and Muhammad suffered at the hands of their enemies? Why Allah failed to send his elite force of angels to fight for Muhammad? So, Satan is able to do something against the "Will" of Allah! Finally it is the Satan who won the war! What kind of sins did the defeated soldiers earn? Were those sins really unpardonable that they called for a devastating defeat at the hands of the enemies? It is also not justified to lay blame on the "Creator" as he only takes the "Credit"! So it is apparent that Allah sent Satan, instead of an army of angels, to "Cause them to backslide and run away from the battlefield"! Nobody is above blame games including the "Creator"! Looking for lame excuses for failures is a foul practice which is widespread among humans, not expected of a "Creator"! This verse is also one of many that goes against the claim that Quran is a divine book revealed and authored by a divine entity! A "Creator", even if he exists, shall never take part in war, directly or indirectly against his own creation; the humans! Neither the "Commander" of the battlefield nor his "Creator" could desist Satan from playing his ploy! The same is true when Satan ousted Adam from paradise!

Verse-166, Ch-3: "AND WHAT YOU SUFFERED ON THE DAY OF THE BATTLE OF UHUD, WAS BY THE LEAVE OF ALLAH, IN ORDER THAT HE MIGHT TEST THE BELIEVERS". This and the verse discussed above are closely related and provide two separate reasons of defeat in the battle of UHUD in which followers of Muhammad fighting for Allah suffered a deadly defeat at the hands of the so-called infidels! In the first verse the blame for the defeat was attributed to Satan who is said to have caused the Muslim fighters to turn their back and flee from the battlefield! The second verse says the defeat was caused by the leave of "Allah" in order that he might test the believers! So, Allah turned the battle field into a testing ground for the believers! Who was the commander in the battlefield? Was he not supposed to take responsibility for the defeat? Nay, since Muhammad claims that Allah has made him victorious by awe (by frightening his enemies) and made war booty lawful only for him among the messengers! But as a messenger his failure is even more humiliating than the defeat at UHUD! He claims to have come for the entire mankind to implement Islamic monotheism on behalf of Allah! How much did he achieve to that end? These verses are aimed at frightening the followers so that they don't flee the war in future leaving Muhammad in a helpless situation at the mercy of the disbelievers! Allah did not keep his promises to help Muhammad with elite forces of angels nor did he frighten his enemies to ensure his victory! Allah and his messenger's war plan was faulty and that of Satan was meticulously drawn! If we are made to believe that Allah had plans to test the believers of their loyalty in the battlefield, then why did he not think of the humiliation of Muhammad as the commander of his forces? The battle that took place at the foot of the mountain UHUD is a historical fact but to give it a divine flavor, the script writers had to struggle a lot to make it look like a Holy-war! All-Knowing Allah did not know the outcome of the battle in advance! Satan won the war decisively! So, the winner takes it all!

Verse-185, Ch-3: "EVERYONE SHALL TASTE DEATH, AND ONLY ON THE DAY OF RESURRECTION SHALL YOU BE PAID YOUR WAGES IN FULL. THE LIFE OF THIS WORLD IS ONLY THE ENJOYMENT OF DECEPTION (A DECEIVING THING)".Every creature is born with a death warrant; destined to meet one's fate! This fact of life is neither spiritual nor philosophical but natural and applies to all creatures! We have been repeatedly told that every living being who tested "Creation" will have to taste death except the "Creator" himself since he has not gone through any process of creation! Chances are there that he might decide to destroy his entire creation and live all alone by himself until he decides to go for a new creation! Surprisingly Allah has decided to pay our "WAGES IN FULL" on the basis of our performance in "THE LIFE OF THIS WORLD" which is "ONLY THE ENJOYMENT OF DECEPTION"! Allah has allowed Satan to live his life, without having to taste death, to mislead mankind until resurrection! Note that Allah has given the Satan a life that spans from Creation to Resurrection! No prophet or messenger was allowed such a massive span of life! Probably among the prophets, Muhammad was the unluckiest to have the shortest life in this world! As this life is "A DECEIVING THING", Allah took him at the earliest opportunity! Humans are naturally inclined more towards recreation than religion! The "Deceptions" created by Satan and his associates received a better response from the crowd! Those who have been trapped by Satan's "Enjoyment of Deception" in this world will have to pay their price in full and will also receive their "Wages in Full" from Allah after resurrection! The "Creator" could easily skip mass trial on the Day of Judgment by resurrecting only those qualified for to enter paradise! All religions use after-death fear as the most effective tool to terrorize human beings! No other creatures worry about hell and heaven as humans do! Animals are really born-free as they have not been "Warned" by so many messengers nor received any "Divine Revelation" from heavens!

Verse-1, Ch-4: "O MANKIND! BE DUTIFUL TO YOUR LORD, WHO CREATED YOU FROM A SINGLE PERSON (ADAM), AND FROM HIM HE CREATED HIS WIFE (EVE) AND FROM THEM HE CREATED MANY MEN AND WOMEN." Well, it is possible to create "Many men and Women" from a couple as Adam and Eve! But their individual creation process was conspicuously unusual and untrustworthy! Allah already created angels from Light and devils from Fire as invisible creatures! Later he planned to create a visible mankind! So he created Adam from Clay and then uttered the word "Be" to breathe life into him! At this point Allah was in a dilemma! His plan to create a mankind needed at least one woman to make a pair with Adam since there was no other woman available! He could apply the same creative method as he did for Adam but he finally opted to create Eve directly from Adam though it looked crazy! Another ridiculous story was manufactured about the creation of Jesus, the so-called "Son of God"! Finally the "Creator" or the story-teller came to the conclusion that it was the semen or, in divine term, the "Despised Water" that could make his dream come true through mating between male and female! This is the only method of procreation universally known to almost all living creatures and acceptable to the mankind! The "Creator" devised and applied unusual modes of creation on Adam, Eve and Jesus! However, prophet Muhammad was born in a usual way! Because at that time the sun was in its prime, the pagans would not buy such myths! All prophets and messengers were dutiful to their Lord save the infidels! But how the marriage between Adam and Eve was solemnized and who pronounced them husband and wife? Adam being the first Muslim prophet must have followed Islamic Sharia Law for marriage? Well, whatever Allah does is Islamic! If the scientists create a man by cloning, as Allah created Eve from Adam, most of the humanity will be on toes to protest! The mankind is dutiful to their "Lord" save the priests; God has forbidden them to take part in procreation!

Verse-15, Ch-4: "AND THOSE OF YOUR WOMEN WHO COMMIT ILLIGAL SEXUAL INTERCOURSE, TAKE THE EVIDENCE OF FOUR WITNESSES FROM AMONGST YOU AGAINST THEM, AND IF THEY TESTIFY, CONFINE THEM (i.e. WOMEN) TO HOUSE UNTIL DEATH

COMES TO THEM OR ALLAH ORDAINS FOR THEM OTHER WAY". Why only women? What about men who commit illegal sexual intercourse? When Muhammad got trapped into conjugal quagmire, Allah sent many verses to pull him out of the wetland! Verse 30 of surah 33 is one those which says; "O WIVES OF THE PROPHET! WHOEVER OF YOU COMMITS AN ILLEGAL OPEN SEXUAL INTERCOURSE, THE TORMENT FOR HER WILL BE DOUBLED, AND THAT IS EVER EASY FOR ALLAH"! In this case Allah did not ask for four witness to testify! Is it possible to find four eye witnesses to fornications? Why only women should be confined until death? Why these verse should not be applicable to wives of the prophet? This verse is said to have been abrogated by Verse 2 of chapter 24 which advocates even harsher punishment: "ORDAINING LASHING FOR THE UNMARRIED AND STONING TO DEATH FOR THE MARRIED WHEN FOUR WITNESSES TESTIFY TO THE CRIME". Confusion arises to the fact who abrogated the verse in question? No divine authority has been referred to for the abrogation! Perpetrators of "Honor Killing" in the Muslim communities may have been inspired by these verses! The most horrific part of this kind of religious killing and beheading is that the execution is usually carried out in front of mass gathering! Allah is also said to be the "Creator of Time"! Yet he could not write a timeless book for the mankind once for all without miracles, abrasion and abrogation? 23 years of time was not enough for a flawless "Revelation"? Despite sending scriptures after scriptures, Allah's messages could not rise above time to be accepted universally! Finding four witnesses to a crime like fornication is not an easy option! Depicting an invisible "Creator" out of imagination is not as difficult as hiding the truth about him!

Verse-45, Ch-4: "ALLAH HAS FULL KNOWLEDGE OF YOUR ENEMIES, AND ALLAH IS SUFFICIENT AS A PROTECTOR, AND ALLAH IS SUFFICIENT AS A HELPER". All-Knowing Allah had full knowledge of the enemies in the battle of UHUD but proved to be insufficient as a "Protector" and also as a "Helper"! Muslim soldiers led by Muhammad, fighting for Allah were defeated and suffered a huge loss of life and property at the hands of the infidels! Eventually Allah tried to shift the blame on Satan for the defeat! If he could play his role both as protector and helper, the world would have been overwhelmed with believers! Probably the "King" of the Universe, sitting in his throne over Seven Heavens, is not able to see the hopeless conditions of his helpless believers all round his "Kingdom"! Another probable reason for Allah's failure as protector and helper could be attributed to the negligence of the angels entrusted to report daily affairs of the world to him! Otherwise the creator Allah could easily reassess his role to be sufficient both as "Protector" and "Helper" for his believers! Undoubtedly the All-Mighty has full knowledge of the safety and the security situation of the Muslim nations of the world! People of Iraq, Syria, Afghanistan, Somalia, Yemen, Palestine and others who believe in Allah raise their hands upwards seeking help from the merciful "WALI" (Protector) living in the heavens! What often comes from the above is a barrage of bullets! Drenched with bloods they shout "ALLAH-HU-AKBAR" before their last breath; for they must die as the believers to get a share of the bounties in paradise! Believers undergoing tests need not worry at all as Allah "HAS FULL KNOWLEDGE" of their awkward predicament! Life of this world is an entertainment of "Deception" only! Paradise is the place for eternal bliss! Hold your patience! When the time is right, Allah will definitely send "Help" and "Protection" for the believers! The Jews, the Christians and all other disbelievers, who are not protected by Allah, enjoy more peace and protection than the Muslims!

Verse-79, Ch-4: "WHATEVER OF GOOD REACHES YOU, IS FROM ALLAH, BUT WHATEVER OF EVIL BEFALLS YOU IS FROM YOURSELF, AND WE HAVE SENT MUHAMMAD AS A MESSENGER TO MANKIND AND ALLAH IS SUFFICIENT AS A WITNESS". "No one can die without Allah's leave"(V. 145 of Ch. 3) and this verse says; "Whatever of evil befalls you is from yourself"! Try to find coherence between these two statements of Allah from your recollection of Abel-Cain murder episode! All catastrophe that play havoc on us come from ourselves! So says the All-Aware "Witness" living in the heaven! Allah refuses to take responsibilities for the devastations! On the other hand, he says; "WE SHALL TEST YOU WITH SOMETHING OF FEAR, HUNGER, LOSS OF WEALTH, LIVES AND FRUITS" (V. 155 of Ch. 2)! Whatever had befallen Muhammad, as regards to his family affairs and illness, Allah had nothing to do with that! But when the matters got out of control, Lord's intervention became imperative! What came from heaven are the verses containing advice how to resolve conjugal matters with his wives! Muhammad was relentlessly busy fighting wars one after another against infidels for which he was not able to put his own house in order! Dozens of wives put him in a difficult domestic problems! Whenever something of "Good" reaches us, we thank God and whenever "Evils" befall us, we blame ourselves! Sometimes Allah too blames Satan for his own failures! For the defeat in the battle of UHUD,

Allah blamed Satan as he is said to have instigated the fighters to backslide and run away! Allah claims he is "SUFFICIENT AS A WITNESS"! The Lord will be "Sufficient" as "Witness" to Muhammad's failure as "MESSENGER TO MANKIND"! It is hard to believe that our "Creator" created us as the source of "Evils"! Allah's Arabic name is "RABB" which means the one and only Lord of the universe and giver of security! Our security is "guaranteed" but how can we get rid of Satanic Evils? It is Allah who has granted "Respite" to Satan to mislead humans to evils until Resurrection!

Verse-82, Ch-4: "DO THEY NOT THEN CONSIDER THE QURAN CAREFULLY? HAD IT BEEN FROM OTHER THAN ALLAH, THEY WOULD SURELY HAVE FOUND THEREIN MANY A CONTRADICTION". Had it been really from a man or a group of man, the Quran as a book of religion would not have gone through such an awful mishandling right from its revelation all the way down to compilation! It is indeed from Allah, the unseen "Author"! To be or not to be that is the Question! The believers who are faithfully blind or blinded by faith would never see any contradictions in the Quran! The cover-up stories, circulated by the loyalists, lack credibility! However, some trustworthiness could be restored if Muhammad had lived until the compilation of the Quran! Why he died long before that? Because his death was not in the hands of his Lord! In the beginning of this English Translation of the Quran, Allah is quoted to have said; "THERE HAS COME TO YOU FROM ALLAH A LIGHT AND A PLAIN BOOK". Interestingly, this "Plain Book" has 114 Surah or chapters and around thirty of them begin with verses composed of some Arabic letters, called the miracles of the Quran, ranging from one to five that bear no meanings for anyone of the mankind including Muhammad to whom it was revealed! Gabriel, Muhammad and his companions spoke Arabic dialect, yet none could make out the meanings of those letters! Surely, there is mystery behind these miracles! In some cases only one letter has been shown as one verse of the chapter! The translators while explaining these Arabic alphabets said; "THESE LETTERS ARE ONE OF THE MIRACLES OF THE QURAN AND NONE BUT ALLAH ALONE KNOWS THEIR MEANINGS". Are these miracles not contradictory to the claim that the Quran is a "Plain Book"? Does the Quran deserve to be defined as a "Plain Statement"? How on earth can a book be called "Plain" If the meanings are not plain to the readers? In a number of verses Allah has claimed to have created the earth and the heavens in six days and in some other verses he said he could create anything just by uttering the word

"Be" in a fraction of a second? He also claims to have created Adam and Jesus by uttering that word (Be) only! Almost every chapter of the Quran contains contradictory verses! One has to read this Quran carefully without being blind-folded by faith to find contradictions, controversies, inconsistencies, incoherence that render the whole Quran all in all a poor composition. For the defeat in the battle of UHUD, Allah first blames Satan and then in another verse he says it happened by his "Leave"! Also after going through the meanings of its texts, a careful reader gets the impression that this Quran has not been composed by a single person or by any divine being! Most importantly the reading generates a conviction in the minds of the readers that whoever may be the author of the Quran, he doesn't deserve to be regarded as the "Creator" of the universe! If investigated thoroughly by some independent theologians, this Quran would reveal many loopholes that will render it redundant as a "Light" for the mankind! How can we lay our trust on a "Creator" who swears by Olives and Figs to say that he is the "Best of Judges"? In some verses he clearly says that the Jews or the Christians who believed in their scriptures and also believe in the "Day of Judgment" are on the right path! And then in another verse he claims Islam as the only religion acceptable to him? Are these not contradictions? Some Islamic expert argue that these verses have been "Abrogated"! Who has the right to abrogate these verses? Surely Allah or the "Author"! Allah has not mentioned anywhere in the Quran that he himself has abrogated those verses! In one verse Allah claims that his one day is equal to a thousand years of world standard time and in another verse he says it is equal to fifty thousand years! Allah promised to give Muhammad the best place in paradise! He promised to lodge his believers in paradise and others in Hell! And then the "Lord" asks Muhammad (Verse 9 of chapter 46) to say to his followers; "I DO NOT KNOW WHAT WILL BE DONE WITH ME OR WITH YOU"? We have found "MANY A CONTRADICTION" in the Quran!

Verse-84, Ch-4: "THEN FIGHT (O MUHAMMAD) IN THE CAUSE OF ALLAH, YOU ARE NOT TASKED (HELD RESPONSIBLE) EXCEPT FOR YOURSELF, AND INCITE THE BELIEVERS TO FIGHT ALONG WITH YOU". Muhammad unequivocally claims that among thousands of messengers, he is the one sent for the whole of mankind! He is the one who has the mandate to speak to Allah on the "Day of Resurrection" on behalf of the mankind! He is the one who visited Allah paradise! He is the one who led Jihad against infidels to establish Allah's religion of

Islam! After having been tasked with so many important assignments, yet Muhammad is not going to be held responsible for his failure as the messenger of mankind! Every believer is obliged to greet him saying; "Oh messenger of Allah, Peace be upon you"! Is this complement paid for his achievement as a peace-maker? Or is it that he is not in peace? Do the Muslims have doubt that Muhammad is not in peace after death despite assurances given by Allah that he would be taken care of? Responding to Allah's call to incite the believers, thousands of terrorist groups are now fully operational all over the planet! Muhammad has been "Tasked" for the whole of mankind without accountability! So, Muhammad has no moral obligation to take any responsibility for atrocities wrought by the radical Islamists on innocent people all over the world in the name of Allah? Allah's justice system allows his messenger to incite the believers to fight for him without taking any blame for the consequences! His commandment asking Muhammad to "INCITE THE BELIEVERS TO FIGHT" reinforces the distrust on his credibility! The people of the scripture say; "NONE SHALL ENTER PARADISE UNLESS HE BE A JEW OR CHRISTIAN" (Verse 111 of chapter 2)! In response Allah asks Muhammad to challenge them and say; "PRODUCE YOUR PROOF IF YOU ARE TRUTHFUL"! Did Allah produce any proof? The mankind is entangled into the sticky fabrics of faiths woven by many "Spiders"; who don't want to be proved wrong! The "Truth" is missing in action!

Verse-86, Ch-4: "WHEN YOU ARE GREETED WITH A GREETING, GREET IN RETURN WITH WHAT IS BETTER THAN IT". What is amusing is not the verse itself but the related Hadith (AL-BUKHARI, Vol. 8, #246) that narrates how the greeting began as a custom in Muslin community: "ALLAH CREATED ADAM IN HIS IMAGE; SIXTY CUBITS (ABOUT 30 METERS) IN HEIGHT. AFTER CREATION ALLAH ORDERED ADAM TO SEE A GROUP OF ANGELS AND GREET THEM SAYING; PEACE BE UPON YOU. THE ANGELS REPLIED BY SAYING; PEACE AND ALLAH'S MERCY BE ON YOU! SO WHOEVER WILL ENTER PARADISE, WILL BE OF THE SHAPE AND PICTURE OF ADAM. SINCE THEN THE CREATION OF ADAM'S OFFSPRING (i.e. STATURE OF HUMAN BEINGS) IS BEING CONTINUOUSLY DIMINISHED UP TO THE PRESENT TIME. FEATURES OF ADAM ARE DIFFERENT FROM THOSE OF ALLAH, ONLY THE NAMES ARE THE SAME, e.g. ALLAH HAS LIFE AND KNOWLEDGE AND POWER OF UNDERSTANDING, AND ADAM ALSO HAS THEM, BUT THERE IS NO COMPARISON BETWEEN THE CREATOR AND THE

CREATED. ALLAH DOES NOT EAT OR SLEEP WHILE ADAM USED TO SLEEP AND EAT". Probably the Satan took advantage of it and induced Adam into eating the "Forbidden Fruits"! This Hadith contains lots of interesting information on physical features of Adam and Allah! Scientists have uncovered fossils of huge dinosaurs but never found any human fossil 90 feet in height! Is this Hadith not enough to confuse the mankind? Allah created Adam in "His Image"! So, Adam resembled his creator, like a son resembles his father! What about Abel and Cane? Surely they resembled their father! When Abel was killed by cane, how his ninety feet body was buried? What is Allah's height? To add more to the confusion the hadith further says, the features of Allah and Adam are not real, similar only in name! So our ancestors were thirty meters (about 90 ft.) in height and since then gradually diminishing! How much time elapsed between Adam and Muhammad? His height has come down to about six feet from ninety feet! Unbelievable indeed! What was the average height of the mummies of the ancient Egyptian royals? Did they resemble Adam in stature? If we keep diminishing at this rate, time is not far off when we might end up being Pigmies or Lilliputians! Jonathan Swift may have borrowed the idea from this story before writing Gulliver's Travels.! But Prophet Muhammad assures us that we will regain our "Shape and Picture" before entering the paradise! Muhammad did not mention from what source he collected the information about Adam's physical features! Many philosophers believe that probably the creator does not have physical existence! But Prophet Muhammad certifies that Allah has "Life", "Knowledge" and "Power" of understanding, as do Adam and his offspring, but those qualities of the "Creator" are not comparable to those of the "Created"! Allah also has "Two Hands" on which he will hold the earth and the heavens on the "Day of Judgment"! So, Allah has all features of a "Man"! Allah did not like to have offspring and as such he did not want to marry! Islamic scholars use "HE" as the pronoun for Allah! All that indicate that Allah belongs to male gender! Allah has shared his attributes (Life, Knowledge and Power of understanding) with his creation! Those attributes have enabled us to question his existence! But the confusion still persists as the Hadith warns us that there can be no comparison between the "Creator" and the "Created"! If we trace out our roots in terms of ancestral heritage, we have to begin with Allah who has imparted his image to Adam and then he, as the father of the mankind, transferred his image to his offspring! We are gradually landing into identity crisis! Our image has a striking resemblance with four-footed apes, not ninety feet tall Adam! But "Creators" would never accept the fact that Monkeys were our forefathers! Darwin on the other hand dismissed Adam-Eve saga as a folklore! However, after the perilous journey, the pilgrims will regain their height, shape and picture of Adam! They don't want to enter into paradise as dwarfs!

Verse-119, Ch-4: "VERILY, I WILL MISLEAD THEM, I WILL AROUSE IN THEM FALSE DESIRES AND CERTAINLY, I WILL ORDER THEM TO SLIT THE EARS OF CATTLE, AND INDEED I WILL ORDER THEM TO CHANGE THE NATURE CREATED BY ALLAH". Satan, emboldened by the "Respite" granted to him by Allah, spoke these words of defiance! If these words are spoken by a man, he would definitely be beheaded by the defenders of Islam! Allah set Satan free to mislead us and decided not to reprimand him! Muhammad may have failed to achieve his target but Satan has done well! He has been able to divert most of mankind away from the path of Allah! What did Satan mean by "SLIT THE EARS OF CATTLE"? A Hadith, (AL-BUKHARI, Vol. 6 #409) explains this verse in greater details; "ALLAH CURSES THOSE LADIES WHO PRACTICE TATOOING AND THOSE WHO GET THEMSELVES TATOOED, AND THOSE LADIES WHO GET THEIR HAIR REMOVED FROM THEIR EYEBROWS AND FACES EXCEPT THE BEARD AND MOUSTACHE, AND THOSE WHO MAKE ARTIFICIAL SPACES BETWEEN THEIR TEETH IN ORDER TO LOOK MORE BEAUTIFUL WHEREBY THEY CHANGE ALLAH`S CREATION". It is Allah who has the absolute right to change his creation! He reduced our height from ninety feet to six and will increase it back to ninety before entering into paradise! Are the Hadith writers misogynist? They targeted only the ladies doing cosmetic beautifications! The Royals including "Custodian of the two Holy Mosques" color their hair and beards to look younger! Even at ninety, beards of the Kings do not turn gray! The Hadith also says; "ALLAH'S MESSENGER HAS CURSED THE LADY WHO USES FALSE HAIR". Satan not only misled the mankind, he also arouse false desires among the ladies as and when he found the opportunity! However, Allah warned messenger's wives well in advance (Verse 30 of chapter 33) so that they don't fall victims to Satan's ploy! For the male believers, Allah has created "HURS"! Each will get two "HURS" as his wives in paradise! Surprisingly there is no mention of such rewards for the ladies!

Verse-129, Ch-4: "YOU WILL NEVER BE ABLE TO DO PERFECT JUSTICE BETWEEN WIVES EVEN IF IT IS YOUR ARDENT DESIRE.

SO DO NOT INCLINE TOO MUCH TO ONE OF THEM BY GIVING HER MORE OF YOUR TIME AND PROVISION SO AS TO LEAVE THE OTHER HANGING i.e. NEITHER DIVORCED NOR MARRIED". This verse highlights the problems often encountered by the polygamists! Allah has approved polygamy and Muhammad has shown the way to his followers! But he himself suffered untold pangs of polygamy that went out of limits and Allah finally sent verses warning his wives with double punishments if they do not stay away from "OPEN SEXUAL INTERCOURSE"! He also advised Muhammad how to deal with his wives amicably spending fair amount of time with them as far as their physical needs are concerned! The verse is about ill-fated husbands who practice polygamy and face continuous domestic unrest from their unruly wives! It is a natural instinct of men to spend more time with one who is relatively attractive, if he has lot of options to choose from! In that situation no man can do perfect justice to their wives! Then who is responsible for this? Allah in the first place should not have allowed polygamy! People live a better life with a single wife! Muhammad, the messenger for the mankind, was given a free choice by Allah to marry as many as he wanted aged between seven to seventy! He even married divorced wife of his adopted son! In that dilemma Muhammad was probably forced to keep some of his wives hanging by not giving them time and attention they deserved! How can we expect a prophet, appointed as a "MESSENGER TO MANKIND" to guide the mankind to the right direction who failed to keep his own house in order? Does the "Creator" of the universe has to pay so much attention to family feuds? Muhammad said there would be only one man to "Look After" fifty women before the Dooms Day! So, "Polygamy" is probably the right step in the right direction! Allah never had a wife, yet he was able to guide messenger as to how he should deal with his multiple wives!

Verse-140, Ch-4: "WHEN YOU HEAR THE VERSES OF ALLAH BEING DENIED AND MOCKED AT, SIT NOT WITH THEM. SURELY ALLAH WILL COLLECT THE HYPOCRITES AND DISBELIEVERS ALL TOGETHER IN HELL."! It is apparent from this verse that people in the pagan period used to sit together to discuss verses of the Quran! In those sittings, hypocrites and the disbelievers used to express their resentment by mocking at the verses of the Quran! Probably the contents of the verses appeared aggressive and threatening to them! Moreover they were reluctant to accept Muhammad as a messenger! In some of the previous verses Allah himself mocked at hypocrites and now he cannot accept his verses being mocked at! Allah should not collect hypocrites from the Jews and the Christians communities together in hell. The enmity between them might reignite the old feud inside the hell since the Christians could never forgive the Jews for Crucifying the "Son of God."! Collection of hypocrites and the disbelievers may not be necessary if Jesus is sent again as a Muslim prophet to rule the world by Islamic Sharia Law! It is said that he would be given only forty years to accomplish his mission which Muhammad and his predecessors had failed do in thousands of years! Hopefully, during Jesus's rule there would be no one to mock at the Quran since new revelation will resume upon his arrival! In addition to that Allah may not have to convene the "Day of Judgment" for trial if Jesus is able to motivate all humans into believing in Islamic monotheism! Though Muhammad expected that his followers would be greater in numbers on the Day of Resurrection, now it seems that Jesus is the one who will have the last laugh! But that will again depend on who leads the mankind since Muhammad is already selected by Allah for the job! Jesus should have the right to lead his men on the Day since he is the one who will make Allah's dream come true! Success of Jesus will unfold failures of all preceding messengers! He will descend with a new set of "Revelation" from Allah which might not be mocked at!

Verse-14, Ch-5: "AND FROM THOSE WHO CALL THEMSELVES CHRISTIANS, WE TOOK THEIR COVENANT, BUT THEY HAVE ABANDONED A GOOD PART OF THE MESSAGE THAT WAS SENT TO THEM. SO WE PLANTED AMONGST THEM ENMITY AND HATRED TILL THE DAY OF RESURRECTION". Enmity amongst the Christians is not as severe as it is amongst the Muslims and is unlikely to end before Resurrection!! What kind of covenant was that; written or verbal? Does the Old and New Testaments contain details of the covenant agreed upon? Is it possible to work out an agreement between the created and the "Creator" who lives over seven heavens? By "Planting" enmity and hatred amongst the Christians, Allah has done exactly the right thing as revenge for not accepting Muhammad as their messenger! A footnote related to this verse says; "THE CHRISTIANS WERE ORDERED IN THE INJEEL (GOSPEL) TO FOLLOW PROPHET MUHAMMAD WHEN HE WOULD COME AS A MESSENGER OF ALLAH TO ALL MANKIND"! All Christians reject this claim outright as planting of enmity among them by Allah has proved to be wrong! Though they are divided into Catholics, Protestants, Orthodox etc. yet they have learnt lessons from the past and respect humanity! To the contrary, the enmity and hatred has grown among the Islamists and

INSHALLAH shall continue to prevail till the End! What is so surprising about Allah is that he never included the Hindus, Buddhist or the Sikhs in his list of enemies by name? Did he not create them? Why the "MESSENGER OF ALLAH TO ALL MANKIND" had nothing to say about them? No Jews or Christians acknowledge existence of such orders or "Covenant" in their scriptures! They, including people of all other faiths, have taken the right course to live a relatively peaceful life in this world by abandoning the path of Islamic Monotheism! As a result, Allah, the so-called "Creator" of the universe has become the "Leader" of the minority! Trust cannot be enforced by threats and temptations! Similarly, truth cannot be established by doubtful Revelation!

Verse-27, Ch-5: "AND (O MUHAMMAD) RECITE TO THEM (THE JEWS) THE STORY OF THE TWO SONS OF ADAM; ABEL AND CAIN IN TRUTH. WHEN EACH OFFERED A SACRIFICE TO ALLAH, IT WAS ACCEPTED FROM ONE BUT NOT FROM THE OTHER. THE LATER SAID TO THE FORMER, I WILL SURELY KILL YOU". What is the use of telling the story of Abel and Cain to the Jews which reflects nothing but shame for Adam and his "Creator"! What is the moral and message of that story? That was not a story of "Sacrifice" but most importantly an ugly start of mankind involving murder between brothers over woman; sex and beauty! Let us recall the famous saying, "MORNING SHOWS THE DAY"! Even in that grave situation, Allah was in need of a sacrifice! Dr. AL-JOHANI, a Saudi, in his book "The truth about Jesus" says; "The essence of Islam, which is the willing submission to the will of God, was revealed to Adam who passed it on to his children"! Dr. Abdullah Al-KAHTANY, another Saudi Islamic Scholar says; "Every newborn child is born on the innate nature (Islam i.e. complete surrender to Allah)! Do these two terms "Willing Submission" and "Innate Nature" relate to Islam? Does Islam allow "Willing Submission"? It rather believes in intimidation! "ISLAM IS ESTABLISHED BY JIHAD": Right from the days of Muhammad Islam resorted to killing, war, stoning to death, beheading, caning etc.! Islam has no room for "WILLING SUBMISSION"! Which scripture was revealed to Adam? What was the significance of that sacrifice? Did Allah order Abel and Cane to make sacrifice in the "Dream" as was the case with prophet Abraham? Did the animals come on earth before Adam? Allah as the "WALI" (protector) of the mankind did nothing to protect Abel! Adam's scripture had no impact on his children! This was the first failure of Allah as a "Protector"! Allah ordained Cain to marry Abel's twin sister but she was not as beautiful as his own twin! After the killing of Abel, obviously an "Illegal" marriage took place between Cain and his own twin sister against the "Will" of the Lord! So by Allah's own account we are the illegitimate offspring of a father who was the first murderer in the history of mankind! In a Hadith (AL-BUKHARI Vol. 9, #6) Muhammad expressed his opinion on this killing saying; "NONE IS KILLED OR MURDERED (UNJUSTLY), BUT A PART OF RESPONSIBILITY FOR THE CRIME IS LAID ON THE FIRST SON (QABIL) OF ADAM WHO INVENTED THE TRADITION OF KILLING ON THE EARTH". Why All-Knowing Allah did not know that a murder was going to take place? Cain was in great trouble as he did not know what to do with the huge ninety foot long body of his brother! Instead of an angel, Allah then sent a "Crow" to teach Cain how to make "The Burial of the Dead"! From previous reading we know that Adam was 30 meters in height and definitely so was his son! It must have been very difficult for Cain to bury the huge body! Muhammad's teaching had little effect on the humanity, instead it emerged as one of the coercive forces of atrocities all over the world! "Cutting Necks" is the easiest option in Islam to eliminate those who oppose it! Adam and Eve story is a cunning way of weaving a fairy-tale about inception of mankind! Many poets joined hands with the prophets and the priests to legitimatize tales of Adam and Eve! Milton, one of the greatest English poets, adapted "Fall of Man" for his great epic thinking he was building on the religious foundation! To him, senses were the gateways of heaven; religion was an ecstasy and not an argument! The world has seen a flurry of works on this mythical story even in the midst of the phenomenal advancement of science! These myths may have motivated Charles Darwin to undertake a global trip to seek truth on evolution! His bold endeavor paid off and convinced most of the mankind of their real origin! Adam and Eve are the Hero and heroine of the divine drama played on the world stage before an ignorant audience! Satan was made the protagonist! None has "Lost" or "Regained" paradise! What the mankind needs most is to regain its Consciousness which was lost in the darkness of the past!

Verse-45, Ch-5: "AND WE ORDAINED THEREIN FOR THEM, LIFE FOR LIFE, EYE FOR EYE, NOSE FOR NOSE, EAR FOR EAR, TOOTH FOR TOOTH, AND WOUNDS EQUAL FOR EQUEL. BUT IF ANY ONE REMITS RETALIATION BY WAY OF CHARITY, IT SHALL BE FOR HIM AN EXPIATION". Even the absolute despots of the medieval era had never thought of making a law of this nature with brutal provision of tit for tat retaliations for not obeying his orders! However, the "Laws" of the "Creator" cannot be compared with those of the created! This verse allows a victim to remit retaliation by way of charity! So, the punitive measures are from the Merciful Allah and the charity is from those who are "Ingrate" by birth! A Hadith (AL-BUKHARI, Vol. 4 #651) quotes Muhammad as saying; "THE BLOOD OF A MUSLIM CANNOT BE SHED WHO CONFESSES THAT NONE HAS THE RIGHT TO BE WORSHIPPED BUT ALLAH AND THAT I AM THE MESSENGER OF ALLAH EXCEPT IN THREE CASES; 1) LIFE FOR LIFE IN CASE OF INTENTIONAL MURDER, 2) A MARRIED PERSON WHO COMMITS ILLIGAL SEXUAL INTERCOURSE and 3) THE ONE WHO REVERTS FROM ISLAM"! Who is a Muslim? The one who unambiguously acknowledges Allah as the only legitimate deity to be worshipped and Muhammad as his messenger! Only believing in Allah does not make you a Muslim! The first example of blood-shed was set by the son of Adam,! Was it not an intentional murder? Adam did not kill his other son in retaliation, though Allah ordained "life for life"! If Adam had killed Cain, there would have been serious consequences for the procreation of the mankind! Adam would be the only man left therein with Eve and their two daughters! Who would marry his daughters? Out of "Doctrine of Necessity", the Lord allowed marriages between brothers and sisters! Allah also says, every child is born with his "Innate religion of Islam"! It implies that the rest of the mankind "Reverted" from Islam to other religion? That is why Allah wants them killed! In the above Hadith, Muhammad justifies their killing! In Islam, killing is the easiest option as revenge!

Verse-54, Ch-5: "O YOU WHO BELIEVE! WHOEVER FROM AMONG YOU TURNS BACK FROM HIS RELIGION (ISLAM), ALLAH WILL BRING A PEOPLE WHOM HE WILL LOVE AND THEY WILL LOVE HIM". Astonishingly, the word "ISLAM" in the bracket is not mentioned in the original Arabic text! It has been added by the translators! This verse is a candid confession from Allah that he has created a people who do not love him! Allah has used mild language to replace those among the believers who might turn their back on religion! But according to Muhammad "THE ONE WHO REVERTS FROM ISLAM" should be killed! The Christian and the Jews had broken their "Covenant" with Allah yet he did not replace them! Rather he has bestowed upon them his blessings to lead a better life than those few who "Love" him! Adam and his offspring are made of Clay; they are not happy with the "Creator"! Satan for being made of a superior material (Fire) refused to prostrate to Adam! So far we have been under the impression that Lord's plan for creating mankind was flawless since he is All-Mighty and All-Knower! He did not expect that such a vast majority of people would turn their back on him and his religion! Now he feels the necessity of creating a new people who would be completely loyal to him with no love lost between them! Allah might have received disturbing reports from his angels about the number of People who really "Love" him is plummeting! If Allah decides to recreate mankind, first of all he should replace old pair of Adam and Eve! Since both of them committed the "SIN" and their son became the first murderer of the human history! As for the Lord's plan-B, i.e. to send Jesus again on earth, he got to be careful about putting old wine into new bottles! This time Jesus should abandon his bachelorhood! The priests who "Love" Jesus have "Abused" tens of thousands of children at various Churches! Adam failed to produce children of his own choosing! Allah also failed to create a people with mutual love between him and his creation, as a result most of them turned their back from his religion (Islam)!

Verse-64, Ch-5: "THE JEWS SAY; 'ALLAH'S HAND IS TIED UP' (i.e. HE DOES OT GIVE AND SPEND OF HIS BOUNTY). BE THEY (JEWS) ACCURSED FOR WHAT THEY UTTERED. NAY, BOTH HIS HANDS ARE WIDELY OUTSTRETCHED. WE HAVE PUT ENMITY AND HATRED AMONGST THEM TILL THE DAY OF RESURRECTION. EVERY TIME THEY KINDLED THE FIRE OF WAR, ALLAH EXTINGUISHED IT, AND THEY (EVER) STRIVE TO MAKE MISCHIEF ON THE EARTH". Allah planted enmity and hatred amongst the Christians before and now that has fallen on the Jews! Why the Jews accused Allah of being miserly is not known. They say, "ALLAH'S HAND IS TIED UP"! Earlier he branded them as the "GREEDIEST PEOPLE"! Allah also warned Muslims not to make friends with them! More than thirteen centuries later, this verse might have motivated Hitler to pour his venom of vengeance on the Jews! To the utter surprise of the Lord, they quickly recovered from the catastrophe and now leading a life much better than their enemies! Look at the lingering conflict between the Arabs and the Jews at the epicenter of all three revealed religions! When did Allah "EXTINGUISHED THE WAR"? Allah's anti-Semitic attitude is vividly visible all over the Quran! Nay! Allah's bounty knows no bound! His "Both Hands" can be outstretched to go round the universe! To illustrate the span of Allah's "Hands", Muhammad, in a Hadith (AL-BUKHARI, Vol. 9 #509) says; "ON THE DAY OF RESURRECTION,

ALLAH WILL GRASP THE WHOLE EARTH BY HIS HAND, AND ALL THE HEAVENS IN HIS RIGHT, AND THEN HE WILL SAY; I AM THE KING". So, the entire mankind will be Resurrected on the "Hands" of "The King" of the Heavens and the Earth! Allah's "Enmity" and "Hatred" planted among the Jews seem to have no impact on them! It is the hatred of Hitler that made the greatest damage to the Jews! It is not the Jews but the Islamists that are consistently striving to do the mischiefs! On the other hand the Jews including Albert Einstein made significant contribution to the advancement of mankind and the civilization!

Verse-66, Ch-5: "AND IF ONLY THEY HAD ACTED ACCORDING TO THE TORAH, THE GOSPEL AND WHAT HAS NOW BEEN SENT DOWN TO THEM FROM THEIR LORD (THE QURAN), THEY WOULD SURELY HAVE GOTTEN PROVISION FROM ABOVE AND FROM UNDERNEATH THEIR FEET". Please note that the Torah and the Gospel are clearly mentioned in this verse but the Quran is within the bracket, why? Because it is also absent in the original text! The real meaning of the verse would reflect a different meaning and significance if the word "Quran" is omitted from it! It is claimed by the Muslim scholars that nothing can be added to or omitted from the Quran by any human being! This is just one of the instances! There are hundreds of them in the translated version of the Quran where many such inclusions have happened! Who authorized the translators to insert words that are not in the original text? Allah, the Creator of the universe, sent all three books of religion for the mankind in the Middle East, precisely in and around Jerusalem, the heart of religious conflicts! Rest of the mankind, who did not receive Torah, Gospel or the Quran, are also getting their "PROVISION FROM ABOVE AND FROM UNDERNEATH THEIR FEET" without bloodshed! The Quran has been described as a "Light from Allah"! In fact this "Light" should have been sent to Africa to enlighten the "Heart of Darkness"! Those who followed Torah and the Gospel are better provisioned than the followers of the Quran! An interesting Hadith (AL-BUKHARI, VOL. 5, # 275) seemingly unrelated has been quoted as the foot note to this verse. It narrates how Muhammad gave answers to "Three Questions" when asked by an elderly man of Medina. The miracle about this Hadith is that no sooner the questions were asked, believe it or not, Allah immediately ordered angel Gabriel to descent from heaven to Medina carrying the answers to three questions for Muhammad! The first question was: "What is the first sign of the "Hour"?" Muhammad, receiving the answers from Gabriel, replied; "AS FOR THE FIRST SIGN OF

THE HOUR, IT WILL BE A FIRE THAT WILL COLLECT OR GATHER PEOPLE FROM THE EAST TO THE WEST". In another verse Allah said, upon arrival of the "Hour" the sun would rise in the West! And the second question was: "What is the first meal, the people of paradise will eat?" In reply to this question Mohammad said, "THE FIRST MEAL TO BE SERVED IN PARADISE WILL BE MADE OF CAUDATE (EXTRA) LOBE OF THE FISH LEVER". In our world Caviar is known to be very testy and costly food prepared from eggs of sea fish! But this heavenly "Fish Lever" may be testier than the Caviar! I am indeed disappointed; I expected something better than the fish lever would be served as the maiden meal in paradise! The third question was: Why does a child attract the similarity to his father or mother?" And the answer to this was: "DURING INTERCOURSE IF THE MAN`S DISCHARGE PRECEDES THE WOMAN`S DISCHARGE, THE CHILD ATTRACTS THE SIMILARITY TO THE MAN AND IF THE WOMAN'S DISCHARGE PRECEDES THE MAN'S, THEN THE CHILD ATTRACTS THE SIMILARITY TO THE WOMAN". So, the parents can mutually determine whether the offspring should resemble their father or mother, just by controlling timing of their sexual discharge? If the fetus is incubated in a test tube then the resemblance could go either way since no sexual discharge takes place in that process! As for the rest of the creatures, we have no idea if this procedure applies to them or not! Allah has taken twenty three years to reveal verses of the Quran but in this case no sooner the questions were asked, Allah immediately sent Arch-Angel Gabriel in a flying saucer at a speed many times faster than light to enable his messenger to give the answers! This instance may be analyzed in the perspective against which the Quran is claimed to have been revealed, memorized, scripted, collected and compiled through a long history of incomprehensive events! The Quran could not have taken long twenty three years for its "Revelation" if it had really come from a divine source!

Verse-69, Ch-5: "SURELY, THOSE WHO BELIEVE (IN THE ONENESS OF ALLAH, IN HIS MESSENGER MUHAMMAD AND ALL THAT WAS REVEALED TO HIM FROM ALLAH), AND THOSE WHO ARE THE JEWS AND THE SABIANS AND THE CHRISTIANS, WHOSOEVER BELIEVED IN ALLAH AND THE LAST DAY, AND WORKED RJGHTOUSNESS, ON THEM SHALL BE NO FEAR, NOR SHALL THEY GRIEVE". This verse clearly says that the JEWS, the SABIANS and the CHRISTISNS are on right path if they believe in Allah and the Last Day and work righteously! Believing "IN HIS MESSENGER MUHAMMAD AND ALL THAT WAS

REVEALED TO HIM FROM ALLAH" has been added in the bracket but not mentioned in the original verse! A Hadith quoted as footnote says that this verse and verse 62 of Surah 2 with similar contents "SHOULD NOT BE MISINTERPRETED BY THE READER AS PROVISION OF THESE VERSES HAVE BEEN ABROGATED BY VERSE 85 of SURAH 3 AND AFTER THE COMING OF PROPHET MUHAMMAD, NO OTHER RELIGION EXCEPT ISLAM WILL BE ACCEPTED FROM ANYONE". Were these verses revealed before Muhammad? Why was it not amended by Allah himself? Why he made double mistakes! Prominent Muslim scholars claim that Islam is the innate religion that Allah has implanted in every new born since Adam! What is the fact? Islam came before or after Muhammad? Who abrogated these verses? Allah did not mention anywhere in the Quran that he has abrogated any verse! Even the verse 85 of surah 3 does not say that other two verses have been replaced by itself! One thing more to be noted that the verse belonging to chapter 3 has abrogated verses from chapter 2 and 5 whereas all three verses are said to have been revealed at one place i.e. Medina! Contents of the two abrogated verses are similar! Why did Allah make same mistake twice apparently in a short span of time? Normally an old law or its provision is abrogated by new one with proper reasoning embodied in it but in this case no such rules have been followed! Two abrogated verses assured Jews, Christians and others of Allah's favor! But the coming of prophet Muhammad has excluded them from Allah's mercy and favor to the contrary he claims to have been sent for the whole of mankind? Well, Allah is able to do all things at his will! An interesting Hadith (AL-BUKHARI, Vol. 8 #621), related to verse 89 of chapter 5 quotes prophet Muhammad as saying; " WE MUSLIMS ARE THE LAST TO COME IN THIS WORLD, BUT WILL BE FOREMOST ON THE DAY OF RESURRECTION". These sayings of Muhammad have two notable segments in it. From the first segment we come to know that there were no Muslims before the Jews and the Christians, which is historically correct as Muhammad was the last prophet! But the history of Islam also claims Adam, Abraham and other prophets as Muslims who are said to have believed in Allah's monotheism! If so, as offspring of Adam, all succeeding generations of humans that stemmed from him would have no other choice but to become Muslims! DR. ABDULLAH AL-KAHTANY, a famous Islamic scholar of Saudi Arabia, in his book "THE TRUTH ABOUT THE ORIGINAL SIN" said: "THE RELIGION BEFORE THE ALLAH IS ISLAM. GOD HAS IMPLANTED HIS OWN RELIGION IN INNATE, WITH WHICH ALL

HUMAN ARE EQUIPPED. THIS IS THE PRIMORDIAL RELIGION, THE ONE AND ONLY TRUE RELIGION! Note the writer used the word "GOD"! Generally the Muslims do not like Allah to be called God! In the same book Muhammad is quoted to have said: "EVERY NEW BORN CHILD IS BORN ON THE INNATE ISLAM; COMPLETE SURRENDER TO ALLAH". Why then Muhammad says "WE MUSLIMS ARE LAST TO COME"? Why did Allah sent "TORAH" and "GOSPEL"? Does it not contradict Muhammad's own statement? Calling Islam as the implanted "INNATE RELIGION" is a perversion of the truth! A creature in the bottom of the ocean is also equipped with innate intellect which enables it to live its life without being blessed by holy books and prophets! Muslim scholars go out of their way to defend Islamic Monotheism with conflicting and contradictory narratives! If every child is born with the innate religion of Islam, then what was the necessity of "Revelation"?

Verse-97, Ch-5: "ALLAH HAS MADE THE KABAH, THE SACRED HOUSE, AN ASYLUM OF SECURITY AND BENEFITS (e.g. HAJJ AND PILGRIMAGE) FOR MANKIND". This KABAH is a small square, stone-built house situated inside the Mecca grant mosque complex. This sacred house was built by Prophet Abraham! It is really unbelievable that Allah, the Creator of the universe, had decided to make such a tiny structure as his monument? Calling it a sacred house as a mark of respect raises no question but how this sacred house serves as an asylum for the benefit of the mankind? Benefit in terms of Hajj and pilgrimage is meant to be for the Muslims only. In no way does this benefit the entire mankind! Moreover less than one percent of world Muslim population at best can afford to perform Hajj, as it is the most expensive of all Islamic rituals! Also, considering the reality on ground, we should not lose sight of a fundamental fact that the words 'Muslim" and "Mankind" are not interchangeable as regards to their meanings. Next, how does this Sacred House serves mankind as an asylum of security? Who seeks asylum at KABAH for security? Lot of questions need to be answered! Curfew had to be imposed around KABAH during lockdown so as to keep it safe from Corona infection! Allah, the "WALI" (protector), has failed to provide protection to KHABA and the pilgrims against virus! Mosques are also called "House of Allah" and the bitter truth is that Allah is not able to ensure safety of his houses from natural disasters! Muslim worshipers do not feel themselves safe even inside the mosques because of sectarian violence! Do the rulers of the Arab world feel themselves safe around the "Asylum of Security? Obviously, security of all nations around KABAH is really scarce unless it is guaranteed from across the Atlantic! This sacred house of Allah is always kept covered in black and no one, except the Royals, is allowed inside! The Royals give it a ceremonial wash once a year. What does this squire building hold inside is a mystery! Why is it not open to public? Only a peace of stone is kept in one corner of that squire building for pilgrims, so that they can kiss it from outside as part of the Hajj rituals! Muslims, wherever they may be, must face KABAH during prayers! Why should they face the "House of Allah" instead of facing the omnipotent Allah himself who is also said to be Omnipresent? As part of Islamic custom, the Muslims sleep keeping their heads towards KABAH! The exception is when they are dead! The body is kept in a North-South direction and also buried in the same position! Why direction is so important for the dead? The KABAH is also important for its strategic location! Allah has built a palace for himself over Seventh Heaven exactly parallel to KABAH! Do the Muslim scientists have the knowledge to prove that claim? Truth of the matter still hangs in the balance ever since the KABAH was built! Before the advent of Islam, the pagans used to place statues of their deities inside that building! Going round KABAH in a naked state was a Pagan ritual and now the Muslims do the same by rapping white sheets of cloths around their body without head dress! The Quran itself testifies that KABAH was indeed a Pagan house of worship! Verse 28 of chapter 7 says; "And when they commit evil deeds (i.e. going round KABAH in naked state and every kind of unlawful sexual intercourse), they say, "We found our fathers doing it and Allah has commanded it on us". Of course Allah has denied having said that! What is evident from this verse is that before Muhammad, Pagans were the masters of Mecca! They had their own religion and worshipped their own deities! Allah and Islam were introduced to them by Muhammad! Though Muhammad failed to convince his own uncle of this new ideology but he was able to establish Mecca as the epicenter of Islam and it provided economic benefits to his successive generations for ages! The Quran says Muhammad is a "MESSENGER OF ALLAH TO MANKIND" and the KABAH is an "ASYLUM OF SECURITY FOR MANKIND"! Do these Quranic claims have any factual reality on ground considering the history of mankind since the so called "Revelation"?

Verse-109, Ch-5: "ON THE DAY WHEN ALLAH WILL GATHER THE MESSENGERS TOGETHER, AND SAY TO THEM; WHAT WAS THE RESPONSE YOU RECEIVED FROM MEN TO YOUR TEACHING? THEY WILL SAY; WE HAVE NO KNOWLEDGE, VERILY, ONLY YOU ARE

THE ALL-KNOWER OF ALL THAT IS HIDDEN OR UNSEEN". To gather all messengers in one place, Allah will have to bring down Adam, Jesus, John, Joseph, Enoch, Aeron, Moses and Abraham from Seven Heavens and Muhammad and others will have to be resurrected from the cracking ground of their graves! All of Allah's messengers were illiterate! They could neither read nor write! Even they could not read the scriptures given to them! "WE HAVE NO KNOWLEDGE" is probably the best answer Allah can expect from his messengers! Because Allah kept most of his miracles hidden and unseen from them! The only exception is Muhammad! He was taken to a space mission to witness paradise and other marvels of Allah's creation! Muhammad is said to have come for the whole of mankind! Can he deny having no knowledge of the response he received to his teaching? Can he forget the response he got from the pagans and his own family members? How can he not remember the unfair treatment he had to face from his unruly wives? Can he not recollect the humiliated defeat he suffered at the hands of his enemies at the battle of UHUD? What is the purpose of gathering all messengers since they have no "Knowledge" of what "Response" they received from the people to their "Teachings"? Adam received a bloody response from his son! Noah's son flatly refused to come on board the ship he built! Abraham's father refused to take lessons from his son! Muhammad's uncle refused to be inducted to Islam! Messengers' answer to Allah's question seems appropriate as they were not told or taught to record responses to their teachings! But Muhammad was exceptionally courageous to draw a bleak picture of the responses he and his two predecessors received from their respective followers saying; (Hadith, AL-TIRMIDI); "THE JEWS WERE DIVIDED INTO SEVENTY ONE FRACTIONS, THE CHRISTIANS INTO SEVENTY TWO AND THE MUSLIMS INTO SEVENTY THREE! ONLY ONE OF THE SEVENTY THREE DIVISIONS OF THE MUSLIMS, THAT REMAINS LOYAL TO HIM, WILL GET ENTRY INTO PARADISE". Look at the divisions in terms of the seniority! Moses's followers divided themselves into 71 fractions, those of Jesus's into 72 and lastly Muhammad's followers divided themselves into 73 fractions! God forbids; if Jesus arrives again as the last messenger of Allah, he might end up breaking the mankind into 74 fractions! See how difficult it is to get an entry into paradise! Out of a total of 216 fractions, only one, which will remain loyal to Muhammad, may get entry into paradise! Allah has employed some angels to report to him about all affairs of the earth on a daily basis! He must have analyzed their reports and got annoyed by poor performance of the messengers! As a result Allah had decided to send Jesus again to drive all humanity into accepting Islamic Rule of Law that Muhammad and others have failed to establish! Are there any conflict of interests between Allah and Muhammad? May be Allah is not aware of the volumes of Hadiths written in the name of Muhammad; hundred times more than all the verses of the Quran combined! If those are compiled into one volume, that will outweigh the "Book of Decree" held with Allah over Seven Heavens! Another dangerous trend prevalent among fanatics is that the Hadith gets precedence over verses of the Quran when a dispute arises on religious matter! As there are many incorrect verses in the Quran, similarly there are many incorrect Hadiths too! The verses of the Quran and the Hadiths don't differ much in terms of their contents, composition and narration! A careful scrutiny will reveal striking similitude between them! "Author" of the Quran and those of the Hadiths seem to have gone through same schooling though they differ in interpretations! It is inconceivable that Allah, "The All Knower" should gather all messengers who have no knowledge of their own achievements?

Verse-1, Ch-6: "ALL PRAISES AND THANKS BE TO ALLAH, WHO ALONE CREATED THE HEAVENS AND THE EARTH AND ORIGINATED THE DARKNESS AND THE LIGHT". Allah "Alone" has written the Quran; deserves all the praises and thanks since he "Alone" created the heavens and the earth and originated the "Light" and the "Darkness"! Allah also denies having created the Satan and devils to help him in the "Creation"! Joining partner to Allah in worship or in the creation is the gravest of all Sins, even graver than the "Original Sin"! Before the creation of the universe he was "Alone" and after its destruction he will stay as such! Why is he so adamant to be "Alone"? Because his "Singularity" is often challenged by a great majority of his creation who still believe in multiple Gods! If we think in the context of the universe, the quantity of light is too little in comparison with the amount of darkness! We are also in the dark about the Dark Matters and Dark Energy! Allah's universe is filled with more "Darkness" than "Light"! Allah thanks Allah; Allah praises Allah for everything he created! How does it sound? The verse above has generated a legitimate curiosity and concern to the claim that Allah alone created the "Earth" and the "Heaven"? If so, why Allah needed tens of thousands of messengers, prophets and angels to implement his Islamic Monotheism over a small number of humans, fewer than the number of stars in the sky? Allah may take credit for creating "Light" since he has made the "Sun" and the "Moon" as "Lamps"! Allah has created only one "Moon" to enlighten his mankind! Whereas he has "Created" hundreds of moons around other planets of the solar system where no believers exist! Allah claims that he brings nigh as a cover for the day! But why he couldn't do it evenly for those living in and around the polar regions? The Quran is also called a "Light" from Allah but it could not enlighten the mankind to praise and thank Allah alone! Then who should take the blame for not being able to unite the mankind to embrace the only religion of Allah?

Verse-2, Ch-6: "HE IT IS WHO HAS CREATED YOU FROM CLAY AND THEN HAS DECREED A TERM FOR YOU TO DIE". Allah said before that created Satan and Jinn from Fire, Adam from dust, Eve from Adam's rib, Angels from light, Jesus from Gabriel's breathing and the rest of the Mankind from semen or in his own words the "Despised Water"! On the other hand he says; "AND WE HAVE MADE FROM WATER EVERY LIVING THING" (Verse 30, chapter 21)! So, the angels, devils and the Jinn are not living things as they are not made from "Water"? No explanation can reach to a logical conclusion about Allah's transcendental creativeness! Now consider all of them together (Adam, Eve, Jesus, Angels, Satan, Jinn and the Mankind) and then think of Allah's different methodology of creation: are they not "LIVING THINGS"? Why did he use different materials other than "Water" for their creation? The "Author" also claims that disbelievers would find lot of contradictions in the Quran if it had been written by anyone other than Allah himself! Contradiction will not be visible to the believers whose eyes are covered by a covering of love and loyalty for Allah! Allah has not mentioned anywhere in the Quran what material he used to make the earth and the heaven! Scientists are sweating profusely to find the elementary particle of which everything, including the universe is made of! Satan being made of Fire became so proud and arrogant that he defied his "Creator" by refusing to prostrate to Adam! The "Author" of the Quran shifted his position on creation of "EVERY LIVING THING" in many different ways! The aim has been to mesmerize people with charming stories on creation! Allah used clay, the cheapest raw material, to create Adam and his offspring! This must have been the reason why the "ASHRAFUL MUKHLUKAT" (Best of all Creation) are physically fragile and prone to a dictionary of diseases! Human's life is as brittle as the pottery of a potter! There is no room for reasoning in religion; it's a heavenly nightmare bestowed upon humanity that came through "Revelation! Do we have to live with it!

Verse-12, Ch-6 states; "SAY (O MUHAMMAD)! TO WHOM BELONGS ALL THAT IS IN THE HEAVEN AND THE EARTH? SAY; TO ALLAH, HE HAS PRESCRIBED MERCY FOR HIMSELF. INDEED HE WILL GATHER YOU TOGETHER ON THE DAY OF RESURRECTION". Since Allah is the "Creator" and the "King" of the universe, obviously everything in it belongs to him! To explain why Allah "PRESCRIBED MERCY FOR HIMSELF", two Hadiths have been quoted! The first hadith (AL-BUKHARI, Vol. 8 #29) quotes Muhammad as saying; "ALLAH HAS DIVIDED MERCY INTO HUNDRED PARTS AND HE HAS KEPT NINETY NINE PARTS WITH HIM AND SENT DOWN ONE PART TO THE EARTH AND BECAUSE OF THAT ONE SINGLE PART, HIS CREATURES ARE SO MERCIFUL TO EACH OTHER, SO THAT EVEN THE MARE LIFTS UP ITS HOOP AWAY FROM ITS BABY LEST IT SHOULD TRAMPLE ON IT". Allah's creature are not so merciful when it comes Jihad! History records cruelties of the Arabs who used to kill their infant female babies lest they would share foods with them! Mercy melts away when hunger sets in! Cruelty of the Merciful Lord knows no bound when dealing with the disbelief in him and his religion! The second Hadith (AL-BUKHARI Vol. 4,# 416) says; "WHEN ALLAH COMPLETED THE CREATION, HE WROTE IN HIS BOOK WHICH IS WITH HIM ON HIS THRONE: VERILY, MY MERCY HAS OVERCOME MY ANGER". How Muhammad came to know of what has been written in the book that has not been revealed to him? What is to be noticed is that the narration of the Hadiths and the Verses is conspicuously complementary and similar in composition and contents! What a fair distribution of mercy! The creator gets ninety nine and leaves only one percent of the total mercy for all of his creatures! Allah swears by Figs and Olives to say that he is the Best of Judges! A tiny fraction of mercy enabled the "MARE LIFTS UP ITS HOOP AWAY FROM ITS BABY"! Probably "All Knowing" Allah is not aware of the fact that lack of little love and mercy causes millions of babies die all across the Earth he claims to have created!

Verse-97, Ch-6 states; "IT IS HE WHO HAS SET THE STARS FOR YOU, SO THAT YOU MAY GUIDE YOUR COURSE WITH THEIR HELP THROUGH THE DARKNESS OF THE LAND AND THE SEA". Using high-tech telescope, so far the scientists have been able to see only about one hundred billion galaxies of our universe and each of those galaxy has around one hundred billions of stars! So what would be the total number of stars visible only in our telescopic spectrum? Now think of the number of people on earth and how many men of the mankind travel through the darkness of the land and the sea to use these stars? How many stars do they really need as guides? I am not good at math yet I can say for sure that Allah has created at least one billion stars for each one of us! Don't you dare say it is too late or too little! Is this what induced the Lord of the universe to create and "Set" trillions of stars for us? Surprisingly enough, the nearest star or the "Guide" is more than four light years away from the travelers and often get out of sight for poor visibility in the night sky! But men on earth have invented much more precise Global Positioning System (GPS) to guide them in all weather conditions rendering Allah's unreliable star-oriented guidance system redundant! Allah has not only made the stars as "Guide" for the travelers but he can also use them as guided "Missiles" to hit the devils! A Hadith(Al-BUKHARI, Vol. 4, chap. 3, P. 282) quoted to explain this verse in greater details, says; "THE CREATION OF THESE STARS IS FOR THREE PURPOSES, i.e. AS DECORATION OF THE NEAREST HEAVEN, AS MISSILES TO HIT THE DEVILS AND AS SIGNS TO GUIDE TRAVELERS. SO, IF ANYBODY TRIES TO FIND A DIFFERENT INTERPRETATION, HE IS MISTAKEN AND JUST WASTES HIS EFFORTS; AND TROUBLES HIMSELF WITH WHAT IS BEYOND HIS LIMITED KNOWLEDGE". So, it is the Hadith writers who have taken a position not to "Let the cat out of the bag" in order to defend Allah, Muhammad and their religion! Humans with limited knowledge want to dig out the "Truth" about the so-called Islamic science! Why are they scared of a "Different Interpretations"? Please note that, out of the three purposes of creating "Stars", Allah wants to use them as "Guide" for the travelers but the Hadith writer wants to use those billions of stars not only as missiles but also as a piece of decoration to decorate the nearest heaven! How many stars Allah needs to decorate the nearest heaven? How many he has "Created"? The term "Nearest Heaven" is itself a vague expression! Out of three functions of the stars stated in the above quotation, only the last one has some commonsense in it! Ships in the sea may be guided by the north stars for navigational purpose or the birds in the sky for migratory flights. As for the first purpose, Allah says he set the stars to decorate "First Heaven"! Does he mean to say other heavens are not "Decorated" with stars? Dividing the so-called seven heavens one over the other by numbers is in itself an unscientific idea! The heaven has been conceived as a canopy over the tiny earth by the "Creator"! PROXIMA CENTAURI, the nearest star is more than four light years away! There are stars millions of light years away from us! The "Light-Year" may not be understood by some readers! The speed of light is three hundred million meters per second! At this speed, the total distance travelled by the light in one year is one Light-Year! Our sun is also a star and the light from the sun takes about eight light minutes to reach the earth! Trillions of stars in the sky are ready to be used by Allah as missiles to hit the devils! It's like using an ICBM to hit a mosquito! Laymen often take meteors for stars falling from the sky! This natural phenomenon misled the "Author" to conclude that Allah is using stars as missiles! This Verse and the Hadith have helped unearth divinity and the fake identity of the "Author" of the Quran! Al- BUKHARI warns us not to find different interpretations of his Hadith with "Limited Knowledge"! Science and civilization must reverse its course by going against the direction of "The Arrow of Time" to see Allah using trillions of stars as missiles to hit the devils on eafth!

Verse-101, Ch-6: States; "HE IS THE ORIGINATOR OF THE HEAVENS AND THE EARTH. HOW CAN HE HAVE CHILDREN WHEN HE HAS NO WIFE"? Allah has every right to be concerned for his bachelorship! Seemingly a male "Creator", he has decided to stay unmarried! This is an unjust allegation leveled against Allah that he has children! He is already having enough trouble maintaining his "Singularity" as the only God to be worshiped! If he had wished to have children, he could easily have created a wife from himself as he created Eve from Adam! He wants to remain aloof from all the trouble of having a family life! Most probably Allah has taken a lesson from his messenger who had an acrimonious conjugal life on this earth and he had to directly intervene by sending verses from heaven! Allah does not sleep, eat or drink! He is above every needs of this worldly life! "NO VISION CAN GRASP HIM BUT HE GRASPS ALL VISION" (Verse 103 of chapter 6)! As far as Muhammad's mission is concerned, Allah seems to have inconsistent stance and reminds him that "FOLLOW WHAT HAS BEEN REVEALED TO YOU (O MUHAMMAD) FROM YOUR LORD AND TURN ASIDE FROM POLYTHEISTS, PAGANS, IDOLATERS AND DISBELIEVERS" (Verse 106 of chapter 6)! If he turns aside from those, how can he bring them to the "Right Path"? He again says; "HAD ALLAH WILLED THEY WOULD NOT HAVE TAKEN OTHERS BESIDES HIM IN WORSHIP AND WE HAVE NOT MADE YOU A WATCHER OVER THEM NOR ARE YOU A GUARDIAN OVER THEM" (Verse 107 of chapter 6)! AND INSULT NOT THOSE WHOM THEY WORSHIP BESIDES ALLAH,

LEST THEY INSULT ALLAH WRONGFULLY"(Verse 108 of chapter 6)! So it is apparent from the above verses that Allah had willed disbelievers to worship others besides him! Muhammad has not been appointed a "Watcher" or a "Guardian" over them! Whereas he wanted his followers to love him more than their children and fathers! He further claims that no Muslim will have his faith complete unless he is acknowledged as the messenger of Allah for all humanity! So the humanity is indeed caught between "Revelation and Resurrection"!

Verse-159, Ch-6 states; "VERILY, THOSE WHO DIVIDE THEIR RELIGION AND BREAK UP INTO SECTS, YOU (O MUHAMMAD) HAVE NO CONCERN IN THEM IN THE LEAST". Allah has acquitted Muhammad of all "Concerns" related to religious divides and break ups! What a great relief for prophet Muhammad! Soon after his demise, Islam, the religion founded by Muhammad himself broke apart into Shia and Sunni Sects! This divide was much worse than the one between the Catholics and the Protestants in terms of violence and hatred! Muhammad failed to implement Islamic monotheism in his lifetime! Besides, he left this world without appointing a legitimate successor to him! His religion begun to split on the issue as to who would be the right person to succeed him! Thousands of sects and factions created in Islam due to diverse interpretations of its so-called revealed verses augmented by different schools of Hadiths! The infighting among these factions is more of a power struggle than religious disagreement! The most common agenda of these violent sects is that they all fight in the name of Allah! Muhammad died leaving his followers divided into seventy there groups, yet Allah has granted him an unconditional "Respite" saying "YOU HAVE NO CONCERN IN THEM IN THE LEAST"! Following his death, Muhammad's close friends and family members got embroiled among themselves in the power struggle! The legacy of Shia-Sunni divide is vividly visible around KABAH and KARBALA! This separation of Islam has turned so violent that they kill themselves inside each other's mosques! Persistent tension in and around the Gulf states is rooted in the Shia-Sunni divide! This dangerous divide could be avoided if Allah had bestowed Muhammad with a son to inherit his legacy! Allah says in verse 6 of chapter 7; "THEN SURELY, WE SHALL QUESTION THOSE PEOPLE TO WHOM THE BOOK WAS SENT AND VERILY, WE SHALL QUESTION THE MESSENGERS"! A close look at this verse and the verse quoted above will reveal how Allah contradicts his own "Revelations"!

Verse-11, Ch-7 says: "AND SURELY, WE CREATED YOU (YOUR FATHER ADAM) AND THEN GAVE YOU SHAPE (THE NOBLE SHAPE OF A HUMAN BEING),THEN WE TOLD THE ANGELS; PROSTRATE TO ADAM, AND THEY PROSTRATED THEMSELVES EXCEPT IBLIS (SATAN)". In another story Allah claimed to have created Adam in "His Image"! Adam was not a short man, his height was thirty meters! Since then, sons of Adam kept loosing height on Allah's will! We just cannot imagine what would be the height of human beings before and after resurrection! According to Muhammad, people qualified to enter paradise will regain their original shape and stature! Allah says he gave sons of Adam "THE NOBLE SHAPE OF A HUMAN BEING". So, Adam's offspring can trace back their resemblance in terms of "Shape" and "Image" to their Creator! But Charles Darwin disagrees with all these changes in our "Shape" and "Image"! He insists our forefathers had the shape of monkeys and apes and with the passage of time, after hundreds of thousands of years, these animals have gained "THE NOBLE SHAPE OF A HUMAN BEING"! Allah commanded IBLIS (Satan) to prostrate to Adam but he refused! Satan's bold reply to his creator: "I AM BETTER THAN HIM (ADAM), YOU CREATED ME FROM FIRE, HIM YOU CREATED FROM CLAY". Allah got annoyed and expelled Satan, saying; "GET DOWN FROM THIS PARADISE". Adam was surely a human being! Why Allah told the angels to prostrate to Adam? Are the angels inferior him? Following his expulsion, Satan requested Allah to grant him respite till the Day of Resurrection. Allah accepted his request and granted him respite! But Satan challenged and warned Allah by saying that he would continue misguiding humans until the Day of Resurrection! Satan feels proud of himself for being made of "Fire"! Why Allah had chosen to create Satan from a superior material like "Fire" and Adam from an inferior material like Clay? Despite being made of "Fire" Satan remains invisible and we feel no heat when he comes to mislead us! The "Fire" is so "Cool"!

Verses-24&25, Ch-7 state; "ALLAH SAID: GET DOWN, ONE OF YOU IS AN ENEMY TO THE OTHER (ADAM, EVE AND SATAN). ON EARTH WILL BE A DWELLING PLACE FOR YOU AND AN ENJOYMENT FOR A TIME. THEREIN YOU SHALL LIVE, AND THEREIN YOU SHALL DIE, AND FROM IT YOU SHALL BE BROUGHT OUT (RESURRECTED)"! All three were punished and expelled from paradise by Allah because of the sin Adam and Eve committed for eating the "Forbidden fruits"! "Satan misled them with deception! What happened to Adam and Eve after going near the tree? Their private parts, which were hidden from them, became manifest and they began to cover themselves with the leaves of paradise" (Verse 22 of chapter 7)! The meaning of the "Leaves of Paradise" has not been explained by Allah! However, whatever has been said in the above verses had no effect at the end! Allah forgave Adam and Eve, and the Satan was granted "Respite" until resurrection to misled the entire mankind save a few who believed in Allah and his messenger Muhammad! Adam and Eve were ordained to produce their offspring but had to face a humiliating procreation process giving birth to the first "Killer" of the mankind! How shall they be brought out or resurrected? Adam is already living his eternal life alone without Eve in the "First Heaven"! He was visited by Muhammad during his mission to Space! Eve may have died on earth and thereby she may be resurrected "Nude, Barefoot and Uncircumcised"! Satan will never die as his "Respite" is not likely to expire before resurrection! Moreover, how Satan can be brought out of cracking graves on the Day of Resurrection since Allah has created him from "Fire"? After his expulsion, Satan warned Allah in verse 16&17 of chapter 7; "THEN I WILL COME TO THEM (HUMAN BEINGS) FROM BEFORE THEM AND BEHIND THEM, FROM THEIR RIGHT AND FROM THEIR LEFT. BECAUSE YOU HAVE SENT ME ASTRAY, SURELY I WILL SIT IN WAIT AGAINST THEM ON YOUR STRAIGHT PATH"! Satan did his job well!

Verse 26&27, Ch-7 state; "O CHILDREN OF ADAM! WE HAVE BESTOWED RAIMENT UPON YOU TO COVER YOURSELVES (SCREEN YOUR PRIVATE PARTS) AND AS AN ADORNMENT. LET NOT SATAN DECEIVE YOU, AS HE GOT YOUR PARENTS (ADAM AND EVE) OUT OF PARADISE STIPPING THEM OF THEIR RAIMENTS, TO SHOW THEM THEIR PRIVATE PARTS"! This clever Satan has outwitted his All-Powerful "Creator" right in front of him in paradise! Did Satan had his own raiment on while stripping our parents of their clothes? Allah, the "Creator" of the earth and the heaven, had lots of flaws in his master plan! In the first place he should not have "Created" Satan! And then instead of punishing him to death, he granted him "Respite until Resurrection"! Was it necessary to have fruit-bearing tree in paradise? We also cannot rule out the possibility that Allah himself had played politics to oust them from paradise! Think for a moment if Adam and Eve had not landed on earth, what would have been the fate of Adam's offspring? It was Allah's game plan that he would bring Adam and Eve to this world so as to facilitate them multiply their offspring into billions! As part of his plan he destroyed all Dinosaurs, before the arrival of Adam! Out of the billions of trillions of celestial objects, he chose our planet earth to implement his "Islamic Monotheism" giving a chance to Prophets, Popes, Priests, poets and Philosophers to rejoice over "Anthropic Principle"! Be it in paradise or in the earth, nudity is natural! We are born naked and we will be "Resurrected" naked! No curse befell Pagans when they used to go round the KABAH in a naked state indulging in all kinds of evil deeds including unlawful sexual intercourse saying: "WE FOUND OUR FATHERS DOING IT, AND ALLAH HAS COMMANDED IT ON US (Verse 28 of chapter 7)"! How would the believers, especially the ladies, feel upon being raised naked showing their private parts? What is the point "Resurrecting" the entire mankind in a naked state? Allah says; Prophet Abraham, not Mohammed, would be the first to get his raiment!

Verse-44, Ch-7 states; "AND THE DWELLERS OF PARADISE WILL CALL OUT TO THE DWELLERS OF THE FIRE SAYING WE HAVE INDEED FOUND TRUE WHAT OUR LORD HAD PROMISED US, HAVE YOU ALSO FOUND TRUE WHAT YOUR LORD PROMISED (WARNINGS)"? THEY WILL SAY 'YES'. THEN A CRIER WILL PROCLAIM, 'THE CURSE OF ALLAH IS ON THE POLYTHEISTS AND WRONG DOERS"! In the subsequent verses Allah narrates that there will be a wall with elevated places between Paradise and Hell! Who would be placed on the elevated wall? Those whose good and evil deeds would be equal in scale! From the elevated places they would recognize people of paradise and Hell by their marks! Those in paradise will have their faces marked with white and those of the Hell will have black faces! People with equal amount of good and bad deeds have been assured of a place in paradise as Allah has decided to give them the benefit of doubt! So far so good but verse # 50 of the same chapter states; "AND THE DWELLERS OF THE FIRE WILL CALL TO THE DWELLERS OF THE PARADISE: 'POUR ON US SOME WATER OR ANYTHING ALLAH HAS PROVIDED YOU WITH'. THEY WILL SAY BOTH WATER AND PROVSION ALLAH HAS FORBIDDEN TO THE DISBELIEVERS"! On the day of Resurrection, death will be brought forward in the shape of a "Black and White" Ram! Allah will order a call-make to kill the Ram to show to the dwellers of Hell and Paradise that "Death" is no more an option for them (BUKHARI, Vol. 6, # 254)! Another Hadith narrated that each of the dwellers of Hell would be enclosed in a "Fire Box" so that they don't see others being tortured! Allah has built "Paradise" with one hundred grades in it with a distance between each grade equal to the distance between the earth and the Heaven (BUKHARI,

Vol. 4, #48)! Will it be sensible to pour water on an "Eternal Fire"? Allah has rightly chosen a "Black and White" ram to represent death, so that neither the "Black" nor the "White" should complain against each other for color discrimination! What messages do these "Revelations" deliver to the mankind?

Verse-54, Ch-7 says; "INDEED YOUR LORD IS ALLAH, WHO CREATED THE HEAVENS AND THE EARTH IN SIX DAYS AND THEN HE ROSE OVER THE THRONE (REALLY IN A MANNER THAT SUITS HIS MAJESTY). HE BRINGS THE NIGHT AS A COVER OVER THE DAY, SEEKING IT RAPIDLY, AND HE CREATED THE SUN, THE MOON, THE STARS SUBJECTED TO HIS COMMAND". We are living in an infinite universe which is still expanding but Allah says he has already finished creation of the Earth and the Heaven in "Six Days"! How Allah spent these "Six days" in "Creation" is given on a "Time-Table" by an eminent Hadith scholar called IBN-QASIR! He said that some Jews from Medina approached prophet Muhammad to ask him questions on creation of the earth and the heavens! In reply, Muhammad is quoted to have said, "Allah created the earth on Sunday and Monday. On Tuesday he created the mountains and all kinds of minerals! On Wednesday he created plants, springs, barren lands etc.! He created the Heavens on Thursday! On Friday Allah had a busy schedule: In the first quarter of the day he created the Stars, Sun, Moon and Angels, and in the second quarter he created all kinds of calamities; in the third quarter of the day he created Adam! Then Adam was placed in paradise and IBLIS Satan was asked to prostrate to Adam but he refused and as a result Satan was ousted from paradise and thus Allah ended his Friday work schedule and on Saturday he took a day off"! This is how Allah finished his "Six Days" in creating the "Earth and the Heaven"! But one thing which cannot escape our attention is that Allah created a "Calendar" before creating everything else so as to sort out a working plan within "Six Days"! Divided mankind has not been able to find a common name for the Lord; the Creator of the universe! Humans call their Lord in many different names: ALLAH, RABB, KHODA, MAULA, GOD, VAGHWAN, ISHAWAR, RAMA and so and so forth!! Shakespeare said; what's in a name! Of course, name does matter! Allah has taken ninety nine names for himself! Oh Lord! Why have you taken long "Six Days" to create the heavens and the earth despite being able to do it in a fraction of a second; only by uttering the word "Be"? Verse 117 of chapter 2 states; "THE ORIGINATOR OF THE HEAVENS AND THE EARTH. WHEN HE

DECREES A MATTER, HE ONLY SAYS TO IT "BE" AND IT IS"! In another verse Allah claimed to have taken two days each for the creation of the earth and the heaven and four days to create sustenance for the earth! May be in this case His Majesty, the "King" of the universe did not like to use his magical power of creation! After having created the heavens and the earth, Allah rose to his throne over seven heavens in a manner that suits His Majesty! But what "Manner" suited his majesty to ascend to his throne is beyond our limited knowledge! Divine science like the divine religion is really difficult for humans to comprehend! We also do not know what "Manner" was used by the Lord to raise Jesus to heaven! But we know for sure that a four-footed mule-like flying animal with two wings, called the "BORAKH", was given to Muhammad to use it as spacecraft for his journey to the Heavens with archangel Gabriel! Can the Lord bring the "Night" as a cover over the "Day" without rotating the Earth? Since his "Earth" is "Fixed and Flat"! He also claims to have affixed mountains on his Earth so that it does not move or shake! The "Sun" often fails to comply command of the Lord in the polar regions; "Night" keeps the "Day" covered for months together! Allah says he created the Sun, the Earth and the Moon but he never claimed to have created other planets and their moons that are part and parcel of our solar system! The reason may be that "The religion with Allah is Islam" and all fundamental Islamic rituals are closely linked to sunrise, sunset and sighting of the moon! The Muslims need only the Sun and the rotating Moon of the earth to perform prayers as ordained by Allah! He created stars to decorate the first heaven; as guide for the travelers and as missiles to hit the devils on Earth if the need arises! Allah says he created the earth first and then he created heavens and other celestial objects using bottom-up principle! So, the Big Bang is a big lie?

Verse-57, Ch-7 states; "AND IT IS HE WHO SENDS THE WIND AS HERALD OF GLAD TIDINGS, GOING BEFORE HIS MERCY (RAIN), TILL WHEN THEY HAVE CARRIED A HEAVY-LADDEN CLOUD. WE DRIVE IT TO A LAND THAT IS DEAD, THEN WE CAUSE WATER (RAIN) TO DESCEND THEREON. THEN WE PRODUCE EVERY KIND OF FRUIT THEREWITH. SIMILARLY WE SHALL RAISE UP THE DEAD". Please note that first part of the verse is narrated by third person singular number "HE" and the rest is by a plural pronoun "WE"! It is difficult to say whether it is a divine problem or a linguistic error! Who sends whirling winds from the oceans as bad omen of devastations? Allah also states; he drives "HEAVY-LADDEN CLOUD TO A LAND THAT IS DEAD"! Had it been so, the world would have seen no deserts at all! The rain is really scarce in and around the motherland of Prophet Muhammad! Most part of the Middle East is dead; dry "Waste Land"! Rain-prayers are held under special Royal Decree to restore dry land to fertility but to no avail! Often the violent wind comes as storms causing death and destructions to punish Allah's creatures who have gone astray: men and women, old and young are "Gone with the Wind" to the land of no return! The "HEAVY-LADDEN CLOUD" is often driven to places where it is not needed! "AR-RAD", the angel in charge of the clouds is quite often misled by Satan! Despite holding vegetation ceremonies, people in the draughty land "DIE WITH THE DYING". Bushfire keeps throwing flames of anger into the sky: "Burning, burning, burning, burning! O Lord! Thou PLUCKEST me out. O Lord thou PLUCKEST"! And the "HEAVY-LADDEN CLOUD DISCEND THEREON" to wash off the ashes of the fallen greenwoods when it is all over! Charred trees drenched with rain of mercy look up in vain to the merciful who had promised; "WE SHALL RAISE UP THE DEAD"! He raised "Son of Mary" unto him! Christ raised Lazarus from the dead to say: "I am Lazarus" come from the dead, come back to tell you all"! Oh Lazarus, please do tell us everything about the eternity and the divinity!

Verse-143, Ch-7 states; "AND WHEN MOSES CAME AT THE TIME AND PLACE APPOINTED BY US, AND HIS LORD (ALLAH) SPOKE TO HIM, HE SAID: OH MY LORD! SHOW ME (YOURSELF), THAT I MAY LOOK UPON YOU. ALLAH SAID: YOU CANNOT SEE ME, BUT LOOK UPON THE MOUNTAIN, IF IT STANDS STILL IN ITS PLACE THEN YOU SHALL SEE ME. SO WHEN HIS LORD APPEARED TO THE MOUNTAIN, HE MADE IT COLLAPSE TO DUST, AND MOSES FELL DOWN UNSONSCIOUS. THEN WHEN HE RECOVERED HIS SENSES HE SAID: GLORY BE TO YOU, I TURN TO YOU IN REPENTANCE AND I AM THE FIRST OF THE BELIEVERS"! Nay! Adam was the first believer! Who is a believer and who is a Muslim? Of course, anybody who believes in Islam, the religion of Allah, is supposed to be a Muslim! According to Muhammad every new born child is born with innate nature i.e. Islam, which means complete surrender to Allah as he has implanted his own religion in innate with which all human are equipped! Moses and his followers were all Jews and Allah is said to have revealed the Torah unto him! According to above verse, Moses, while still being the prophet of the Jewish people, wanted to see Allah! A Hadith of THIRMIDHI states that "The appearance of Allah to the mountain was very little of him. It was approximately equal to the tip of one's little finger as explained by the Prophet"! So, the little appearance of Allah made the mountain collapse; Moses fell down unconscious! What would happen to the entire mankind when Allah will appear before them on the Day of Judgment? In Verse 163 of chapter 6 Muhammad claims: "I AM THE FIRST OF THE MUSLIMS"! And again in Verse 12 of chapter 39 he says; "I AM COMMANDED IN ORDER THAT I MAY BE THE FIRST OF THOSE WHO SUBMIT THEMSELVES TO ALLAH AS MUSLIMS"! Why Allah sent Torah and Gospel to Moses and Jesus if they were Muslims? Why he miraculously demolished a mountain to make Moses say: "I AM THE FIRST OF THE BELIEVERS"? Do these statements make sense? Who is the first believer and who is the first Muslim?

Verse 203, Ch-7, states; "AND IF YOU DO NOT BRING THEM A MIRACLE ACCORDING TO THEIR PROPOSAL, THEY SAY: WHY HAVE YOU NOT BROUGHT IT?" A Hadith (AL-BUKHARI, Vol. 4, #831)narrates; "THAT THE PEOPLE OF MECCA (QURAISH PAGANS) REQUESTED ALLAH`S MESSENGER TO SHOW THEM A MIRACLE, AND SO HE SHOWED THEM THE SPLITTING OF THE MOON". Muhammad never claimed that Allah had bestowed magical power upon him! Rather he said all prophets were sent with miracles but him (BUKHARI, Vol. 9, #379). Can the Muslim scientists explain this phenomenal event with Islamic science that the splitting of the moon did really take place? Did Muhammad repair the split after the miracle? Armstrong and his colleague never reported to have seen any split in the moon after the historic Apollo mission! Some skeptics from the Muslim community had commented that the astronauts did see the split but did not report it as they were Christians! Thanks be to All-Mighty Allah! After "Splitting" the moon, Muhammad was able to bring back the two pieces together to restore the original shape of the moon, otherwise it could have devastating impact on time and tide including Islamic rituals that are linked to lunar months! Moon is indeed the luckiest heavenly object to have been linked to divine rituals by the prophets; over-praised by poets for its luminous beauty! If you believe in Islam, you have to believe in the miracles! Even after seeing the "Miracle", did the Arab pagans change their position on Islamic monotheism? Miracle is not science but religion! Humpbacked mankind with a burden of sins; terrified by the horrific Day of Judgment is slowly moving forward to the City of God! To regain freedom of mind and soul, it must shake off the unbearable load that has come from the unseen! Let the "Dream of the Rood" tell the truth; was it not Jesus that it Crucified? Who did make the

"Fall of Man" happen? Satan or the God? We need "To have squeezed the universe into a ball: To roll it towards some overwhelming question"! The ball is in the court of the Lord!

Verse-39, Ch-8 states; "AND FIGHT THEM UNTILL THERE IS NO MORE DISBELIF AND POLYTHEISM, AND THE RELIGION (WORSHIP) WILL ALL BE FOR ALLAH ALONE (IN THE WHOLE OF THE WORLD) Is this not a dangerous proposition! Allah is asking his loyal believers to fight off every other faiths and religion so that only Islam is established in this world! Allah wants all mankind to worship him alone! Does it not contradict what Allah said in verse 256 of chapter 2 that "THERE IS NO COMPULSION IN RELIGION"? And in verse 6 of chapter 109, Allah instructed Muhammad to tell the disbelievers; "TO YOU BE YOUR RELIGION, AND TO ME MY RELIGION! Why does Allah often contradicts himself? The spirit of accommodation should have been adapted right from the beginning of Islam which could save millions of innocent lives all over the world! More interesting is the related footnotes in which some Islamic religious scholars have expressed their opinion to explain the above verse as follows; "THAT WILL BE AT THE TIME WHEN JESUS WILL DESCEND ON EARTH AND HE WILL NOT ACCEPT ANY OTHER RELIGION EXCEPT ISLAM". Does it matter so much whether Jesus accepts any other religion or not? When Allah said the same thing in verse 85 of chapter 3 that "AND WHOEVER SEEKS A RELIGION OTHER THAN ISLAM, IT WILL NEVER BE ACCEPTED OF HIM"! How many of the mankind have accepted Islam? But a Hadith (Al-BUKHARI, Vol. 3, #425) quotes Prophet Muhammad giving a more elaborate explanation of the same verse, saying; "SURELY, THE SON OF MARY (JESUS) WILL SHORTLY DESCEND AMONGST YOU PEOPLE (MUSLIMS) AND WILL JUDGE MANKIND JUSTLY BY THE LAW OF THE QURAN AND WILL BREAK THE CROSS AND KILL THE PIGS AND ABOLISH THE TAX TAKEN FROM THE JEWS AND THE CHRISTIANS BY THE MUSLIM GOVERNMENT". Does it not tantamount to conceding a humiliating defeat by Allah and Muhammad along with all other prophets that came before him during the dark period? Yet Allah awarded him the best place in paradise! Why than All-knowing Allah revealed the Quran to Muhammad which was to be implemented by Jesus ultimately? Though the verse, the footnote and the Hadith are related, yet they give three different accounts of the same event! Does Allah have any plan to send Jesus with a new scripture or a modified version of the Quran? Allah's original plan to have one religion for the whole world was not flawless! In place of Muhammad, Allah could have send Jesus in the beginning for the job! The descend of Jesus on earth is of course a good news for some but at the same time it is a bad news for the Christians and the Jews since he is going to convert them to Islam and will rule this world with Islamic Laws! In this verse Allah has given Jesus a directive that he must clear this earth of all other religions except Islam! The Hadith also says that Jesus will break the cross, kill the pigs and abolish taxes imposed on the people of scriptures by the Muslim rulers! Breaking the cross and killing of the pigs will not help Jesus implement Islamic monotheism! What about Churches and synagogues? Should they remain intact? During Muhammad`s time, Allah could have sent verses asking Muslim leaders not to levy taxes on non-Muslims! Under Jesus's rule all mankind will be required to embrace Islam as they will have no other choice! So, instead of Muhammad, Jesus should be called the last and the best Prophet! The "Crucified Son of God" is coming back from heaven to this world on a face-saving mission to salvage the sinking ship of Allah's religion! Christians are also eagerly waiting for the return of the Messiah! They are comforted with the assurances that hereafter Messiah shall return "To reward His faithful, and receive them into bliss, whether in Heaven or Earth shall all be paradise, far happier place than this of Eden"! As yielding to temptation brought the "Fall of Man", yielding to Muhammad's assurances might lead the mankind to another disastrous consequence as he totally failed to materialize his mission! The "Messenger for Mankind" left this world untimely leaving behind chaos and confusion that led his followers to an endless fighting along the sectarian divides!

Verse-60, Ch-8 says; "AND MAKE READY AGAINST THEM ALL YOU CAN OF POWER, INCLUDING STEEDS OF WAR (TANKS, PLANES, MISSILES, ARTILLERY) TO THREATEN THE ENEMY OF ALLAH", Allah has choked out a modern war plan using sophisticated war machines to threaten his enemies! Are these war machines included in the original text of the Quran? Do the translators have right to add them in the verses? since Islamic Scholars firmly declare that nothing can be added to or subtracted from the Quran by human being! Did tanks, planes and missiles exist at that time when these verses were revealed? May be Allah knew that in foreseeable future those would be invented! But Allah did not know that his enemies would be the first to make such deadly weapons much ahead of his believers! In military might, enemies of Allah are thousand times more powerful than his followers! Allah in a previous verse claimed to have made billions of stars to use them as missiles to kill devils! Why can't he use them to kill his own enemies? The translators have added many words and phrases at their own accord in the brackets almost in every verse of this English version of the Quran! Muslim scholars are trying to win a lost battle resorting to tricks and tactics! This English translation of the Quran will take quite a different look and emerge as a book of chaos and confusion if those additional words in the brackets are deleted and the manufactured Hadiths are removed from it. Probably one of the objectives of writing this Quran was to praise Allah as the only deity worthy of worship! Allah has been mentioned in this book more than 3000 times! Besides this, another aim that received the highest attention is to establish Muhammad as the best human being on earth! Eventually, doubts expressed by the Arab pagans will become true and prove that the Quran is not a revealed book; rather written by some people who had little knowledge about the science! How Allah, the "Author" of the Quran, could think of using "Stars" to demolish devils on earth? What would be its impact on humans and his chosen religion?

Verse-73, Ch-8 states; "AND THOSE WHO DISBELIEVE ARE ALLIES OF ONE ANOTHER, AND IF YOU, (MUSLIMS OF THE WHOLE WORLD} DO NOT DO SO i.e. TO BECOME ALLIES AS ONE UNITED BLOCK UNDER ONE MUSLIM KHALIFA (RULER) FOR THE WHOLE MUSLIM WORLD, TO MAKE VICTORIOUS ALLAH`S RELIGION OF ISLAMIC MONOTHEISM, THERE WILL BE WARS, BATTLES, OPPRESSION, CORRUPTION AND A GREAT MISCHIEF ON EARTH." Allah has rightly predicted the consequences of Muslim nations for their failure to unite under one KHALIFA! Those unfortunate consequences are now vividly visible in the Muslim world especially in and around the land of "Revelation" where most of the Muslim nations are concentrated! What a contrast and contradiction from the Lord of the universe? When thousands of prophets and messengers including Muhammad have utterly failed to unite the Muslims, how a KHALIFA or a King is going to translate that mission impossible into a success? In this verse Allah sees alliance among the disbelievers and disintegration among the believers! So, it would be difficult to implement Islamic monotheism unless all Muslim communities of the world are united under a single KHALIFA (Muslim ruler)! How can the mankind build trust on Allah who could not send a messenger or a prophet capable of uniting the Muslims under one leadership and now he expects a "KHALIFA" to do that? His "Best" and the

"Last" messenger, who is said to have been sent for the entire mankind, left this world leaving entire population of the world disintegrated and that might have forced Allah to reconsider sending Jesus on earth again to implement his "RELIGION OF ISLAMIC MONOTHEISM"! OSAMA-BIN LADEN, AL-BAGDADI tried to become KHALIFA of the Muslim world but Allah, like Jesus, raised them unto him! What the enemies of Allah killed is their incarnation! Angels entrusted to protect them also fled to the heaven! Why Allah is now talking about only the Muslim nations? Has he abandoned the idea of implementing Islamic Monotheism over the entire mankind? To that end he sent Muhammad but he failed hopelessly to unite the mankind with his messages! Allah's next move is to send Jesus Christ as a Muslim ruler to rule the world under Islamic law! AL-TABARI, a noted Hadith expert quotes Muhammad as saying; "WHEN YOU ALL MUSLIMS ARE UNITED AS ONE BLOCK UNDER A SINGLE MUSLIM RULER AND A MAN COMES UP TO DISINTEGRATE YOU AND SEPARATE YOU INTO DIFFERENT GROUPS, THEN KILL THAT MAN". Muhammad advises Muslims to "Kill that Man" whoever comes to disintegrate them! In fact, it was his legacy that disintegrated the Muslim nations! Killing is another despicable legacy of Islam which they inherited from the sons of Adam, the so called "First Muslim Prophet"! Another Hadith from "ABU-SAID-AL-KUDRI" states; "IT IS A LEGAL OBLIGATION FROM THE QURAN AND THE PROPHET`S STATEMENT THAT THERE SHALL NOT BE MORE THAN ONE KHALIFA FOR THE WHOLE MUSLIM WORLD". Does Allah still have a plan to unite and rule "The whole Muslim world" under one KHALIFA? What is said in this verse will never materialize before Resurrection! Some Muslim nations in the Middle East are said to be governed by Islamic Sharia Law! Do they follow above verses of the Quran? In fact those rulers, given the geopolitical realities, have already abandoned the hope of uniting all Muslims under one KHALIFA as it's a dream that will never come true! The division among the KINGS and the KHALIFAS of the Muslim Gulf States, around the birth place of Muhammad, is wider than the gulf itself! What is common among these royalties is the dependence on disbelievers for their security and existence! The dream of establishing a KHILAFAT under a single KHALIFA is nothing but a Utopian Scheme! Sky has a limit; "Dream" has none! How "All-Knower" Allah, who also claims to be the "Creator of the universe", kept sending thousands of unrealistic verses as "Revelations" for the mankind that has nothing in common! 'Unity in Diversity' may be possible only in Paradise!

Verse-20, Ch-9 states; "THOSE WHO BELIEVED AND EMIGRATED AND STROVE HARD AND FOUGHT IN ALLAH`S CAUSE WITH THEIR WEALTH AND THEIR LIVES ARE FAR HIGHER IN DEGREE WITH ALLAH". Allah wants to reward those believers adequately who have made supreme sacrifices in his cause, by giving them higher grades to live an eternal life in paradise! In reference to Hadith (AL-BUKHARI, Vol. 4. #48) Muhammad describes paradise saying; "PARADISE HAS ONE HUNDRED GRADES WHICH ALLAH HAS RESERVED FOR THOSE WHO FIGHT IN HIS CAUSE, AND THE DISTANCE BETWEEN EACH OF TWO GRADES IS LIKE THE DISTANCE BETWEEN THE HEAVEN AND THE EARTH. AL-FIRDAUSE IS IN THE MIDDLE AND HIGHEST PART OF PARADISE. ABOVE AL-FIRDAUSE IS THE THRONE OF THE MOST GRACIOUS(ALLAH) AND FROM IT GUSHES FORTH THE RIVERS OF PARADISE". The most important information about the paradise is that it has one hundred grades! Each grade is apart from the other like the distance between the earth and the heaven! Here the word "Heaven" is somewhat misleading! However, we know the distance between the earth and the sun is one Astronomical Unit (AU) which is very close to 150 million Km. The distance from the sun to its farthest planet Neptune is 30 AU. If "Heaven" stands for the space beyond the last planet of our solar system, we can safely assume that the total distance from the first to the hundredth grade of the paradise is more than 3000 AU. Another way to look at it is the so-called "First Heaven" which Allah has decorated with stars and the nearest star (PROXIMA CENTAURI) is more than four light years away from the earth! So, from the beginning to the end this one hundred grades of the paradise will occupy a distance of more than four hundred light years! This is really a short distance in comparison with the light we receive from galaxies millions of light years away! But Allah on the other hand claims to have created only "Seven Heavens"! I don`t like to involve too much mathematics in it, yet one can roughly assume the size of the paradise! As per Islamic claim the paradise has eight gates! Allah is not a socialist! Pious believers will be classified according to the sacrifice they made in the cause of Islam! Each one of them will be awarded the grade he deserves! AL-FIRDAUSE is the highest grade of paradise but located in the middle! MAQAM-MAHMOOD, a palace Allah has specially built for Muhammad only, may be located in it! Yet Muhammad clearly said in verse 9 of chapter 46 that he was not sure what would happen to him and his followers after death! Above the highest grade is the throne of

Allah from where the rivers of paradise gushes forth! That may be a reason why time and again Allah defined paradise in the Quran as the "GARDEN UNDER WHICH RIVERS FLOW". Muhammad and Allah will be living there as close neighbors! In another verse it was claimed that Allah lives in his palace which is above and parallel to the KHABA at Mecca! All these conflicting accounts about paradise and Allah's house makes the mystery murkier and create a puzzle that can only be resolved by a devoted Muslim architectural engineer or one who is an expert in Islamic science! What about the Hell? Are there similar grades too? If the believers cannot attain equal grades in paradise because of their differences in performance, then disbelievers should also be treated with different degree of punishment in the hell as par the gravity of the crime! What is the distance between the hell and the paradise? A "Black and White Ram" will be slaughtered between the Hell and Heaven to inform the dwellers that the "Death" is no more an option for them! Dwellers of the Heaven will be "RECLINING UPON THE COACHES LINED WITH SILK BROCADE AND THE FRUITS OF THE TWO GARDENS WILL BE NEAR AT HAND" (Verse 54 of Ch. 55)! Those who disbelieve in Allah, Islam, Quran and the Day of Judgment will behold the torment "AND WE (ALLAH) SHALL PUT IRON COLLARS ROUND THE NECKS OF THOSE WHO DISBELIEVED" (Verse 33 of Ch. 34)! Can the mankind get rid of the 'Religious Iron Collars Round its Neck' on earth? No way! This is the impact of the "Revelation"!

Verse 54, Ch-9 says; "THEY COME NOT TO THE PRAYERS EXCEPT IN A LAZY STATE, AND THEY OFFER NOT CONTRIBUTIONS BUT UNWILLINGLY". It is because the timing of the prayers is not right! Especially the early morning prayer which begins at dawn between 4 to 5 a.m. before sunrise! If anybody gets late to attend prayer at fixed time, it will not be accepted of him by Allah or his reward will be curtailed! Who wants to skip this late night sound sleep? It is even more troublesome in the winter! Most of the prayers are closely linked to sunrise and sunset! What would happen to those who might be living near North or South poles where often the sun does not rise for months together? It is evident through confession that Allah's religion did not receive spontaneous response from larger section of people in terms of prayers and contributions! Most of the Muslims attend these prayers out of frustrations, finding no way out! Threats frighten them and temptations befool them! Muhammad expressed his anger and disgust in the following Hadith(AL-BUKHARI, Vol. 1 # 626); "IF THEY KNEW THE REWARDS FOR PRAYERS, THEY

WOULD CERTAINLY PRESENT THEMSELVES AT THE MOSQUE EVEN IF THEY HAD TO CRAWL". Surely, the believers would crawl themselves at the mosque "If they Knew" and lay their trust on promises made to them by both Allah and his messengers! Lack of trust is at the root of mismanagement of all failed faiths! None of the gods could send trustworthy messages and messengers to build confidence among the followers! To a great extent displeased and disappointed, Muhammad in his inflammatory language added more by saying; "I INTENDED (WAS ABOUT) TO ORDER THE CALL MAKER TO TAKE A FIRE FLAME TO BURN ALL THOSE MEN ALONG WITH THEIR HOUSES WHO HAD NOT YET LEFT THEIR HOUSES FOR PRAYER IN THE MOSQUES". Muhammad was ordained to act as a "Plain Warner"! But his inflammatory language depicted him as an irritant, merciless Jihadist! Whereas Allah claims; "THERE IS NO COMPULSION IN RELIGION" (Verse 256 of Chapter 2)!

Verse-5, Ch-10 states; "IT IS HE WHO MADE THE SUN A SHINING THING AND THE MOON AS A LIGHT AND MEASURED OUT FOR IT STAGES THAT YOU MIGHT KNOW THE NUMBER OF YEARS AND THE RECKONING." It is "He" (Allah) who made the sun as a "Shinning Thing" and the moon as a "Light" and also as a calendar for reckoning of the years! If we think in terms of scientific truth, the role played by the sun and the moon in the life of all living creatures is indispensable! This so-called "Shinning Thing" is continuously emitting vital energy for the entire creation! A deity or a human, whoever has written this verse had absolutely no knowledge of the functioning of the solar system! He cannot be regarded as the "Creator" by any means! The role being played by the sun to sustain life on earth has been ignored out of ignorance by the author of the Quran! He repeatedly stressed that the sun and the moon are created as source of light and for reckoning! How can he be dubbed as the "Creator" of the universe? He even does not know that the moon has no light of its own rather it reflects the light emitted by the sun! Even if he claims to have made the moon as the reflector of sunlight, yet the moon cannot give off light uniformly in its thirty days journey around the earth! Role of the moon as a reckoner reflects an Arab-Islamic socio-cultural tradition as many of the Islamic rituals are linked to different stages of the revolving moon! Mankind invented calendar for reckoning of the number of years at least a thousand years before the revelation of these verses! Does the "Author" of the Quran know how a star or the sun is born in the space? Does he know how radioactivity or the nuclear fusion make the sun a "Shining Thing"? The sun, the earth and the moon were born around five billion years ago! When did the so-called revelation take place? He also claims to have made "THE MOON AS A LIGHT"! The real identity of the "Author" of the Quran and the so-called "Creator" is evident from the ignorance exhibited in this verse! Truth is light, clouds cannot hide it forever!

Verse-19, Ch-10: states; "MANKIND WERE BUT ONE COMMUNITY (i.e. ON ONE RELIGION; ISLAMIC MONOTHEISM), THEN THEY DIFFERED (LATER)". Why did Allah reveal Torah and Gospel (Verse 65 of Ch. 3) if the mankind were already inducted into Islamic monotheism? This is an invented lie to say that mankind were born on one religion! All religions, like political parties, were created by man on earth and none has come from heaven! A supplementary Hadith (AL-BUKHARI, Vol. 2, #467) quotes Muhammad as saying; "EVERY CHILD IS BORN ON TRUE FAITH OF ISLAMIC MONOTHEISM (i.e. TO WORSHIP NONE BUT ALLAH ALONE), BUT HIS PARENTS CONVERT HIM TO JUDAISM OR CHRISTIANITY OR MAGIANISM; AS AN ANIMAL GIVES BIRTH TO A PERFECT BABY ANIMAL. DO YOU FIND IT MUTILATED?" Animals are not mutilated as they are born free! They don't need to care about creator; hell or Heaven! They are happy with one life on earth! If the mankind were one community, then how did it divide itself into so many? Allah in the Quran has claimed multiple times to have sent prophets and messengers to every nation with the message of his monotheism! Why did they fail to bring all under so-called Islamic monotheism? Who should be held responsible? Different revelations at different time to different messengers created the divisions among mankind. Acknowledgement of this fact in the above verse itself creates doubt whether any revelation has taken place at all! We are not aware of any success story of any messenger or prophets about unification of humankind on this earth! They came down on earth and then left this world to receive their rewards at luxurious resorts in the heavens! According to Muhammad's statement every child is implanted with Islamic monotheism before being born and it was also Muhammad who said Muslims were the "Last" to come but will be foremost on the day of Resurrection! Do we have to live with this kind of contradictory statements and worship Allah obediently forever? When Muhammad departed from this world, what percentage of the mankind he could leave behind indoctrinated in Islamic monotheism? Animal babies are also born exactly the same way but without any faith injected into them! They are

"Born Free" and not mutilated physically or spiritually! An animal baby can stand on its feet right after birth as it has not been implanted with heavy load of religion! Every human being should have been given the right to choose his own religion without being implanted with one which he may not like! Automatic transmission of faith from parents to offspring has disintegrated the mankind as Allah has given us no choice! Dr. ABDULLAH AL-KATHANY, an eminent Saudi scholar claims; "ALLAH HAS IMPLANTED HIS OWN RELIGION (ISLAM) IN INNATE, WITH WHICH ALL HUMAN ARE EQUIPPED"! If so, why Allah sent different messengers with different books of religion to different nations? This double standard is in fact an innate nature of the religious believers in general across the world! In reference to verses 4&5 of chapter 53, Dr. AL-JOHANI, a Saudi Islamic expert says; "HE (Muhammad) DOES NOT SPEAK OUT OF HIS OWN FANCY. HE UTTERS WHAT IS REVEALED TO HIM." Muhammad in clear terms claimed (AL-BUKHARI, VOL. 1, # 331)that "THE EARTH HAS BEEN MADE FOR ME AND MY FOLLOWERS A PLACE FOR PRAYING". "I HAVE BEEN GIVEN THE RIGHT OF INTERCESSION ON THE DAY OF RESURRECTION"? Are these not fanciful utterances? Where in the Quran Allah gave him such assurances? How Muhammad demanded that the believers must "Love" him more than their father, children and the mankind? Verse 252 of chapter 2 says; "AND SURELY, YOU ARE ONE OF THE MESSENGERS (OF ALLAH)! Muhammad again claims that no Muslim will have his faith complete unless he believes in him as the messenger of Allah! This also implies that a Muslim or a believer can have no direct connection with Allah bypassing Muhammad! He was given the prophethood as a "Plain "Warner"! But in reality he raised himself to a God-like deity in terms of religious allegiance and loyalty?

Verse-99, Ch-10 states; "AND HAD YOUR LORD WILLED, THOSE ON EARTH WOULD HAVE BELIEVED, ALL OF THEM TOGETHER. SO, WILL YOU (O MUHAMMAD) THEN COMPEL MANKIND UNTIL THEY BECOME BELIEVERS?" Why should then the prophet compel mankind to become believers against the "Will" of his Lord? If this was the intention of the Lord, then why did he send Muhammad as messenger to mankind? Muhammad claims that every child is born in this world on true faith of Islamic monotheism! If so, why Allah says " HAD YOUR LORD WILLED" only then all on earth would have become believers? So, efficacy of his injected innate religion to the humankind has gone down to its lowest level or might have lost its way in the oblivion? It seems that the HADHITS and the VERSES are not complementary to each other! Muhammad even expressed his intent to burn people in their houses who did not come out to attend prayers in the mosques! Allah is then said to have sent verse 109 of chapter 10 probably to pacify his angry messenger saying; "AND (O MUHAMMAD) FOLLOW THE REVELATION SENT UNTO YOU AND BE PATIENT TILL ALLAH GIVES HIS JUDGMENT". Oh dear Lord! Please with hold your judgment! Bestow upon mankind impunity from all ambiguities and contradictions! Free mankind from religious imprisonment; stop playing game from the "THRONE"! Let truths and facts prevail against fantasy, delusion and illusions! If Allah did not want all of mankind to turn believers, then why he decided to send Jesus again back to earth to convert all humans to Islam and rule the world in Islamic laws? Allah and his messenger claim that all humans are born Muslims but their parents convert them to other religions! Could any human being act against the will of the Lord who consistently claiming to be the real "Creator" of all creations? When it became clear to Allah that the mankind was not going to accept his monotheism, he decided to take his messenger unto him! Hope, Nightmare that pervaded the darkness of time shall vanish with the sunshine in the days to come!

Verse-6, Ch-11 says; "AND NO LIVING CREATURE IS THERE ON EARTH BUT ITS PROVISION IS DUE FROM ALLAH. AND HE KNOWS ITS DWELLING PLACE AND ITS DEPOSIT. ALL IS IN A CLEAR BOOK; THE BOOK OF DECREES WITH ALLAH". Since the inception of life on earth billions of living creatures including human being have died of hunger, famine, drought and devastations as their "PROVISION" was not "Due" from Allah! He claims to have created the earth in "Two" days but has taken "Four" days to create its sustenance! Yet billions of his creation have died for lack of food! What had happened to those that died of hunger was also written in the "Clear" book of Allah as nothing can happen against his "Will"! Though disgruntled, yet victims of deadly calamities accept Godly curses as "Acts of God"! All predators created by Allah, adapt "Might is Right" policy; kill one another for consumption, since "Killing for Living" is a divine provision "Decreed" by Allah for them! Among the humans, very few are vegetarians! Animals are killed by man for food and sometimes sacrificed in the name of the Lord to pave the way for paradise! Allah, the "King" of the universe has a written constitution; "THE BOOK OF DECREES" (AL-LAUH AL-MAHFUZ) for all creatures of his Kingdom! This book may also be called the "Constitution of the Universe"! All divine statutes and decrees are said to be written in that "Book of Decrees", also known as the "The Clear Book", held by Allah himself in his palace over Seven Heavens! The plain book (Quran), revealed by Allah for the mankind, to a large extent, is "Unclear" as it contains lots of miracles and abrogated verses! Very shortly Jesus will touch down on earth from heaven for his second mission! This time hopefully the Lord will not make second mistake! Jesus should be equipped with a "Clear Book" with clear instructions so that he finds no difficulty inducting whole of mankind into Islamic monotheism! Otherwise, Jesus, the "Son of Mary" might have to face a "Second Crucifixion" at the hands of those who lovingly call him "Son of God"!

Verse-35, Ch-11 states; "THE PAGANS OF MECCA SAY; HE (MUHAMMAD) FABRICATED THE QURAN. SAY; IF I HAVE FABRICATED IT, UPON BE MY CRIMES, BUT I AM INNOCENT OF ALL THOSE CRIMES WHICH YOU COMMIT". This verse is about an allegation against Muhammad brought by the pagans of Mecca that he fabricated the Quran! As usual Muhammad flatly denies the allegation! Despots on earth, following the footsteps of the prophets, also deny all allegations if brought against them without trying to refute them with justifications! Both political and religious bureaucracy use denial as an effective weapon of self-defense! Allah accordingly advised Muhammad to say to the Pagans that he was innocent of the crimes of fabricating the Quran! The allegation of fabrication of the Quran began from the day of its inception and continues till today! The seeds of doubt lie in the peculiar process of revelations! From revelation until compilation, the Quran changed hands many times involving ALLAH the "Author", GABRIEL the message carrier, MUHAMMAD the recipient, then the messages passed on to sixty five associates of Muhammad who acted as scribes, and then the manuscript was handed over to ABU BAKAR, UMAR, HAFSA, ZEYD IBN THABIT and UTHMAN! Prof. M.M. Al-AZAMI of U.K. Islamic Academy says that ZEYD IBN THABIT was present in person while angel Gabriel was reciting the Quran to Muhammad during the month of Ramadan! So, the story has managed at least a witness to revelation! If one witness is enough to vindicate "Revelation, then why is it mandatory to have four witnesses against fornication? The most genuine doubt is cast by the untimely death of Muhammad! Why Allah being so powerful did not allow Muhammad to compile the Quran in his life time? Some Muslim scholars say that thorough proof reading of the manuscript was done by experts after collecting it from different sources! No proof reading can ever validate or authenticate contents of a book when the writer or in this case, the recipient himself is dead! It is more so difficult when the parchments, on which these dictations had been drafted, were scattered into different hands and remained unbound for long time! What ABU BAKAR did was to collect all parchments into one volume and verified their accuracy against "WHAT WAS WRITTEN BY OTHERS AND MEMORISED BY THE PROPHET`S COMPANIONS". Another doubtful aspect of the Quran`s coming into being is that it had to be resurrected from the "Memories" of many unreliable sources! Allah narrated the verses to angel Gabriel who had to memorize them to pass on to Muhammad and then he along with many of his companions memorized those verses to dictate them to the scribes! How is it possible to preserve authenticity of the original texts simply by collecting them from memories of so many persons involved? The arrangements of the chapters and the verses are neither chronological nor logical! It has been clearly stated that the Quran was revealed in a tribal dialect of the QURAISH people! So, we can conclude that Allah and angel Gabriel also spoke QURAYSH dialect, at least for revelation purpose! Coincidently Muhammad too spoke the same language as he himself belonged to that QURAISH tribe! An interesting piece of story about collection of the Quran is narrated in an Islamic journal called "Islamic Relief" published from CA, U.S.A. It says, "SOME SCHOLARS SAY THAT THE FIRST COMPILATION OF ZAID'S WAS WRITTEN ACCORDING TO ALL SEVEN "AHRUF", OR MODES, IN WHICH THE QURAN WAS ORIGINALLY REVEALED. THESE AHRUF WERE THE MOST COMMON ARABIC DIALECT IN WHICH ALLAH PERMITTED THE PROPHET TO RECITE THE QURAN"! The Quran lost credibility because of the puzzling story behind its revelation and compilation! Why non-Arab Muslims are not allowed to recite these verses in their own language during prayers? Is it forbidden by any "Decree" from Allah? How Muhammad himself allowed people to recite the Quran in their own dialect? There are many verses in the Quran that are really embarrassing! Discussed below is one of those verses!

Verses-77, Ch-11 narrates; "AND WHEN OUR MESSENGERS CAME TO PROPHET LOT, HE WAS GRIEVED ON ACCOUNT OF THEM AND FELT HIMSELF STRAITENED FOR THEM (LEST THE TOWN PEOPLE SHOULD APPROACH THEM TO COMMIT SADOMY WITH THEM). HE SAID; THIS IS A DISTRESSFUL DAY". What an embarrassment! The poor prophet Lot was in the horns of a dilemma! His people were gay and preferred man over woman for sexual gratification! On the other hand when some Messengers from Allah came to see Lot, he was grieved and straightened for them lest his people should approach the messengers for sodomy! He advised his people in the next verse (#78) saying; "O MY PEOPLE! HERE ARE MY DAUGHTERS (WOMEN OF THE NATION), THEY ARE PURER FOR YOU. SO FEAR ALLAH AND DISGRACE ME NOT WITH REGARD TO MY GUESTS. IS THERE NOT AMONG YOU A SINGLE RIGHT-MINDED MAN?". This verse has drawn a bleak picture of the state of the un-Islamic affairs prevailing during the rule of the said prophet! In reply to the proposal put forward by the prophet Lot, his people said; "SURELY YOU KNOW THAT WE HAVE NEITHER ANY DESIRE NOR NEED OF YOUR DAUGHTERS, AND INDEED YOU KNOW WELL WHAT WE WANT" (Verse 79 of Ch. 11)! An article published in an Islamic periodical called "ISLAMIC RELEIF" from C.A, U.S.A. says; "WHEN A MAN SLEEPS WITH ANOTHER MAN, THE EARTH ROARS AND CRIES OUT TO ALLAH, AND THE ANGELS RUN TO THEIR LORD AND COMPLAIN TO HIM ABOUT THE OUTRAGEOUS ACT THEY HAVE WITNESSED"! Millions of such "Outrageous" acts take place every day all over the world, but none has heard of any roars of the earth! So, the history of the sodomy dates back to the ancient culture of Islamic Rule and continues till today unabated! LGBT movement is gaining momentum across the world! During prayers, if the IMAM recites these verses inside the mosques, mixed reactions of the believers standing behind him will create a shock wave in their minds! These verses are not recited by the IMAMS at religious gathering!

Verse-114, Ch-11 states; "AND PERFORM AS-SALAT (PRAYERS) AT THE TWO ENDS OF THE DAY AND IN SOME HOURS OF THE NIGHT. VERILY THE GOOD DEEDS REMOVE THE EVIL DEEDS". This verse deserves a careful attention as in it Allah clearly asks believers to perform prayers at the "TWO ENDS OF THE DAY"! This obviously refer to the MORNING and the EVENING of the day and which also mean two obligatory prayers during daytime! Exact date and time of the revelation of this verse cannot be ascertained in any way but the million dollar question is whether it was revealed before or after the so-called space mission of Muhammad? Because it was during his meeting with Allah that the number of obligatory prayers is said to have been reduced from fifty to five after a lot of arguments with him! This verse belongs to chapter 11 and the story of the space mission is mentioned in chapter 53! Both of which are claimed to have been revealed at Mecca! Did the Muslims offer fifty obligatory prayers before Muhammad's ascend to heaven? How a Muslim could fulfill this obligation? Next part of the verse reads "IN SOME HOURS OF THE NIGHT" which also mean one more prayer sometimes at night! So this makes a total of three obligatory prayers without any ambiguity as the verse specifically mentions three stages; "Two ends of the day" and "Some hours of the night" within the twenty four hour cycle! But the translators by their own accord claim that it refers to five prayers! Despite this being a clear verse, Muslims everywhere offer five obligatory prayers! Though Allah denies having burdened his men with religion, yet he originally ordained fifty obligatory prayers in a day for all Muslims, a mammoth obligation that his followers did find impossible to perform! There is also an interesting story narrated by Hadith (AL-BUKHARI, Vol. 6. #209) quoted with this verse; "A MAN KISSED A WOMAN AND THEN CAME TO ALLAH`S MESSENGER AND TOLD HIM OF THAT. SO THE DIVINE REVELATION WAS REVEALED TO THE PROPHET". What a luck! Revelation of this verse occurred instantaneously as soon as the crime was reported to Muhammad! By the way, kissing a woman against her will was not considered a crime since neither Allah nor Prophet Muhammad recommended any punishment for the perpetrator! Rather he was asked to perform SALAT (prayers) so that good deeds will remove his evil deeds! What a great example of Islamic justice! The man who kissed the women asked Muhammad if the instruction was valid only for him? Muhammad replied; "IT IS FOR ALL THOSE OF MY FOLLOWERS WHO ENCOUNTER A SIMILAR SITUATION"! Kissing a woman, a crime committed willingly or unwillingly, has been amicably solved by Allah and Muhammad jointly, setting an example for the entire mankind and particularly for the Muslim community! It is not mentioned whether any verse was revealed for the woman kissed! What has been revealed has no mention of the woman and her complaint against the man? It is also not clear about the relationship between these man and woman? Definitely she was not his wife! In that case what justice was done to the victim who has been kissed? What does the Islamic Justice System say about kissing a woman against her consent? Why the punishment has not been mentioned by Allah in that verse for the man? Instead he has been asked to perform Prayers? This verse is one of the "Unclear Verses" of the Quran! Whenever Muhammad is confronted with social or religious issues, Allah immediately sends his angel with verses to solve the problem? Despite the prompt action in this matter, yet Allah has taken twenty three years to reveal the Quran! After the death of Muhammad, his associates and the successors had taken around fifteen years to compile different segments of the Quran into a complete manuscript! The end result is a Quran that still contains "Abrogated", "Unclear", and "Entirely Unclear" verses along with many meaningless "Miracles"!

Verse-118, Ch-11 states; "AND IF YOUR LORD HAD SO WILLED, HE COULD SURELY HAVE MADE MANKIND ONE NATION OR COMMUNITY FOLLOWING ONE RELIGION i.e. ISLAM, BUT THEY WILL NOT CEASE TO DISAGREE". So it was Allah's will that he did not want the mankind to live as one nation or community under Islamic monotheism since they would not cease to disagree! What a contradiction to his own statement! Why All-knowing "Creator" did not know in advance that disbelievers would not cease to disagree! If Satan could make Adam eat the forbidden fruits in paradise, why can't Allah make the disbelievers agree with him! In a previous verse Allah urged all Muslims to unite under one KHALIFA or one Muslim ruler to counter all moves by the disbelievers! Now Allah seems to have changed his mind and decided to send Jesus again on earth to convert entire mankind to Islamic monotheism? Yet the blindfolded Islamic scholars find no deviation in the verses of Allah! To highlight the misleading contradiction I have to quote DR. AL-JOHANI again who said; "THE ESSENCE OF ISLAM, WHICH IS THE WILLING SUBMISSION TO THE WILL OF GOD, WAS REVEALED TO ADAM WHO PASSED IT ON TO HIS CHILDREN. ALL FOLLOWING REVELATIONS TO NOAH, ABRAHAM, MOSES, JESUS AND FINALLY MUHAMMAD WAS IN CONFORMITY WITH THAT MESSAGE"! Allah has tried his utmost to bring the mankind to his cherished monotheism but failed utterly! To illustrate another example of contradiction I would like to quote DR. ABDULLAH AL-KAHTANY who said; "INDEED, GOD HAS DONE ALL THIS AND EVEN MORE! HE HAS IMPLANTED HIS OWN RELIGION IN INNATE, WITH WHICH ALL HUMAN ARE EQUIPPED. How can Allah now say "IF YOUR LORD HAD WILLED"? It is apparent from the beginning to the end of the Quran that Allah, the self-styled "Creator" of the universe, had done his best to make the mankind accept Islamic monotheism but failed with humiliation! So it is pointless to try to unify all Muslims under one "KHALIFA"! The verse testifies that the Lord did not want us to live like one nation!

Verse-119, Ch-11 states; "EXCEPT HIM ON WHOM YOUR LORD HAS BESTOWED HIS MERCY.". This verse is a continuation of the previous one. Allah ends this verse with a note of warning for those who disagree; "SURELY I SHALL FILL THE HELL WITH JINN AND MEN TOGETHER". A Hadith quoted to explain this verse says; "TO SHOW MERCY TO THE GOOD-DOERS, THE BLESSED ONES WHO ARE DESTINED TO PARADISE, AND NOT TO SHOW MERCY TO THE EVIL-DOERS, THE WRETCHED ONES WHO ARE DESTINED TO HELL". Oh, the believers! Whether you are bound to hell or heaven, it all depends on Allah's mercy and will! Allah can take whole of the mankind either to the hell or to the heaven as he wills! Apparently this was not his intention! In one of the previous verses Allah said he would use hypocrites as "Fuel" for hellfire! One more thing seems weird is about the Jinn, a creature that are made of "Fire"! Where do they live? Is the Quran revealed for them too? Is Muhammad also their messenger? Did Muhammad see them? How the invisible Jinn, being made of "Fire" are going to be punished in the hellfire? Burn "Fire" with fire? What is the language of the Jinn? Do they speak Arabic too? Allah says; "VERILY, WE HAVE SENT IT DOWN AS AN ARABIC QURAN IN ORDER THAT YOU MAY UNDERSTAND" (Verse 2 of Ch. 12). The Quran was actually revealed in QURAYSH dialect since prophet Muhammad was also from that tribe! Allah, the creator of the universe, took the decision to reveal his messages for the mankind and the Jinn in a tribal dialect! Allah himself was already conversant with QURAYSH language and taught that dialect to angel Gabriel so that he could deliver the messages to Muhammad! No doubt that Allah was not aware of the fact the entire mankind did not speak in Arabic vernacular and Muhammad was in no way equipped with necessary skills to turn it into an universal language! Muhammad was sent as a messenger to mankind but Allah appears to be more focused on the Arabs. By all considerations, the Quran is "FOR THE ARABS, OF THE ARABS AND BY THE ARABS"!

Verse-103, Ch-12, states; "AND MOST OF THE MANKIND WILL NOT BELIEVE EVEN IF YOU DESIRE IT EAGERLY." In the next verse (#104) Allah correctly defines his Book: "IT (THE QURAN) IS NO LESS THAN A REMINDER AND AN ADVICE UNTO THE ALAMIN (MEN AND JINN)"! People pay little heed to reminder and advice! Yes, Allah's prediction has come true! He is really All-Knower! Most of the mankind believe in other religions except Islam! Billions of Chinese and others neither believe in religion nor believe in the existence of a creator! This is the reality! Lord's angels who are tasked to give him day-to-day reports on all affairs of the earth, might mislead him with misinformation! Oh, Lord, there are plenty of reasons to doubt success of your plan B, i.e. sending Jesus again to implement Islam to rule over entire mankind! To some extent the timing favored the prophets! When you did sent those prophets, that was the age of darkness; people in general used to believe in Magic, Myths, Mystery and Miracles! Moreover the science was in its infancy! A fool will always find some greater fools to admire him but all people cannot be befooled for all time! Old Jesus will have real hard time answering a host of hard questions from the disbelieving community on religions and creation! Theologians from all kinds of faiths might embarrass "Son of God" on the question of his most talked-about controversial 'Father-Son" relationship with Allah! Allah's denial of having fathered Jesus was not so much of a controversy as compared to Mary's claim of being pregnant without having her having touched by any human being! Gabriel played a controversial role in Mary's pregnancy coming to her disguised as a man! The mystery behind Mary's pregnancy is yet to be unfolded! Jesus after his arrival from heaven might be able to resolve controversies about his mother's "Virginity" and his "Crucifixion" once for all! Allah says Jesus will come as a Muslim ruler and that might make the mystery much more murkier than what it is now!

Verse-2, Ch-13 says; "ALLAH IS HE WHO HAS RAISED THE HEAVENS WITHOUT ANY PILLARS THAT YOU CAN SEE. THEN HE ROSE ABOVE THE THRONE IN A MANNER THAT SUITS HIS MAJESTY. HE HAS SUBJECTED THE SUN AND THE MOON TO CONTINUE GOING ROUND, EACH RUNNING ITS COURSE FOR A TERM APPOINTED". Allah raised Jesus unto him from this world and Jesus raised Lazarus from the dead! Now Allah claims to have "Raised the Heavens" but did not mention from where? He also takes a lot of credit for creating the heavens! These two terminology i.e. "Raising Heavens" and "Creating Heavens" have indeed created confusion as to their real meanings! This verse belongs to a chapter of the Quran called "The Thunder". Eliot, a Catholic Christian, wrote in a different context, "WHAT THE THUNDER SAID"! Elliot described his poem "The Waste Land" as a personal and wholly insignificant grouse against life! The reality is that he who created "Life" in "The Waste Land" is nowhere to be found! It is also he who has subjected the "Sun" and the "Moon" to continue going round the "WASTE LAND" and then he rose over to his "THRONE OVER SEVEN HEAVENS WHICH HE

RAISED WITHOUT PILLARS"! Even if he wished to raise the Heavens on pillars, where would he affix the pillars? In a previous verse Allah also said that his throne was "On" the water! That may be the reason why Allah this time "Raised" his throne from water to heavens! On the Day of Judgment eight angels will bear the "THRONE" of the Lord! When human beings for the first time planned to launch satellites, ISS and other devices into space, they never thought of placing them on "Pillars"! Even the children do not question how birds fly in the sky; why balloons need no pillars! But what "MANNER SUITED HIS MAJESTY" to ascend to his throne shall remain a mystery until Resurrection! Unfortunately Allah made the same mistake as Aristotle, both saw the sun moving round the earth! What meets the eye is not always the truth! The sun is defying Allah's commandment! Allah has "SUBJECTED THE SUN AND THE MOON TO CONTINUE GOING ROUND EACH ON ITS COURSE FOR AN APPOINTED TERM" since they are serving his believers as "Lamp" and "Time keeper"! The appointed term for the moon is about thirty days around the earth but that of the sun is hundreds of millions of years around the galaxy! Does Allah have any knowledge how force of gravitation works? Allah claims to have "Spread out" the earth but Einstein says it is not flat but curved! Curvature of the "Space-Time" makes all celestial objects move around one another! It is unthinkable to raise anything on pillars in space! Allah doesn't care about other planets of the solar system going round the sun as those are not related to his religion of Islam! What really happens is the movement of more than a billion stars around a mighty black hole at the center of the Milky-Way, along with our solar system once in a millions of years! Allah is not able to see the earth moving round the sun, how can he perceive movement of stars and galaxies? These unfounded assertions about the cosmos is termed by the Islamic experts as "Tidbits from the science of the Quran"! "The sun, with a diameter of 864000 miles and its mighty force of gravitation, holds the eight known planets in their elliptical orbits. In addition, the solar system has nearly two hundred satellites orbiting the planets; thousands of millions of asteroids and meteors and it measures 7,350,000,000 miles across! The next division of space is our galaxy: an aggregation of about 100 billion stars! Our sun is an average star in this galaxy known as the "Milky Way'. Light takes only over eight minutes to travel from the sun to the earth! The galaxy itself is so vast that the light takes 100,000 years to travel from one edge of it to the other! The so-called "Science of the Quran" says, Allah created the "Sun" as the "Lamp" for the human being and "Stars" as the "Missiles" to hit the devils on earth! The angels may have fly back to the "THRONE" over "Seven Heavens" to say to the Lord that the human beings reject his "Science of Creation" as they have reservation on "Revelation" as well!

Verse-3, Ch-13 says; "AND IT IS HE WHO HAS SPREAD OUT THE EARTH, AND PLACED THEREIN FIRM MOUNTAINS AND RIVERS. HE BRINGS THE NIGHT AS A COVER OVER THE DAY". Long ago probably in 340 B.C, Aristotle predicted that the earth is round and not flat as it appears! Albert Einstein says that the Space-Time is wrapped and all planets including the earth are round and follow an elliptical orbits around the sun. But Allah, the "Creator" of the universe, holds a different view! After creating the earth he spread it out to place mountains and rivers on its level surface! It is really difficult to place mountains and rivers on an orange-shaped uneven earth! The Lord with his extra-ordinary engineering skill decided to affix mountains and rivers on the surface of the earth so that it neither moves nor shakes! We have no idea what Allah did to the planet Earth when it broke into continents and islands! But it is the tremors and the tsunami; the shakers and the movers, that often make mockery of Allah's plan! For what strategic reason Allah placed the Himalayan mountain range in Nepal is beyond conviction! It is also not known why Allah did not explain and claim to have placed a huge furnace at the core of the earth burning day and night at a temperature almost equal to that of sun's surface! Knowingly or unknowingly, Allah, while spreading the earth, has torn apart its surface into millions of isles of different size and shape! That has also been a key factor in dividing the mankind into different nations with diverse colors and creeds! The rivers have occupied a very important place in Allah's creative strategy! The reason behind this could be the severe shortage of water in the desert where the messengers had to ask people to look up to sky for rain! And Elliot, the religious poet, had to say; "HERE IS NO WATER BUT ONLY ROCK! Moreover, Allah, the author of the Quran, is well aware of the hardship of the desert people! He has built "GARDENS OF PARADISE UNDER WHICH RIVERS FLOW"! There are also four rivers overflowing with "SWEET WATER", "MILK", "HONEY" and "WINE" in paradise! Most prominent of the rivers in paradise is "AL-KAUTHAR" whose banks are made of tents of hollow pearls! Believe it or not, though the Nile and the Euphrates are located in the Middle East but originated in the paradise, so says the Quran! Allah may have forgotten to mention about the vast oceans that have tens of thousands of mountains affixed at their bottoms! Oh Lord, please do not spread out the bottoms of the oceans as rising sea level might cause millions to face "DEATH BY WATER"! The Lord of the universe deserves our admiration for bringing the night as cover for the day! But why couldn't he do it with equal proportion for all of us? Why day and night are not same around the polar regions of the earth as at the equator? Sheikh Muhammad, an Islamic scholar while explaining a "FATAWA", published in a periodical called "Islamic Relief" said; "A MENTALLY CHALLENGED PERSON WILL GO TO PARADISE AND IF A CHILD IS BORN LACKING IN MENTAL FACULTY OR BRAIN-DAMAGED THEN HE IS MUSLIM"! Will he still be regarded as Muslim if born in a Jewish family? All of mankind are not mentally retarded or brain-damaged as to claim a place in paradise! If I live in and around the North or South pole, I have to see the "Night" spread out against the sky for months together "Like a patient etherized upon a table": Shining "Days" not dying under the cover of the "Night"! As a Muslim, how can I remember my "Creator" to pay my "Debts" five times in the morning, evening and night? Surely, some FATAWA and HADITH experts will come up with solution to this problem on behalf of Muhammad and Allah, based on "Islamic Science"! Allah claims to have "Raised" the Heaven without pillars but why he is not able to stop the Earth from "Moving" without affixing thousands of mountains on it? Is it that the "Islamic Science" works only for the Heaven and not for the Earth? The mankind does not deserve to be brain-washed for an eternal life in paradise nor does it deserve to be burned eternally in the Hell! No doubt the "Revelation" itself has revealed its real identity!

Verse-13, Ch-13, says; "AND 'AR-RAD' (THUNDER) GLORIFIES AND PRAISES HIM, AND SO DO THE ANGELS BECAUSE OF HIS AWE. HE SENDS THUNDERBOLTS, AND THEREWITH HE STRIKES WHOM HE WILLS, YET DISBELIEVERS DISPUTE ABOUT ALLAH". This "Thunder" is an angel! He is the in-charge of clouds and he drives them as ordered by Allah and he glorifies his praises! Let's see what does the Hindu God say as opposed to Islamic Allah: "Then spoke the Thunder"; the Creator God instructs the lesser gods to "Control" their unruly nature; men to "Give" alms despite their natural miserliness; the cruel demons to "Sympathize"! The Hindu God asking demons to sympathize but Allah, the Merciful Lord of the heavens might have thought that the mankind could easily be frightened into obedience with thunderbolts! "Alas, I have been struck a mortal blow"; cried Agamemnon aloud when struck by his wife!

But this time the "Creator" himself strikes mortal blow to his creation using "Thunderbolts"! Thunder is a great killer of mankind but it "GLORIFIES AND PRAISES" Allah! Does it kill the disbelievers only? Does thunder have life? Does it have to go to "Hell" if it fails to glorify Allah? The Lord is using deadly thunderbolts to strike disbelievers who "DISPUTE ABOUT ALLAH"! So, "THIS DAY NO RANSOM SHALL BE TAKEN FROM YOU (HYPOCRITES), NOR OF THOSE WHO DISPUTE AND DISBELIEVE IN THE ONENESS OF ALLAH AND ISLAMIC MONOTHEISM (Verse 15 of Ch. 57)"! Allah in another verse has categorically said he would not accept an earth-full of gold as ransom to set free a hypocrite from torment on the Day of Judgment! In fact All-Mighty Allah has brought his own stature down to that of an ordinary being by receiving glorifications and praises from lifeless thunders and talking of ransom as a way of getting rid of punishments! But the truth of the matter is crystal-clear that both thunders and the thunderbolts are secular in actions! The disbelievers in a way should be thankful to Allah that he is not using stars as missiles to strike point blank, because Allah has created those stars as missiles to strike the devils only! This concept of using stars, thunderbolts and thunders from the sky to shoot down enemies may have inspired some super powers on earth to adapt this idea of militarization of the space as part of modern warfare! Allah generally uses threats to generate fear to implement his religion over mankind and to secure his position as the only Creator of the earth and the heavens! Allah despite having so many deadly weapons at his disposal did no harm to the Jews who crucified "The Son of God" mercilessly on the rood! The reason is simple; he did not believe in that crucifixion! Allah rather "Sympathized" with Hitler, the Demon, who had thrown millions of Jews into the inferno as fuel for fire to mitigate his hatred! Similar is the plan of action drawn up by Allah to use men as "Fuel" for hellfire! After all, Elliot, the Anglo-Catholic poet expressed Christ's agony in the Garden of Gethsemane, his imprisonment, trial, and death on the Cross, in the poem "What the Thunder Said; "HE WHO WAS LIVING IS NOW DEAD; WE WHO WERE LIVING ARE NOW DYING"! We are dying to please our "Creator" who has promised to give us an unending lease of life posthumously! Nothing can get out of "Space-Time", says the scientists and similarly we cannot get rid of the "Spiders' Net" faithfully woven with fabrics of faiths by the home-grown "Weavers"! So, thunder is the voice of the creator God; so says the poets and the prophets! "THUNDER" reveals the "Truth"! Thunder tells the tale of the "Two Worlds"! Medieval Churches in England opposed all remedies for curing her sickness; declared heretics must be burned to death! Modern age saw tens of thousands of children abused in the churches! The intellectual community dwindled into insignificance! Not only the Christians but the mankind as a whole stood: "Between two worlds, one dead, The other powerless to be born"! What the humanity needs most is salvation from the Threats and Temptations that came down on earth from heaven through divine "Revelation"!

Verse-15, Ch-13 states; "AND UNTO ALLAH (ALONE) FALLS IN PROSTRATION WHOEVER IS IN THE HEAVEN AND THE EARTH, WILLINGLY OR UNWILLINGLY, AND SO DO THEIR SHADOWS IN THE MORNING AND IN THE AFTERNOON"! If all in the heaven and the earth must fall in prostration unto Allah alone, then why he wanted Satan to prostrate to Adam? Allah is also against having a partner to him! This, according to Allah's own law, constitutes the highest degree of crime! Who are in the heavens now? Most prominent among the prophets and the messengers are currently living in different heavens of the "Seven Heavens"! Adam is in the first heaven which Allah has decorated with "Stars"! This is also the nearest from the earth but farthest from Allah! On some special "Day" and at the third quarter of each night he descends to the so-called first heaven! "Islamic Science" did not elaborate on the time-line! When it is morning in Saudi Arabia (Approximately 4 a.m.), it is mid-day in Australia and evening in America! And then imagine what it is like around the polar regions! This first heaven also acts as the launching pad for the "Missiles" (stars) that Allah uses to hit the devils! Most probably in the pre-historic era, Allah fired a very small "Missile" to hit the devils but instead it killed all dinosaurs! The second heaven is jointly shared by Jesus and John; in the third heaven lives Joseph; Enoch lives in the fourth heaven; Aeron is in the fifth; Moses is in the sixth and in the seventh, which is nearest to Allah, lives Abraham; the chief architect who built KABAH, the house of Allah at Mecca! Prophet Muhammad met all of them during his space mission! Prophet Muhammad has not been allotted any of those Seven Heavens, instead he was buried in Mecca! However, Allah claims that these prophets and messengers, along with trillions of celestial objects and their shadows prostrate to Allah, sometimes willingly and sometimes unwillingly in the morning and in the afternoon! The Quran is a "Plain Book" and a "Plain Statement" but Allah has written it in a "Language" that falls far short of comprehension!

Verse-41, Ch-13 states; "SEE THEY NOT THAT WE GRADUALLY REDUCE THE LAND (OF THE DISBELIEVERS BY GIVING IT TO THE BELIEVERS IN WAR VICTORIES) FROM ITS OUTLYING BORDERS. AND ALLAH JUDGES, THERE IS NONE TO PUT BACK HIS JUDGMENT AND HE IS SWIFT IN RECKONING". In reality it is the believers who are losing their land gradually! The readers will face no hurdle to understand how the statement of this verse contradicts reality on the ground! Has this verse been written by a sane entity? It is nothing but a flagrant distortion of the facts! Oh Lord, verily, we have been seeing this battle between believers and disbelievers decades after decades in and around the holy land of Jerusalem, not far from Mecca, the heartland of Islam! Palestinians, the believers losing their lands to the Jews, the disbelievers! They have been forced out of their "OUTLYING BOARDERS" to make rooms for the Jews who not only disobeyed Moses but also refused to accept Jesus as a messenger, calling him an imposter! At the end they "Crucified" the "Son of God" alias the "Son of Mary"! How many war Muslims have won since the dawn of Islam? How much of the land of the earth belongs to believers in Allah? The total land occupied by the Muslims, the believers, may not be more than ten percent of the total land of the earth! Yet success of the Lord lies in the fact that these believers still prefer to die shouting "ALLAH-HU-AKBAR"! The battle between the followers of Muhammad and Moses might continue until the arrival of Jesus! He will have to make a choice between "WAR AND PEACE"! Jesus stands a slim chance to make peace unless he comes with a revised divine plan from the "BOOK OF DECREE" held with Allah to convert the Jews, the Christians and others to Islamic Monotheism! The land Allah gave to the Palestinians is now under enemy's occupation! Allah's Judgment has been overturned by the disbelievers; the Jews are at the wheel! Yet Allah says; "THERE IS NONE TO PUT BACK HIS JUDGMENT? Contents of this verse in enough to undermine the factuality of the divine "Revelation"!

Verse-1, Ch-14 says; "THIS IS A BOOK WHICH WE HAVE REVEALED UNTO YOU (MHUAMMAD) IN ORDER THAT YOU MIGHT LEAD MANKIND OUT OF DARKNESS (DISBELIEF AND POLYTHEISM) INTO LIGHT (ONENESS OF ALLAH AND ISLAMIC MONOTHEISM)". This verse is directly addressed to Muhammad to remind him of his prime task that Allah has entrusted to him! Logically this verse should have been the first verse of the Quran! What has really happened is exactly the opposite to what Allah expected from Muhammad! Allah, the Lord of the heaven, sent a lot of messengers with many divine "Books" but the disbelief and polytheism prevailed over mankind since the beginning till today! People at large rejected Islamic monotheism! Thanks be to Allah that after all he has realized the futility of sending messengers with books to that end! Why Allah did not bestow sufficient time and talent to his last messenger Muhammad to lead the mankind out of "DARKNESS INTO LIGHT"? How an illiterate man undertake such an impossible mission? Allah revealed the Quran at a place which was relatively less dark! The "Book" should have been revealed at a place in and around the "Heart of Darkness" in Africa if his prime target was to remove real darkness and bring forth an enlightened mankind! Peaceful co-existence of a diversified people will only come through polytheism; not through monotheistic menace! Monopoly of monotheism has never been well-received by the mankind! Polytheism, as opposed to monotheism, is much more democratic and inclusive. Verse 4 of chapter 14 says; "AND WE SENT NOT A MESSENGER EXCEPT WITH THE LANGUAGE OF HIS PEOPLE IN ORDER THAT HE MIGHT MAKE CLEAR THE MESSAGE FOR THEM"! Allah has appreciable sense of humor! In the same verse he continues to say, "THEN ALLAH MISLEADS WHOM HE WILLS AND GUIDES WHOM HE WILLS". What was the language of Adam? What "People" did he represent? What messages did he receive from his "Creator" for his offspring? It is not just the Satan who misleads mankind but Allah as well! Satan and Allah joined hands in misleading whom they "Will' and as a result followers of Muhammad are in minority! So, it is evident from the above verse that the mankind were divided right from the inception in terms of Language, Color, Creed and Culture! Allah, as the "Creator" of the earth and the heaven should have taught one language to all messengers for the unification of the mankind! Monotheism has failed to unify the mankind! Muhammad knew only a tribal dialect of the QURAYSH people; he never had gone through schooling of any kind in his lifetime! He neither spoke an international language nor Arabic was spoken by people internationally! Was he in any way equipped with necessary wisdom to play the role of a global leadership to impact the whole of mankind? Why the Lord nominated an unlettered man as the messenger to mankind to "MAKE CLEAR THE MESSAGE"! In the verse, Allah made his objective clear to Muhammad i.e. to bring mankind out of darkness into light! And in the same chapter he says, "ALLAH MISLEADS OR GUIDES WHOM HE WILLS". Does this statement of Allah make any sense? If it was his "Will", then what was the necessity of sending so many messengers with ambiguous messages to so many nations? Could he not "LEAD" or "MISLEAD" people of his choice according to his "WILL" from heavens? Why Allah has to mislead mankind since he has granted license to Satan to do that? The "Plain Book" is full of abrogated, inconsistent, contradictory, unclear, and unscientific verses written with total disregard to chronological discipline! It contains many "Miracles" that are understood only by the "Author"! The messenger, who was supposed to lead mankind into light, plunged himself into darkness of Jihad, war, killing, polygamy, conjugal chaos, etc.! "Messenger to mankind" left the world with "Overwhelming" failures! What percentage of mankind is now "STRAIGHTENED"? How many of them say in one voice; "NONE HAS THE RIGHT TO BE WORSHIPPED BUT ALLAH"?

Verse-27, Ch-14 states; "ALLAH WILL KEEP FIRM THOSE WHO BELIEVE, WITH THE WORD THAT STANDS FIRM IN THIS WORLD AND IN THE HEREAFTER. ALLAH WILL CAUSE TO GO ASTRAY THOSE WHO ARE POLYTHEISTS AND WRONG DOERS AND ALLAH DOES WHAT HE WILLS". We already know how Allah is going to deal with the disbelievers based on his dictatorial principle; "ALLAH DOES WHAT HE WILLS"! Allah is a despot, an absolute dictator! He acts like a cruel monarch to bring entire mankind to his knees unchallenged! We can say nothing about hereafter but what is the number of believers that Allah has been able to keep firm with his words in this world? Allah has caused others to go astray and as a result the polytheists are much greater in numbers in the world of his own making! An interesting Hadith, quoted as the footnote to this verse in reference to "TAFSIR IBN HATHIR, says; "IMMEDIATELY AFTER THEIR DEATH TWO ANGELS, NAMELY; 'MUNKAR' AND 'NAKIR' WILL COME TO THE GRAVES TO ASK THREE QUESTIONS: Q. 1. "WHO IS YOUR LORD"? Q. 2. "WHAT IS YOUR RELIGION"? Q. 3. "WHAT DO YOU SAY ABOUT THIS MAN (MUHAMMAD) WHO WAS SENT TO YOU"? The answers to first and second questions are ALLAH and ISLAM respectively! As for the third question, the believers may find it difficult to answer, since except his contemporaries, none has seen Muhammad! His image is strictly forbidden to be printed in any form of artistic expression as it is considered blasphemous! Muhammad must be present with the angels in person at the graves during interrogation! If those deceased are brought back to life for questioning inside the graves, only than both believers and disbelievers will be able to answer the last questions! Believers would say; "THIS MAN MUHAMMAD IS ALLAH'S

MESSENGER AND HE CAME TO US WITH CLEAR SIGNS AND WE BELIEVED IN HIM". The disbelievers will not be able to answer these three questions! So, right in the grave itself their fate will be decided! General perception is that we would only get back our life after resurrection for final judgment! But this Hadith says we will be brought back to life again in the grave, although briefly for interrogation! So the souls will enter the body soon after the burial! But what would happen to those that are cremated? It is also clear that we will have our "Second Life" followed by "Second Death" in the grave! Bodies of the many disbelievers are burnt to ashes after death! Some even preserve the ashes in the urn making it even more difficult for the angels to do the questioning! How angels are going to handle these remains? What questions would be asked to those in the graves who would die after "Second Coming" of Jesus? For them the correct answer to the last question should be Jesus, not Muhammad or the question itself be changed entirely and the Angels detailed to interrogate them need to be briefed accordingly! Otherwise a serious misjudgment might occur during evaluation process of the answers to those three questions! Verse 48 of chapter 14 states; "ON THE DAY WHEN THE EARTH WILL BE CHANGED TO ANOTHER EARTH AND SO WILL BE THE HEAVENS, AND THEY (ALL CREATURES) WILL APPEAR BEFORE ALLAH". Look "EVERYMAN"! "How the Father of heaven SENDETH death to summon every creature to come and give account of their lives in this world"! Long, long ago, all the dinosaurs died a sudden death in this earth without knowing that they have to appear before Allah to give account of their life in a Neo-Earth! In an earlier verse Allah said he would hold the Earth and the Heavens on his hands on the Day of Judgment! Let there be no question at all! What the creator does is above question! All answers to all questions will be given upon resurrection on the Day of Judgment! Until then hold your patience! Now the creator says he will recreate the earth and the heavens but all of his creatures will have to appear before him, probably unchanged, in his changed Earth! May be the sublime shall create a new universe for the grand trial to take place or he may even move us to another universe that already exists beyond the "Lot-Tree", the last boundary of our present universe! Science also talks about multiverse! If Allah wants to replace this "Resting Place" with new one, he will have to change its "Canopy" as well! Allah will also have to rebuild his Throne, his Palace and the Paradise to give them a new look as part of the Neo-Heavens! What about the Hell? Everything in the heaven will undergo the "Change"! There is valid reason for these changes! All little human beings who would qualify for an eternal life would be remolded into giant statures with their heights increased to "Thirty Meters" before being admitted into paradise! Adam was thirty meters in height and for that matter his offspring, who lost their height in this earth gradually, must regain that height to match with that of their "Father"! The Earth has to be changed for another good reason as Allah wants the sun to rise in the West on the Dooms Day! The easiest way would be to hold the "Trial" at our nearest planet, the Venus where the sun always rises in the West! Allah has not mentioned whether these changes will affect our solar system, the galaxies or the universe as a whole? He has obviously neglected the moon which has served his chosen religion by reckoning the days and nights for all kinds of prayers and rituals! He always kept one half of the moon out of our sight! Probably that part of the moon is the one Muhammad had to split open to show the miracle to the people of Mecca! Would he also change trillions of stars that he wanted to use as missiles to hit the devils? It is a matter of real concern that despite having so many "MISSILES", Allah has not been able to restrain Satan or the Devils from misleading the mankind! He let Satan go off the hook! Like a coin, every statement of Allah has two sides": He "WILL KEEP FIRM" his words with believers and will "CAUSE OTHERS TO GO ASTRAY"! One more important aspect of this verse is about "ALL CREATURES"! Why should they be asked to appear before Allah? Do these creatures have religions as humans do? Which prophet is going to lead them on the Dooms Day? According to the Quran Prophet Muhammad will lead both Man and Jinn (A creation created by Allah from fire) on the Day of Resurrection!

Verse-49, Ch-14 states; "AND YOU WILL SEE THE CRIMINALS, DISBELIEVERS, POLYTHEISTS BOUND TOGETHER IN FETTERS WITH THEIR HANDS AND FEET TIED TO THEIR NECKS WITH CHAINS". Allah claims that he has implanted his religion of Islamic monotheism innately into every new born starting from Adam! Unlike animals, humans are born mentally bound in fetters of faiths! Now the Merciful "Creator" wants them, who have been led astray by the Satan, bound physically with their hands and feet tied to their necks with chains! A chilled sensation is bound to run through the spine after reading the graphic description of the verse above which narrates one of the most disturbing episodes how human beings will be subjected to brutal treatment by their "Creator"! Allah has already declared them "Criminals" before holding trials on the

Day of Judgment! These criminals, polytheists and disbelievers should understand what a horrific ordeal awaits them after death! Those who did not believe in Allah, Muhammad and Islam were resentful of being handcuffed here on earth, will now have their hands and feet tied to their necks with chains on the Day before the merciful Judge! Even Americans did not treat the Afghans in such a cruel manner at the Cuban island! "No! I am not the Crown Prince, nor was meant to be! I can't tear body of my critique into pieces and then deny having done that! Probably Shakespeare's mind was going through some kind of spiritual crisis that suddenly turned his genius from comedy to tragedy! But the greatest tragedy on humanity will be played on the Day of Judgment by the "Creator"! Guess what comes next! "THEIR GARMENTS WILL BE OF PITCH, AND FIRE WILL COVER THEIR FACES (Verse 50 of chapter 14)"! The pilgrims with loads of sins on their back will follow "The road winding above among the mountains; which are mountains of rock without water"! The Lord will be seated on his "Throne" while the criminals bound in fetters will be waiting to hear the "Judgment" from the "Merciful" Lord of the Heavens and the Earth!

Verse-9, Ch-15 says; "VERILY, WE, IT IS WE WHO HAVE SENT DOWN THE DHIKR (i.e. THE QURAN) AND SURELY WE WILL GUARD IT (FROM CORRUPTION)". If I rewrite this verse as follows; "Verily, I, it is I who have sent down the Quran and surely I will guard it from corruption"! It would have been much better if Allah could guard the Quran from confusion arising out of singular and plural pronouns used to refer to himself! Allah, as the only "CREATOR" could neither guard the earth from destruction nor could he guard mankind from corruption! The Quran is probably the most corrupt book of religion in terms of revelation, composition, compilation, collection, correction, confusion, contradictions, abrogation, myths, mystery and miracles! We could lay belief on this verse if Allah could keep his promise to Muhammad! Allah is said to have assured Muhammad that he would be kept alive until all crooked disbelievers are "Straightened"! Ultimately this proved to be wrong! Allah even did not allow him enough time to edit the Quran to raise it above all doubts! A foot note to this verse says; "THIS VERSE IS A CHALLENGE TO MANKIND AND EVERYONE IS OBLIGED TO BELIEVE IN THE MIRACLES OF THE QURAN. IT IS A CLEAR FACT THAT MORE THAN 1400 YEARS HAVE ELAPSED AND NOT A SINGLE WORD OF THE QURAN HAS BEEN CHANGED, ALTHOUGH THE DISBELIEVERS

TRIED THEIR UTMOST TO CHANGE IT IN EVERY WAY, BUT THEY FAILED MISRABLY IN THEIR EFFORTS. AS IT IS MENTIONED IN THE HOLY VERSE BY ALLAH; WE WILL GUARD IT! AND HE HAS GUARDED IT. ON THE CONTRARY ALL THE OTHER HOLY BOOKS (TORAH AND GOSPEL) HAVE BEEN CORRUPTED IN THE WAY OF ADDITIONS, SUBTRUCTIONS AND ALTERNATIONS IN THE ORIGINAL TEXT"! Allah has downgraded his position, both as an "Author" and also as a "Creator" by challenging the "Mankind" that he claims to have "Created? If he has guarded the Quran so eagerly, why did he not do that for Torah and Gospel? If anyone thinks the Quran has not been corrupted, then he is living in fool's paradise! Those blinded by loyalty to Allah will not see it! Corruptions and controversies began right from the first verse of the Quran itself! Can any Islamic scholar claim that the Quran has been chronologically compiled? Is this not scripted from unreliable memories of some illiterate persons! Was it edited by the recipient himself? Who is responsible for meaningless miracles, abrogation and unclear verses? Are these works of the Lord of the universe? What Aristotle, Plato, Socrates, Ptolemy and others wrote hundreds of years before the coming of Muhammad, needed no God to guard their immortal works on Science and Philosophy! What the Ancient Egyptians wrote on the tombstone still survives uncorrupted! "Beowulf", probably the first long poem in English was composed by an unknown author around the time of so-called divine revelation! Manuscript of this historic book of poem still survives in the British Museum! History of the Quran from revelation to compilation spread over more than thirty years! The entire composition of the Quran is based on "Memories"! The corrupting has begun right from the first verse (BISMILLAH......) of the first chapter itself! Is this the verse revealed first? Did Allah allow this verse to be used as a separator between each chapter? Who inserted punctuations in the text of the Quran? Did Allah began writing this book in his own name? Muhammad is said to have been sent for the whole of mankind, if so why the Quran is revealed in QURAISH dialect? Repetitions of similar verses with similar contents genuinely generate a feeling that it has not been written single handedly, rather the Quran appears to be a group-composition! The question is not about corruption as it is for revelation! Here I have to quote Elliot again; "To have squeezed the universe into a ball; To roll it towards some overwhelming question"! Universe is expanding in all directions to find the answer to that

"Overwhelming Question"! Elliot was not a prophet but even as a poet he kept his belief intact and passed "Through the iron gates of life" to enter into paradise!

Verse-16, Ch-15 states; "AND INDEED WE HAVE PUT THE BIG STARS IN THE HEAVEN AND WE BEAUTIFIED IT FOR THE BEHOLDERS". Confusion again arises about words such as "Heaven", "First Heaven" and the "Nearest Heaven"! This is another example of repetitions of verses on the same subject! There are a number of verses on stars in the Quran! Allah or the author mistakenly took these giant stars for flowers! He could not have made such mistakes if he really had lived in his throne on Seven Heavens! A splendid show of massive fireworks takes place when a star explodes as Supernova, lighting the space million times brighter than the sun! Is this the decoration Allah is talking about? But anyone who has no knowledge of the universe and the space may use stars for decoration as the poets do! Allah claims he has beautified the heavens with stars since the "BEAUTY LIES IN THE EYES OF THE BEHOLDERS". This quotation would have pleased All-mighty if it could be written as "BEAUTY LIES IN THE EYES OF THE BELIEVERS". Why Allah has created trillions of stars for a tiny number of beholders? The believers can see only a very small number of stars on a clear sky at night! May Allah order his angel-in-charge of clouds (AR-RUD) to keep the sky clear, so we could see more of them! Allah has planted these stars beyond human reach so that no disbelievers can ravage these blooming "Flowers"! The nearest star is more than four light years away from the beholders! Allah, being in his "Throne" over seven heavens, has deprived himself of this spectacular starry blossom of the nearest heaven! If the need arises, he has the option to use them as missiles to strike the devils! Does Allah know how much of energy these stars produce? Do they produce energy for beautification? These kind of verses clearly draw a line of separation between the "Author" of the Quran and the presumptive "Creator" of the heavens and the earth! To Allah, the Sun is a "Lamp" and to the rest of the creation, it is the lifeline! Those who worship Sun as God deserve respect for not being misled by "Revelation"!

Verse-26, Ch-15 states; "AND INDEED, WE CREATED MAN FROM DRIED (SOUNDING) CLAY OF ALTERED MUD". And for this reason IBLIS Satan refused to prostrate to ADAM, when ordered by Allah, since he was made of "Smokeless flame of fire", a superior material far better than "Dried sounding clay of altered mud"! Thanks be to Allah that he has taken enough pains to process ordinary clay into "ALTERED MUD" to create humans! Potters on earth also undertake similar process to produce quality products out of stinking rotten clay! Allah seems to have done a lot of experiments in creating life! He began creation first by uttering the word "Be" and then "Breathing" through sleeves, and in succession he used Water, Mud, Altered mud, Dust, Despised Water of Semen, Flameless Fire, Light etc.! In addition to all of these, Allah claims to have made "Wives" from their "Husbands"! What material Allah used to create other creatures like animals, birds, insects, virus etc. has not been mentioned! Plants too have life! What about them? Our curiosity knows no bound to know what material Allah himself is made of! Probably he is made of flammable light as the mountain over which he appeared to talk to Moses burnt to ashes because of the intense heat! Our "Creator" knows everything about us, unfortunately we know very little about him! The only information we know about him is that he is not "Created" by any Creator! As part of his grand scheme of creation, Allah has employed various methods to create all living beings! Humans are supposed to be the "BEST OF CREATION" but he has used one of the worst materials to create them! On them he hopes to implement his Islamic monotheism! The Satan, Devils, Angels and Jinn are made of better materials! To the astonishment of all, Allah, the "Creator" has not been able to create a single man out of the entire mankind including his dearest friend Muhammad, who could live his life without suffering from diseases! Why? Because the Lord "Created" us from "Dried Altered Mud"! Is he not the "Best of Creator"?

Verse-27, Ch-15 states; "AND THE JINN, WE CREATED AFORETIME FROM THE SMOKELESS FLAME OF FIRE"! Allah has used special materials such as fire, light etc. to create Angels, Satan and Jinn! Whereas for Adam and his offspring, the ASHRAFUL MUKHLUKAT (Best of all creations), Allah has chosen an inferior material like Mud and "despised Water"! Although he dried and altered the mud into "Sounding Clay" yet the body of a human being is as brittle as a pottery and harbors numerous diseases! This is why human's life is so short and frail! Prophet Muhammad's life is a great example of this fragility! His "Creator" has given him everything but longevity! Allah cut short his life to save him from further humiliations! It shows how the mankind has been victim of Allah's negligence right from the inception! What is even more surprising is that Allah has shifted from his earlier claim that he created man from "WATER! Genetic code or DNA tests have revealed nothing to support

Allah's claim that we are made of mud! Jinn may have been made from smokeless fire but why are they invisible? They could have been made visible like the fireflies! Logically we find no reason behind the creation of "Jinn and Man" together to live in one planet! Being the closest neighbors, yet there is no mutual interactions between the Jinn and Man as Allah has built an invisible "Great Wall" between them! For the Jinn, Allah could have made a separate planet giving them a new book of religion! Do they believe in Islam? Allah has assigned different tasks to all angels! Satan has been granted "Respite" to mislead man until Resurrection! What purpose do the Jinn serve for Allah? The answer is; "ALLAH CREATES NOTHING WITHOUT PURPOSE"! Sun is the only star directly linked to our sustainability, so do not raise the question why he created trillions of other stars! He created them to decorate the nearest heaven! Those "stars" are his "missiles"! If you believe not, then you are heading for a life in the inferno forever! It may be mentioned that the Jinn are also equally affected by the "Revelation"!

Verse-99, Ch-15 says; "AND WORSHIP YOUR LORD UNTIL THERE COMES UNTO YOU THE CERTAINITY (DEATH)." Worship until death is what has been ordained by Allah for the believers! Learning to worship Allah begins at seven and if still unwilling, give the child a good beating after ten, so says Muhammad! Even on death bed a Muslim is obliged either to recite or listen to verses of the Quran so that he dies with IMAAN (belief)! All Islamic prayers are mostly physical! Meditation or mental devotion cannot please Allah! Muhammad, in a Hadith related to this verse (BUKHARI, Vol. 8,# 362), cautions his followers not to long for death even when a calamity befalls them! In case the calamity gets unbearable then he should pray to Allah; "O ALLAH! LET ME LIVE AS LONG AS LIFE IS BETTER FOR ME AND TAKE MY LIFE IF DEATH IS BETTER FOR ME". What happens to those who die before being able to speak or say those words to Allah? Unfortunately the death has never been able to establish itself as a better choice over life for any creature on earth leave aside the humans! The kings and the queens of the ancient Egyptian civilization did not want to die and they built pyramid hoping the souls would enter their body to live another life inside that huge structures! It is a welcome option only when life gets heavier than death! Probably Muhammad also did not want to die so soon! Deadly diseases coupled with conjugal chaos that prompted his departure earlier than schedule pending his most important task; inducting all humans into Islam, the only religion acceptable to Allah!

I would rather advise every believer in Islam to take the shortest route to paradise; worship All-Mighty Allah only in the night of "AL-QADR" (The Night of Decree)! At this night Allah comes down to "First Heaven" and reward for this one night worship would be more than worshipping him for 83 years! But you have to search that "Night" in the five odd nights of the last ten days of the month of Ramadan! Please avoid being around polar regions where it may be even more difficult to find that blessed "Night"!

Verse-8, Ch-16 states; "AND (HE HAS CREATED) HORSES, MULES AND DONKEYS, FOR YOU TO RIDE AND AS AN ADORMENT. AND HE CREATES (OTHER) THINGS OF WHICH YOU HAVE NO KNOWLEDGE". These animals are basically used as beasts of burden and not as adornment! However, the horse is an exception! Rich and Royal Arabians are very much fond of horses! Arabian horses bred from high quality species are adorned world-wide! Yet we cannot give much credit to the "Creator" of the universe for creating these animals! Why Allah is silent about the creation and destruction of the Dinosaurs? Allah does deserve credit for creating "BORAQ", an animal bigger than a donkey and smaller than a horse, which carried Muhammad to the heavens and back just in one night! Moreover Allah questions humans: "DO THEY NOT LOOK AT THE CAMELS, HOW THEY ARE CREATED? AND AT THE HEAVEN, HOW IT IS RAISED? (Verse 17&18 of Ch. 88). Is the creation of camels and heavens comparable? Yet considering the fact that the Quran was revealed in Arabic in Arabia, the camel as the "Ship of the Desert" had played a crucial role in the life of the messengers and their ancestors besides providing much needed milk and meat as sustenance! As we all know Allah begun creating living things with a pair of man and woman (Adam & Eve) and afterward he created (Verse 143&144 of Ch. 6), "EIGHT PAIRS: OF THE SHEEP TWO; OF THE GOATS TWO; OF THE CAMELS TWO; AND OF OXEN TWO (MALES AND FEMALES)" In relation to this verse, Prophet Muhammad narrated a story (BUKHARI, Vol. 5, # 15) in which a cow and a wolf are said have spoken in the language of a human being! Then the prophet ordered a congregational prayer, read out another Hadith (ABU SAID AL-KHUDRI, Vol. 3, page 83); "By Him (Allah) in whose hands my soul is, the day of resurrection will not be established till beasts of prey speak to the human beings, and the stick lash and the shoe laces of a person speak to him and his thigh inform him about his family as to what happened to them after him"!

Verse-15, Ch-16 states; "AND HE HAS AFFIXED INTO THE EARTH MOUNTAINS STANDING FIRM, LEST IT SHOULD SHAKE WITH YOU, AND RIVERS AND ROADS, THAT YOU MAY GUIDE YOURSELVES". The "Creator" who did "Raise" the Heaven without pillars, now needs to affix mountains on earth "LEST IT SHOULD SHAKE"! The science of the Quran shakes us more than the earth itself that the mankind can hardly stand erect! The creator Allah has already mentioned about his marvelous engineering skill in a previous verse; affixing mountains and rivers into the earth! Roads have been added in this verse! This earth, with many mountains and oceans affixed on it, rotating on its axis and also going round the sun in its own orbit! No mountain can prevent surface of the earth from shaking, if hit by quakes or tremors! The mountains themselves are not immune to shaking! Trillions of celestial bodies and asteroids floating freely in the space having no mountains affixed on them! What meets the eyes is not always the truth! Allah has special fascination for rivers in the world as well as in paradise! Let me quote DR. MAMDOUH N. MOHAMED from "Islamic Relief"; "Among specific examples of the after-life, the prophet Muhammad often used images of heaven to motivate his followers. The Arabian Peninsula in general has very little rain and does not support vegetation readily. As such, the Quran very readily offers the reward of beautiful gardens with rivers flowing beneath them"! What this quote has unfolded contradicts the verse 57 of chapter 7 which says; "AND IT IS HE WHO SENDS THE WIND AS HERALD OF GLAD TIDINGS, GOING BEFOR HIS MERCY (RAIN). TILL WHEN THEY HAVE CARRIED A HEAVY-LADDEN CLOUD. WE DRIVE IT TO A LAND THAT IS DEAD, THEN WE CAUSE WATER (RAIN) TO DESCEND THEREON"! Thousands of dead deserts will testify against Allah's claim! The real author of the Quran seems to have come from Arabian roots and as such Allah has built all gardens in "Paradise" under which rivers flow! Water was really scarce during "Revelation"!

Verse-20, Ch-16 states; "THOSE WHOM THEY (POLYTHEISTS, PAGANS, IDOLATERS etc.) INVOKE BESIDES ALLAH HAVE NOT CREATED ANYTHING, BUT ARE THEMSELVES CREATED". Allah claims the earth and the heaven and everything between them is created by him! This verse surely testifies that all polytheists and their deities are also created by Allah! So, Allah being the only "Creator" has created his own rivals who are disobedient to him! The "One and Only" who is not "Created" is ALLAH himself and the rest of all creation needed to be

"Created" by a "Creator"! The polytheists, pagans, idolaters, Satan and the deities are all enemies of Allah! But the problem is that he is not able to fight against them despite being an "All-Powerful All-Mighty"! Is the Lord self-created? Is he created out of nothing? Our creator doesn't need a creator but we sure do! Adversaries have gone as much as to say; Allah "Created" Muhammad and Muhammad "Created" Allah! Who is the creator of those gods that polytheists worship? Allah claims that he is the creator of all creations and he creates none without "Purpose"! So, can we not say Allah himself created his own rivals exactly the way he created Adam and Satan for two opposing purposes? Others say the creator doesn't exist at all! If the Mighty Lord can be created without a creator, why every tiny creature needed creator? Skeptics say, sponsors of all faiths have created their respective "Creators" as they desperately needed one to build their dogmatic empires around a mighty invisible divine deity! Muhammad needed an invisible Allah over his head to convince the pagans who right from the outset dismissed him as a messenger! Many had branded him as an imposter who fabricated the Quran! Who would then listen to his "Good Words" on rewards and punishments after death? All sponsors of faith lodged their "Creators" over the sky, far from the meddling crowds; named those imaginary "Creators" differently and then painted them as the ultimate power with different shades and colors to serve their purposes!

Verse-79, Ch-16 states; "DO THEY NOT SEE THE BIRDS HELD (FLYING) IN THE MIDST OF THE SKY? NONE HOLDS THEM BUT ALLAH. VERILY, IN THIS ARE CLEAR PROOFS AND SIGNS FOR PEOPLE WHO BELIEVE (IN THE ONENESS OF ALLAH)".Those days are long gone when people used to be amazed by seeing the "BIRDS HELD (FLYING) IN THE MIDST OF THE SKY" as human beings are habituated to seeing the giant stars and galaxies floating; held in the sky without pillars! How these "PROOFS AND SIGNS" are related with the "ONENESS OF ALLAH? This could also be the work of multiple Gods! This claim of oneness or singularity of the creator has kept the entire mankind fighting against those who differ on this question ever since the dawn of humanity! Flying machines invented jointly by two brothers are also held in the sky! Not necessarily everything has to be created by "One and Only"! What is both amazing and charming is the extra-ordinary feat of flying these birds display during their long-haul flight from Siberia to Australia and back! More amazing is the flight of millions of beautiful butterflies flocking together more than two thousand miles from Canada to Mexico! Every year they make it to their respective destinations successfully as they don't need to bother about hell or heaven! Neither the birds nor the butterflies received guidance from heaven through angels or messengers! Most of the believers and the pilgrims, burdened with sins, lose their way trying to make it to the paradise! Allah claims that he has provided provisions for every creature he created! Then why these little birds have to fly thousands of miles for food and survival? Allah in verse 6 of chapter 11 assures: "AND NO MOVING (LIVING) CREATURE IS THERE ON EARTH BUT HIS PROVISION IS DUE FROM ALLAH. AND HE (Allah) KNOWS ITS DWELLING PLACE AND ITS DEPOSIT"! Birds living in Siberia have their winter supplies in Australia! Trees are not moving creatures! Who gives them food? All celestial objects float in space! Who holds them? The "Quranic Science" has failed to explain the phenomenon!

Verse -99, C-16 says; "VERILY! HE (SATAN) HAS NO POWER OVER THOSE WHO BELIEVE AND PUT THEIR TRUST ONLY IN THEIR LORD (ALLAH)" If this verse is true, then how Satan misled Adam into eating forbidden fruits in paradise? Does it not imply that Adam, the first "Muslim" prophet and father of mankind, did not have trust in Allah? Contrary to what has been stated in the above verse, either the Satan was more powerful than Allah or Adam did not put his trust in his Lord! Allah gave respite to Satan and he challenged Allah by saying that he would continue to misguide mankind until Resurrection! Satan has still retained his power over man and has been able to divert most of the mankind away from Islamic Monotheism! Muhammad, the messenger for all mankind lost the battle! He could not bring the mankind into confidence about Islamic monotheism! In this battle of beliefs, Satan has won decisively against Allah! Angels as the trusted agents of Allah failed to assist messengers and the majority of mankind sided with the Satan! No problem! Allah has made the Hell with seven doors and large enough to fill it with men and Jinn as he wanted! And the Jihadists driven by the illusion, fighting in the name of Allah, are divided and killing for living an eternal life in paradise with "Wine and Wives" of supreme qualities! Sometimes fairy-tales seem more credible than divine fictions! Milton, despite having full trust in his Lord, characterized Satan as the hero of his poem! Birth of Messiah provoked the rebellion of Satan and his associates! Their defeat and expulsion from Heaven paved the way for building Pandemonium! Creation of the Earth gives the Satan the prospect of revenge until the Resurrection! Allah, God or the "King" of the heavens are all equally responsible for the ultimate defeat they suffered in the hands of the Satan! "Fall of man" led to Fall of Mankind! The majority still believes in this fallacy that has fallen on them as "Revelation" from heaven!!

Verse-1, Ch-17 states; "GLORIFIED BE ALLAH WHO TOOK HIS SLAVE (MUHAMMAD) FOR A JOURNEY BY NIGHT FROM MASJID-AL-HARAM (MECCA) TO MASJID-AL-AQSA (JERUSALEM) THE NEIGHBOURHOOD WHEREOF WE HAVE BLESSED, IN ORDER THAT WE MIGHT SHOW HIM OUR PROOFS, EVIDENCES, LESSONS, SIGNS etc."! This verse, like many of its kind, is a mixture of direct and indirect speech! Someone is expressing his desire that Allah deserves to be glorified for taking Muhammad on a journey from Mecca to Jerusalem by night. Rest of the verse is narrated in direct speech by "We", that refers to Allah himself! Why it had to happen at night? Did the journey happen in the dream? Muhammad's space mission to seven heavens also took place at night when he was in a state between "Sleep and Wakefulness"! For that impossible journey to Heaven, Allah did not wish to be glorified! For this short journey from Mecca to Jerusalem, Allah needs to be glorified! Here we may recall that Allah taught Adam names of everything before sending him to this world from paradise! In this case Allah is too late to show Muhammad his "Proofs, Evidences, Lessons and Signs"! This journey by night from Mecca to Jerusalem may have served as a rehearsal for his journey to space! After returning from that journey by night, Muhammad tried to describe his experiences to the people of his own tribe but they did not believe him! In Muhammad's own words (AL-BUKHARI, Vol. 5. #226); "WHEN THE PEOPLE OF QURAYSH DID NOT BELIEVE ME, I STOOD UP AT A COMPOUND NEAR KABAH AND ALLAH DISPLAYED JERUSALEM IN FRONT OF ME AND I BEGAN DESCRIBING IT TO THEM WHILE I WAS LOOKING AT IT"! It was really a miracle! City of Jerusalem, which is nearly a thousand kilometers away from Mecca, was displayed to Muhammad on a seemingly digital platform by a giant video screen in 7th century A.D.! If the Pagans did not believe the story, how people of this modern time will place their trust in it? The incredible story is indeed unbelievable! Jerusalem has a lot of religious and cultural heritage sites including relics of ancient Jewish and Christian era besides AL-AQSA mosque! Jerusalem could be reached on foot or by riding a horse-like animal, like the one Muhammad used for his space mission! What proofs and evidences Allah wanted to show to Muhammad at Jerusalem are also not described in the verse! What lessons to learn from there? It is said,

"Some people have greatness thrust upon them" and some try to achieve that thru magic or miracles! Muhammad's travel to space, his journey by night to Jerusalem and splitting of the moon are all aimed at imparting "Greatness" into his personality so as to achieve people's confidence in him as messenger of Allah! "Motivating Without Pause" is an article written by DR. MAMDOUH N. MOHAMED about the prophet's motivational strategy in a periodical called "Islamic Relief" published from CA, U.S.A. It says; "The prophet Muhammad was a strong believer in the use of motivation technique. During the first thirteen years as a prophet, he focused on forming a core group of believers who were strong and committed to his message! In the following ten years in Medina, the prophet focused on building a community and this involved much different motivation strategies"! It is apparent from this essay that Muhammad had formed two separate groups in Mecca and Medina who were sincerely dedicated to his messages! Probably these two "Core Groups" scripted the verses of the Quran and accordingly those verses have been categorized as "MAKKI" and MADANI"! The writer further adds saying; "He did not become tired of being the source of motivation for his followers throughout his life. Motivational techniques of Muhammad include the stories on his visit to space, the splitting of the Moon, visit to Jerusalem by night, his demand for love from the believers, his claim as being the only messenger to mankind, his right to intercede on Dooms Day, and his claim that none can enter paradise without accepting him as the messenger of Allah! Yet all of his motivational techniques have failed to "Straighten" the majority of mankind including his own uncle!

Verse-45&46, Ch-17, state; "AND WHEN YOU (MUHAMMAD) RECITE THE QURAN, WE PUT BETWEEN YOU AND THOSE WHO BELIEVE NOT IN THE HEREAFTER, AN INVISIBLE VEIL"! WE HAVE PUT COVERING OVER THEIR HEARTS LEST THEY SHOULD UNDERSTAND THE QURAN, AND IN THEIR EARS DEAFNESS"! Has this been a wise decision? Rather the disbelievers should have been allowed more and more opportunities to listen to what Muhammad has to say about the Revelation" he received from Allah! This was definitely a strategic mistake as it has gone against the propagation of Islam! Allah himself has prevented disbelievers from understanding the Quran by rendering them "Deaf" and putting an "Invisible Veil" between the messenger and the disbelievers! "Invisibility" is a hallmark of the "Creator"! Can anyone trust in such a divine deity, claiming to be the Creator of the universe? Eventually Prophet Muhammad, as the last in the series of messengers, failed to implement Allah's Islamic monotheism! Jesus is ultimately ordained by Allah as his last "Hope" to make the mission possible! Another question that remains unanswered is how prophet Muhammad could recite the Quran when it was not bound or compiled in one volume in his life-time? He might have read some verses instantly composed by himself like the bards of the ancient cultures! Many of the promises Allah made about life in this world have gone unfulfilled! The disbelievers are indeed in the driving seat and enjoying "EVERY GOOD THING IN THIS WORLD"! It would be wrong to blame disbelievers for not believing in an uncertain life in the hereafter! The "Invisible Veil" of darkness that exists between the creator and the created is the apple of discord! Why on earth a "Creator", who claims to have created everything alone including the universe, instituted such a messy strategy to implement a simple faith among his own creation despite being assisted by so many messengers, prophets and angels? Is it customary for the creator to stay mysteriously hidden behind the veil? Mankind, equipped with immense power and potential, might one day bring the "Truth" to light which may be hiding behind the Dark Matter that for now seems beyond human reach but surely not outside human intellect! A Hadith (Al-QURTUBI, Vol. 10. #269) related to this verse says; "IF THIS VERSE (45 of chapter-17) IS RECITED BY A REAL BELIEVER OF ISLAMIC MONOTHEISM, HE WILL BE SCREENED FROM A DISBELIEVER. (ALLAH KNOWS BETTER)"! The Islamic scholars know it better that this kind of miraculous screening will never happen in real life! If every Muslim is tested on the basis of this verse, not a single "REAL BELIEVER OF ISLAMIC MONOTHEISM" will be found on this earth who could "BE SCREENED FROM A DISBELIEVER" after reciting this verse! To avoid embarrassment, if challenged, the Hadith ends with the words "ALLAH KNOWS BETTER" in the bracket! It is a common practice with the Islamic scholars and theologians to leave all inexplicable matters to Allah who stays beyond horizon; out of reach! They add a number of suffix and prefix to the Arabic expressions that are said to have a wealth of meaning and finally the veil fails to hide the real intention! With respect to the same verse (45 of Ch. 17) an interesting story about "AN INVISIBLE VEIL" is narrated by IMAM QURTUBI, a Hadith writer: When chapter # 111 was being revealed to Muhammad, a woman with hostile intent came to see him when ABU BAKR was also present with the prophet! ABU BAKR requested Muhammad to get away to avoid being seen by the woman! After a conversation with ABU BAKR, she left and did not see Muhammad! Later Muhammad said to ABU BAKR; "AN ANGEL WAS SCREENING ME FROM HER"! The angel is invisible and made of 'Light", how he screened Muhammad? According to the revealed verse, the woman who came to see Muhammad was the wife of his uncle ABU LAHAB! She used to bring slander against Muhammad! Allah; the Lord has put an invisible "Veil" between Muhammad and the disbelievers and as a result the messenger could not turn them into believers! Thus the "Revelation" failed to receive overwhelming response!

Verse-58, Ch-17 states; "AND THERE IS NOT A TOWN (POPULATION) BUT WE SHALL DESTROY IT BEFORE THE DAY OF RESURRECTION, OR PUNISH IT WITH SEVERE TORMENT. THAT IS WRITTEN IN THE BOOK OF OUR DECREES". So, all townships along with their population will come under destruction before resurrection in accordance with what is written in his "Book of Decrees", says Allah! ABDULLAH BIN MASOOD, an Islamic Hadith expert has provided a short explanation by quoting some justifiable reasons for destruction from a book of reference "TAFSIR-AL- QURTUBI", says; "IF THE PEOPLE OF A TOWN INDULGE IN ILLIGAL SEXUAL INTERCOURSE AND PRACTICE USUARY OF ALL KINDS, ALLAH PERMITS ITS DESTRUCTION"! The proper justification for destruction of the towns that was missing in the revealed verse of Allah is now available in the book of his defenders! The Quran is the "Child" of a mother book known as "AL-LAUGH-AL-MAHFUZ" or "The Book of Decree" and it is held under the sole custody of Allah himself over Seven Heavens! Definitely Allah is also the "Author" of that "Book of Decree" since there is no partner to him who could undertake writing such a "Book" that is meant to govern the whole of the universe! Call it a "CONSTITUTION" or a "LAW", Allah cannot defy his own "Decree"! Abdullah has categorically mentioned that all towns and their people would be destroyed by Allah's permission if they indulge in "Illegal sex" and "Usury"! How did the scholar come to know of these reasons for destruction since those are well-guarded secrets with Allah, written in the "Book of Decree"? Allah's unequivocal declaration (THERE IS NOT A TOWN (POPULATION) BUT WE SHALL DESTROY IT), surely includes the cities of Mecca and Medina where two holy mosques are located! The "Custodian" of the two holy mosques will be watching the divine demolition helplessly! So, at the end, prior to Resurrection, these two holy cities will also plunge into illegal sex and usury! If the City of Mecca is destroyed, than the "KABAH", the so-called house of Allah has to go with it? Allah has guaranteed security of the city of Mecca and the house of KHABA! Is this not a complete contradiction to what Allah has been saying all along the Quran that after resurrection he would hold a mass trial on the "Day of Judgment" and accordingly people will be either rewarded or punished! In another verse Allah said that he would change this entire earth and the heaven and create new ones! If that is his ultimate plan, then what is the point destroying those towns and their population? Here we may recall Allah's plan "B" under which Jesus is destined to come back to earth before Resurrection to implement Islam in its totality! If he succeeds in his mission, Allah may not have to destroy all towns and their population for illegal sex and usury! Does it not forecast that Allah's plan "B"; to administer all affairs of the earth by Islamic Law, is also going to fail? Destruction and creation are two sides of the same coin! But destruction is much easier than creation! Creation of this universe is said to have begun about fourteen billion years ago and the solar system came into being nearly nine and half billion years after that! So far our tiny Earth is the only planet of the solar system known to be congenial to breeding life in the entire universe! Of all the creatures, man are the most intelligent being living in it! For whatever reasons, these intelligent beings have become tools of the divine games orchestrated by some unseen Creators believed to be living in the heavens! Each one of those masterminds has chalked out different rules of games from behind the scene and employed many visible and invisible umpires to blow the whistles if the rules are broken! The most lucrative rewards for the winner includes an infinite life in paradise with "Wine and Wives" of the most superior quality! The loser goes to hell for a never-ending life inside the inferno! Allah says destruction will happen before the Day of Resurrection! Can the mankind be scared of destruction when it is busy unfolding mystery of creation? Is it not unfortunate that the mankind has a Creator who takes pride in both destruction and creation?

Verse-64, Ch-17 states; "AND BEFOOL THEM GRDUALLY THOSE WHOM YOU CAN AMONG THEM WITH YOUR VOICE (i.e. SONG, MUSIC AND ANY OTHER CALL FOR DISOBEDIENCE), MAKE ASSAULTS ON THEM WITH YOUR CAVALRY AND INFANTRY, SHARE WITH THEM WEALTH AND CHILDREN AND MAKE PROMISES TO THEM; BUT SATAN PROMISES THEM NOTHING BUT DECEIT". From a different angle the Lord and the "Author" of this verse appears to be guilty of inciting his adversary, the Satan, to act against his own ambition! Do these words have really come from the merciful originator of the mankind?

Allah has formulated a sophisticated strategy combined with a modern war-plan for Satan as to how he should make assault on Adam's offspring! We may recall Allah's principle of creation; he creates nothing without Purpose! So, the purpose behind the creation of Satan is becoming more and more evident as Allah never says anything for nothing! And to the utter astonishment of all, Satan has fulfilled his assignment with a spirit of dedication as ordained by Allah! In terms of performance, success of Satan has exceeded far beyond that of all the messengers! In another verse, Allah, the sublime, expressed his intent to fill the hell with disbelievers and hypocrites to use them as fuel for hellfire! Probably, to that end Allah is giving Satan a green signal to go ahead as planned! Music lovers should not be treated as disbelievers! Most of the humans except a few loves to hear music! Without music our life on earth is unthinkable! Man and music are inseparable! Verses of the Quran have not been revealed only for humans but also for Satan and Jinn! Satan, as directed by Allah in the above verse, has played his part very well by using his "Cavalry" and "Infantry"! Allah considers music as the voice of the Satan and treats it as a punishable "Sin"! The Satan helped disbelievers attain superior arms and army so that the believers can never retain their "Honor", "dignity" and "Land" even after uniting under one "KHALIFA"! This is the downside of the "Revelation"!

Verse-106, Ch-17 states; "AND IT IS A QURAN WHICH WE HAVE DEVIDED (INTO PARTS) IN ORDER THAT YOU (MUHAMMAD) MIGHT RECITE IT TO MEN AT INTERVALS. AND WE HAVE REVEALED IT BY STAGES (In 23 yrs.)". Could it not be recited in stages if revealed all at a time? Division of the Quran into parts itself testifies how intelligent is Allah as an author! Allah originally divided the Quran into only seven parts so that one could recite it in one week and then his followers divided that into thirty chapters in order to recite it one month! In addition they have added punctuations and Surah separator which Allah, as the author, failed to incorporate into the Quran! Allah took twenty three years to reveal the Quran in stages to facilitate Muhammad to recite it to men at intervals! It was indeed very thoughtful! Was it then easy for the Muslims to attend fifty obligatory prayers at mosque every day as ordained by Allah in the beginning? But why Allah did not reveal the entire Quran into the heart of Muhammad just by uttering the word "Be" or by breathing through his mouth? Some chapters of the Quran have hundreds of verses while some have only three to four! Some verses are composed of as few as one to five Arabic letters, known as miracles of the Quran and their meanings are understood only by the "Author" himself! This skillful planning of writing and revealing of the messages by the Lord has not been able to impress the mankind, instead generated huge amount of confusion about the charismatic creator of the universe! Prof. M.M. AL-AZAMI of UK Islamic Academy, in his book "THE HISTORY OF THE QURANIC TEXT FROM REVELATION TO COMPILATION" has narrated some of the important events from "REVELATION TO COMPILATION" as they happened one after another: (1) Allah, the creator of the universe, has authored the Quran that has been derived from another book known as the "Book of Decree" which is held by himself at his throne over seven heavens (2) He is said to have revealed the Quran to Prophet Muhammad from heavens through an angel called Gabriel; (3) It was revealed in the month of Ramadan. (4) ZAID IBN THABIT, a trusted companion of Muhammad, used to be present while the angel read the verses to Muhammad. (5) The Quran was revealed in QURAYSH, a tribal dialect since Muhammad belonged to that tribe. (6) Allah took twenty three years to reveal the Quran in stages so that Muhammad could dictate that to his scribes. (7) Muhammad had many companions who used to memorize the verses besides 65 scribes who recorded his dictations. (8) The Quran was drafted during Prophet's lifetime on parchments, wooden planks and palm leaves. (9) Those parchments were not bound in a book during his lifetime because of continuous flow of revelation. It had to wait until prophet's mission had been completed. (10) The prophet used to instruct the scribes about the placement of the different verses as they were revealed. (11) However, there is difference of opinion among the scholars whether the arrangement of the chapters also goes back to the prophet himself and the order of surah or chapters is not mandatory for Muslims during recital of the Quran. (12) The compilation of the Quran in the form of a book took place during the reign of ABU BAKR and the task of compilation was entrusted to ZAID IBN THABIT. (13) Other people were also asked to bring what they had written down of the Quran after having directly heard it from the prophet. (14) After compilation, the book remained under the custody of ABU BAKR. (15) After his death it was passed on to UMAR, the second ruler, and then to HAFSA, the wife of Muhammad who was also the daughter of UMAR. (15) ABU BAKR also verified accuracy of the book against what was written by others and memorized by prophet's companions. (16) However, the pronunciation of the words of the Quran was prevalent in various dialects as because the prophet allowed it out of necessity. (17) When UTHMAN came to power, he took custody of the book from HAFSA to standardize pronunciation of the Quran in the QURAYSH dialect. (18) UTHMAN appointed a committee of twelve from among the QURAYSH and assumed to have made eight copies that were sent to various provinces along with official reciters to ensure authenticity of the texts and pronunciation! (19) Later a number of reading aids have been added including the Surah separator BISMILLA...... (20) In the beginning the Quran was divided into seven parts but two centuries later it was again divided into thirty parts and in addition to that, dots and vowel marks were also added! The Quran is often dubbed by the Muslim scholars as a "Complete Code of Life", a "Plain Book", a "Plain Statement" and a "Miracle" from Allah! All has been done to this book to save it from extinction "IN THE NAME OF ALLAH, THE MOST GRACIOUS, THE MOST MERCIFUL". Probably, Quran is the only book in the history of mankind that has undergone so many "Operations" under the knives of hundreds of "Doctors" and what finally they "Delivered" is a total stranger! Does it seem logical that Allah divided the Quran in stages for Muhammad to complete the reading in 23 years! In the above discussion it has been claimed by the Islamic scholars that order of the chapters is not important during recitation of the Quran! Revelation could not have happened disorderly! A ten to twelve year old child can memorize the entire Quran in a period of twelve months or even less than that. But why Muhammad, a matured young man in his prime needed long 23 years to complete dictating the Quran to his scribes? This Quran raises more questions than answers! The biggest question that has no answer is that why Allah did not allow Muhammad a few more years to compile the book himself in his lifetime? The zigzag history of the Quran itself testifies that it has been "Engineered and Manufactured" by a number of cunning quacks who took twenty three years to complete their "Operation"! The messy history of the Quran, from revelation to compilation, also testifies that it could not have been "Authored" by a divine "Creator" of the Earth and the Heaven whose very existence has not been established yet! The unusual and untrustworthy history of compilation of the Quran itself dispossess "Revelation" as a hoax!

Verse-1, Ch-18 says; "ALL THE PRAISES AND THANKS BE TO ALLAH, WHO HAS SENT DOWN TO HIS SLAVE (MUHAMMAD) THE BOOK (QURAN) AND HAS NOT PLACED THEREIN ANY CROOKEDNESS"! Who "Praises" and "Thanks" Allah in this verse? Allah himself? Of course it is not prophet Muhammad either! Undoubtedly, an unknown third person is narrating these words! The archangel Gabriel, who brought down the verses from Allah to prophet Muhammad, flying back and forth between the Earth and the Heavens, probably did not face any hurdles in his way through the space except that he had to make innumerable sorties in his twenty three years assignment! So, the revelation may have been quite smooth and straight! Why did Allah send so many letters (ALIF, LAM, MIM etc.) of QURAISH dialect as miracles with the verses? Why did he not make clear the meanings of those letters even to the messenger himself? But the real "Crookedness" began soon after the demise of Muhammad when his successors started to piece together shattered segments of the Quran from various unknown sources! Islamic "Gurus" always claim that Muhammad is the last prophet and the revelation stopped with his death! The assumed "Author" has never mentioned in the Quran that this is the beginning of the revelation or this is the end of it! Yet Allah sees no "Crookedness" in the Quran as if he had not seen the messy handling of the composition and the compilation process! He ignored all of the anomalies that took place with respect to the so-called "Complete Code of Life" for the mankind! So, either the Allah has no connection with the revelation or he himself does not exist! Is the Lord happy with the present "State of the Islamic Monotheism"? Allah said he had not placed any "Crookedness" in the Quran! Let me quote just one: Allah asks Muhammad to say, "NOR DO I KNOW WHAT WILL BE DONE WITH ME NOR WITH YOU" (V. 9 Ch. 46): Allah promised to give Muhammad the highest place in paradise and Muhammad promised to take his followers with him!

Verse-6, Ch-18 says; "PERHAPS, YOU WOULD KILL YOURSELF (O MUHAMMAD) IN GRIEF, OVER THEIR FOOT STEPS, BECAUSE THEY BELIEVE NOT IN THIS NARRATION (THE QURAN)". Why Muhammad? The one who "Authored" and "Revealed" the Quran deserves to be "Killed" out of frustration! But he is "Eternal"! I don't think Muhammad would have taken such a bad decision as to kill himself since none of his predecessors set an example of this nature! Allah was deeply offended by the allegation brought by the Jews, Christians and the Pagans that "ALLAH HAS BEGOTTEN A SON" (verse 4 of chapter 18)! Allah is so annoyed on this issue that his anger reverberates throughout the Quran! Creator Allah categorically said in verse 35 of chapter 19 that "IT BEFITS NOT HIS MAJESTY (ALLAH) THAT HE SHOULD BEGET A SON"! Allah is not ready to hand over his "Empire" to his children! Allah also said in plain verse that Muhammad is only a warner and will not be held responsible for others! The prophet has been assured of the highest place in the paradise and Allah has forgiven his past and future sins! He received total amnesty from Allah! Thanks be to Muhammad that he had chosen to die a natural death even though prolong illness compelled him to die at 63! It would have been a complete disaster for Muhammad to "kill" himself in grief only because the disbelievers did not believe "In the narration of the Quran"! Why should prophet Muhammad take the blame? Allah has already assured him that he will not be held responsible for his failures! Besides, the prophet was leading a life surrounded by a host of young beautiful wives! Allah has bestowed upon him a free choice to marry as many times as he wants to! Moreover, Muhammad himself has instructed his disciples not to long for death even if the calamity becomes unbearable! Jesus is the apple of discord over his parentage! Different accounts of his relationship with the Lord has adversely impacted three major religions on earth! Allah says the "Son of God" is actually the "Son of Marry"! People in general do not believe in Allah's narratives and "Revelation"!

Verse-8, Ch-18 says; "AND VERILY WE SHALL MAKE ALL THAT IS ON IT (EARTH) A BARE DRY SOIL (WITHOUT ANY VEGETATION OR TREES)". In the preceding verse (Verse 7 of chapter 18) Allah said; "VERILY! WE HAVE MADE THAT WHICH IS ON EARTH AS AN ADORNMENT FOR IT, IN ORDER THAT WE MAY TEST MANKIND AS TO WHICH OF THEM ARE BEST AT DEEDS"! Now the Lord says, if the mankind fails the "Test", he would turn this "Adorned" earth into a "BARE DRY SOIL" which will produce no vegetation or trees! So, we are victims of double punishments; one before death and the next after the Grand Trial on the Day of Judgment! To punish his dear creation Allah wants to turn this "Greenland" into a dry "Waste Land" although we have neither killed the "Fisher King" nor any vegetation God! Allah may ask angel AR-RA'D, entrusted to drive the clouds to different places when ordered by his master, to make his dream come true! If the earth is made a "A BARE DRY SOIL WITHOUT VEGETATION" by Allah, then the mankind might turn to Pre-Christian fertility myths and rituals to celebrate vegetation ceremonies! They may even undertake a quest for the "Knight", like the one undertaken for the "Holy Grail", who could regenerate the dead king and restore his land to fertility! What Jesus would do on this dry land? Will he arrive as the vegetation god to regenerate green vegetation on this a barren land? Even the begging for rain in prayers will be of no avail!

These kind of contradictory and conflicting verses have much to do with the distrust that has been prevailing about Allah and his religion since the so-called Revelation! But we should not forget that it was Allah who made this earth and as such he is entitled to adorn it or turn it into a dry land as and when he "Wills"! Two third of earth is water! More than half of the land has already turned into desert! Verily, on a "Dry Soil", all religions will die out and the Lord will be relieved of his personal grouse against his disloyal "Creation"! Then only the Question will become clear whether he created religion for man or man for religion!

Verse-31, Ch-18 States; "FOR THEM WILL BE EDEN, PARADISE (EVERLASTING GARDEN) WHEREIN RIVERS FLOW UNDER THEM, THEREIN THEY WILL BE ADORNED WITH BRACELETS OF GOLD, AND THEY WILL WEAR GREEN GARMENTS OF FINE AND THICK SILK. THEY WILL RECLINE THEREIN ON RAISED THRONES, HOW GOOD IS THE REWARD, AND WHAT AN EXCELLENT DWELLING RESTING PLACE". The coining of the words and the composition of the verse bear clear evidence that these are not the works of a divine creator! Why Allah's all Gardens have to have Rivers flowing underneath them? Probably he wants to assure the people, who lived around the place where the revelation is said to have taken place, that they will not face the scarcity of water as they do here in the dry desert! These heavenly treasures such as "BRACELETS OF GOLD", "GREEN GARMENTS OF SILK", "RAISED THRONES " etc. do not raise our fascination at all! Man-made worldly luxuries are much better than those of paradise in terms of beauty and bounty! Spending this life only to be adorned with bracelets of gold in afterlife makes no sense! Gold and silk are very ordinary materials widely available here on earth! Allah built gardens under which rivers flow in paradise over Seven Heavens! Our experts on earth can build gardens under Seven Seas! Queens on earth wear jewels of finest quality and their garments are made of golden fibers! The crowns are adorned with specially crafted precious pearls! What makes the paradise exceptionally attractive is the "HURS"; two each for every male dwellers! But it is not that simple as it sounds! There is an overpass between Heaven and Hell which is sharper than a sword and thinner than a hair! People will cross it in a manner concordant with their deeds: "Some will pass like a winged horse, some like a stallion, and some will gallop! Others will just walk, and still others will crawl on it. A group will fall into fire and be caught with hooks"! Would you not still like to go to Paradise? Prepare yourself like a stallion or winged horse so that you don't fall into fire and be caught with hooks!

Verse-51, Ch-18 states; "I (ALLAH) MADE THEM (IBLIS AND HIS OFFSPRING) NOT TO WITNESS (NOR TOOK THEIR HELP IN) THE CREATION OF THE HEAVENS AND THE EARTH AND NOT EVEN THEIR OWN CREATION, NOR WAS I (ALLAH) TO TAKE THE MISLEADERS AS HELPERS". Thanks be to Allah for regaining his singularity as the "Creator"! In this verse "I" is Allah, not "WE", as was the case with most of the verses of the Quran! Allah has directly referred to himself in the first person singular number "I", but why? All along the Quran, save a few verses, he used plural pronoun "We" to refer to himself! Why this change? Allah acknowledges the fact that he created IBLIS (SATAN) AND HIS OFFSPRING as misleaders! Allah did not want them to witness the creation of the Earth and the Heaven nor did he seek their help in the creation! IBLIS and his offspring are born-misleaders as Allah created them to be! They were not created as scientist or engineers to help Allah in the creation! Yet Satan successfully misled Adam to commit the sin! "SIN IS BEHOVELY"; necessary element to the divine plan! Though IBLIS did not help Allah directly in the creation, yet he got Adam ousted from paradise as part of Allah's master plan! Allah than ordained Adam to set in motion the procreation process on earth and as a result mankind began multiplying into millions! Satan, after being respited by the Lord, promised to mislead mankind and he has done his job well! In other words IBLIS has helped Allah have a small number of believers on his side in return for the respite! Allah "Cursed" him many times but could not "Cure" him since Allah did not like to break his promise that allows Satan to continue misleading the mankind until Resurrection! As regards to prophet Muhammad, Allah's promise to keep him alive until all "Crooked" people are "Straightened" has gone in vain! If we impartially evaluate the achievement of Satan and messengers, Satan is far ahead of them! At present what is the ratio between the Muslims and the Non-Muslims on this planet? The actual ratio is bound to get even wider if it is evaluated against the Muslims who actually believe in Allah! It was also claimed in a previous statement that Jesus, the "Son of God" or the "Son of Mary" will shortly arrive as a Muslim; energized with a new set of ideas and vision, to implement Allah's Islamic monotheism! This ambitious mission of Allah might not see the light if Satan continues to mislead mankind the way he did in the tenure of Muhammad! Was it not possible to implement Allah's

Islamic monotheism without the creation of Satan and his offspring? Nay! Since the Lord needed some kind of pretext to expel Adam from paradise! Naturally Adam would not have opted to come down to this pandemonium at his own accord abandoning the pompous life he was leading with Eve in the Heaven! To this end, Allah planed in advance and planted a tree of "Forbidden fruit"! Allah disregarded the advice of the angels not to create man as they would do mischief therein! Perhaps the Satan could read Allah's mind and both of them in a secret deal decided to oust Adam and Eve from paradise! Everything worked as planned and finally Adam and Eve came down to earth to produce their offspring! Allah also expelled Satan but with a Respite so that he could mislead Adam's offspring until Resurrection! In reference to above verse, let us see what Allah said about Satan: "GET YOU DOWN, ALL, (ADAM, EVE, AND SATAN) WITH ENMITY BETWEEN YOURSELVES. ON EARTH WILL BE A DWELLING PLACE FOR YOU AND AN ENJOYMENT FOR A TIME (Verse 36 chapter 2)! "FOLLOW NOT THE FOOTSTEPS OF SATAN. VERILY, HE IS TO YOU AN OPEN ENEMY (Verse 168 of chapter 2)! "SATAN THREATENS YOU WITH POVERTY AND ORDERS YOU TO COMMIT EVIL DEEDS, ILLEGAL SEXUAL INTERCOURSE (Verse 268 of chapter 2)! "There are many more verses on Satan in the Quran! Good or bad, Allah does not create anything without a "Purpose"? Satan is lucky to have been created from "Fire"! Even if he is put into hellfire for his misdeed, "Fire" will not burn "Fire"! All human being, except the pious Muslims, are destined to be put into Fire; so says the Lord in his "Revelation"!

Verse-109, Ch-18 states; "SAY (O MUHAMMAD) IF THE SEA WERE INK FOR WRITING THE WORDS OF MY LORD, SURELY, THE SEA WOULD BE EXHAUSTED BEFORE THE WORDS OF MY LORD WOULD BE FINISHED, EVEN IF WE BROUGHT ANOTHER SEA LIKE IT FOR ITS AID". Allah, the Lord of the universe, is asking his messenger to inform the mankind that not just one but two seas of ink would not be enough to write words of his Lord! Though the size of the sea is not mentioned, yet we may assume it to be as big as the Arabian sea as the "Author" of the Quran seems to be more familiar with life in Arabian peninsula! In place of "Seas", the Lord could have used "Oceans", as big as the Atlantic or the Pacific, so that his greatness would appear much more amplified! If the water of these two oceans were turned into ink, probably the Lord will not feel short of ink to write all words about him! Except the Quran, we have no other evidence of Allah's autobiographical works so as to assess the amount of ink he might need to write all of the words about him! The Quran is a small book of moderate size having only about three hundred pages! A human being can write a book of that size in less than a month! Why the Lord would need more than two seas of ink? Because he is used to writing thousands of adjectives and words of appreciation for himself! The Quran although very small in size contains ninety nine names of Allah! Besides that he repeated one verse 31 times in chapter No. 55 alone! May be in Allah's consideration this verse is not like any other in terms of its meaning and significance which reads; "THEN WHICH OF THE BLESSINGS OF YOUR LORD WILL YOU BOTH (JINN AND MEN) DENY?" From what perspective and strategic importance this verse demanded so many repetitions again and again? No reason has been assigned! Allah's name alone has occurred more than three thousand (3000) times in the Quran! If the repeated verses and the words are omitted, the size of the Quran will reduce to that of a small "Note Book"! Surely Allah did not live in a digital world while writing the Quran, otherwise he could compose all the words about him on a super computer without the need for a "Sea of Ink"! We do not know how the Jinn would react but the mankind in general and the Muslims in particular must not deny the blessings of the Lord after thirty one reminders just in one chapter! To be frank, besides blessings, we cannot deny the "ACT OF GOD" that comes in the form of curses and calamities upon entire creatures round the clock around the globe! Of course, we have no knowledge of the "Book of Decree" (AL-LAUH-AL MAHFUZ) held by Allah over Seven Heavens! Only Allah knows how many seas of ink he needed to write that book! Thanks be to Allah, that he has not written down everything about himself in the Quran! Otherwise it would have been quite impossible for Allah to finish revelation before Resurrection at the speed the Quran was revealed to mankind which took twenty three years! Bad luck for the elderly people of that dark period who witnessed the revelation of the first verse, might not have lived another twenty three years to see the last verse being revealed! Those who were just born in the beginning of the revelation had to wait nearly forty years to understand and see the revelations compiled in the form of a book! The creator Allah, being the creator of "Time" who can accomplish anything just by uttering the word "Be", should not have taken long twenty three years to reveal the Quran! Allah in his defense stated that the Quran was revealed in stages so that Muhammad could recite them to his people at ease! Revelation of a divine book, containing only few hundred pages of information, took twenty three years! Is this believable? It is acceptable to those who have their brains displaced! The universe has no end and as such all water of the earth would surely be exhausted to write everything about the "Creator" of an endless universe! Who would write that book? Definitely not the one who "Wrote" the Quran since he had chosen a messenger for his "Revelation" who could neither read nor write! The "Creator" of all that exists has preferred to use the "Sea of Ink" to showcase his greatness!

Verse-20, Ch-19 states; "SHE (MARY) SAID: HOW CAN I HAVE A SON, WHEN NO MAN HAS TOUCHED ME, NOR AM I UNCHASTE?". That is why Allah sent Gabriel disguised as a man with all human attributes so that he could "Touch" her, if need be, when breathing through sleeves fails to make her conceive the "Baby"! It's like a million dollar question asked by Mary to angel Gabriel that has found no acceptable answer since then! It is also evident from Mary's question that, by then it became known to the entire mankind that a child or a baby cannot be born without sexual mating between male and female! So, in that reality how can she deliver a baby as a virgin without being "Touched" by any man? Allah is directly responsible for her disgrace to the people of the land she was living! Her question to Gabriel was both legitimate and reasonable! But the proposition for conception to an "Untouched woman" in that manner was both unthinkable as well as unbelievable! But Gabriel replied; "YOUR LORD SAID (Verse 21 of Ch. 19), IT IS EASY FOR ME (ALLAH)"! But to say the least, it is difficult for human being to understand! The Quran, in Allah's words is a miracle but what happened to Mary concerning Jesus's birth is the real miracle! The Lord sent angel Gabriel to Mary with the glad tiding of a son but she was taken aback! Why the name of Allah is in the bracket? Neither Allah nor Gabriel could realize the impact of naming and shaming a young girl by making her pregnant irrespective of the means involved! Were the people in her society able to comprehend such divine disposition? People in general should not be blamed for reading something between the lines of the verse above? What consequences she would face from amongst the people and the society she lived in? See how considerate is Allah, the Lord of the universe! If Allah could create Adam and Muhammad without naming or shaming anyone, why could he not do that for Jesus? The first footnote related to this verse says; "WE (ALLAH) BREATHED INTO THE SLEEVES OF HER SHIRT THROUGH OUR ANGEL GABRIEL AND THUS SHE CONCEIVED". The second footnote says; "IT IS SAID THAT GABRIEL HAD 'MERELY' BREATHED INTO THE

SLEEVE OF MARY'S SHIRT, AND THUS SHE CONCEIVED. WE MADE HER AND HER SON (JESUS) A SIGN FOR THE MANKIND AND JINN"! What is the lesson for Jinn in this verse? Is it possible to breath one for another? As Allah says "WE BREATHED", then he should not have denied being father of Jesus! Actually it was Gabriel who did the breathing into Mary's sleeve! Logically Gabriel is supposed to be the "Father of Jesus! Since Mary's conception occurred, as is claimed, through the breathing, not semen! But according to Islamic explanation Mary received the "Breath" of Allah through Gabriel into her sleeves and obviously from their it reached into her womb to germinate the fetus of "Jesus" and later she delivered the baby as the "Son of Mary", not as the "Son of God" or "Son of ALLAH"! Gabriel has been deprived of his right and thrown out of the arena in the fight for the fatherhood of Jesus! Angels are made of light whereas men are made of mud yet Allah changed GABRIEL into a complete man and sent him to Mary to breath into her sleeves on his behalf! In this weird circumstances how fatherhood of a child can be ascertained? DNA test is not an option here! We have a number of options open to us to assume that; (a) Allah is the father of Jesus (b) Gabriel is the father of Jesus or (c) Jesus has an unknown father! Archangel Gabriel, who came to Mary after being transformed into a complete man in all respects, may have done "Something" more "Credible" besides "Merely breathing into her sleeves"! Since he was bestowed upon all biological features of a young man including sexuality and Mary was a young beautiful virgin! Gabriel delivered all messages to Muhammad as an angel, why he was changed into a "Man" merely to breath into Mary's sleeve? ZACHARIA, a man who used to look after Mary, asked her; "How comes this to you? Mary replied; "From Allah" (V. 37, Ch. 3)! Thus, Allah claims to have made Jesus "A SIGN FOR THE MANKIND AND JINN"! Did Jesus work for the "JINN" too? How the Christians would react to this "Revelation"?

Verse-30, Ch-19 states; "VERILY I AM A SLAVE OF ALLAH. HE HAS GIVEN ME THE SCRIPTURE AND MADE ME A PROPHET". When Mary returned to her people, they accused her of adultery! To defend herself Mary pointed to the child to inquire about the truth! Surprisingly, the baby Jesus began to speak the words stated in the above verse! The Lord made Jesus a "Prophet" while still a "Baby"! On the other hand Allah's last and the best messenger Muhammad was appointed a prophet when he was forty! Allah also bestowed upon Jesus the ability to talk while he was in his cradle! Question may arise how he got this feat as a baby? Most probably it was infused into him when archangel Gabriel, disguised as a man, "Breathed" into Mary's sleeve for conception! Allah also claims to have created Jesus by uttering the word "Be" only as he did the same for Adam! This unique ability of baby Jesus may also be compared with a calf that immediately stands on its feet looking for its mother for sucking her breast! Allah has deprived human babies of that unique feature! We may also recall that Adam, the father of mankind did not go through the ordeal of babyhood as he was created as an adult with 90 meters in height! It is unfortunate that the God could not send any message to his "Son" cautioning him that he was heading for a cruel "Crucifixion"! But a Christian poet expressed his anguish over unwillingness of the Cross to play its part in "Crucifixion" in the poem "THE DREAM OF THE ROOD"! Most of the miracles happened with prominent prophets: Adam's fall from paradise; Noah's making of the Boat, Abraham's dreadful dream to kill his toddler, Moses's Q&A session with Allah; Birth of Jesus; Muhammad's meeting with Allah and splitting of the moon etc.! Muhammad claims to have met Jesus in the second Heaven during his space mission! Then how could Jesus say; "PEACE BE UPON ME, THE DAY I WAS BORN, AND THE DAY I DIE, AND THE DAY I AM RAISED UP ALIVE (V. 33:Ch. 19)"! Oh, Jesus, you don't have to die! You are destined to come again in this world! You will be Raised up again alive!

Verse-39, Ch-19 states; "AND WARN THEM (O MUHAMMAD) OF THE DAY OF GRIEF AND REGRETS, WHEN THE CASE HAS BEEN DECIDED, WHILE THE POLYTHEISTS AND DISBELIEVERS ARE IN A STATE OF CARELESSNESS AND THEY BELIEVE NOT". Leave aside the polytheists and the disbelievers, even the believers would not listen to a messenger when he says to them, "I KNOW NOT WHAT WILL BE DONE WITH ME OR WITH YOU" (Verse 9 of Ch. 46)! So, Muhammad is not aware of what awaits him and his followers after death! He has been dictated by Allah, the "Creator", to say these words to his followers! Allah himself put Muhammad in a state of embarrassment! Muhammad narrates a mythical story of great significance in a hadith (AL-BUKHARI, Vol. 6, #254) at the footnote of this verse to send a message to the dwellers of Hell and Paradise about eternal life therein; "ON THE DAY OF RESURRECTION, DEATH WILL BE BROUGHT FORWARD IN THE SHAPE OF A BLACK AND WHITE RAM. A CALL-MAKER WILL DRAW ATTENTION OF THE PEOPLE OF THE HELL AND THE PARADISE! THEREUPON THEY WILL STRETCH THEIR NECKS AND LOOK AT THE RAM CAREFULLY. THE CALL-MAKER WILL INTRODUCE THE RAM TO THEM, SAYING; 'THIS

IS DEATH'! THEN THE RAM WILL BE SLAUGHTERED IN FRONT OF THEM! THE KILLING OF THE RAM IS MEANT TO SEND A MESSAGE TO THE PEOPLE OF HELL AND PARADISE THAT DEATH IS NO MORE AN OPTION FOR THEM; THEY WILL LIVE THERE FOR ETERNITY". So death is "Killed", long live the mankind hereafter! The long and the short of this parable is to evoke fear and frenzy among people disloyal to Allah and Muhammad as a religious ploy! This is basically an imagery; a descriptive representation of death intended to generate horror in the minds of the readers! Why death has to be incarnated into a "BLACK AND WHITE RAM"? Is this not a weird idea to represent death in a live animal and then killing that animal to send the message to the dwellers of hell and paradise that death is not an escape for them anymore! It clearly shows that Allah or the Lord has ran out of ideas! We cannot assess how big is the Hell but science does tell us that each star can be used as "Hell" if the Lord wants to! The Quran tells us that the paradise is made of 100 grades with eight doors for its dwellers! The distance between each grade is equal to the distance between the earth and the heaven! The hell has seven doors! We can also imagine their vastness from the fact that the whole of mankind would be lodged in these two dwelling places! When a single call-maker would call upon them to see the "BLACK AND WHITE RAM" being killed; will it be possible for them to "STRETCH THEIR NECKS AND LOOK AT THE RAM? Will this huge assembly of men and women be able to see the "RAM" and listen to the caller all at a time? Will the caller blow a horn like the one by angel ISRAFEEL on the Dooms Day? Why it became so imperative for Allah to send his message this way? Will the message get through? Moral of this ridiculous mythical story seems incapable of serving the purpose! At the same time it is not difficult to evaluate the poor intellectual background of the story teller as his story lacks both relevance and reality in terms of the message it wants to send! Can anyone, even with very limited knowledge find trustworthiness of this story with respect to life in the hereafter; sending a message to the entire humanity by killing an animal? Muslims have been advised to view death with a completely different attitude: Death is a good reminder of the fact that man is God's eternal creature whose most important part of life takes place only after he dies! Muhammad said; "OFTEN THINK OF DEATH, THE PLEASUR'S TERMINATOR"! Why not to think of it as the beginning of a life full of lust and luster? Eliot said nothing about what would happen to so many "Death had undone"? Dawn of a New Day has not been able to do away with the darkness! Mythical stories are still able to mesmerize the mankind! Rings in the ears of dead and living alike, the last line of Donne's holy sonnet: "AND DEATH SHALL BE NO MORE: DEATH, THOU SHALT DYE"!

Verse-30, Ch-21 says; "HAVE NOT THOSE WHO DISBELIEVE KNOWN THAT THE HEAVENS AND THE EARTH WERE JOINED TOGETHER AS ONE UNITED PIECE, THEN WE PARTED THEM? AND WE HAVE MADE FROM WATER EVERY LIVING THING. WILL THEY NOT THEN BELIEVE?" In a previous verse Allah claimed to have made the earth "First" then he rose over to space in a manner suitable to his majesty to create the Heavens! These two terms "HEAVENS" and "SEVEN HEAVENS" in the Quran have always created confusion as to their real meanings and numbers! These seven heavens are also said to have been built one upon another! Do they mean universe? Similarly the term "EARTH" also gives birth to ambiguity! Earth is a planet of our solar system where life exists! But why Allah is completely silent about other seven planets? No doubt, the earth and the heavens look separated! They had to be since Allah wanted to make the earth a resting place for mankind and the Seven Heavens for Adam, Moses, Jesus, Abraham and other prophets! Above the seven heavens Allah made a palace for himself! Why he made seven heavens and only one earth is also not logical! So, the Creator and the created can't live together! But the disbelieving scientists say that this universe was born out of a Singularity called the BIG BANG more than thirteen billion years ago! Energy released from the BIG BANG transformed into millions of trillions of galaxies, stars, planets etc.! O Lord! Have you not separated the Mars, Jupiter and other planets from the heavens? The Sun, at the center of the solar system, keeps all planets rotating around it by its gravity but Allah says he has separated only the earth from the heaven! Scientifically it does not make any sense! Rather he claims to have made the sun as a "Lamp"! The Lord is excessively focused on the planet earth! Allah has created living creatures from many different materials such as clay, dust, mud, semen, fire, light, etc.! At last he has added water to his long list of materials that "EVERY LIVING THINGS" are made of! Allah said he created Jinn and Devils from "Fire" and angels from "Light"! Are they not living things? If so, how on earth he is claiming to have created "EVERY LIVING THING FROM WATER'? Again in verse 54 of Ch. 25 he states; "AND IT IS HE WHO HAS CREATED MAN FROM WATER"! Are men not included in "Every living thing"? Scientists are not interested in what material the "Living Things" are made of; instead they are looking for that ultimate particle or the so-called God particle of which "EVERYTHING IS MADE OF"! Though Allah is capable of creating everything from anything and anything from everything, yet he seems to have no knowledge of elementary particles other than the dust! Why Allah has taken billions of years after separating the "EARTH" from the "HEAVENS" to create life on earth? Whereas uttering the word "Be" by Allah would have been more than enough for the entire "CREATION"! The Book of Genesis claims that the universe was created before five thousand years B.C.! Allah claims that the earth and the heavens were joined together as one unit but he did not mention at what point of time he separated them! Verse 3 of Ch. 10 says; "SURELY, YOUR LORD IS ALLAH WHO CREATED HEAVEN AND THE EARTH IN SIX DAYS AND THEN ROSE OVER THE THRONE"! Verse 7 of Ch. 11 says; "AND HE IT IS WHO HAS CREATED THE HEAVEN AND THE EARTH IN SIX DAYS AND HIS THRONE WAS ON THE WATER"! Verse 4 of Ch. 32 says; "AND IT IS HE WHO HAS CREATED THE HEAVEN AND THE EARTH AND ALL BETWEEN THEM IN SIX DAYS"! Verse 38 of Ch. 50 says; "AND INDEED WE CREATED THE HEAVENS AND THE EARTH AND ALL BETWEEN THEM IN SIX DAYS AND NOTHING OF FATIGUE TOUCHED US"! If we sum up all these verses what we get is: Allah created the heaven and the earth in six days and then he rose to his Throne that was on water. Allah could have created all things just by uttering the word "BE" instead of working for "Six Days"! He began his Creation on Sunday and finished on Friday! Though "Nothing of Fatigue Touched Allah" yet he decided to take a day-off on Saturday! As a mark of respect for the "Lord", Saturday should be observed as a weekly holiday universally!

Verse-2, Ch-22, states; "THE DAY YOU SHALL SEE IT, EVERY NURSING MOTHER WILL FORGET HER NURSING, AND EVERY PREGNANT ONE WILL DROP HER LOAD AND YOU SHALL SEE MANKIND AS IN A DRUNKEN STATE, YET THEY WILL NOT BE DRUNKEN". An article written by SHEIKH MUHAMMAD CHAIRI in a periodical called "ISLAMIC RELIEF" published from CA, USA. mentioned more horrors of the Day of Judgment; "EARTH TREMBLES AS GROUND RIPS APART, THE TEMPEST OF HORROR PULSES TEARS SURGE, AS THE DARK LOCKS OF BEBES FALL ASHEN RUNNING, PETRIFIED, SCATTERED AND NUMB". The writer of this article, a blind defender of Islam, has given a terrified description of the Day of Judgment like an eye witness! Whatever happens to Earth, I have nothing to fear since Allah said he would hold the Earth on his hands on the day of Judgment! What else could be more secure than Allah's hands? I would like to mention some of the striking events to enable readers to form their own opinion regarding this so-called Day of judgment! "THE ANGEL WHO IS GIVEN THE TASK OF BLOWING OF THE HORN, TO ANNOUNCE THE ARRIVAL OF THE DAY, IS NAMED ISRAFEEL; THE BEST DAY ON WHICH THE SUN RISES IS FRIDAY; ON FRIDAY ADAM WAS CREATED; ON IT HE WAS ADMITTED INTO PARADISE; ON IT HE WAS CAST OUT OF IT; AND THE HOUR (THE DAY OF JUDGMENT) WILL ARRIVE ONLY ON A FRIDAY; ALLAH PLACES IN EVERY HUMAN BEING A BONE WHICH THE EARTH CAN NEVER CONSUME AND FROM WHICH CREATURES WILL BE RECONSTRUCTED ON THE DAY OF RESURRECTION; THE FIRST TO BE BROUGHT BACK TO LIFE AND EMERGE FROM THE CRACKING GRAVE WILL BE THE PROPHET MUHAMMAD; WHEN THEY ARE GATHERED, ALL PEOPLE WILL BE BAREFOOT, NUDE AND UNCIRCUMCISED; THE FIRST PERSON TO GET COVERED WITH CLOTHES WILL BE ALLAH`S INTIMATE FRIEND ABRAHAM AND NEXT WILL BE MUHAMMAD; DISBELIEVERS WILL BE GATHERED FALLEN ON THEIR FACES—BLIND, DUMB AND DEAF; A PERSON WILL BE GIVEN HIS BOOK EITHER IN HIS RIGHT HAND IF HE IS UPRIGHT OR IN HIS LEFT IF SINFUL AND WILL BE TOLD TO READ THEIR RECORDS". This description seems like an extract from a horror fiction! Bad luck for Muhammad; his birth and death did not happen on the best day; the Friday! Nobody, particularly his followers on earth would dare to find Muhammad in a naked state! It is strictly forbidden and considered an act of blasphemy to build or create Muhammad's image in any art form! But the entire humanity will see him naked upon resurrection until he gets his nudity covered! On the Day of Judgment Allah is going to hold a trial to deliver his verdict on our conduct as humans in this life! Amidst terror and fear can we expect a fair trial? The total number of believers and disbelievers, since the beginning of mankind until the so-called Day of judgment, may exceed thousands of trillions and more! Severe tempest will make the pregnant mothers drop their loads! Men and women will be scrambling back and forth with loads of vice and virtues on their backs! The mankind will be in a drunken state, yet not drunk, toddling around to see their fate hanging in the balance between hell and heaven! Sounds of the "Horn" may not reach everyone in that noisy gathering of men and animals! The sun will rise in the West if Allah is able to reverse the rotation of the earth or he may hold the "Trial" on planet Venus where the sun rises in the West! Will it matter whether the sun rises in the East or the West when the earth itself will be destroyed? Who named the days? Does "Friday" matter so much to a perishing humanity? What significance does "Friday" hold for the moment of destruction? The whole universe will perish except Allah! Where does Allah live then? Does he have an abode outside the universe? Or he might have created another universe only for himself? Allah has implanted a bone in every creature that cannot be consumed by earth and they will be reconstructed from that bone! Do we have any scientific proof as to ascertain which bone, out of two hundred and six bones of human body, is not consumable by earth? What would happen to those who are cremated? Fire cannot be expected to spare any bone of the body during cremation! What method would be followed to resurrect and reconstruct them? The most weird decision is that Allah is going to raise all men and women naked from the Cracking Graves! We were born naked as such we should be raised naked! It might look like a sea of men and women roaming nude on the beaches! All creatures save the humans will have an advantage since they don't have to worry about being clothed upon resurrection! The Islamic Sharia Law is so strict about woman's nudity that it does not allow a man even to look at a woman! The trial on the Day of Judgment is supposed to be held on individual performance of Islamic monotheism! So, what is the point in holding this trial when the very foundation of Islam is collapsed! A rehearsal of this kind of breach of Islamic isolation between men and women may be witnessed during Hajj in Mecca! Around the KABAH, groups of men and women, also known as "Guests of Allah" entangled, pushing one another to seek blessings from the Lord! On the Day the first man to be resurrected is Muhammad. Fair enough! But he will have to wait for his turn to get a piece of cloth as Allah's intimate friend Abraham would be the first to have his nudity covered! By the way, is Abraham also going to be raised from the grave? Abraham is the one who greeted Muhammad at sixth heaven when he was on his space mission to meet with Allah over Seven Heavens! What about Jesus? Is he not going to be raised unto Allah after his second mission on earth? Adam and other prominent prophets are currently living at different heavens whom Muhammad met during his space journey! How are they going to be resurrected from the Cracking Graves? So, where lies the truth? What is the use of giving books of records to the disbelievers if they are raised "Deaf, Dumb and Blind"? Allah will surely deliver the best judgment on the "Day" as he swears by the figs, olives, mount Sinai and the city of Mecca that he is the Best of Judges (Ch. 95)!

Verse-63, Ch-22 says; "SEE YOU NOT THAT ALLAH SENDS DOWN WATER (RAIN) FROM THE SKY, AND THEN THE EARTH BECOMES GREEN? VERILY, ALLAH IS THE MOST KIND AND COURTEOUS, WELL ACQUINTED WITH ALL THINGS". What makes us skeptical about this verse is the fact that the part of the world, where so many messengers with divine books were sent, was almost dry and dead! The land was not green but gray! During the period of "Revelation" People of the land, believers and disbelievers alike, had to walk miles after miles to fetch a bag of water to quench their thirst! Does this verse reflect the reality on ground? Allah in a previous verse has already threatened to make this earth "A BARE DRY LAND WITHOUT VEGETATION"! The Islamic world, during the rule of those prophets, consisted of nations clustered around Arabian peninsula! May be the Lord had ordained; "HITHERTO SHALT THOU COME, BUT NO FARTHER"! And by the grace of Almighty, most part of their "KINGDOM" became infertile as the angel in-charge of clouds was not ordered by Allah to "SEND DOWN" water on that drought-stricken desert! Looking for water desperately, these desert people often get deceived by mirage! Yet many of them do not abandon worshipping the "ONE" up in the sky above their head! They invented "ABLUTION", a form of mandatory purification of the body with dust as part of preparation for prayers! The Hindus use "Holy Water" of the sacred river Ganga to wash off their sins! The river is often seen carrying dead bodies of man and animal! However, to the believers, the water is always clean and sacred! The scarcity of water was so severe that people in that dry land of the prophets probably had to go without a wash for days! What a great example of love and loyalty to Allah! And it is he who turns green into gray and gray into green! He sure does! Allah ordered Americans, the disbelievers to come to the desert and dig out the liquid "Gold" from underneath the dry land for the Islamic believers and that liquid gold made the barren land go green, hundreds of years after the revelations! And for that matter the believers pay "GRATITUDE' to Allah and "CURSE" the Yankees; the enemies of Allah! Whether Allah makes the earth a "GREEN LAND" or a "WASTE LAND", it all depends on his "WILL"! The clouds are created in the sea and then they go up to come down on earth as rain! Allah has appointed an angel, AR-RA`D by name, who is entrusted with the task of driving the clouds where the rain is needed! To our utter disappointment and distress, the distribution of rain is neither proportional nor well-planned! This angel should be held accountable for the mismanagement of the distribution of rain! These verses were revealed on that dry land that was devoid of green vegetation! Imported technology from the disbelievers has given a bit of greenish look to the desert that hitherto has been producing only dates for the survival of the believers and the pagans alike! The dry lands of the Middle East, especially in and around the birth place of Muhammad, are frequently over looked by the angel who drives the clouds! The rainfall is very scarce around the "Holy Land"! Together they invoke Allah during "Rain-Prayers" to rain his mercy upon them! When the flames of bushfires play havoc across the vast landscape of this "Resting Place", the angel in-charge goes on vacation! Flames of fire fiercely engulf all it can and thereafter comes the rain when it is all over! Yet the mankind got to say, "ALLAH IS THE MOST KIND AND COURTEOUS AND WELL AWARE OF OUR NEEDS"! It is difficult to imagine, Dylan Thomas, a poet of twentieth century said "Death shall have no Domain"! Like a prophet, the poet goes on to say "Destruction is not destruction but a guarantee of immortality, of perpetual life in cosmic eternity"! By now he must have realized that death has undone him forever and destruction cannot guarantee immortality! The Merciful creator of the "Time" and "Death" has imparted immortality only to himself! The Lord is ever-lasting and the rest is perishable! Long live "The Most Kind and Courteous" Lord!

Verse-66, Ch-22 says; "IT IS HE, WHO GAVE YOU LIFE, AND THEN WILL CAUSE YOU TO DIE, AND WILL AGAIN GIVE YOU LIFE ON THE DAY OF RESURRECTION. VERILY MAN IS INDEED AN INGRATE". In other words the "Creator" admits his failure to create a "Grateful" mankind that would pay their gratitude to him unquestionably! The all-knowing creator did not know that man would one day become ingrate indeed! In this verse Allah knowingly or unknowingly has made a mistake! According to Islam we are supposed to have another "Life" and "Death" in the grave, although for a short period prior to resurrection! After the first death, two angels will be appointed by Allah to come to the graves for seeking answers to three most important questions! During that interrogation in the graves, we would get our life back, at least for a brief moment, so that we can answer those questions! Obviously, after that Q&A session we will have our second death in the graves! Then only we will have our third and the last "Life" on the Day of Resurrection! So, Allah will give every believer three lives and two deaths before reaching the final destination;

the "Hell" or the "Heaven" for a deathless life! Mankind will live there forever an eternal life, since "Death" incarnated as "WHITE AND BLACK RAM" will have been killed in front of all dwellers of the hell and heaven to send a clear message that "Death" is no more an option for them! Question may arise why Allah chose black and white colors for the Ram? Probably with the killing of this "White and Black" ram, Allah also intends to make sure that the racial discrimination between black and white ends for good and does not cripple communal harmony in the life hereafter! The only exception is Jesus Christ as far as death is concerned, he will have two lives on earth with no deaths, as he will be raised up alive, as before, unto Allah if the situation for second crucifixion arises again! In the process of creation Allah has not been democratic at all, he created us like an absolute dictator without our consent! Allah claims to have created humans only to appreciate him unequivocally! So after resurrection, fate of every human being will be decided on the degree of praise and appreciation he did for his creator in this life! The entire humanity will be hurt by the harsh comment (MAN IS INDEED INGRATE) Allah has made in the last part of this verse! Who should take the blame for creating "AN INGRATE MAN"? Allah has again made an unfair assessment calling mankind ingrate! As a matter of fact it is not the mankind but the "Muslims", who believe in Islamic fanaticism, are the real ingrate! After coming out from darkness to light they begin to implement Islam on Christian land by stabbing and shooting followers of the "Son of Mary" and the Jews inspired by the Jihadi verses in the Quran! Before the bloodshed they never forget to shout "ALLAH-HU-AKBAR" as they think they are fighting for Allah! Oh Lord, this life of man on earth has been one of severe struggle from the beginning to the end! A relentless fight against a dictionary of diseases caused by bacteria, waves of viruses made our life as hard as it could be! The physiques of the "ASHRAFUL MUKHLUKAT" (the best of all creations) are so fragile that it can hardly fight against pandemics that come one after another probably machinated by Satan as he has been blessed by the Lord with a "License" to do mischief and mislead mankind until Resurrection! Ingratitude is one of the many innate ingredients that has been bestowed upon us by the creator during creation! In an open letter to the periodical called "Islamic Relief, CHERINE ABDULLAH-SMITH says; "All mankind is from Adam and Eve, an Arab has no superiority over a non-Arab; a white has no superiority over black! Learn that every Muslim is a brother to every Muslim and that the Muslims constitute one brotherhood"! Allah has given life to all mankind! Muslims all over the world will have to suffer from inferiority complex unless they learn to integrate themselves with the rest! "Muslims constitute one brotherhood" and "All mankind is from Adam and Eve"; these two expressions clearly demonstrate that the believers loyal to Allah are not indeed "AN INGRATE MAN"!

Verse-35, Ch-24 says, "ALLAH IS THE LIGHT OF THE HEAVENS AND THE EARTH. THE PARABLE OF HIS LIGHT IS AS A NICHE AND WITHIN IT A LAMP, THE LAMP IS IN A GLASS, THE GLASS AS IT WERE A BRILLIANT STAR, LIT FROM A BLESSED TREE, AN OLIVE, NEITHER FROM THE EAST NOR FROM THE WEST, WHOSE OIL WOULD ALMOST GLOW FORTH, THOUGH NO FIRE TOUCHED IT". This parabolic description of Allah's "LIGHT" deserves appreciations from literary point of view! Scientifically it is totally insignificant! It might look inconceivable, yet Allah's light will glow forth, "Though no Fire Touched it", exactly the way mother Mary conceived Jesus "Though no man Touched her"! Again, not to be forgotten that each Arabic word has a "Wealth" of meanings by virtue of which the Islamic experts will provide a meaning of the word "Light" that will even illuminate every "BLACK HOLES" of the universe to establish Allah as the "Light" of the heaven and the earth! The light that we get from the Sun is enough for the earth! In this verse, Allah, the so-called "LIGHT OF THE HEAVENS AND THE EARTH" has been depicted in a demeaning parable of a lamp, oiled by an olive tree that glows like a brilliant star fuelled by olive oil! A star glows brilliantly because of its consistent nuclear reaction. Whoever has drafted this verse has not done justice to Allah. The Creator deserved a much more realistic and sophisticated PARABLE other than a mere lamp lit by olive oil! Did Allah really write this verse? Does the word HEAVENS in the verse mean the entire universe? Scientists say more than ninety percent of the universe is filled with DARK MATTERS that do not reflect light! Allah is emitting his light like a lamp enclosed in a glass as a brilliant star! This parable is so insignificant that Allah's light lost its luminance amidst billions of bright stars! How Allah's parabolic lamp will light up the heavens? The Quran, referred to as the "Light" from Allah to Muhammad, could not show the mankind how to come out of the darkness! The parabolic lamp lit from an olive would glow forth and show the loyalists path to Paradise!

Verse-2, Ch-25, says; "HE TO WHOM BELONGS THE DOMINION OF THE HEAVENS AND THE EARTH, AND WHO HAS BEGOTTEN NO

SON, AND FOR WHOM THERE IS NO PARTNER IN THE DOMINION. HE HAS CREATED EVERYTHING AND HAS MEASURED IT EXACTLY ACCORDING TO ITS DUE MEASUREMENTS". Allah has begotten no son since he did not have a wife! But the Lord has many enemies who often portray Mary as the mother of the "Son of the Lord" although he merely breathed into her sleeves through angel Gabriel and thus she conceived Jesus, the "Son of God"! Allah, as an absolute dictator has absolutely made sure that there should be no partner in his domain to challenge his authority! Allah "Created" everything "Alone" as he needed no partner to help him! It raises lot of questions why he needed help from the angels, Satan, messengers and prophets to implement his monotheism over mankind since he is sufficient to accomplish all by himself? He categorically denied having taken any help from Satan in the process of creation! Most of what have been said in this verse are repetitions, except the claim that Allah created everything "EXACTLY ACCORDING TO ITS DUE MEASUREMENTS"! Allah's "DOMAIN" is comprised of the "HEAVENS" and the "EARTH" only! Because Allah needed to build a Paradise, a Hell, a Home for himself over seven heavens and a resting place for the mankind on earth! What about the universe which is still expanding? Has it not yet reached its "DUE MEASURMENTS? Why he created other planets in our solar system? A much smaller solar system, comprising of just one sun and one planet with one moon going round it, would have been more than enough to implement Islamic monotheism over the mankind! What was the necessity to create seven heavens? One would have been enough for one "Creator"! Does his domain include the entire universe with billions of galaxies packed with stars and celestial objects into it? Have they been created with "DUE MEASUREMENTS? Was it necessary to create Adam thirty meters long in height? How many stars Allah needed to decorate the nearest heaven? Are the stars made with due dimension to use them as missiles to hit the devils? Are the Devils bigger than the Stars? Should the bullets be bigger than the targets? Were the Dinosaurs created in due measurements? May be Allah did not like their physiques and later he decided to destroy them using floating asteroids as "Missiles"! Though Adam's name is mentioned time and again but surprisingly, there is no mention of dinosaurs at all in the Quran! Who came first to this world, Adam or the dinosaurs? It will not be an exaggeration to assume that Allah sent dinosaurs to this earth and then killed them altogether with a single strike as part of an experiment to ascertain survival of the fittest! And then Allah sent only eight pairs of different cattle like camels, cows, goats, sheep etc. with due measurements for the entire mankind! Are the world population evenly distributed with "Due" consideration? What about innumerable virus and bacteria? Were they bestowed upon mankind by the "Creator" in "Due" proportions? How many diseases and calamities do the mankind need? Death of a baby before being born is also ordained by the merciful "Creator" with "Due Consideration"? The deities are more dangerous than the devils for the mankind! To be honest, all "Invisible" and "Unseen" entities, who carry out their mission staying beyond our vision, have proven to be detrimental to humanity! None of the basic elements of life is duly distributed with "Due Measurements" as claimed in the divine verses! Verse 18 of Ch-23 says: "AND WE SENT DOWN FROM THE SKY WATER (RAIN) IN DUE MEASURE"! This statement from Allah does not reflect the truth! Which part of the world gets rain in due proportion? What causes droughts and floods? Verse 70 of Ch-56 says; "IF WE WILLED, WE VERILY COULD MAKE IT (WATER) SALT AND UNDRINKABLE. WHY THEN DO YOU NOT GIVE THANKS TO ALLAH"? Thanks be to Allah for making 98% water on earth 'Salt and Undrinkable'! Please do not lose patience! There are plenty of rivers in the Gardens of Paradise that are overflowing with delicious Water, Wine, Milk and Honey!

Verse-4, Ch-25 states; "THOSE WHO DISBELIEVE SAY; THIS QURAN IS NOTHING BUT A LIE THAT HE (MUHAMMAD) HAS INVENTED, AND OTHERS HAVE HELPED HIM AT IT. IN FACT THEY HAVE PRODUCED AN UNJUST WRONG (THING) AND A LIE". Nay! The Quran is not an unjust lie nor has it been invented! What has been invented is its "Revelation" and that is "A LIE"! The Quran is a truth and the truth is that it has been written, most probably by a group of associates led by Muhammad! He had a group of associates who were sincerely dedicated to his ideology! Since the leader failed to command widespread allegiance and respect from the masses, they attributed authorship of the Quran to an unseen entity living in the heaven! This verse is the summation of all the allegations brought against prophet Muhammad and his associates since the revelation of the verses! The verse deserves to be considered as an unequivocal confession made in plain language but not so for those who have been thoroughly "Brain Washed" by love and loyalty toward Allah and Muhammad! Does the unseen "Creator" of the earth and the heaven have to be a "Writer" to write a small book and then reveal it through an invisible angel to an illiterate man? There is no other instance of this scale where the creator, even if he exists, could be questioned for his mishandling of an ideology! To find the truth, what it takes is a comparative assessment between the writer of the book and the creator of the universe! Not only the Arab Pagans but disbelievers of both old and modern times have cast their doubts on the so-called "Revelation" of the Quran! This Quran would have found greater acceptance and credibility as a book of social reforms and justice, from the people without claiming to have been revealed from the heaven! This unseen, unproven and untrustworthy chain of revelation has nothing but blind faith as support for its sustainability as the "Work" of a divine "Creator" whose very existence itself is not beyond doubts! Death of Muhammad, before being able to edit and compile the book, has dented the trustworthiness of the revelation to the extreme! If a creator does exist, call him by any name, his way of doing things to a great extent has become obvious to the mankind through science and commonsense! Why a divine entity, thought to be the creator of the universe, should resort to such a messy means of communication to propagate his message for the mankind? Did he face such complex situation while creating the universe? Allah, time and again, claimed in his "Book" to have created the entire creation alone! Why then he needed thousands of prophets and angels to implement a "Law" into action? In the verse next to this, Arab Pagans described Quran as the "TALES OF THE ANCIENTS"! It should better be called "A TALE OF TWO CITIES" because all of Muhammad's religious maneuvering including some of the battles he fought took place in and around the two cities; Mecca and Medina! In addition to this, all of 114 Surah of the Quran are said to have made landfall in these two holy cities! Why Allah, the Lord of the heaven decided to send down his message for the whole of mankind in these two small desert cities is also a matter of concern! Muhammad was ousted from Mecca by the pagans and he took shelter in Medina and later he again took control of Mecca! Moreover most of his religious maneuvering took place around these two cities! The Quran retold similar stories, with some turn and twist, regarding twenty prophets including Adam, Noah, Abraham, Moses, Jesus that were already narrated in other scriptures! There was also the story of a "Whistle Blower" who is said to have abandoned Christianity to become a Muslim and worked with Muhammad as one of his scribes! He later left alleging that the texts of the Quran were not revealed as claimed by prophet Muhammad, rather they were drafted by him and other scribes! The whistle blower was later killed by the followers of the prophet! Pagans dubbed the Quran as

"AN UNJUST WRONG THING" and "AN INVENTED LIE"! Who can mitigate these allegations against the Quran?

Verse-61, Ch-25 states; "BLESSED BE HE WHO HAS PLACED IN THE HEAVEN BIG STARS, AND HAS PLACED THEREIN A GREAT LAMP (SUN), AND A MOON GIVING LIGHT". Prophet Muhammad in a Hadith made it clear that one of the purposes of creating "Stars" was to decorate the "First Heaven"! This verse states that the "Blessed" has placed Big Stars in the Heaven and then he placed a "Great Lamp" (Sun), and a Moon giving light! Any reader who has very basic knowledge about space science, would not need any explanation of this verse! The stars are "Big" and the Sun is a "Great Lamp"! There are stars in the sky that are tens of thousands of times bigger than the Sun! But one thing is obvious that writer of these verses had absolutely no knowledge about the real functioning of the celestial bodies of the space! What an ordinary observer can see with naked eyes is a vast sky filled with stars, the sun and the moon! For an ordinary onlooker it is next to impossible to think of the real functioning of the sun and the moon! They only see them revolving and giving light like lamps, during day or night for the benefit of the people on earth! What is said in the above verse; a "Great Lamp (Sun), and a "Moon giving Light", has been drafted from that plain perspective and simple observation! What meets the eye is not always the truth! Did the author of the "Book" understand the different roles the "Sun" plays both as a source of light and as a source of energy? Understanding sun's role as a source of light is of course not a rocket science but most intelligent human being took thousands of years to discover sun's role as source of energy for life on earth! These two observations clearly demonstrate the difference of intellectual capability of the science and the faiths! The verse also mentions that Allah has "PLACED IN THE HEAVEN BIG STARS", if so, then who placed the great galaxies in the heaven? Why Allah as the "Creator" could not "See" the Galaxies? May be the Galaxies were created by some other Creator? Nay! "ALLAH ALONE CREATED THE EARTH AND THE HEAVEN"! He is alone and unrivalled!

Verse-3, Ch-26 states; "IT MAY BE THAT YOU (MUHAMMAD) ARE GOING TO KILL YOURSELF WITH GRIEF, THAT THEY DO NOT BECOME BELIEVERS IN YOUR MESSAGE OF ISLAMIC MONOTHEISM". The same message was conveyed in verse 6 of chapter 18 which states; "PERHAPS YOU WOULD KILL YOURSELF (O MUHAMMAD) IN GRIEF,

OVER THEIR FOOTSTEPS (OVER THEIR RUNNING AWAY FROM YOU) BECAUSE THEY BELIEVE NOT IN THIS NARRATION(THE QURAN)! It is obvious that two different persons expressed Muhammad's anguish in two different sets of words! Allah's own admissions testify the level of frustration both he and his messenger had to endure because of the poor response they received to their message of Islamic monotheism! Allah would have to bear responsibility if Muhammad had killed himself with grief! The most appropriate advice from Allah to his messenger, in that time of grief, should have been; "Keep your Cool (O Muhammad)! A Hadith narrates that once Muhammad got very upset over poor turnout of the devotees at the mosque! His rage was so immense that he wished to order the call-maker of the mosque to burn those men along with their houses who did not come to mosque to attend the prayers! The actual grief that would have killed Muhammad did not come from his failure as a messenger but his failure as a husband of dozens of young and old wives who could give him neither a happy conjugal life nor a "Son of Muhammad" to succeed his dominion! Probably this led him to declare himself as the "Last" messenger leaving his mission and vision in complete disarray! Talking of prophet Muhammad's character, Dr. M.H. DURRANI, a Pakistani Islamic scholar says; "He was never rude, nor spoke a severe word to anyone"! Not cataract but excessive love and loyalty that makes one go blind! Does the "Creator of the Universe" have to send different scriptures with different messages at different times to different nations in different languages only to instill Islamic monotheism? Is it not time to come out of "The Cloud of Unknowing"?

Verse-61, Surah-27 says; IS NOT HE (BETTER THAN YOUR GODS) WHO HAS MADE THE EARTH AS A FIXED ABODE, AND HAS PLACED RIVERS IN ITS MIDST, AND HAS PLACED FIRM MOUNTAINS THEREIN, AND HAS SET A BARRIER BETWEEN THE TWO SEAS (OF SALT AND SWEET WATER)? The bracketed words; "Better than your Gods" in this verse have acknowledged the existence of other Gods! Of course Allah is better than those Gods since he is the one "WHO HAS MADE THE EARTH AS A FIXED ABODE"! But the "Best" among the Gods is "He" who has made the earth as a "ROTATING ABODE" on its axis altering day into night and vice versa and then he made it revolve on its orbit around the sun at least once in a year! The earth is basically a planet of the solar system constantly functioning as an abode for all forms of life including an intelligent entity like us. Since its inception the earth has never stopped being active about its axis. The concept of making the earth as a "Fixed Abode" and a "Resting Place" for mankind by Allah stands nowhere amidst the mystery unfolding day by day behind the creation! Also the better God is "He" who has placed Seas and Oceans in the midst of the earth. And the one who has placed only "Rivers" in paradise cannot claim to be better than other Gods! In another verse Allah claimed to have placed mountains on the earth so that it doesn't shake! Indiscriminate placement of mountains to stop the Earth from shaking and moving, may be the brainchild of a novice! Which sea on earth has sweet water? Water coming out of ZAMZAM (a sacred well near KABAH) is also salty! Pilgrims take home ZAMZAM water as an antidote against diseases that has proven to be totally ineffective! Where is the "Barrier" that separates the two "Seas" of salt and sweet water? Romantic Coleridge in a supernatural voice expressed his poetic truth: "And we did speak only to break the silence of the sea"! Millions of Albatross flying over the water also broke the silence of the sea to say, it's all salty but sweet! A God in need is a better God indeed!

Verse-64, Ch-29 states; "AND THIS LIFE OF THE WORLD IS ONLY AN AMUSEMENT AND A PLAY! VERILY, THE HOME OF THE HEREAFTER—THAT IS THE LIFE INDEED, IF THEY BUT KNEW". Even after visiting the paradise Muhammad knew not what would be done with him and with his followers in the hereafter! Verily, what is said in this verse about home of the hereafter sounds like distant music that lost its melody on the way! Shakespeare should not have written so many comedies to celebrate life that is "Only an amusement and a play"! This verse is making a comparison between the real life that we live here and a life beyond horizon which is not only out of reach but also out of sight! All information about the eternal life in paradise are trapped inside the divine "Black Hole", since no light is able to pass beyond the divine horizon! As for the believers, the Quran is a great source of words of temptations and entertainments about life of the hereafter! Yet, as usual, the people have mistrusts and misgivings about things unseen! Muhammad is said to have paid a visit to Allah over seven heavens, so he is an eye witness to "THE HOME OF THE HEREAFTER"! Adam who was created in paradise and presently living in the " First Heaven" might have some knowledge about the life of the hereafter! It is only Jesus, the "Son of God" who could give a detailed description of the home hereafter when he comes back to earth to rule the mankind in Islamic way so that the entire mankind would enjoy the amusement of the life hereafter! But the Christians are comforted with the assurance that Messiah shall return "To reward his faithful, and receive them into bliss, whether in Heaven or Earth, for them the Earth shall all be Paradise, far happier place than this of Eden"! In a related Hadith (AL-BUKHARI, Vol. 4, #468) Allah's Messenger Muhammad says, "THE FIRST GROUP OF PEOPLE WHO WILL ENTER PARADISE WILL BE GLITTERING LIKE THE MOON ON A FULL-MOON NIGHT. THEY WILL NEITHER SPIT NOR BLOW THEIR NOSES NOR RELIEVE NATURE! EVERY ONE OF THEM WILL HAVE TWO WIVES; THE MARROW OF THE BONES OF THE WIVES' LEGS WILL BE SEEN THROUGH THE FLESH OUT OF EXCESSIVE BEAUTY. THEY WILL NEITHER HAVE DIFFERENCE NOR ENMITY AMONGST THEMSELVES; THEIR HEARTS WILL BE AS IF ONE HEART AND THEY WILL BE GLORIFYING ALLAH IN THE MORNING AND IN THE AFTERNOON"! If Allah could take the mankind into confidence about such an entertaining life with alluring attractions, he could have easily made all of them accept Islamic monotheism with hundred percent success! As par this Hadith no woman will be included in the "FIRST GROUP"! Not even Eve, Mary or wives of Muhammad? Because each one of them will receive "Two Wives"! Is this not an unfair treatment to ladies? It is also possible that no lady of the land could qualify to be included in the first group or none of them would do well to earn such a favor from Allah during trial on the Day of Judgment! However, those lucky males, destined to enter paradise at the first opportunity, will glitter like "THE MOON ON A FULL-MOON NIGHT! Will they enter paradise at night? This parable does not seem befitting to them! Because moon has no light of its own and totally dependent on the sun for its shine! If they enter during daytime, the sunlight will take away their glint! Allah, the All-Mighty, could also make them glitter like supernova! It is claimed that Adam's offspring will regain their father's gigantic physical statures before entering paradise! So, a man or woman of thirty meters height will definitely need a lot of foods! Yet they will be exempted from relieving nature! How will they dispose their waste? May be they will be equipped with a new metabolic system! Here on earth man and woman are almost equal in number. If every man gets two wives in paradise, to be fair, every woman should also get two husbands of similar beauty and attributes! But as par Allah's Law, woman gets half of what a man gets as father's inheritance and If the same rule is applied in the paradise, then women will probably get half of what a man gets i.e. one husband each! The concept of "One man one wife" is not an acceptable norm in paradise!

Those lucky guys who would be admitted into paradise are expected to be mostly with Islamic background and polygamy is a way of life in Muslim community! Allah allowed Muhammad to set the precedence of polygamy! So, having two wives in paradise for an eternal entertainment seems quite reasonable and logical! Will those males undergo any changes in their physical appearance? All-knowing Allah must have thought about it already! Otherwise, if an ugly-looking man enters into paradise, he may be rejected by those ladies whose bone marrow is visible through their flesh because of excessive beauty! This verse further says that dwellers of paradise will have no differences among themselves and will stay there as man of one heart! Will that be possible? Allah has already created difference by building the paradise with one hundred grades! People in lower grade might be jealous of those in upper grades! In the paradise they will also be free from boredom of glorifying Allah five times a day starting from early morning until going to bed at night! They will glorify Allah only "IN THE MORNING AND IN THE AFTERNOON" in paradise so that they get more time to spend with their excessively beautiful wives! The "Night" will be entirely at the disposal of the romantic dweller of the paradise to enjoy his time with Two Wives! So, we may safely assume that there will be sunrise and sunset as they happen in our solar system! This paradise might be located in another planet of a different solar system! If the paradise is built on a "Fixed Abode" unlike the rotating earth, than there may be problem! However, we should not lose sight of the fact that Allah is able to do all things at his will! All rewards in paradise will be given in proportion to one's spiritual performance in "THIS LIFE OF THE WORLD WHICH IS AN AMUSEMENT AND PLAY"! But the Lord is assuring the believers of a life hereafter with more amusement and fun! The mankind is on the horns of a dilemma since it can neither abandon this life nor can it be sure of the everlasting amusement of the life hereafter!

Verse-21, Ch-30, states; "AND AMONG HIS SIGNS IS THIS, THAT HE CREATED FOR YOU WIVES FROM AMONGST YOUESELVES, THAT YOU MAY FIND REPOSE IN THEM, AND HE HAS PUT BETWEEN YOU AFFECTION AND MERCY. VERILY, IN THAT ARE INDEED SIGNS FOR A PEOPLE WHO REFLECT". What happened between Muhammad and his wives is one of the greatest "Signs" that testifies how much of marital "Repose" he enjoyed in this "Resting place" Allah has made! Muhammad's home was not a place of conjugal harmony! His wives failed to behave like "The Merry Wives of Windsor"! Allah himself had to intervene by sending more than seven verses (Ch. 33} to Muhammad to settle the disputes between him and his acrimonious wives! Though Allah put "AFFECTION AND MERCY" between husbands and wives so that they "MAY FIND REPOSE" amongst them, yet the marital acrimonies have continued unabated! Besides biological fitness, a strong bond between husband and wife can only be cemented by love, not by "AFFECTION AND MERCY" alone! "Love" between two young man and woman, in Islamic point of view, is a taboo! The Mankind needs a collective resurrection of consciousness! DR. SALWA RASHED, who is a contributor to the magazine "Islamic Relief" says; "THE PROPHET MUHAMMAD GAVE US THE BEST EXAMPLE IN HIS LIFE WITH HIS WIVES"! In verse 32 of Ch. 33, Allah warns; "O WIVES OF THE PROPHET! YOU ARE NOT LIKE ANY OTHER WOMEN. BE NOT SOFT IN SPEECH, LEST HE IN WHOSE HEART IS A DISEASE (OF EVIL DESIRE FOR ADULTRY) SHOULD BE MOVED WITH DESIRE"! Verse 30 of Ch. 33 says; "O WIVES OF MUHAMMAD! WHOEVER OF YOU COMMITS AN OPEN ILLEGAL SEXUAL INTERCOURSE, THE TORMNT FOR HER WILL BE DOUBLED AND THAT IS EVER EASY FOR ALLH"! Read between the lines to see how the prophet set "Best Examples" with dozens of wives aged between seven to seventy! Eventually Allah had to save his messenger from further embarrassment! The Prophet died when he was only sixty three; probably "BEFORE THE TERM APPOINTED FOR HIM!

Verse-22, Ch-30 states; "AND AMONG THE SIGNS IS THE CREATION OF THE HEAVENS AND THE EARTH, AND THE DIFFERENCE OF YOUR LANGUAGE AND COLORS. VERILY, IN THAT ARE INDEED SIGNS FOR MAN OF SOUND UNDERSTANDING". Allah's knowledge of the heavens and the earth, as evident from the so-called science of the Quran, is so shallow that the credit for the creation of the universe cannot be attributed to him based on the factual evidence of the natural science! In Allah's own words, this tiny planet of earth is a "Fixed Abode" which he has "Spread Out" to affix mountains and rivers so that it does not shake! Each of the Seven Heavens Allah created is now home to his prominent Prophets; Adam, Jesus, John, Joseph Abraham, Moses, Aaron etc. who have been bestowed a second life and probably they don't have to be Resurrected! All of them greeted Muhammad in their respective heaven while he was on his way to meet Allah at his palace (AL-BAIT-UL-MAMUR) over seven heavens! No doubt the differences in language and colors are signs of creative excellence but they also have a down side; they play a divisive to the unity of humanity. This world would have been a much better place to live if Allah could create a mankind with no differences in color and language! The history of creation may be summarized in Allah's own words: "Allah is the one and only creator who has created Seven heavens and an Earth! Then he created a Sun and a Moon as sources of light and reckoning! He then created one pair of man and woman to generate a mankind imbued with an innate religion of Islam"! Why than the diversity of color, language and religion has taken place? It has created chaos and cracks in the unification of mankind! Obviously things have gone out of his control! Identity of a person, in terms of his language, color and creed determines his position in the society and the treatment meted out to him is also in proportion to that social standing! All-knowing Allah did not know the fall-out from the multi-colored and multi-lingual humanity would be so devastating! If Allah could send Islam as a universal religion, why couldn't he send a universal language? He rather claims that he sent this Quran for the mankind in Arabic so that everybody understands its meanings! By his own admission Allah claims to have created the mankind with differences in color and language and unfortunately these two nationalistic traits of human beings have impacted the mankind to become fascist and racist! The angels who are responsible to report to Allah about all affairs of the earth on a daily basis may have failed to inform him on ugly nature of racism on earth! We know now from the Quran that Allah speaks Arabic but what about his color; Black or white? Could he not avoid making multi-colored mankind so that Dr. King wouldn't have to die for saying; "I have a dream"? And his "Dream" is still lingering in limbo! Though the white Shakespeare had special fascination for a "Dark Lady", yet he said, "From fairest creatures we desire increase"! In the land of the Red Indians, immigrated White Supremacists do not think the "Black lives matter"! But why? Because the Lord failed to create enough "MAN OF SOUND UNDERSTANDING"! This world would have been free of racial discrimination originated from skin colors, if our "Creator" could create a monochrome mankind! As man of understanding we may conclude that the difference in language and color is the work of Allah or he has no control over the functioning of the nature! Does the nature work against his "Will"? A disobedient nature also implies an absence of a creator! Nature works by its own set of rules! I have to quote again CHERINE ABDALLAH-SMITH from "Islamic Relief" who said; "An Arab has no superiority over a non-Arab nor a non-Arab has any superiority over an Arab; a White has no superiority over Black nor a Black has any superiority over White"! This is an overstatement! Allah by his own admission says he has sown the "Seeds" of the difference of language and colors among the human beings! Allah's religion is Islam; his language is Arabic! We have no knowledge of his "Color"!

Verse-6, Ch-31 states; "AND OF MANKIND IS HE WHO PURCHASES IDLE TALKS (MUSIC, SINGING) TO MISLEAD MEN FROM PATH OF ALLAH WITHOUT KNOWLEDGE AND TAKES IT (QURAN, THE PATH OF ALLAH) BY WAY OF MOCKERY. FOR SUCH THERE WILL BE A HUMILIATING TORMENT IN THE HELL-FIRE". So, music and singing is not the way of Allah! The Way of the Lord is different! A section of the mankind, irrespective of religious allegiance, sing devotional songs to please their Lords! Out of affinity, "NOT BY WAY OF MOCKERY", they think music paves the way to the Lord! Melody of music is the medicine of mind that resonates with heart and souls! Why Allah opposes music? Many believers of Islam sing verses of the Quran in melodious tune! Without music, this world would instantly become a Hell! Allah could have used music as one of the temptations, along with beautiful Wives and Wines for the dwellers of paradise! An eternal life in paradise without music would tantamount to a life in desert without water! However, some Arabians enjoy Belly-dance with melodious music in the deserts close to the epicenter of Islam! They surely have forgotten that "THERE WILL BE A HUMILIATING TORMENT IN THE HELLFIRE"! Allah warns his creation with humiliating torment if they take the Quran or the path of Allah by way of mockery! Allah himself called disbelievers "Despised Monkeys" and mocked at them! What if they follow the suit of their creator? In a related hadith (AL-BUKHARI, Vol. 7, #494) Prophet Muhammad is quoted to have said; "FROM AMONG MY FOLLOWERS THERE WILL BE SOME PEOPLE WHO WILL CONSIDER ILLEGAL SEXUAL INTERCOURSE, THE WEARING OF SILK, THE DRINKING OF ALCOHOLIC DRINKS, AND THE USE OF MUSICAL INSTRUMENTS AS LAWFUL. AND FROM THEM THERE WILL BE SOME WHO WILL STAY NEAR THE SIDE OF A MOUNTAIN, ALLAH WILL DESTROY THEM DURING THE NIGHT AND WILL LET THE MOUNTAIN FALL UPON THEM AND HE WILL TRANSFORM THE REST OF THEM INTO MONKEYS AND PIGS AND THEY WILL REMAIN SO TILL THE DAY OF RESURRECTION"! Why Muhammad calls them his "Followers" who indulge in illegal sex, wear silk, drink alcohol and use musical instruments? Probably they are the ones who would ultimately, as predicted by Muhammad, divide his nation into

73 groups and at the end only one of those groups will stand by his side and follow his teachings! Consensual sex, which is considered illegal and un-Islamic, is much more morally acceptable as opposed to "MUTAH" (a temporary marriage for sexual gratification), and sex with slaves that one's "RIGHT HAND POSSESS"! Prophet Lot was an unlucky prophet who could not prevent his people from practicing wide spread sodomy! He said to his people (Verse 81 of Ch. 7); "VERILY, YOU PRACTICE YOUR LUST ON MEN INSTEAD OF WOMEN"! Drinking alcohol without getting drunk is neither harmful nor unlawful. What makes the use of silk and musical instruments unlawful is not convincing at all! Every form of music brings calm and tranquility as opposed to religious chaos and confusion! Wearing silk or playing music is not a crime under any human jurisprudence! All-Merciful Allah shows no mercy and awards death penalty by crushing mountains on them! These so-called "Criminals" should never go near the mountains! Why Allah has preferred night over day as the right time to make the mountains fall upon the wrong doers is also beyond our limited knowledge! Those who considered themselves lucky to have escaped the crush, are in fact not so lucky as they would be transformed into "Monkeys and Pigs" to stay as such until Resurrection! Charles Darwin said that the evolution process took hundreds of thousands of years to gradually transform monkeys into humans but Allah can transform them back into monkeys just by uttering the word "Be"! Do these monkeys and pigs stand a chance to be resurrected? Why not? All creatures will be "Resurrected" on the Day of Judgment to stand a trial before the "Sublime"! The Lord has clearly indicated of this trial in his "Revelation"!

Verse-10, Ch-31 says; "HE HAS CREATED THE HEAVENS WITHOUT ANY PILLARS THAT YOU SEE, AND HAS SET ON THE EARTH FIRM MOUNTAINS LEST IT SHOULD SHAKE WITH YOU". Since no pillars are attached to the Heavens, the universe is expanding at an unstoppable acceleration! Are there pillars below the Earth? Despite setting the firm mountains on earth, it still shakes with us when struck by quakes! Tremors make the tectonic plates drift along with the mountains! Narration of this verse clearly demonstrates that the " Author" of the Quran and the " Creator " of the Heavens are not the same entity! We do see the heavens hanging as we see the balloons floating in the air without pillars! Where would the Lord affix the pillars to hold the heavens? Allah says he has created the sky as the canopy of the earth, without raising any pillars! Does Allah have the engineering excellence required to raise the heavens on pillars? The "Author" of the Quran seems devoid of knowledge how the gravitational forces work? When humans began planning to launch satellites into orbits, no scientists suggested such a weird idea of putting them on pillars. Oh, Lord, how big is the universe? How big is the heavens? How much of it is visible to us? Will it be possible to hold Seven Heavens on pillars? Imagine the huge number of pillars you would need to support each of the Seven Heavens as, according to your statement, each one of the seven heavens is built one over another like a seven storied building! Will it be possible to affix pillars under an expanding universe? To erect pillars you have to bring its expansion to a halt? How the "Firm Mountains" will stop a rotating planet from shaking while the mountains themselves are shaken by the tremors! Thanks be to Allah that he has not built the Heavens on pillars! The mankind is not shaken by the gravitational waves, that come travelling through the space-time, as much as by the shocking "Revelations" that come from the "Creator" of the heavens; the All-Knowing Allah! Allah's science of creation creates confusion among the disbelievers!

Verse-27, Ch-31 says; "AND IF ALL THE TREES ON THE EARTH WERE PENS AND THE SEA (INK TO WRITE WITH) WITH SEVEN SEAS BEHIND IT TO ADD TO ITS SUPPLY, YET THE WORDS OF ALLAH WOULD NOT BE EXHAUSTED". Verse 109 of Surah 18 may be quoted here for comparison. In this verse Allah directly asking Muhammad to say; "IF THE SEA WERE INK FOR WRITING THE WORDS OF MY LORD, SURELY, THE SEA WOULD BE EXHAUSTED BEFORE THE WORDS OF MY LORD WOULD BE FINISHED, EVEN IF WE BROUGHT ANOTHER SEA LIKE IT FOR ITS AID"! After a close look at the contents of these two verses, what becomes conspicuously evident is that they were written by two different persons! Both of these verses are said to have been revealed at Mecca! The composer who made the mistake in chapter 18, by asking for only one more additional sea of ink to write the words of his Lord, has been corrected in chapter 31 saying that seven seas of ink would be exhausted to finish writing all the words of the Lord! The Lord as the "Author" of his own book, is not expected to give two different narratives of the same subject! Another observation we can make from many instances of this kind that this Quran has not come from any divine source! A divine being, if exists at all, cannot go out of his way in self-appreciations! He takes "pride" in everything he claims to have "Created"! Whereas "Pride" is one of the seven deadly cardinal sins that, according to medieval theology, entails spiritual death! What these verses deliver is nothing but utter sycophancy! Composer of the verse 109 of chapter 18 has shown some sense of rationality when he thinks "Another Sea" of ink would be enough to add to the one he already has! But the composer of verse 27 of chapter 31 says it would not be enough even if all trees of the Earth were pens! Besides, he would need "Seven Seas" of ink probably for the reason that his Lord Created "Seven Heavens"! These are not allegories like the "Dances of the Seven Deadly Sins"! These are verses "Revealed" by the Lord the heavens to show the mankind the "Right Path" to paradise!

Verse-4, Ch-32 states; "ALLAH IS HE WHO HAS CREATED THE HEAVENS AND THE EARTH, AND ALL THAT IS BETWEEN THEM IN SIX DAYS. THEN HE ROSE OVER THE THRONE IN A MANNER THAT SUITS HIS MAJESTY"! This verse has been repeated many times in the Quran! However, there are some verses to this effect which give a different account of the divine creation! Verse 9 of chapter 41 says; "SAY (O MUHAMMAD) DO YOU VERILY DISBELIEVE IN HIM WHO CREATED THE EARTH IN TWO DAYS? In this verse Allah is asking Muhammad to say to the disbelievers, who set up rivals unto him in worship, whether they believe in the creator who has created the earth in two "Days"? Now we are clear about the fact that Allah created the Earth in two days! And the next verse (10 of Ch. 41) states; "HE PLACED THEREIN (i.e. the Earth) FIRM MOUNTAINS FROM ABOVE IT, AND HE BLESSEED IT, AND MEASURED THEREIN ITS SUSTENANCE FOR ITS DWELLERS IN FOUR DAYS EQUEL IN LENGTH"! Here we have another important piece of information that Allah took "Four Equal Days" to create sustenance for the dwellers of the earth! And again in verse 12 of the same chapter Allah says; "THEN HE COMPLETED AND FINISHED FROM THEIR CREATION (AS) SEVEN HEAVENS IN TWO DAYS AND HE MADE IN EACH HEAVEN ITS AFFAIR. AND WE ADORNED THE NEAREST (LOWEST) HEAVEN WITH LAMPS (STARS) TO BE AN ADORNMENT AS WELL AS TO GUARD (FROM THE DEVILS BY USING THEM AS MISSILES AGAINST THE DEVILS)"! In the first verse Allah claims that he created the Earth, Heaven and all that is between them in "Six Days"! Then he says he took only "Two Days" to create the Earth! Next he claims that he took "Four Days" to arrange sustenance for the dwellers of the earth! And lastly he created Seven Heavens only in "Two days"! All of mankind is in a puzzle about divine creation! Allah could create everything he intends to only by saying "Be" and the things come into being without delay! We are created by the "Creator" to be tested and tried on the basis of our love and loyalty for him!

Verse-5, Ch-32, states; "HE MANAGES AND REGULATES EVERY AFFAIR FROM THE HEAVEN TO THE EARTH, THEN IT (AFFAIR) WILL GO UP TO HIM, IN ONE DAY, THE SPACE WHEREOF IS A THOUSAND YEARS OF YOUR RECKONING (RECKONING OF WORLD'S TIME)! One day of Allah is equal to "A Thousand Years" of our time! In verse 4 of chapter 70 Allah claims that his one day is equal to "Fifty Thousand Years" of world standard time! This is the real problem! The Creator and the created live in a different time zone and as a result, actions and reactions do not happen on real time-scale! Why Allah increased his one day from "A Thousand" to "Fifty Thousand" years is not clear at all! However, what is clear is that these verses have been drafted by two different individuals! Another probable reason may be that Allah was staying at different heavens when these verses were written! Allah himself acknowledged that he often comes down to the "First Heaven" from his " Throne" over "Seven Heavens" as and when he "Wills"! We cannot expect an immediate response from him who manages all affairs of the world unless we are able to synchronize our time with that of the "Manager"! So this huge time difference is the reason why we don't get any help from Allah when we need it most! The mankind is now faced with a number of catastrophic problems! Did the angels inform Allah of these disasters? An appropriate response from Allah may take one thousand years to reach the earth! Everything in the earth or in the heaven is created by Allah and he creates nothing without a purpose! Pandemics and problems are also created by Allah with a definite "Purpose"! We cannot rule out the possibility that one day he may send the "Recipe" for vaccines, to fight against viruses, to one of his most trusted devotees in the dream! The "Dream" plays very important part in Islam! Prophet Abraham was tested for his loyalty to Allah through a dreadful dream! Many Muslims in the Islamic world sell medications claiming to have received the recipe in the dream through divine blessings! Why the coronavirus is attacking believers and disbelievers without discrimination is a mystery? Believers had to stop going to mosque and KABAH to avoid being infected! This KABAH, called the house of Allah, is not immune from virus attack! How good is Allah as a WALI (protector)? Do the promises made by Allah in his verses about life hereafter make sense? His verses and words seem to have lost credibility in totality! Allah has prescribed an antidote for mankind against all kinds of diseases known as "AR-RUKYAH" which is:

"A DIVINE SPEECH RECITED AS A MEANS OF CURING DISEASE. IT IS A KIND OF TREATMENT i.e. TO RECITE SURAH AL-FATIHA (THE FIRST SURAH OF THE QURAN) OR ANY OTHER SURAH OF THE QURAN AND THEN BLOW ONE'S BREATH WITH SALIVA OVER THE SICK PERSON'S BODY-PART"! A man of average common sense will be able to evaluate the disastrous impact of "BLOWING ONE'S BREATH WITH SALIVA" as an antidote against infectious diseases! All believers including the Mullahs, Imams and Islamic scholars should try this divine treatment by reciting the "DIVINE SPEECH" to prove its efficacy! If they are able to prove its effectiveness and get cured by this treatment from the All-Mighty, their job would be much easier to convince disbelievers to believe in the Islamic monotheism for a disease-free eternal life with never-ending entertainments in paradise! Thereby the entire mankind will be fully convinced how Allah "Manages and Regulates" every affair from the heaven to the earth"! A Hadith narrated by AL-BUKHARI quotes the prophet as saying that "The Hour (Dooms Day) will not begin until knowledge is taken away"! I think the Hour for the believers has already begun! Otherwise how can anyone suggest to recite some verses from the Quran and then "Blow one's breath with saliva" as an antidote against diseases"? It is prescribed by the Islamic medical science for those who believe in Islamic Monotheism! Does it work? It doesn't matter whether it works or not but believing in it is what matters most for the pious people as this "Belief" is key to their success!

Verse-7&8, Ch-32, states; "HE BEGAN THE CREATION OF MAN FROM CLAY, THEN HE MADE HIS OFFSPRING FROM SEMEN OF DESPISED WATER (MALE AND FEMALE SEXUAL DISCHARGE)". After creating angels from light; devils and Jinn from fire, finally Allah had chosen to create man from "Clay"! Allah did not use the best of materials to create "AHSHRAFUL MUKFLUKAT", the best of his creation! Co-incidentally the believers in traditional faiths also make their deities from clay! In many other verses he claimed to have created man from mud, dust, water etc. Then Allah decided to create Adam's offspring from "Semen of Despised Water" with only one exception! Allah did not want the "Son of Mary", widely believed to be the "Son of God" (Allah denies having fathered him) to be created from "Despised Water"! So, Allah sent Gabriel, disguised as a man to breathe a combination of X+Y chromosome into Mary's garments on his behalf, so as to make Mary conceive Jesus into her womb and deliver the baby in a solitary place far from the meddling crowd!

We, the mankind, as a whole feel offended and disgusted for being born of "Despised Water"! However, Allah also created the "Best" of the humans; his last messenger from that "Despised Water"! If Jesus comes to this world again with a New Quran, (since the Old Quran like Old Testament could not unite mankind) I would humbly request Allah to expunge the word "Despised" from the new version of the Quran. Almost all living creatures including humans are dependent on semen for procreation! Allah, by branding semen as "Despised Water" has not only insulted his own creation, instead he augmented the doubts on his own credibility as the "Creator"! But we cannot deny the fact of immense pleasure that is hidden in the sexual union between the males and females! All living beings resort to this method as it combines procreation with pleasure! Some disobedient creatures pay more attention to pleasure than procreation! Mating as a means of procreation has been a wise decision, otherwise every creature would suffer from boredom multiplying their offspring from clay or mud! The procreation process would have come to a close long ago! Adam and Eve may have been trained and advised in paradise how to make physical relation to produce offspring from "Despised Water! Islamic scholars claim that Allah has implanted his own religion, with which all humans are equipped and Islam is a "Complete Code" of life! Does the word "Life" only means the human life? What surprises us is that how the rest of the living creatures including those of the pre-historic time (dinosaurs and their contemporaries) came to know of this pleasurable procreation process through "Despised Water" having no prophets or messengers appointed with divine verses to educate them? Surely, it is the Nature that implanted in them the process of producing offspring from mating between male and female! Plants and trees do have life, yet they have different methods of multiplying themselves! It is not the so-called "Act of God" rather the "Act of Nature" that takes care of itself through its innate mechanism! In verse 104 of Ch. 21, Allah reiterates his promise saying; "AND (REMEMBER) THE DAY WHEN WE SHALL ROLL UP THE HEAVEN LIKE A SCROLL ROLLED UP FOR BOOKS. AS WE BEGAN THE FIRST CREATION, WE SHALL REPEAT IT. IT IS A PROMISE BINDING UPON US. TRULY, WE SHALL DO IT"! Is it the right way to destroy the heaven? However, if the Lord begins his creation again, we hope he will not create man from "Clay"! We are living this life struggling day and night against tens of thousands of diseases! The "Creator" has created immense number of virus and bacteria that we are not able to deal with! Muhammad, the "Best" of human being had to die suffering from incurable diseases leaving his job undone! His health broke down so quickly because he was not created from the "Best" of materials! All those angels that the Lord appointed for our "Protection" have utterly failed to do their job and those detailed to report to him on a daily basis also failed! They kept "All-Knowing" Allah in the dark!

Verse-13, Ch-32 states; "AND IF WE HAD WILLED, SURELY WE WOULD HAVE GIVEN EVERY PERSON HIS GUIDANCE, BUT THE WORD FROM ME TOOK EFFECT THAT I WILL FILL HELL WITH JINN AND MANKIND TOGETHER"! For what reason Allah has appointed angel for every person? To lead or mislead? Then why did the Lord send so many prophets and messengers with so many scriptures to every nation on earth? It is now obvious that Allah could give "HIS GUIDANCE" to "EVERY PERSON" if he "WILLED" but he refrained from that because of his firm determination to fill the hell with "JINN AND MANKIND"! In Allah's consideration filling hell with Man and Jinn got preference over sending them to paradise for an eternal life! All-Knowing Allah may have sensed in advance that "ONE HUNDRED GRADES OF PARADISE" might not be fully occupied for lack of believers in his monotheism! So, he is fully determined to fill the hell with disbelievers along with Jinn! What seems weird is that the so-called "JINNKIND" and the "MANKIND" are created from two different genetics! One is visible and the other is not! The Jinn are made of "Fire" and men are made from Clay! Can these two co-exist in the hellfire? Will it not be disturbing to All-Merciful Allah to see his creation thrown into fire? This verse reflects nothing but lack of sanity! It is his "Will" that takes precedence over everything else! Dr. AL- JOHANI, an Islamic scholar from Saudi Arabia says; "The essence of Islam, which is the "Willing" submission to the "Will" of God, was revealed to Adam who passed it onto his children"! Adam was first to defy Allah by eating forbidden fruits and then his son became the first murder of the mankind! Present state of the humanity on earths will testify what Adam passed on to his children! Allah "Willed" to create Satan alongside Adam to mislead him! This verse is enough to invalidate all "Revelations" since Adam! If he had willed, surely, Adolf Hitler could let go every Jews free but the words from him took effect that he would fill gas chamber with Jews to implement his "Will"!

Verse-6, Ch-33 states; "THE PROPHET IS CLOSER TO THE BELIEVERS THAN THEIR OWNSELVES AND HIS WIVES ARE THEIR

MOTHERS (AS REGARDS RESPECT AND MARRIAGE). THIS HAS BEEN WRITTEN IN THE ALLAH`S BOOK OF DIVINE DECREE (AL-LAUH AL- MAHFUZ)"! Out of respect a priest is often called a "Father" by the devotees and Adam is also "Father" of the mankind! Any leader who earns freedom for his people is called Father of the nation! So, naturally, Muhammad by virtue of being the best of all messengers, also becomes "Father" of all believers since his wives are also their "Mothers" as ordained by Allah in his "Book of Divine Decree"! What surprises the believers is the fact that their "Father" took too many wives, young and old ranging from seven to seventy! And their first "Mother" was fifteen years older than their "Father"! The believers in Islam must feel themselves lucky to have dozens of "Mothers" besides their own! They may also feel ashamed of dire warning their "Mothers" received from Allah, threatening them with double punishments if they indulge in "Open illegal sexual intercourse" and do no behave themselves well with their husband, the prophet! Probably for this reason Allah has forbidden all believers not to marry Muhammad's widows after his death since marriage between mothers and sons is highly immoral! A Greek tragic play portrayed a royal who had to suffer severe wrath from God for unknowingly marrying his mother! Muhammad was appointed a messenger by Allah and made it clear that he was to act as a "Plain Warner"! Allah says in verse 40 of Ch. 33; "MUHAMMAD IS NOT THE FATHER OF ANY MEN"! Most importantly he claims that no believer is a true Muslim and his worships will not be accepted by Allah unless he believes in his messages and recognizes him as the messenger of Allah! Believing in Allah and believing in Muhammad are both mandatory for the Muslims! Allah warned Muhammad not to transgress his limits! Yet he had chosen to become a Semi-God by being "Closer to the believers than their own selves"!

Verse-30-33, Ch-33, state; "O WIVES OF THE PROPHET! WHOEVER OF YOU COMMITS AN OPEN ILLEGAL SEXUAL INTERCOURSE, THE TORMENT FOR HER WILL BE DOUBLED! WHOEVER OF YOU IS OBEDIENT TO ALLAH AND HIS MESSENGER WILL BE REWARDED TWICE AND WE HAVE PREPARED A NOBLE PROVISION FOR HER IN PARADISE. YOU ARE NOT LIKE ANY OTHER WOMEN AND BE NOT SOFT IN SPEECH LEST ADULTERERS SHOULD BE MOVED WITH EVIL DESIRE, BUT SPEAK IN AN HONORABLE MANNER. AND STAY IN YOUR HOUSES, AND DO NOT DISPLAY YOURSELVES LIKE THAT OF THE TIMES OF IGNORENCE". These verses speak volumes! Each word and sentence demands a careful attention of the readers to grasp the real meanings that are hidden between the lines! Knowing that Muhammad was unable to discipline his wives, Allah felt it necessary to reveal a code of conduct for them! When Allah revealed verses through angel mentioning "AN OPEN ILLIGEL SEXUAL INTERCOURSE", it sure does indicate that something of grave nature has happened or about to happen behind the scene? And as a result he threatened them with double punishments! And also assuring them of double rewards if they remain loyal and obedient to both Allah and Muhammad! Wives of Muhammad did not observe good mannerism while talking to strangers! Allah had to caution them to speak in an honorable manner so that their talking does not arouse evil desire in the hearts of the adulterers! They have been advised to stay indoors! Why on earth Allah issued a decree from his "Divine Book of Decree" proclaiming wives of Muhammad as the "Mothers" of all believers? Did all of them possess a dignified personality? Did all of them possess clean and spotless characters? Allah claims to have put "Mercy and Affection" between husbands and wives so that they live in harmony! Now it is evident from prophet's life, leave alone the rest of the mankind, how harmonious life he lived with his wives! The reason is obvious! Polygamy was one of the root causes of Muhammad's unhappy conjugal life! He took too many wives, young and old, from various backgrounds! Included among his many wives was a divorcee of his slave; an adopted son! Probably his younger wives got more unruly when Muhammad became incapacitated due to multiple diseases! His mental distress too adversely affected his physical fitness to meet the demands of the younger wives! Thanks be to Allah, the "Creator" of the universe, for paying minute attention to his messenger's unfortunate family affairs! The prophet who has utterly failed to manage his own family affairs cannot be expected to bear the burden of being the only messenger for the whole of mankind! The next verse will unfold one of the many situations created with divine blessing from Allah to facilitate Muhammad with more options to marry more woman of his choice! In the situation when Muhammad sank himself into a deep trouble with his acrimonious wives, Allah should have asked him to stop marrying immediately! After the death of his first wife KHADIJA, Muhammad married SAUDA, an old lady of seventy who was almost double his age! The reason given for the marriage is that she was one of the early converts to Islam and her husband died in the hands of the enemies of Islam and she deserved a shelter! Could he not give shelter to that old lady of seventy as his mother os as a sister?

Muhammad married AISHA, the daughter of ABU BAKR, when she was only six or seven! Many of the reasons given for this marriage are: ABU BAKR was the first man to embrace Islam; he accompanied Muhammad on a dangerous journey from Mecca to Medina exposing himself to death; prophet wished to honor him and cement their friendship! Who on earth would believe that the friendship can be cemented by marrying his minor daughter? Even a man of ordinary intellect would not go for such a ridiculous option! Could he not adopt her as his own daughter to provide her with love and security she deserved? Could he be respected as the "Messenger of the whole of Mankind"?

Verse-37, Ch-33 states; "WHEN YOU SAID TO HIM (ZAID, A FREED-SLAVE AND ADOPTED SON OF MUHAMMAD) 'KEEP YOUR WIFE TO YOURSELF, AND FEAR ALLAH' BUT YOU (MUHAMMAD) DID HIDE IN YOURSELF THAT WHICH ALLAH WILL MAKE MANIFEST, YOU DID FEAR THE PEOPLE WHEREAS ALLAH HAD A BETTER RIGHT THAT YOU SHOULD FEAR HIM. SO WHEN ZAID, THE MANUMITTED SLAVE AND ADOPTED SON OF MUHAMMAD HAD ACCOMPLISHED HIS DESIRE FROM HER, WE GAVE HER TO YOU (MUHAMMAD) IN MARRIAGE SO THAT THERE MAY BE NO DIFFICULTY TO THE BELIEVERS IN FUTURE TO MARRY THE WIVES OF THEIR ADOPTED SONS"! This verse is not explicit in narrating the real story behind Muhammad's weakness towards the wife of his adopted son ZAID-BIN-HARITHAH! Muhammad is said to have manumitted him and later adopted him as his son probably for the reason that Muhammad had no son of his own! This wife of ZAID being young and attractive caught attention of Muhammad but fearing criticism from others he kept his desire within himself! All-Knowing Allah came to know the intention of his messenger and accordingly decided to "Give her in Marriage" to Muhammad to "Accomplish" his desire! Circumstances surrounding this embarrassing marital story of Muhammad forced ZAID to divorce his wife! It was done in a way as if Muhammad had nothing to do with it but to obey the order of Allah in order to set an example before the believers; paving the way for them, so that they also can marry wives of their adopted sons in future after divorce! How many people did have adopted sons? And how many of them would have wanted to marry wives of their adopted sons? So, Allah correctly read what is in Muhammad's mind and accordingly sent verses to facilitate his marriage! Leave aside the Prophets, even an ordinary man would not have married his adopted son's wife! What standard of ethics the "MESSENGER TO MANKIND" has set for the mankind? Was he really sent by Allah to bring mankind from darkness into light as is claimed in the "Revelations"?

Verse-50, Ch-33 states; "O PROPHET (MUHAMMAD), WE HAVE MADE LAWFUL TO YOU YOUR WIVES, TO WHOM YOU HAVE PAID THEIR BRIDAL MONEY AND THOSE SLAVES WHOM YOUR RIGHT HAND POSSESSES, AND DAUGHTERS OF YOUR PATERNAL AND MATERNAL UNCLES AND AUNTS WHO MIGRATE WITH YOU AND BELIEVING WOMAN WHO OFFERS HERSELF TO THE PROPHET AND THE PROPHET WISHES TO MARRY HER; A PRIVILEGE FOR YOU ONLY, NOT FOR THE REST OF THE BELIEVERS"! Allah sent Muhammad as the messenger for the entire mankind and now he sends a special marriage privilege applicable only for him! As opposed to Allah's blessings for prophet Muhammad, Buddha, the sponsor of Buddhism, in his Fire Sermon counsels his followers to conceive an aversion for the burning flames of passion and physical attractions to live a holy life! Whereas Merciful Allah has bestowed upon Muhammad more and more options to marry as many as he wants to, without hiding his desires within himself! Did Allah bestow such favors to any of the messengers who came before Muhammad? His first wife Khadija was a wealthy woman, fifteen years older than him and Muhammad came from relatively poor family. We have no idea how much bridal money he paid to that wealthy lady? We also don't know what "Matrimonial Verses" from the Quran were recited during their marriage? Because he "Revelation" of those verses contained in the Quran is said to have began after fifteen years of Muhammad's marriage with Khadija! It may be mentioned here that recital of verses from the Quran is mandatory under Islamic legal system! Was it right for a prophet to have sex with slave-girls whom his "RIGHT HAND POSSESSED" if not motivated by hidden desires? I have no idea what these words "RIGHT HAND" mean in Arabic? Probably it means buying slaves with due payments? This fact also unfolds the prevalent slave-trading, like any other commodity, among the Arabs during the ministry of Muhammad chiefly to use those slave girls as an object of sex! How his subjects would react if a king marries his maid servant while the Queen is still his legal wife? Slave trading was rampant during Prophet Muhammad's rule! Were they not ASHRAFUL MUKHLUKAT? Muhammad was also granted a free hand to marry anyone of his cousins, paternal or maternal, who migrated with him! In addition to that he was also allowed to marry other believing woman "WHO

OFFERS HERSELF TO THE PROPHET"! The most eye-catching part of this verse, which might raise your eye brow, is "A PRIVILEGE FOR YOU (MUHAMMAD) ONLY, NOT FOR THE REST OF THE BELIEVERS! This exclusive privilege granted to prophet Muhammad by Allah may have adversely affected his physical and mental health! Among the women he married ranged from minor girls to elderly women including manumitted slaves with total disregard to their background! The accumulative effects of these indiscriminate marriages deteriorated his health to the extent that after suffering from lingering diseases he died a premature death at 63! Revealing a code of conduct by Allah to Muhammad, to regulate his sexual life with his multiple wives in verse 51 of chapter 33, did not have desired effect as Muhammad's death could not be delayed by divine decree! Dr. M.H. DURRANI, an Islamic scholar from Pakistan says; "So we find that the prophet showed by his marriages that in normal circumstances, the Muslims should live with one wife, but may take more than one in particular circumstances arising out of inopportune conditions provided they do justice"! Islamic scholars around the Muslim world turn a blind eye to the facts about Muhammad's life! Did Allah advise him to stay with one wife? Rather Allah revealed many verses giving a free choice to Muhammad to marry as many as he wanted and he was the only person to have received that exclusive privilege! Mr. DURRANI has gone as far as calling Muhammad a "God-like Character" saying, "This is the Character of God, yet he was a human being"!

Verse-51, Ch-33 states; "YOU (O MUHAMMAD) CAN POSTPONE THE TURN OF WHOM YOU WILL OF YOUR WIVES, AND YOU MAY RECEIVE WHOM YOU WILL. AND WHOMSOEVER YOU DESIRE OF THOSE WHOM YOU HAVE SET ASIDE HER TURN TEMPORARILY, IT IS NO SIN ON YOU TO RECEIVE HER AGAIN; THAT IS BETTER THAT THEY MAY BE COMFORTED AND NOT GRIEVED, AND MAY ALL BE PLEASED WITH WHAT YOU GIVE THEM. ALLAH KNOWS WHAT IS IN YOUR HEARTS"! This verse has vividly indicated the in-most facts about prophet Muhammad's conjugal life that led to consistent brawling between him and his wives! Allah issues more advice and instructions to Muhammad saying that he has the right to reject or chose any one of his wives to keep company with him in a manner so that others are not grieved! In plain language Allah has passed his instructions to his messenger with plenty of options to choose from! Allah even had to advise his "Messenger for Mankind" how and when to postpone and resume "Turn" of his wives!

He, as the only husband of a group of wives, has the absolute right to select one from amongst them with whom he wants to sleep! As for others whose turns have been postponed should be comforted! The bitter rivalry between wives to receive romantic attention from husband is not unusual in a polygamous family! Jealousy among wives gets more and more ugly if the age-gap is abnormally wider between husband and wives! By giving him free choice to marry as many as he wanted, Allah put Muhammad in a difficult situation that he ultimately failed to fulfill: His mission to implement Islamic monotheism over whole of mankind! I quote DR. M.H. DURRANI again, who says; "It is said that Christ changed water into wine, but he could not change the nature of his disciples into what he desired them to be"! What about Muhammad? Could he change the nature of his followers? It seemed that Muhammad had an insatiable urge for marriage and that forced Allah to caution Muhammad by revealing another verse (52 of Ch. 33) to avoid marrying other women even if their beauty charms him!

Verse-52, Surah-33, states; "IT IS NOT LAWFUL FOR YOU (MUHAMMAD) TO MARRY OTHER WOMEN AFTER THIS, NOR TO CHANGE THEM FOR OTHER WIVES EVEN THOUGH THEIR BEAUTY ATTRACTS YOU, EXCEPT THOSE SLAVES WHOM YOUR RIGHT HAND POSSESSES"! Allah has granted enough leverage to Muhammad about his desire to marry women of different age whose beauty attracted him! Allah wants him to put an end to it but yet allows him to go for those slaves that his "Right Hand" possessed! And also in the verse next to this, Allah warns believers, who frequented Prophet's house for various purposes, not to annoy him since he did not like their manner of talking, attitude when they talked to his wives! May be some of those loyal visitors had ill intentions for which Allah says; "IT IS NOT RIGHT FOR YOU THAT YOU SHOULD EVER ANNOY ALLAH'S MESSENGER, NOR THAT YOU SHOULD EVER MARRY HIS WIVES AFTER HIS DEATH" (Verse 53, Ch. 33)! Allah allowed Muhammad to marry divorced wife of his adopted son and his first wife, Khadija, was also a divorcee! He even married a widowed lady of seventy! Why then Allah asks others not to marry Muhammad's wives after his death? Is this a fair judgment to deprive young widows who might still feel sexual needs? Have they not been deceived of their rights to raise a family of their own in this life since Muhammad failed to give them one because of his health conditions? In a previous verse Allah promised to give "Double Rewards" to prophet's wives in paradise who would stay loyal to him! If they marry again after his death, they might risk losing that offer of "Double Rewards"! From these verses what we get is a bleak picture of prophet's problematic marital life which had gone bad to worse with the passage of time! These physical and mental constraints led to serious illnesses that he had to suffer before his death! He left the "Revelations" in disarray, scattered, unedited and his mission undone! He had to spend more time as "Manager" of the ladies in his Harem than as a "Messenger" for the mankind! I cannot conceive of a notion that an all-knowing "Creator" would ever appoint a "Messenger" to implement his monotheism over mankind who has been totally entangled in a long family feud that remained unresolved till his death! The Creator Lord upon whose advice he acted could neither cure his diseases nor could he extend his life-span though he is "Expanding" the universe relentlessly! Due to this expansion of the universe, I don't know why, the image of the "Creator" is getting smaller and smaller as the universe is getting bigger and bigger! On one hand the scientists are unfolding complex composition of the universe and on the other hand, the divine verses losing their relevance to the reality! A large number of people still think that a compromise may be reached between humanity and the divinity through a workable understanding! Now it seems that divine deities show no flexibility to accommodate realities of the changing world! Do they still hope to put the clock back? Many of the champions of the Churches have abandoned the path of God and are being misled by Satan to engage in immoral activities pertaining to tens of thousands of sex abuses involving minors! The papal regime meted out insult and injustices to the pioneer scientists like Copernicus and Galileo! But the time is not far away when all religious institutions will crumble to their dooms because of their unholy practices and disrespect for the scientific discovery and inventions! There are people who still believe that a star may be used as missile to hit the devils on earth and think they are on the right path to paradise and the rest must get set for a life in the inferno! But for God's sake do not raise a question against them! All believers and faithful are spiritual brothers as they are inter-related by a network of dogmas and have a common goal to reach the City of God! Muhammad said; "BOTH IN THIS WORLD AND IN THE HEREAFTER, I AM THE NEAREST OF ALL THE PEOPLE TO JESUS. THE PROPHETS ARE PATERNAL BROTHERS" (BUKHARI, VOL. 4, #652)!

Verse-1, Ch-35 "ALL THE PRAISES AND THANKS BE TO ALLAH, THE ONLY ORIGINATOR AND THE ONLY CREATOR OF THE HEAVENS

AND THE EARTH WHO MADE THE ANGELS MESSENGERS WITH WINGS, TWO OR THREE OR FOUR. HE INCREASES IN CREATION WHAT HE WILLS. VERILY, ALLAH IS ABLE TO DO ALL THINGS"! So, the angels are not flightless creatures? Allah created them from "Light"! They should be able to travel at the speed of light! Why do they need wings? We, the mankind, are deprived by Allah of the vision to see the angels! In fact believing in the unseen has been the greatest hurdle in believing in the Allah himself! Allah uses angels as messengers for communications between the heavens and the earth! Our forefathers also used pigeons with only two wings to send messages from one place to another! Since Allah increases in creation, he made angels with "Two, Three or Four" wings probably to increase their endurance as they had to travel between the Earth and the Heavens millions of times! Archangel Gabriel alone had to make thousands of journeys back and forth in twenty three years to deliver the "Revelations" from Allah to Muhammad! Millions of years ago the Dinosaurs with huge body had only two wings to fly! Even smaller birds are able to fly from Siberia to Australia and back with only two wings! If Allah wants he can equip his angels even with three wings though he has not created any bird with three wings! Allah's theory of the aerodynamics differs substantially from that of humans! Allah claimed that he created angels from "Light"! Does anything made of light need wings to fly? Photons, the particles of light, are practically weightless and can travel at the speed of 300 million meters per second! Why the "BORAKH", a donkey-like animal was used to carry Muhammad to space? To make the story more credible, Gabriel, the most prominent angel messenger Allah has ever made, should have been fitted with three or four wings to fly Muhammad to meet with Allah at his palace over Seven Heavens since Allah is able to do all things!

Verse-41, Ch-35 States; "VERILY! ALLAH GRASP THE HEAVEN AND THE EARTH LEST THEY SHOULD MOVE AWAY FROM THEIR PLACES, AND IF THEY WERE TO MOVE AWAY FROM THEIR PLACES, THERE IS NOT ONE THAT COULD GRASP THEM AFTER HIM"! Allah needs to "GRASP THE HEAVEN AND THE EARTH" since he did not raise them on pillars! Are they not tied together? May be or may be not! Who has the answer to that metaphysical question: "Of what supreme almighty power; Is the great arm, which spans the east and west; And tacks the center to the sphere"? If the earth and the heaven move away from each other, will they go out of his control? Will it be very difficult for Allah to bring them back?

Nay, Allah is able to do all things at his "Will"! Either the Lord has lost his grip on the universe or Edwin Hubble lost his faith in God and did prove that the universe is expanding at an unstoppable acceleration! The little boy having fun with his balloon, suddenly lost his grip and looking helplessly at the balloon disappearing out of his sight! The child understands that pulling the string would not bring his balloon back to him! Our "Creator" is now in a similar situation looking helplessly at the expanding universe going passed the "Lot Tree"! Yet he hopes to roll all the heavens up with his "Right Hand"! Why the earth should move away despite being affixed with millions of mountains by Allah on its surface? They would not have moved away if Allah had affixed them on pillars! What Hubble said does not support Allah's claim! We have no knowledge on which Galaxy Allah made his abode over Seven Heavens but certainly we know for sure that it is going away from our Milky way to a point of no return until and unless "Big Crunch" happens! This expansion seems relentless as "THERE IS NOT ONE THAT COULD GRASP THEM AFTER HIM"! Also Allah seems unaware of any other planets inside or outside the solar system! His focus is concentrated only on the planet Earth! Probably his chief interest is all about us; to turn his best of creation into a monotheistic mankind! The "Creator Allah" has not talked about the existence of any planet in the Quran with or without living creatures! So, we are the first and we are the last! This is a disheartening news for those scientists who are busy looking for extra-terrestrial creatures in space! The "Creator" has wasted his time and energy creating such a huge universe only for the offspring of Adam! A Hadith (AL-BUKHARI, Vol. 6, #336), quoting Allah's messenger, states; "ON THE DAY OF RESURRECTION, ALLAH WILL GRASP THE WHOLE PLANET OF EARTH BY HIS HAND AND ROLL ALL THE HEAVENS UP WITH HIS RIGHT HAND AND THEN HE WILL SAY, I AM THE KING, WHERE ARE THE KINGS OF THE EARTH? The contents of the above verse and the Hadith do not supplement each other! The word "GRASP" in the verse expresses a present indefinite action and the same word in the Hadith indicates an action in future? Why Allah needs to grasp the earth and the heaven on the Day of resurrection again as they are already in his grasp? If an Arab Islamic scholar is asked to explain the meaning of the word "GRASP", he would definitely say that the word has a wealth of meaning in Arabic language and would explain its meaning in a manner so as to insist that Allah's science is far beyond human knowledge! Allah wants to be the "King" on the Day of Resurrection after he "ROLLS ALL

THE HEAVENS UP WITH HIS RIGHT HAND"! We come across another confusion when the verse says; "ALLAH WILL GRASP THE WHOLE PLANET OF EARTH BY HIS HAND"! Does the word "HAND" stands for his "LEFT HAND" since his "RIGHT HAND" will remain engaged holding the Heavens! So far the All-Mighty Allah was boasting himself of being the "Creator" of the heavens and the earth! Then who holds a superior position in terms of divine protocol; the "King" or the "Creator"? And after declaring himself a "King", Allah would inquire, "WHERE ARE THE KINGS OF THE EARTH? May Allah be kind enough to ask "WHERE ARE THE PROPHETS? As all of them, like the Kings, failed to live up to their tasks! To give a little account of their failures, I may begin with Adam, the first prophet: He committed the gravest "Sin" in collaboration with Satan in paradise and then he failed to prevent the murder of his first son by the second! Noah failed to take his disobedient son aboard the great "Boat" he made under direct supervision of Allah! Prophet Lot had led a people who were all sodomites! They refused to listen to their prophet who advised them to take the women instead of men! Ordered by Allah in a "Dream", Prophet Abraham displayed ultimate cruelty by deciding to slaughter his minor boy to show his love for his Lord! Mosses failed to prevent the Jews from crucifying Jesus! Arguably Jesus fled to his father in heaven leaving Crusaders fighting against the Muslims! And Muhammad, the so-called last prophet set examples of multiple failures: Child marriage, patronizing slavery and slave sex, marrying wife of his adopted son, practicing polygamy, failing to persuade his own uncle into believing in Islam, leaving the revealed verses scattered all over the places in different hands and last but not the least he left this world saying his followers would be divided into 73 sects! Yet he is said have come for the whole of mankind! Does prophet Muhammad deserve all the privileges and pleasures Allah promised to give him in paradise? A story-teller must be smart enough to hide the truth or he got to be honest to tell the truth! Why Allah is not able to "Grasp" all galaxies in their original places? Why are they moving away from each other? Allah claims that none but "HIM" who can keep them together in their places? If the galaxy (Milky Way) is moving, can the earth stay at its position on the Space-Time? Is there any Muslim scientist who can prove otherwise with the help of Islamic Science? Out of millions of trillions of celestial objects, the Lord, from day one, has been paying too much attention on the Earth only, why? Because the Lord himself is not aware of any other planet harboring life in it! Excessive focus on our planet alone by all kinds of celestial entities has led a group of intellectuals to believe in the so-called "Anthropic Principle" as if the Earth is the only place in the universe "Created" as a testing ground for humans to qualify for an amusing eternal life in paradise!

Verse-38, Ch-36 states; "AND THE SUN RUNS ON ITS FIXED COURSE FOR A TERM APPOINTED. THAT IS THE DECREE OF THE ALL-MIGHTY, THE ALL KNOWING". It has been established by the renowned scientists of modern civilization across the world, that the SUN takes hundreds of millions of years to go round the center of gravity of the Galaxy it belongs to! The galaxy itself is drifting along the vast Space-Time with the expanding universe! Light takes one hundred thousand years to travel across a medium size galaxy from one end to the other! There is no mention of any "Galaxies" in the entire texts of the Quran! How Allah has fixed the course of the sun for a term appointed? If he means that the "Sun" is running its course around the earth for a term appointed, then we have nothing to say about the "Science of the Quran"! Surprisingly, Allah always talks about only one "Sun" as he seems to have created just one for this universe! Since his believers need just one, as four out of five obligatory prayers are closely linked to different stages of the sun during the day! Did Allah, the creator, mention anywhere in the Quran when the solar system came into being? When did Allah sent Adam on Earth? Why did he take so long to reveal his verses? What he claimed over and over again that he took only "Six Days" to create the earth and the heavens and then he rose over to Seven Heavens on his "Throne" that was floating on water before! Is this a credible "Decree" from the so-called "Creator" that he "FIXED THE COURSE FOR THE SUN TO RUN FOR AN APPOINTED TERM" around the Earth? Allah believes that the sun "Rises" in the east and "Sets" in the west! Allah will make the "Sun" rise in west on the Dooms Day while the "Earth" and the "Heaven" will be held on his "Both Hands"! Allah also claims he has made the Sun as a "Lamp", though it serves as the source of energy for the entire living creatures of this earth! In Allah's vocabulary the "Sun" is a lamp and the stars are "Missiles"! My grandma still believes that the stars have been created by Allah as flowers to decorate the sky!

Verse-39, Ch-36 says; "AND THE MOON, WE HAVE MEASURED FOR IT MANSIONS TO TRAVERSE TILL IT RETURNS LIKE THE OLD DRIED CURVED DATE STALK". Allah has "Measured" for the moon "Mansions to Traverse" for reckoning of the days and months for the entire mankind! Allah also allowed Muhammad to "Split" the moon to show his charisma! Is it created for "Reckoning" only? The "Creator" knows not that the moon has far-reaching impact on time and tide! From Lord's point of view the moon has even more important role to play for the believers to perform Islamic rituals like Ramadan, Hajj etc. depending on the different "Mansions" of the moon! Though the moon plays an indispensable role in the life of his believers yet Allah made the "Moon Giving Light" dependent on the sun forever! Those eligible to enter paradise shall also shine like the "FULL-BLOWN-MOON"! However, affluent royals living in the luxurious mansion need not worry since the celebration of honeymoon is not linked to the journey of the moon around the planet earth! The beginning and the ending of Ramadan happens when the moon returns like "THE OLD DRIED DATE STALK"! Sometimes the Lord makes the full-blown moon look like the "Holy Grail" and then he reduces it to look like a "Dried Date Stalk"! What a dull and dry simile of the moon from its creator! Though the poets are not prophets, yet they would be the ones to be disheartened by this resemblance! But as a reckoner, the moon is much less accurate than the Atomic Clock in terms of precision made by humans to run their affairs! Why Allah has chosen "DATE STALKE" as an example? Because "DATE" was one of the most familiar staple foods in the desert where the "Revelations" took place! Often Allah's thinking reflects much of the Arabian life and culture that flourished in and around the desert! He created lots of rivers in paradise in order to avoid scarcity of water the believers had gone through in the holy land! Allah looks neither "Global" nor "Universal" in handling the affairs of the earth! He bears an Arabian trait!

Verse-40, Ch-36, says; "IT IS NOT FOR THE SUN TO OVERTAKE THE MOON, NOR DOES THE NIGHT OUTSTRIP THE DAY. THEY ALL FLOAT, EACH IN AN ORBIT"! Whatever we have learned from Galileo, Einstein, Hawking and others must be thrown into hellfire and begin reading the science of Quran to gather new knowledge about divine miracles! Race between the "Sun" and the "Moon" is not only ridiculous but a childish proposition that they would either "OVERTAKE" or "OUTSTRIP" one another! Anybody whose thinking is limited to circling of the sun and moon around the earth that resembles Ptolemy's cosmological model of the second century A.D. may have conceived the idea of a race between the sun and the moon! Probably the mass of the sun would be thousands of millions of times more than that of the moon! Though these two are heavenly bodies, yet a race between a nuclear furnace and a cold satellite is beyond imagination considering their huge differences in terms of mass, distance and speed! The moon makes one revolution on its orbit around the Earth in about thirty days and the sun takes millions of years to go round the center of gravity of the Galaxy! If we make a comparison between the two orbits of the moon and the sun, it would be easier to identify who could say; "IT IS NOT FOR THE SUN TO OVERTAKE THE MOON"! This misconception may have been originated out of ignorance about Solar and Lunar eclipses! The night will never outstrip the day as they are two sides of the same coin! Do "THEY ALL FLOAT, EACH IN AN ORBIT"? The "Author" who scripted these verses had absolutely no knowledge how the night and the day occur on this planet! Misconception about astrophysics has led mankind into believing metaphysics; a world of emotions undermining reasons and reality! "THE WHOLE OF CREATION SHAKES OFF NIGHT; AND FOR THY SHADOW LOOKS, THE LIGHT" says, Vaughan; the metaphysical poet! And Allah says; "SHADOWS ALSO FALL IN PROSTRATION UNTO HIM" (V. 15, Ch. 13)!

Verse-41-49, Ch-37 state: "FOR THEM (BELIEVERS) THERE WILL BE A KNOWN PROVISION IN PARADISE, FRUITS; AND THEY SHALL BE HONOURED IN THE GARDEN OF DELIGHT FACING ONE ANOTHER ON THE THRONES. ROUND THEM WILL BE PASSED A CUP OF PURE WINE—WHITE, DELICIOUS TO THE DRINKERS. NETHER WILL THEY HAVE ANY DISEASE FROM THAT, NOR WILL THEY SUFFER INTOXICATION THEREFROM. AND BESIDE THEM WILL BE CHASTE FEMALE (WIVES) RESTRAINING THEIR GLANCES DESIRING NONE EXCEPT THEIR HUSBANDS WITH WIDE AND BEAUTIFUL EYES, DELICATE AND PURE AS IF THEY WERE HIDDEN EGGS WELL PRESERVED!" This verse, like a well- scripted episode of a romantic play, describes aromatic life in paradise resonating nightclub luxuries on earth! Every male dreams of a life as the one exactly highlighted in the verse above! Who can resist the temptations and the promises of such a pompous life overflowing with entertainments? Astonishingly enough, all ingredients of a lavish life in paradise mentioned in the above verses are widely available on this earth! Wealthy men and women including the Kings and the Queens lead a life in this world, not less pompous than the one Allah offers to the believers in paradise! However, the big difference between the two is that one is short-lived and the other is eternal! If each of the male believers enjoys company of "Chaste Wives" in paradise, the female believers, to be fair, should also be provided with "Chaste Husbands" of similar attributes! Allah has used extra ordinary words and phrases defining the beauty of these "CHASTE FEMALE"! These Wives "WITH WIDE BEAUTIFUL EYES, HIDDEN LIKE WELL-PRESERVED EGGS" will desire none except their husbands! Is there room for evils in paradise? Why not? Satan did the worst mischief of his life by misleading Adam and Eve in paradise in the presence of the "All-Knowing" Allah! He is witness to what Satan did to the "Parents" of mankind! It is now apparent that the creator Allah "Created" this universe only to implement Islamic Shariah Law in this planet!

Verse-102, Ch-37 says; "WHEN HIS SON WAS OLD ENOUGH TO WALK WITH HIM (ABRAHAM), HE SAID; O MY SON! I HAVE SEEN IN A DREAM THAT I AM SLAUGHTERING YOU (OFFERING YOU IN SACRIFICE TO ALLAH), SO LOOK WHAT YOU THINK! HE SAID, O MY FATHER! DO THAT WHICH YOU ARE COMMANDED, YOU WILL FIND ME PATIENT"! Though an animal calf is able to walk with its mother just after birth, but a human baby takes about two years to be "OLD ENOUGH TO WALK" with his father! For argument's sake the age may be increased to eight or nine, yet that age is not enough for a boy to understand the horrors of killing and the significance of a divine sacrifice that came in a dream from the one and only merciful Allah! Because Allah wants to take boy's life through "Slaughtering" to test his father's love for him! In religious arena everything is possible and age is not a factor here! We may recollect the Quranic version of the story about Jesus; while still in his cradle he began to talk and proclaimed himself a prophet bestowed with a scripture! In ancient times before the dawn of civilization primitive people used to sacrifice humans, especially the young children, to please their blood-thirsty Gods! Similarly Allah tested Prophet Abraham for his love and loyalty toward him in that cruel, primitive method! However at the last moment Allah decided to stop Abraham from slaughtering his minor boy! Pre-historic evidences suggest that the Gods of the ancients also preferred young boys or girls for their appeasement. It is unusually astonishing that a minor would respond to such a barbaric proposition from his own father to kill him in the name of Allah? Was the boy matured enough to understand the rewards and horrors of such sacrifice? However, we cannot forget the unexpected that happened when Allah made baby Jesus spoke from his cradle to say that his mother was not guilty of adultery! However, he did not claim himself to be a "Crown Prince" of Allah's "Kingdom" though his disciples call him a "Son of God"! Science has totally rejected the dream as a reflection of reality of life! Does Islam have any means to take dreams for granted? Did Allah himself come down to earth from heavens to stop the slaughter at the last moment? Allah claims that he has sent messages to all Prophets through angels! If so, what was the problem that this time Allah resorted to dreams to apprise Abraham of his desire? Allah might have felt awkward to deliver this pathetic message directly through an angel to a father to kill his dearest son! So, Allah, the All-Merciful does have sympathy! Muslims across the world take this "Dream" as a "Decree" from Allah! Accordingly they are obliged to perform Hajj and celebrate EID-UL–AZHA by sacrificing animals instead of their sons! One question naturally creeps up into mind why this "Dream" was shown to prophet Abraham long before the "Revelations"? By all consideration, Muhammad should have been shown the "Dream" since he was the only messenger entrusted with the task of implementing Islamic monotheism on mankind! Did Muhammad have a boy of his own to sacrifice? Nope! He was so unfortunate that despite having so many wives, Allah did not bless him with a son and Muhammad died with this misery in his life! This was the cause that prevented him to nominate a heir to his dynasty and resulted in the worst religious divide between his followers into Shia and Sunny! Leaving all questions aside, "The Pilgrim's Progress goes on, carrying a burden of sins and terrified by the Day of Judgment reaches the "City of God" for salvation! The salvation is not that easy to come by! Pilgrims have to make several rounds around the "KHABA" wearing white robes! Arab Pagans used to do in naked states! Another important aspect of this salvation process is to throw stones at the monument of "Satan" and during the process many pilgrims lay their lives due to stampede! Do the pilgrims try to kill Satan by stoning him to death? No Way! Allah has granted respite to Satan until the "Day"! Believers will have to believe that a boy, barely old enough to walk, can say to his father; "DO THAT WHICH YOU ARE COMMANDED" by Allah?

Verse-3, Ch-38 says; "HOW MANY A GENERATION HAVE WE DESTROYED BEFORE THEM! AND THEY CRIED OUT WHEN THERE WAS NO LONGER TIME FOR ESCAPE". There is indeed no escape for any creature on earth save the few prophets who are currently living at different heavens of the Seven Heavens! The "Creator" is more efficient in destruction than creation! Every creation is destined to destruction after an appointed term except the "Creator" himself! In the preceding verse of the same chapter, Allah states; "NAY, THOSE WHO DISBELIEVE ARE IN FALSE PRIDE AND OPPOSITION"! In this verse Allah has issued a dire warning to his opposition saying, he destroyed "MANY A GENERATION" before them! Destruction of generations after generations manifests neither pride nor prudence except arrogance! It is rather a flat confession of failures to execute faiths despite sending thousands of prophets and messengers since the expulsion of Adam and Eve from paradise! Opposing the above claim can we not say that after the transformation of man from apes, the humans have continued to survive generation after generation till today? It is the Dinosaurs, not human being that faced the complete destruction on earth! Destruction seems to be the easiest option with Allah as is the killing with the Jihadists! This verse is a clear indication that no civilizations in the past had accepted Allah's invitation to join his religion! And Allah, the Lord of the heavens proudly says; " THEY CRIED OUT WHEN THERE WAS NO LONGER TIME FOR ESCAPE"! Despite crying out for help, Jesus could not escape crucifixion as help did not come from any direction, right or left, up and down! None could help Adam from being misled by Satan! When millions of Jews cried out for help to escape Hitler's annihilation, no help came from the heaven! Allah had a valid reason to stay away, since the Jews are his arc enemies! The world has witnessed lots of massacres in the name of Allah and many more yet to come until Resurrection? Allah seems more focused on revenge! Take it or leave it, Allah thinks whatever "Good" things happen to humans come from him and for the "Bad" things, he lays the blame on man and Satan! But Allah did help his dearest friend Muhammad when his conjugal life was falling apart and, for some mysterious reason, he refrained from helping him during his prolong sufferings due to illness! Allah eventually bestowed "Death" upon him much ahead of his other contemporaries though it was easier for the Lord to raise him to heaven alive! It is said that his body was cut open and washed with Holy water of ZAMZAM before his journey to Seven heavens, yet he suffered from diseases for so long! A short comparative study about Allah's narratives regarding Jesus and Muhammad will reveal some striking facts how he dealt with both of them; Jesus was created in Mary's womb through Gabriel and soon after delivery he was made to speak for himself! Allah claims to have raised him to heaven before Crucifixion and promised to send him again to this earth to accomplish the mission that Muhammad left in disarray! So, Jesus is going to have a second life on earth and probably will never face death or destruction! On the other hand Muhammad was born and raised in a poor family! Orphaned and was made to live on other's mercy! Baby Muhammad was even deprived of his mother's milk! He had to marry a wealthy widow, fifteen years older than him for financial support! Fought wars to establish Islam amidst lots of harassment and eventually died a premature death! Despite being promised the best place in paradise, he was not bestowed a peaceful conjugal life on earth! So, Muhammad, the last and the best of messengers could neither escape hardship of this life nor the inevitable end; the death! He might have cried out "WHEN THERE WAS NO TIME FOR ESCAPE"! The "Time-Creator" has set the term of death for all living creatures save a few prophets! Allah destroyed many generations before, yet the mankind continued to grow without pause since the days they evolved out of four-footed apes into twin-legged homo-sapiens! Every generation of man is smarter than its predecessor!

Verses-18&19, Ch-38 state; "VERILY, WE MADE THE MOUNTAINS TO GLORIFY OUR PRAISES WITH DAVID AFTER THE MID-DAY TILL SUNSET AND AFTER THE SUNRISE TILL MID-DAY". SO DID THE BIRDS ASSEMBLED: ALL OBEDIENT TO HIM AND GLORIFIED ALLAH'S PRAISES ALONG WITH HIM"! In some previous verses Allah affirmed that he affixed mountains on the earth to stop it from shaking! He burnt a mountain to ashes when he descended on it for a direct conversation with Mosses! Revelation also began in a cave inside a mountain! Then he used mountains to crush upon the sinners to punish them! Luckily or unluckily, those who escaped the crush were transformed into pigs and monkeys and they will remain as such until the resurrection! Now Allah has given the mountains an additional task, i.e. to glorify his praises with prophet David from sunrise to sunset! Good thinking; David and the mountains have been relieved of nightly glorifications! Do the mountains have life? Do they listen to Allah? Now mountains have been made to maintain a bond with the prophet in glorifying their "CREATOR"? How did David feel about it, honored or offended? If asked, the defenders of Islam would go out of their way to defend Allah, Muhammad and the Quran against everything they say or do! "Allah never does a thing wrong" is a preconception that leads them to make controversial conclusions! When they fail to explain something or answer any question, they leave it to the "Unseen"! Why do the birds have to glorify Allah along with Prophet David? Do they stand a chance to lead another life hereafter in the Hell or Heaven? You be a prophet, a mountain or a bird; your vocation must be to a life of prayers, meditation and glorifications! Paraphrasing of these verses has been done with total disregard to commonsense and it unfolded his incompetence as an "Author" whoever he may be! To be a good Muslim and a believer in Islam, you have no other options but to do as "DID THE BIRDS ASSEMBLED" and accept everything unquestionably as the "Truth, nothing but the truth"!

Verse-27, Ch-38, states; "AND WE CREATED NOT THE HEAVENS AND THE EARTH AND ALL THAT IS BETWEEN THEM WITHOUT PURPOSE! THAT IS THE CONSIDERATION OF THOSE WHO DISBELIEVE! THEN WOE TO THOSE WHO DISBELIEVE (IN ISLAMIC MONOTHEISM) FROM THE FIRE"! There is a definite "PURPOSE" behind every creation and that is a clear message from the creator stated in his "Clear Book"! Billions of years have elapsed since the "Big Bang", yet the humans have not been able to find the "Purpose" behind the creation of such a huge universe for a small mankind to live a life with innate religion of Islamic monotheism! Obviously every creator, human or divine, gets a kind of satisfaction and a glory for achievement which gets amplified if done with a noble purpose. The Lord created Satan to mislead Adam in heaven and his offspring on earth! As opposed to darker side, creation of Satan also has a brighter purpose! If Satan did not mislead our "Father", the "Fall of Man" would not have happened and we would not been here on earth; the Pandemonium! John Milton found temptation as an eternal conflict between good and evil in his "Paradise Lost"! Subsequently he presented foiling of temptation as the cause of man's restoration in the "Paradise Regained"! So, invisible Allah has created everything, including invisible viruses, with a definite "Purpose" for the benefit of his outstanding creation; the "ASHRAFUL MUKHLUKAT"! Among the insects, what purpose do the mosquitoes serve for humanity? Do they inject divine "Messages" to the mankind? Verse 26 of the chapter 2 states; "ALLAH IS NOT ASHAMED TO SET FORTH A PARABLE EVEN OF A MOSQUITO OR SO MUCH MORE WHEN IT IS BIGGER OR SMALLER THAN IT" to teach a lesson to the ingrate disbelievers! But the mosquitoes going against divine decree adapt secular policy and bite believers and disbelievers alike! And for what "Purpose" he created dinosaurs on earth has not been mentioned in the noble Quran! May be it is in the "AL-LAUH-AL-MAHFUZ"; the "BOOK OF DECREE" held with Allah himself over Seven Heavens! Could we not lead an Islamic life on earth without mosquitoes? These visible mosquitoes in collaboration with the invisible viruses, wage war one after another against humanity to sabotage Allah's plan to implement Islamic monotheism! But one thing to be noted that these enemies to the mankind, like all other creations, believe in secularism unlike Allah! He doesn't want his believers to be secular! The Lord as the one and only "WALI" (protector) of the universe could not protect holy places of Islam from virus attack! His own house, the KABAH is no exception! Allah said he had destroyed many generations before for not believing in him and his messengers! The devils, also created by Allah, are to blame for this as they misled those generations into destruction! Is this not a paradox? Despite sending prophets for every nation, Allah had to take the ultimate decision to destroy those nations? Besides deadly diseases, all calamities created by the creator are also causing destruction of mankind! When a vaccine is found for a virus, a new variant surfaces with new strategy to reinforce the attack on humans! Who creates them and for what "Purpose"? If the trend goes on, Jesus on his second coming may find Allah's "KINGDOM" turned into a barren land, as he intended, devoid of mankind long before the Day of Resurrection! All pandemics are secular in nature and have no connection with divinity! Like the "Creator" they also have one "Purpose": Destroy generation after generation! Yet we are sanguine of a victory over virus! Allah says he has not only created the Earth and the Heaven but "ALL THAT IS BETWEEN THEM"! There are trillions of galaxies and other celestial bodies in the vast space in between the earth and the heaven! We the disbelievers are completely in the dark about the "Purpose" of those creation! Are those essential to implement Islamic monotheism? We, the disbelievers are still not convinced for what "Purpose" the "Creator Allah" created "THE HEAVEN AND THE EARTH AND ALL THAT IS BETWEEN THEM"! If it is only for the "Purpose" of implementing "ISLAM", then the Quran is obviously not telling the whole truth!

Verse-75, Ch-38 says; "O IBLIS (SATAN)! WHAT PREVENTS YOU FROM PROSTRATING YOURSELF TO ONE (ADAM) WHOM I HAVE CREATED WITH BOTH MY HANDS." What happened in paradise between Allah and Satan is narrated at the later chapter of the Quran! Ok, better late than never! Probably Allah did not use his two hands while creating Satan! His answer to his creator was both logical and straight forward! Satan being made of "Fire" felt it demeaning for himself to prostrate to "One" made of "CLAY"! Moreover he has been granted to live a life until resurrection that no prophet or messenger was given! I have quoted this verse to stress on the words "Both My Hands" which definitely indicate Allah has two hands like the human being! Allah also claimed to have created Adam in his own "Image"! He "Grasps" the earth and the heavens by his "Both Hands" so that they don't move away from their places! These two "Hands" of Allah will also be used on the Day of Resurrection to hold the Earth on one hand and the Heavens on the other! Allah could have more "Hands" for himself like he increases the "Wings" of the angels (two, three or four) as and when he feels necessary! We may recall Darwin as it was he who said the humans evolved from four-legged monkeys! Gradually, through a lengthy process of evolution, two of the four legs changed into two hands! But Allah has never claimed to have "Two legs" since he did not have to go through that process of evolution as he emerged out of nothing with "Two Hands"! But we may again recall the "Fact" that Allah created Adam in his own "Image" who sure did have two legs! Religious facts and fictions got more and more "Crooked" by the God-loving intellectual interventionists! Who can "Straighten" them who believe that a "Lot-Tree" demarcates the outermost boundary of the universe? The soul of mankind is drifting with the space-time in an uncharted territory that has no boundary condition inside or outside the universe! Every believer is obliged to prostrate to none but Allah! Why Satan was asked to prostrate to Adam?

Verse-4, Surah-39 states; "HAD ALLAH WILLED TO TAKE A SON (OFFSPRING), HE COULD HAVE CHOSEN WHOM HE WILLED OUT OF THOSE WHOM HE CREATED"! Allah, the "Father of Heaven" does not consider human beings as his "Offspring"! Allah being himself the "Creator", could have as many "Wives" as he wanted in order to take offspring of his own choosing! Did Allah mean to have offspring without getting married? Nay, he has chosen to stay single and flatly denied having fathered Jesus! He took an exceptional step to have a son-like prophet by Mary in order to level him as "Son of Mary"! Allah as the "Creator" does not like to be leveled with fatherhood and own a son since he is not willing to hand his "Kingdom" over to any successor! Adam was created as a "Single" man and later on, the Lord took the decision to create Eve from Adam in order to give him a wife to free him from loneliness! Probably Satan plotted to oust them from paradise out of jealousy as he was not allowed to have a wife of his own and he succeeded in making them "Fall" from paradise to the "Pandemonium" where they began raising a family of mankind! What about prophet Muhammad? Did he not wish to have a son? Probably not! He being the "Last" messenger, did not want an inheritor! If Allah had blessed Muhammad with a son to succeed him, probably many of the sectarian problems could have been avoided which have torn apart the entire Muslim community! In another verse Allah has openly declared that he neither has a wife nor has any offspring! Though there is no clear admission of his gender identity, yet circumstantially, taking references from above verses, we may assume that the "Lord" of the universe is a "Male"! His physical stature is quite like that of Adam as Allah said he created Adam in his own "Image"! As offspring of Adam, we do possess "Image" of our "Father"! If we trace back our parentage, it will definitely reach up to the "One" living over Seven Heavens! But Allah says, "Man are ingrate"! If Allah had willed to have a "Son", Jesus could have been the best choice!

Verse-6, Ch-39 says; "HE HAS CREATED YOU ALL FROM A SINGLE PERSON (ADAM), THEN MADE FROM HIM HIS WIFE (EVE). AND HE HAS SENT DOWN FOR YOU OF CATTLE EIGHT PAIRS (TWO PAIRS EACH OF SHEEP, GOATS, OXEN AND CAMELS). HE CREATES YOU IN THE WOMBS OF YOUR MOTHER; CREATION AFTER CREATION IN THREE VEILS OF DARKNESS. SUCH IS ALLAH YOUR LORD. HIS IS THE KINGDOM. HOW THEN ARE YOU TURNED AWAY?" This verse is a complete reversal of the general concept of creation that it is the female that gives birth to offspring of both sex! But Allah began his first creation of humans from a male i.e. he made Eve from Adam! And then this couple (Adam and Eve) as the first parents of human being began the process of procreation! When Adam could be made from mud or clay, then why Allah had to create his wife (Eve) from his rib? Both Adam and Eve had no mother, so that their creation did not take place in "THREE VEILS OF DARKNESS" of their mother's wombs! For obvious reason Allah had to resort to a unique way of creating Adam and Eve as he needed at least one pair of man and woman to kick start the creation of mankind! If a farmer wants to set up a poultry farm, he must begin with a pair of chicks at the least! When the creator decided to create a mankind, he did not have a pair of man and woman readily available anywhere in the universe! So, he was left with only one option i.e. to create them by any means available to him! And taking no help from any quarter, not even from angels or Satan, Allah alone created the earth and the heavens and then he made Adam and Eve to make his dream come true! Allah claims to have created all creatures but why he took the decision to send down two pairs each of sheep, goats, oxen and camels only? One pair would have been more than enough to meet the needs, since a single pair of human beings (Adam and Eve) has multiplied into billions! Life in those days was totally unsustainable in the dry land of the desert without these animals! Those were the sources of meat and milk and also means of transportation! How can we forget the "Ship of the Desert"? Besides, camels are also used by the "Believers" for racing with minor boys bound on their backs! Wealthy Sheiks do not use their own children but hire minors from poor countries! Allah always claims that he makes all decisions considering needs of the people "WITH DUE MEASUREMENTS"! Were these eight pairs of animals seemed enough to cater to the needs of the people? Another essential four-footed animal that has been excluded is the monkey; our forefather! Oh, God; blasphemy is looming large! Darwin is the one who should be charged with blasphemy for his theory of evolution that goes against the Lord's creative strategy! Arguably twin-legged Adam is still widely believed to be the "Father" of mankind! So Darwin should be the first to enter the inferno! It is also not clear why Allah excluded the most famous Arabian horse from the list of animals he sent on earth? What about the Dinosaurs? Probably these pre-historic animals came before Allah took the decision to send Adam and Eve to this planet! Surprisingly enough, the creator has not disclosed how and where he created all these animals! What material are they made of? How they were brought down to earth! Also not understood is the fact who sent other millions of species on earth? He creates "IN THE WOMBS OF MOTHERS, CREATION AFTER CREATION IN HIS KINGDOM", yet people turned away from him! The "Creator", after making "CREATION AFTER CREATION", becomes a "Destroyer" and continues to destroy "GENERATIONS AFTER GENERATIONS"! Creation and Destruction are the two vividly visible features of the invisible God of life and death! Then comes the Resurrection at the end of the road! He will bring people back to life for the Day of Judgment to sort out those who had been misled by Satan in this world! What would be the fate of the Satan? He might get away with another "Respite"! Whatever may be the message from the Lord, yet the "VEIL OF DARKNESS" stands between him and his creations!

Verse-28, Ch-39 states; "AN ARABIC QURAN WITHOUT ANY CROOKEDNESS THEREIN IN ORDER THAT THEY MAY AVOID ALL EVIL WHICH ALLAH HAS ORDERED THEM TO AVOID". Of course, this is "AN ARABIC QURAN" without any doubt but to be more precise it should be called "An Arabic Quran" authored by Allah; revealed in Arabic dialect (QURAISH) through an Arabic speaking angel to an Arab Messenger! I think no Islamic expert can deny the vast difference that exists between modern Arabic language and the QURAISH dialect! This Quran is dedicated to the Arabs and can be defined as a book "FOR THE ARABS, OF THE ARABS AND BY THE ARABS"! So, all those involved in the revelation process, including Allah, the creator of the universe, were conversant with QURAISH dialect! As for the crookedness, please look at more than thirty Surah of the Quran that began with some Arabic letters (ALIF, LAM, MIM, SIN etc.) known as "Miracles"! The Quran, often referred to as the "Plain book" and "The Plain Statement", unequivocally states; "THESE LETTERS ARE ONE OF THE MIRACLES OF THE QURAN AND NONE BUT ALLAH ALONE KNOWS THEIR MEANINGS"! The Arabs, including Muhammad, to whom the Quran is said to have been revealed for the mankind, are totally in the dark about the meanings of these so-called miracles! Allah claims that he does everything with "Purpose"! If so, then what is the purpose of sending these miracles to the mankind? Would it be a punishable crime if someone doesn't believe in meaningless miracles? Can any Islamic scholar, including Grand Mufti of Mecca, explain the "Purpose" and the meanings of these miracles to the mankind? The verse also claims that the Quran has been sent in Arabic so that they (People of Arab) "MAY AVOID ALL EVILS"! Evils of the past (Sodomy, Slavery, slave-sex, honor-killing, beheading, MUTAH or the temporary marriage for sex) to some extent still prevail in the Arab world! Allah sent this "Arabic Quran without any crookedness therein" to straighten all crooked people so that they follow the straight path to heaven!

Verse-9, Surah-41 states; "SAY (O MUHAMMAD), DO YOU (DISBELIEVERS) VERILY BELIEVE IN HIM WHO CREATED THE EARTH IN TWO DAYS"? Allah commanding Muhammad to ask disbelievers if they really believe in "Him" who has created the earth in "Two Days"? Surely, Muhammad received negative response from them since they have been accused of setting up rivals with Allah! The root cause of unsatisfactory response lies in the fact that Allah often gives inconsistent statements about his power and ability! Allah, in a number of verses claimed that he could create anything just by uttering a word "Be" in a fraction of a second since he is also the creator of "Time"! Verse 35 of chapter 19 STATES; "WHEN HE DECREES A THING, HE ONLY SAYS TO IT 'BE'—AND IT IS"! Verse 59 of chapter 3 says; "HE CREATED ADAM FROM DUST, THEN SAID HE UNTO HIM, 'BE', AND HE WAS"! Why then Allah, the "Creator" took "Two" days to create the earth? If Muhammad had asked this question to his followers, they would surely have given positive answers as they knew believing blindly in the unseen was a precondition for revealed religions! The believers also had to believe when Allah said he created the earth and the heaven in "Six" days (Verse 54 of chapter 7)! They also believed when Allah claimed to have taken only "Four" days to create sustenance for the dwellers of the earth (Verse 41 of chapter 10)! In one of the verses, Allah said his "One" day is equal to "A Thousand" years of world standard time and in another verse he increased that to "Fifty Thousand" years! He can do it since he is also the "Creator of Time"! The message is clear; believe blindly for an eternal life in paradise or go to hell to face the music! DR. AL-JOHANI from Saudi Arabia commented that "Most educated people have come to a conclusion that one can't be a scientist or an educated person and be a Christian. Thus many philosophers, scientists and the majority of the people lost hope of reconciling religion and science"! Light and darkness cannot co-exist! Science is truth, truth beauty!

Verse-10, Ch-41 states; "HE PLACED THEREIN (THE EARTH) FIRM MOUNTAINS FROM ABOVE IT, AND HE BLESSED IT, AND MEASURED THEREIN ITS SUSTENANCE (FOR ITS DWELLERS) IN FOUR DAYS EQUAL IN THE LENGTH OF TIME FOR ALL THOSE WHO ASK ABOUT ITS CREATION"! Allah as the creator has taken lots of credit for placing mountains as pegs on the surface of the earth without placing pillars underneath! Was it necessary? He also made the mountains glorify his praises along with Prophet David! Allah has a great liking for mountains and rivers and he has dedicated many verses on them to highlight their importance! What is so eye catching in this verse is that the Lord has taken long "FOUR DAYS EQUEL IN THE LENGTH OF TIME" to measure and manage sustenance for the dwellers of the earth! We have no idea as to what time-frame he is referring to! Allah himself being the "Time-Creator" does not have to be bound by time! In verse 9 of Ch. 41 Allah stated that he took only "TWO DAYS" to complete the creation of the earth and then he began ascending towards the Heavens! We have no idea how long the "Day" of Allah is in real time since he lives over "SEVEN HEAVENS" on a different time zone! We live in a solar system that has eight planets and each of them has its days not equal in the length of time! From these Quranic verses we can conclude that Allah or the "Creator" has taken more time(four days) for preparing a "Meal" for the dwellers of the earth and less time(two days) to make a "Home" for them! Verse 14 of Ch. 29 says; "AND INDEED WE SENT NOAH TO HIS PEOPLE, AND HE STAYED

AMONG THEM A THOUSAND YEARS LESS FIFTY YEARS"! Noah was sent for his people only, yet Allah gave him 950 years to live whereas prophet Muhammad is said to have been sent as the "Messenger for whole of Mankind" with a life span of only sixty three years! Yet Allah claims: "I AM AD-DAHR", meaning to say "I AM THE CREATOR OF TIME"! Yet Allah failed to allocate enough time to Muhammad, the messenger for all mankind, in accordance with the task given to him!

Verse-11, Ch-41 states; "THEN HE ROSE OVER TOWARDS THE HEAVEN WHEN IT WAS SMOKE, AND SAID TO IT AND TO THE EARTH; COME BOTH OF YOU WILLINGLY OR UNWILLINGLY. THEY BOTH SAID; WE COME WILLINGLY"! Having finished the creation of the "Earth" and its "Sustenance" for the dwellers, Allah rose over to heaven, when his palace over Seven Heavens was yet to be made! Whereas he claims to have taken "Six" days to create the "Earth and the Heavens" together! Whatever it may be, when he decided to go to space "IT WAS ALL SMOKE"! Who then created that "SMOKE"? Where did it come from? Was it caused by the "BIG BANG"? It is really difficult to say when the mankind will come out of this "SMOKE"! However, Allah then invited the "SMOKE" and the "EARTH" to join him in his journey towards heaven willingly or unwillingly! Luckily, "They both said; we come willingly"! Think of the consequences if anyone of them had declined to accompany the "Creator"! The Quran has been dubbed as a "Plain Book" but the contents of this verse is so foggy that even the greatest of scientist on earth will be at a loss to understand the gist of it! DR. AL-JOHANI says again; "Scientific facts are just one source of our knowledge of God. The other source is "Revelation" as it is contained in original teachings of Jesus and in the present text of the Quran. Both religion and true scientific knowledge are from the same source: God. So he won't contradict himself"! Anyone who sees both religion and revelation with preconception will never find contradictions! Why should God contradict himself since he has sent no revelation! His existence itself is still debated! Does science accept the creation of humans as stated in Adam-Eve saga? What is "Seven Heavens"? What is "AR-RUKYAH"? How did "MIRAJ" happen? Did Muhammad "Split" the moon? Are these scientific facts? Religious scholars try to bridge the gap between the science and dogma with ridiculous explanation to impart legitimacy to their religion! Facts and fictions will never get along! Science has no room for myths and miracles!

Verse-12, Surah-41 states; "THEN HE COMPLETED AND FINISHED FROM THEIR CREATION (AS) SEVEN HEAVEN IN TWO DAYS AND HE MADE IN EACH HEAVEN ITS AFFAIR. AND WE ADORNED THE NEAREST (LOWEST) HEAVEN WITH LAMPS (STARS) TO BE AN ADORNMENT AS WELL AS TO GUARD (FROM THE DEVILS BY USING THEM AS MISSILES). SUCH IS THE DECREE OF HIM THE ALL-MIGHTY, THE ALL-KNOWER"! Please go back to your childhood when you may have read "TWINKLING, TWINKLING LITTLE STAR; HOW I WONDER WHAT YOU ARE'! Before going into detail discussion on this verse may I draw attention of the readers to the expressions "HE COMPLETED", "HE MADE" and "WE ADORNED"! Suddenly "HE" changes into "WE"! As per English grammar "HE" and "WE" are not interchangeable! Which of these two pronouns refers to ALLAH and who is the "Author" of these verses? In many places of the Quran, Allah claims to have created the "Earth" and the "Heaven" in six days! Then he claims he created the "Earth" in "Two" days, and then he took "Four" days to arrange "Sustenance" for its dwellers and finally he completed creation of the so called "SEAVEN HEAVENS" in another "Two Days"! So, in total it comes to "Eight" days instead of six! The creation of the "Earth" and the "Heavens" have taken two days each and the arrangements of "Sustenance" for the dwellers alone has taken four days! Allah's plan of creation seems to have made disproportional time-allocation for the projects he had undertaken! Allah as the "Time-Creator" has not been able to make a comprehensive time-table for his "Creation"! Are the "Seven Heavens" and the "Earth" similar in design and dimensions that each one of them should take equal time (two days each) to be created? Why arrangement of "Sustenance" for the dwellers of the earth should take "Four Days"; twice the time taken to create the Earth? How the smoke and the earth responded to Allah's call to accompany him willingly or unwillingly? Did he infuse life into them? Does Allah expect this intelligent mankind to believe in everything he says and have faith in things unseen and unfeasible? For arguments sake, if we accept the claim that Allah is able to do all things, then he should have given us the capacity to comprehend them unambiguously! Allah says he has adorned the lowest heaven with stars for beautification! Does Allah mean to say upper heavens have no stars? He also says, if need be, he will use them as missiles against devils! Super powers on earth are also planning to deploy missiles in space and may have borrowed the idea from Allah! Surely, Allah knows how big a devil is, does he really know how big is a star? If a star is used as missile, then how big should be its target? How big is this Earth compared to a star? Authors of these verses, out of ignorance, may have taken asteroids and meteors for stars that often fall on earth from the sky like missiles! The misleading figure of "Days" presented by Allah in the time-table for the creation of the "Earth", its "Sustenance" and the 'Seven Heavens" must have infuriated the state of mind of the great Persian poet Omar Khayyam to write his famous RUBAIYATS (Quatrains) as a free thinker almost eight centuries ago! Despite being a great mathematician and astronomer himself, Khayyam could not arrive at any definitive conclusion about Allah's astronomy and his time-scale with respect to "CREATION" and probably that led him to take a position against bigotry and fanaticism; "The importance of learning to solve the mystery of life, the domination of man's will by forces outside of himself, the injustice of the doctrine of eternal punishment, and the wisdom of a skeptical attitude towards the unseen" have compelled him to launch a religious revolt through his literary works of extra-ordinary beauty that entered so deeply into the public consciousness! Here comes the famous verse 24 of chapter 59 from Allah which states: "HE IS GOD-- THE CREATOR, THE MAKER, THE GIVER. TO HIM BELONGS THE BEAUTIFUL NAMES. EVERYTHING IN THE HEAVENS AND EARTH GLORIFIES HIM"! The "Mountains" and the "Shadows" are no exception; they too glorify their "Creator"! What pleases the Lord most is appreciations and glorifications!

Verse- 46, Ch-41 states; "WHOEVER DOES RIGHTEOUS GOOD DEED, IT IS FOR HIS OWNSELF, AND WHOEVER DOES EVIL, IT IS AHAINST HIS OWNSELF". In a footnote, attached to this verse, Muhammad narrated a parabolic story concerning the fate of the followers of these three sister religions; "The example of Muslims, Jews and Christians is like the example of a man who employed laborers to work for him from morning till night for specific wages. They worked till mid-day and then said; we do not need your money which you have fixed for us and let whatever we have done be annulled! The man said to them; don't quite the work, but complete the rest of it and take your full wages. But they refused and went away (like the Jews who refused to believe in the Message of Jesus). The man employed another batch after then and said to them; complete the rest of the day and yours will be the wages I had fixed for the first batch. So, they worked till the time of afternoon prayer. They said; let what we have done be annulled and keep the wages you have promised us for yourself! The man said to them; complete the rest of the work as only a little of the day remains but they refused (like the Christian who refused to believe in the message of Muhammad). Thereafter he employed another batch to work for the rest of the day and they worked for the rest of the day till the sunset, and they received the wages of the two former batches. So that was the example of the Muslims, who have accepted willingly the light of Islamic monotheism and the legal ways and guidance brought by prophet Muhammad" (BUKHARI, VOL. 3, #471)!Though the message of this story is clear, yet a supplementary footnote gives a "Bad Tidings" for the Jews and the Christians: "The Jews refused to believe in the message of Jesus, so all their work was annulled! Similarly, the Christians refused to believe in the message of Muhammad and thus their work was annulled too"! The Jews and the Christian's journey to paradise will meet a disastrous end in the inferno! Muhammad will lead his men to Eden under which rivers flow!

Verses-49 & 50, Ch-42 state; "TO ALLAH BELONGS THE KINGDOM OF THE HEAVENS AND THE EARTH. HE CREATES WHAT HE WILLS. HE BESTOWS FEMALE (OFFSPRING) UPON WHOM HE WILLS AND BESTOWS MALE UPON WHOM HE WILLS. OR HE BESTOWS BOTH MALES AND FEMALES, AND HE RENDERS BARREN WHOM HE WILLS"! This natural phenomenon regarding the birth of the babies is common to all living creatures, humans and animals alike. By instinct every man and woman want to be parents. Because of social stigma or customs in the orthodox society, people in general, Arabs in particular, preferred male child! Most of the Arabs, out of disgust and disliking, used to bury their female child alive in the old days which continued even after the arrival of Muhammad! In every nations or generations of mankind, it is a common reality that some families have only female child, some have males and some have both male and female children! Very few of them go barren for medical conditions! More or less this applies to all species of creation universally! This general norms has been attributed to the "Will" of the "King" of the earth and the heavens! Allah watching from above the Seven Heavens could not stop the brutal burial of the female babies in the land of the "Revelation" despite sending so many prophets and messengers to warn them! Yet Allah did not stop giving them female babies! Allah has already declared he did not wish to be a "Father" of any offspring! Allah by all consideration appears to be a "Male" and "Male-Friendly"! In the procreation process some go barren too, as Allah's "Will" doesn't allow them to have babies for unknown reasons or apparently he made some mistakes in their making! As of now parents cannot chose gender of their offspring since this is directly linked to the naturally selected combination of X and Y chromosomes of both parents. So, it was Allah's "Will" that Muhammad could not leave behind a male child to inherit his legacy! It was also Allah's "Will" that a son of Adam became the first murderer in the history of mankind and the murder took place over his greed to marry his own twin sister against Allah's "Will"! Though marriage between brothers and sisters is forbidden in Islam yet necessity of time compelled Allah to refrain from enforcing that "Decree"! So in Islamic point of view the mankind began its maiden voyage through an illegal marriage! Even the "Creator" is not free from mistakes and exceptions! The greatest failure of the "Creator" is that he has not been able to create a single man to live his life in this "Resting Place" free of diseases! Take it or leave it, the bitter truth is that Allah with his "Two Hands" have created people who ultimately became disloyal to him in large numbers! Yet thanks be to Father Adam, the so-called first prophet of Islam, that he did not kill his baby girls as the Arabs are used to, otherwise the procreation process of humans would have come to a halt for good! "HE CREATES WHAT HE WILLS" is a bold pronouncement aimed at bringing entire creation under his domain! No question should be asked why he created dinosaurs in the beginning on earth! What a huge creation this massive universe is; only to raise an ingrate mankind? Allah says; "AND I (ALLAH) CREATED NOT THE JINN AND MAN EXCEPT THEY SHOULD WORSHIP ME ALONE (Verse 56 of Ch. 51)! The Shia-Sunni divide was created mainly by Allah's "Will" for not bestowing Muhammad with a male child! Soon after his demise his followers engaged in heinous debate as to who should succeed him to lead the entire Muslim community! Some suggested that Muhammad's father-in-Law and his best friend ABU BAKR should succeed Muhammad! ABU BAKR is also lucky because, he is known to be "The One Who Allah freed from the Fire"! Others were in favor of choosing a heir to Muhammad's dynasty from his blood-line! The obvious choice was ALI, a cousin and Son-in-Law of Muhammad! At last he became the fourth KHALIPH but was killed due to religious politics! Why none of Muhammad's wife could leave behind a male child? Because Allah "Bestows male upon whom he wills"!

Verses 1-4, Ch. 43: State; " HA-MIM. BY THE MANIFEST BOOK (i.e. THE QURAN THAT MAKES THINGS CLEAR). VERILY, WE HAVE MADE IT A QURAN IN ARABIC THAT YOU MAY BE ABLE TO

UNDERSTAND (ITS MEANING AND ITS ADMONITIONS). AND VERILY IT (THE QURAN) IS IN THE MOTHER OF THE BOOK(i.e. AL-LAUH-AL-MAHFUZ) WITH US, INDEED EXALTED, FULL OF WISDOM"! The first verse is composed of two Arabic letters only! The second verse says the Quran makes things clear! Instead of making their meanings clear, the Quran claims that meaning of these Arabic alphabets are only known and understood by Allah, the "Author", since these are the "Miracles" of the Quran! I think in some previous pages I have already discussed these so-called Miracles! Does it make sense to reveal such verses from heaven by Allah? Even Muhammad, the messenger for the mankind was also in the dark about their meanings! Is this not enough to conclude that Allah's words and actions do not complement one another? All those involved in the chain of revelations (Allah, Gabriel, Muhammad and his associates) do surely speak Arabic! And for that reason Allah "MADE IT A QURAN IN ARABIC"! In addition to this he also claims that this Quran is for the entire mankind! Allah is not aware of the fact that the entire mankind do not speak Arabic! Next two verses (6&7) of this chapter recorded Allah's admission that; " AND HOW MANY A PROPHET HAVE WE SENT AMONGST THE MAN OF OLD AND NEVER CAME THERE A PROPHET TO THEM BUT THEY USED TO MOCK AT HIM"! If anyone of them had asked Muhammad to explain the meaning of those Miracles, what answer did he have to satisfy them? Should they not mock at him! Why did he not ask their meaning from Gabriel? Or he should have rejected them as being meaningless to mankind! Even Allah himself is a mocker and a curser! He mocked and cursed the disbelievers for not believing in his verses! The way Quran made its landfall on the surface of the earth is indeed a "Miracle"!

Verses 43-48, Ch-44: State; "VERILY, THE TREE OF ZAQQUN (A HORRIBLE, ACCURSED TREE IN HELL) WILL BE THE FOOD OF THE SINNERS. LIKE BOILING OIL, IT WILL BOIL IN THE BELLIES. LIKE THE BOILING OF SCALDING WATER. IT WILL BE SAID; SEIZE HIM AND DRAG HIM INTO THE MIDST OF BLAZING FIRE, THEN POUR OVER HIS HEAD THE TORMENT OF BOILING WATER"! Even in the midst of blazing fire, the merciful "Creator" has not deprived the sinners of "FOOD" and "DRINKS"! The Food will be made from accursed, horrible tree in Hell and the Drinks will be provided of scalding water! Allah also says in verse 50 of chapter 7 that " THE DWELLERS OF THE FIRE WILL CALL TO THE DWELLERS OF PARADISE: POUR ON US SOME WATER

OR ANYTHING THAT ALLAH HAS PROVIDED YOU WITH"! Will it be possible for a sinner from hell to call the dwellers of paradise for help? Are these two located side by side? Allah mentioned that he has made the Paradise with eight doors and it has 100 grades in it! The distance between each grade is as much as the distance between the earth and the heaven! Why should the sinners be treated with mercy "WHO TOOK THEIR RELIGION AS AN AMUSEMENT AND PLAY (Verse 51 of chapter 7)"! Human beings neither asked Allah for "THE LIFE OF THE WORLD" nor a "RELIGIN"! He bestowed upon them "Life" and "Religion" at his own will! Allah is generous to the believers who did not take this life and religion as amusement! In verse 52 of chapter 7 he promises them an eternal life "AMONG GARDENS AND SPRING, DRESSED IN FINE AND THICK SILK FACING EACH OTHER. AND WE SHALL MARRY THEM TO 'HUR' WITH WIDE LOVELY EYES"! Who are the "HURS"? They are "Very fair females created by Allah as such, not from the offspring of Adam! They will have their hymens intact as no man or Jinn ever has had sex with them"! Mind you believers! Don't be so overexcited to celebrate "Honeymoon" with HURS! To get their company, you have to pass over a bridge across the Hell sharper than the sword! Only those lived in Faith shall make it to the "City full of dreams"!

Verse-24, Ch-45 states; "AND THEY (POLYTHEISTS) SAY: THERE IS NOTHING BUT OUR LIFE OF THIS WORLD, WE DIE AND WE LIVE AND NOTHIG DESTROYS US EXCEPT TIME (AD-DAHR). AND THEY HAVE NO KNOWLEDGE OF IT; THEY ONLY CONJECTURE"! It would not be an exaggeration to say that all religions are made of conjectures born out of imagination! This polytheistic view on life expressed in the above verse is purely scientific and upheld by those who have faiths in religious democracy and freedom! The most certain thing in life is death and the most uncertain is the time that measures life! "Death" is a point of no return! So far "DEATH HAD UNDONE" many but none has returned to life! If life did not exist before creation, it is unlikely to exist after destruction! Though it is hard to believe whether soul has its own existence in any form! Yet none but the condition in and around the body tells the soul to escape from the "WHEEL OF EXISTENCE"! Soul does not stay in a fallen body! Death follows no command or calendar! The allurement of a life hereafter is a hoax based on countless conjectures! To be a bit more specific, it would not be an exaggeration to say that all religions, which claim divine connections, are based on imagination and conjectures! The following Hadith, out of thousands of this kind, may be analyzed to see the truth of the matter in relation to the doctrinal outbursts! ABU HURAIRAH, a prominent Islamic scholar of the past (AL-BUKHARI, Vol. 6, #351) referring to Muhammad quotes Allah as saying; "THE SON OF ADAM ANNOYS ME FOR HE ABUSES TIME THOUGH I AM THE AD-DAHR (CREATOR OF TIME), IN MY HANDS ARE ALL THINGS, AND I CAUSE THE REVOLUTION OF DAY AND NIGHT. I AM THE CREATOR OF TIME, AND I MANAGE THE AFFAIRS OF ALL CREATIONS INCLUDING TIME. ONE SHOULD NOT ATTRIBUTE ANYTHING WHETHER CHEERFUL OR DISASTROUS TO TIME"! This hadith involves prophet Muhammad, the narrator ABU HARAIRAH, the Hadith writer AL-BUKHARI and finally Allah, the Lord himself! First of all how Muhammad came to know of what was going on in the mind of the Lord as the "Creator" of time? This statement did not come to him as a revealed verse through Gabriel! Did Allah authorize Muhammad to speak for him? ABU HURAIRAH is quoted to have heard Muhammad saying this when he was alive! Then, after hundreds of years how AL-BUKHARI could write this Hadith as an authentic expression of Allah? What was his source of information? Allah's concept of time is based on the revolution of day and night! Alternation of day and night is the effect not the cause! What causes the night to change into day is the rotation of the earth on its axis facing the sun. Allah said he created moon as a time-keeper for reckoning! Even the Muslims across the world get confused and their rituals become chaotic during the RAMADAN and the EID-UL-FITR due to imprecise appearance of the moon at different places on earth! The moon travels around the planet elliptically and appears at different time-zone at different time for the entire mankind, not for the Muslims only! So, Allah as the creator of the "Time" could not ensure precision and accuracy of his time keeper! Yet Allah claims in verse 13 of chapter 55; "THE SUN AND THE MOON RUN ON THEIR FIXED COURSES EXACTLY CALCULATED WITH MEASURED OUT STAGES FOR EACH (FOR RECKONING)! Unlucky are those who live in and around North or South poles as they are not able to use sun and the moon for reckoning! Countries in these polar regions do not see the sun setting for months nor do they see the moon in their night sky! How the Muslims, if any, living there would perform prayers that are closely linked with the revolutions of the sun and the moon? GPS, a human endeavor, works with more precision on the basis of the General Theory of Relativity of Albert Einstein, who was a Jew, an arc enemy of Allah and the Muslims! Allah claims that he is the creator of time! Does time exist alone? Einstein doesn't agree! Muhammad warns that "ONE SHOULD NOT ATTRIBUTE ANYTHING WHETHER CHEERFUL OR DISASTROUS TO TMIE"! But Einstein says time and space are inseparable and together they form the fourth dimensions which he calls "SPACE-TIME"! So, what Einstein attributed to time is definitely "CHEERFUL", not "DISASTROUS"! Apparently Allah seems to have no control over "Time" as he failed to extend life-span of Muhammad and that did irreparable damage to the credibility of the so-called Revelations and the Quran as a whole! Allah also claims that his one "Day" is equal to a thousand years of "World standard time" and for some unknown reasons he extended that "Day" to fifty thousand years in another verse! So, no creatures on earth, including humans have real-time connection with the "Creator"! The "Creator" lives over so-called "Seven Heavens" which lies in a different time-zone and as such any response to our requests from him might take millions of years to reach the earth even at light speed! However, as the creator of time, he might consider sending his responses at a speed faster than light! Believe it or not, there are instances when Allah instantaneously sent his verses to Muhammad to solve problems encountered by him! But what comes between facts and fiction is the "Time" (twenty three years) taken by the "Time-Creator" to reveal his "Book"! Many Islamic scholars unrealistically define the Quran as a "Complete Code of Life" for the mankind though there is no mention of "Genetic Code of Life" anywhere in the Quran! Gabriel, who brought down the verses from Allah to Muhammad, should have been affixed with more "Wings", since Allah could increase the number of wings of his angels at his "Will" to increase the speed! Now for the sake of truthfulness, we may recall that the same angel Gabriel was sent to take Muhammad on a journey to heaven! It is claimed that the journey began at night and Muhammad came back to earth the next morning! If we compare these two events i.e. revelation of the Quran and the Space mission, we find that one has taken long twenty three years and the other one has taken less than twenty three hours! Answers to these queries lie in the "Science of Quran " which can only be answered by Allah himself!

Verse-9, Ch-46 states; "SAY (O MUHAMMAD). "I AM NOT A NEW THING AMONG THE MESSENGERS (i.e. I AM NOT THE FIRST MESSENGER) NOR DO I KNOW WHAT WILL BE DONE WITH ME NOR WITH YOU. I ONLY FOLLOW THAT WHICH IS REVEALED TO ME, AND I AM BUT A PLAIN WARNER"! Allah orders Muhammad to say, "I am not a new "Thing" among the messengers" to mean that he is not the first messenger! This verse is a plain statement of a "Plain Book"! In this verse Muhammad appears to be shifting his earlier stance probably suggested by his Lord! So far the Quran and the Hadiths have been describing Muhammad as "The best Prophet", "The best Messenger", 'The last prophet' and a "Friend of Allah" and only "Messenger" for the entire mankind entrusted to lead his followers to paradise! Now he has been advised by Allah to admit that he is only a "Plain Warner"! How does a so-called "Plain Warner" makes it "Mandatory" for his followers to believe in him and his messages to be a "Muslim"? Believing only in Allah doesn't make one eligible for an entry into paradise unless he or she believes in Muhammad as the messenger of Allah! The most important part of this verse is; "NOR DO I KNOW WHAT WILL BE DONE WITH ME NOR WITH YOU"! This verse clearly sends a discouraging message to the entire community of Muslims who might be thinking that the "PARDISE IS GAINED", but now they may find the "PARADISE IS LOST" and hangs in the balance! Because the "Imam" or the messenger, who has been assuring his followers of an eternal life in paradise with HURS, himself is not sure of his own fate after death! What has created suspicion in Muhammad's mind? The Quran testifies that his past and future sins have been forgiven by Allah and also he has been assured of the best place in paradise! He would be the first to be resurrected! Among the prophets he will be the one to have the honor to intercede with Allah on the day of Judgment! "TIRMITHI" an authority on Islamic affairs says, "THE FIRST TO BE BROUGHT BACK TO LIFE AND EMERGE FROM THE CRCKING GRAVE WILL BE THE PROPHET AND HE WILL SAY 'I AM THE MASTER' OF ADAM'S OFFSPRING ON THE DAY OF RESURRECTION, THE FIRST FOR WHON THE TOMB CRACKS, THE FIRST INTERCEDER"! Another Hadith quotes Muhammad as saying that Allah has made this "Earth" only for him and his followers to pray! To restore conjugal happiness of Muhammad, Allah sent many verses (Chapter-33) warning his wives of dire consequences if they think of open illegal sex with others except their husband! Moreover Allah has assured him that he will not be held responsible for others' misdeeds! Millions of his followers around the world say "Peace Be upon Him" whenever they utter his name! Every call-maker after the call recites a verse to remind Allah to deliver on his promises he made to Muhammad! How can Allah ignore their wishes but to keep Muhammad in peace! What is this "MAQAM-MAHMUD"? As per Hadith (BUKHARI, Vol. 6, # 242) "THIS

IS THE HIGHEST PLACE IN PARADISE, WHICH WILL BE GRANTED TO PROPHET MUHAMMAD AND NONE ELSE"! Why alone? Will he not be rewarded with "Two Wives" or "HURS" as his mates in his MAQAM? In fact Muhammad deserves more than just two! Even on this earth he had dozens of wives! He was assured of his "Reward" while still alive! He will be the first to be resurrected though he will be second in line after Abram to receive "Clothes" to cover his nudity! It is really unfortunate that a prophet like Muhammad will have to wait naked, though briefly, on the Day of Resurrection to receive his clothes! Muhammad is listed among the prophets who have "Strong Wills"! He also visited paradise and met with Allah in his life-time! What else he needs to be sure of his success after death? What consolation he has for his followers? There are plenty of such contradictory verses in the Quran which loyalty-bound Islamic scholars do not see! The messenger to mankind at the last moment has given up all hopes as his Lord asks him to say: "Nor do I know what will be done with me or with you"! Similarly, the "Sons of Adam" do not know what would be done with them posthumously!

Verse-15, Ch-47 states; "THE DESCRIPTION OF THE PARADISE WHICH THE PIOUS HAVE BEEN PROMISED IS THAT IN IT ARE RIVERS OF WATER THE TASTE AND SMELL OF WHICH ARE NOT CHANGED, RIVERS OF MILK OF WHICH THE TASTE NEVER CHANGES, RIVERS OF WINE DELICIOUS TO THOSE WHO DRINK, AND RIVERS OF CLARIFIED HONEY (CLEAR AND PURE) THEREIN FOR THEM IS EVERY KIND OF FRUIT AND FORGIVENESS FROM THEIR LORD. THOSE WHO SHALL DWELL FOR EVER IN THE FIRE WILL BE GIVEN TO DRINK BOILING WATER SO THAT IT CUTS UP THEIR BOWELS"? At least we are assured by Allah that, unlike the earth, paradise is free of bacteria and as such the Water, Milk, Honey and Wine will not be contaminated! Rivers have very special place in the Paradise! Why on earth these rivers have to be filled with drinks? Allah could have preserved those drinks in glittering jars made of pure gold or any other precious metal! Are the dwellers of paradise going to drink while swimming in the rivers? Besides excessively beautiful wives, there will be rivers of Honey, Milk, Water and Wine and various kinds of fruits for them! A casino in Las Vegas or a cruise ship over Atlantic is much better equipped than Allah's paradise for entertainment! If they don't have to relieve nature in paradise, they should have been relieved of eating and drinking too! Allah could have easily devised an eternal life for them to live without food and drinks!

Let them have "EVERY KINDS OF FRUITS" but why "FORGIVENESS"? Dwellers of paradise must have gone through the "DAY OF JUDGMENT" already! Sinners will be given boiling water to drink so that it cuts up their bowels; "LET THEM DRINK AS THEY BREWED"! It is beyond human conviction how one can "DWELL FOR EVER IN THE FIRE". We are used to seeing rivers of water on earth. Humans do not nurture such weird ideas as to make rivers of milk, honey and wine! Besides these four rivers, the paradise also has a unique river called "AL-KAUTHAR", the banks of which are made of tents of hollow pearls but it is not mentioned what kind of fluid flows down that river! Probably "TENTS OF HOLLOW PEARLS" are meant to provide lovely shelters to the amorous lovers dwelling in paradise who might celebrate honey-moon and occasionally go for a walk along the banks like the beach goers! Muhammad is said to have been amazed by the beauty of this river during his visit to paradise and Allah gave it to him as gift! In addition to this, Muhammad was also apprised of two hidden rivers and two apparent rivers; the Nile and the Euphrates, all of which have originated from the "Lot-Tree", located at the utmost boundary of the seventh heaven! People living on the banks of the Nile and the Euphrates will be happy to see their rivers in the paradise after the destruction of the earth! Sorry indeed for the countries living on the banks of the Nile are quarrelling over sharing of its water! They don't have to fight in paradise for water as Allah has created lots of rivers therein! What they need to do is to accept Allah's monotheism without any hesitation! But what is the point cutting up the bowels of the sinners with boiling water while they are already burning in "Fire"? Broadly speaking, people are increasingly becoming dissatisfied with Islamic ideas and practices all over the world because it actively encourages radicalization in the name of their Lord using threats and temptations as the tools to achieve its goal! Intimidation is a way of life in Islam and killing is the easiest option! Democracy and humanity are the most heinous enemies of Allah's religion! All terror groups like Taliban, ISIS, Al-Qaida and others with similar agenda have joined hands to turn the earth into a Paradise! Let the terrorists fight among themselves until they find the road to "Paradise"! At the end, the victory will be of theirs who earnestly believe in just one life, not more! Osama Bin-Laden was actively involved in the planning and execution of Twin-Tower explosion and finally got killed in Pakistan! He was a Jihadist, fighting on behalf of Allah to implement Islamic rule all over the globe! Surprisingly, Allah did not send an army of angels to shield him from disbelievers nor did the Lord raise Osama unto himself alive like Jesus!

Verse 12, Ch-49: States; "O YOU WHO BELIEVE! AVOID MUCH SUSPICION; INDEED SOME SUSPICIONS ARE SINS. AND SPY NOT, NEITHER BACKBITE ONE ANOTHER". To add more light on this verse, Muhammad is quoted to have said (BUKHARI, VOL. 8 #92); "BEWARE OF SUSPICION, FOR SUSPICION IS THE WORST OF FALSE TALES; AND DO NOT LOOK FOR OTHER'S FAULTS AND DO NOT DO SPYING ON ONE ANOTHER"! Would anyone amongst the believers or disbelievers find any significant difference between what has been said by Allah in his revealed verse above and what has been narrated by Muhammad in the quoted Hadith? I may draw your attention to the word "Suspicion" which has been stressed equally by Allah in his verse and Mohammad in his Hadith! Do they look different in terms of their narrative skill and intellectual background? Do we not deserve to see an extra-ordinary writing skill of our "Creator" when he emerges as an "Author" of a book? Probably, in order to frighten his followers, a story is told by Muhammad in reference to a Hadith (BUKHARI, VOL. 8, #78); "Once Muhammad was passing by two graves and he found those persons being tortured in their graves! One of them was being tortured for not using soil to dry up his penis after urination and the other one was being punished for calumnies! Then Muhammad planted two green branches of date-palm tree on their graves and said their punishment may be abated till those branches get dried"! This remission from torture may be short-lived as the green branches will soon get dry in the intense heat of the desert! Allah's saying in the above verse: "SPY NOT, NEITHER BACKBITE ONE ANOTHER"! Whereas Allah himself (V. 3 Ch. 66) spied on private matters of Muhammad's wives! A secret talk between two wives of Muhammad (HAFSA and AISHAH) was made known to him by Allah! Is this not an invasion of privacy? Does it not tantamount to spying and backbiting? The Lord has defied his own verses! Do we still have to believe that the Allah is the "Author" of the Quran?

Verses 6&7, Ch-50: State; "HAVE THEY NOT LOOKED AT THE HEAVEN ABOVE THEM, HOW WE HAVE MADE IT AND ADORNED IT, AND THERE ARE NO RIFTS IN IT? AND THE EARTH! WE HAVE SPREAD IT OUT, AND SET THEREON MOUNTAINS STANDING FIRM AND HAVE PRODUCED THEREIN EVERY KIND OF LOVELY GROWTH (PLANTS)"! We have looked at the heaven but could not come to any definite conclusion as to who made it? As for adornment, Allah has mentioned a number of times that he has adorned the "First Heaven" with shining stars! What about other Heavens of the "Seven Heavens"? Are they not adorned with stars? May be those are decorated with galaxies! Rifts are everywhere in this universe! Even our tiny planet of earth is not free from rifts! While trying to spread the earth, Allah has torn its surface into millions of isles and the mountains are also not evenly placed! Seventy percent of the earth is water and almost half of the rest thirty percent is barren deserts! Lovely growth has not been able to eliminate hunger from the "Resting Place" made by Allah! We may quote some more verses to highlight the futility of Allah's statements! Verse 17 of this chapter says; "REMEMBER THAT THE TWO RECEIVERS (RECORDING ANGELS) RECEIVE (EACH HUMAN BEING), ONE SITTING ON THE RIGHT AND ONE ON THE LEFT TO NOTE HIS OR HER ACTIONS"! Ok, good enough! But according to verse 4 of surah 86; "THERE IS NO HUMAN BEING BUT HAS A PROTECTOR OVER HIM OR HER(i.e. ANGELS INCHARGE OF EACH HUMAN BEING GUARDING HIM, WRITING HIS GOOD OR BAD DEEDS)"! All in all each of us has three angels with us all the time! Two for recording our deeds, good or bad, and the third angel is acting as our security! We cannot see those angels even at night despite being made of light! Probably the angels are made of a kind of light whose frequency is beyond our visible spectrum! They report our actions to All-Mighty on a daily basis at a speed faster than light! So far scientists have not found definite proof of any object that can travel faster than light! They should read the Quran!

Verse-24, chapter-51: states; "HAS THE STORY REACHED YOU, OF THE HONOURED GUESTS OF ABRAHAM"? Who were the guests? Three angels; the famous Gabriel along with another two! Abraham was taken by surprise, yet he exchanged greetings with them and offered a roasted calf to his guests of honor! Abraham got a bit scared as the guests showed no interest to eat the food served! The angels said "fear not", we have brought glad tidings for you from the Lord that you will be blessed with a son having knowledge about Allah and his religion of True Monotheism! Then his wife came forward shouting in loud voice said "I am a barren old woman!" When the angels noticed some fear over the face of Abraham, they told him that they are Allah's messengers. And they also gave the glad news to his wife SARA that she will give birth to a son (Isaac)! She again expressed her surprise saying; "How can I bear a child?" At that time she was approximately 99 years old! The angels replied; "EVEN SO SAYS YOUR LORD. VERILY, HE IS THE ALL-WISE, THE ALL-KNOWER (Verse 30 of chapter 51)!" Should anyone have any doubt how a 99 year old is going to deliver a son? All-Powerful Allah assures all skeptics: "VERILY, OUR WORD UNTO A THING, WHEN WE INTEND IT, IS ONLY THAT WE SAY UNTO IT 'BE'—AND IT IS (Verse 40 of chapter 16)"! This story may have refreshed the memory of the readers of an almost similar story about Mary being conceived to give birth to Jesus! The same Gabriel is involved but this time he was not changed into a man and did not have to breath into SARA's garments on behalf of Allah! Another big difference is in the age of Mary and Sara! Mary was a pretty young lady while Sara was 99 years old! However, science of Allah is not to be weighed in with that of human's! A Hadith (BUKHARI, VOL. 4, #467) quotes Allah as saying; "I have prepared for my pious slaves things which have never been seen by an eye, nor heard by an ear, or even imagined by a human being"! Did Muhammad not "Hear", "Feel" or "See" the "Things" when he visited Paradise?

Verse-12, Ch-53 states; "WILL YOU THEN DISPUTE WITH HIM (MUHAMMAD) ABOUT WHAT HE SAW DURING MIRAJ (ASCENT OF THE PROPHET TO THE SEVEN HEAVENS WITH HIS BODY AND SOUL)"! Nothing has gone right with Prophet Muhammad about his actions from revelation to propagation of messages in his life-time! The so-called "MIRAJ", Muhammad's journey to space had always looked like a mission impossible, generated dispute and distrust among the people of all walks of life except a few ardent believers, ever since the time it is said to have taken place! The pagans even rejected Muhammad's claim of visiting Jerusalem by night which was less miraculous than the "MIRAJ"! Poet T.S. Elliot said, "I am no prophet"! He was an ardent believer of Catholicism and also had devotion to mythology! He poetically envisaged his bald head being brought in upon a platter! But why? According to Matthew, John the Baptist was beheaded by King Herod and his head was brought in upon a silver dish to please his queen! As for Prophet Muhammad, the angel Gabriel brought "Wisdom" and "Belief" from heaven upon a "Golden Tray" that must have been better than the "Holy Grail" of Jesus! The poets and the prophets have lot of things in common! A great majority of famous poets on earth are mystic and believe in divinity like the prophets! Tagore, a great mystic poet of India, spent much of his time and talent looking for a "God of life" who, he thought, sent him here on earth to sing for him! When the end came, he got very scared and surrendered to the will of the

"God of Death"! A Hadith (Al-BUKHARI, Vol. 4, #429) related to this verse, narrates a long story on "MIRAJ" (Ascent of Muhammad to seven heavens with his body and soul) but I have tried to cut it short keeping the sum and substance of the story intact. "Once, while Muhammad was in a state between 'Sleep and Wakefulness' in his house, Gabriel came to him with a golden tray full of "Wisdom" and "Belief! His body was cut open from throat to the abdomen and washed with ZAMZAM (a well, believed to be the source of holy water inside the KHABA complex at Mecca) water! Then Gabriel performed an operation like open-heart surgery to fill his heart with that wisdom and belief! AL-BURAQ, a white animal smaller than a horse and bigger than a donkey was brought and they both, Muhammad and Gabriel, begun ascending to the space riding on that animal! When they reached the nearest heaven, the gate keeper welcome them there and prophet Adam greeted Muhammad by saying "Welcome O Son and a Prophet"! On the second heaven, Muhammad met Jesus and John who greeted him saying, 'Welcome O brother and a prophet"! On the third heaven Muhammad saw Joseph! On the fourth heaven he met with Enoch! Upon reaching fifth heaven, Muhammad found Aaron there! On sixth heaven he met Moses who was weeping for the fact that his followers will be less in numbers than those of Muhammad in paradise! On the seventh heaven Muhammad was greeted by Abraham who said, "Welcome O son and a Prophet" and then Muhammad was shown the house of Allah (AL-BAIT-UL-MAMUR) by Abraham who also informed Muhammad that in the house of Allah seventy thousand (70,000) angels perform prayers every day and each day a new batch of angels replace the old one! Then Muhammad was shown the Lot-Tree at the utmost boundary over the seventh heavens and none can pass beyond that tree! Edwin Hubble probably did not read the Quran, otherwise he could have known that the expansion of the universe would come to a halt near that "LOT-TREE" as nothing can pass beyond that tree! Four rivers flow from this Lot-Tree, of which two are apparent and other two are hidden! The apparent two are the "Nile" and the "Euphrates". The last episode of this mythical and magical story is about how Allah fixed 'five daily obligatory' prayers for the Muslims! It is said that Allah fixed the number at 'fifty' before Muhammad's ascend to heaven! While Muhammad was descending on his way back to earth, he again met Mosses on sixth heaven who advised Muhammad to go back to Allah and have the number of prayers reduced since people will not be able to put up with such difficult obligation!

Muhammad had to make several journeys to and fro between sixth and seventh heavens to have the numbers of obligatory prayers reduced! First time Allah reduced the number to forty, then to thirty, then to twenty, then to ten and finally it came down to five! Moses again advised Muhammad to go to Allah for further reduction but Muhammad said he surrendered to Allah's final offer!" This mythical story is all about questions and queries with no answers whatsoever! Was it not possible by Allah to take Muhammad to space by any other means? How he raised Jesus? Allah has not given the mankind "Wisdom" and "Belief" on a golden tray to believe that a donkey-like animal can travel to space! Why the "Creator Allah" bestowed upon us a brain with billions of neurons in it which cannot accept his "Truth" as truth? Though the ultimate goal of all religions is to have a brain-washed humanity on earth but at the end the brain will overwhelm the bullies! These sort of events can happen in dreams or in a state of intoxication! According to the hadith Muhammad was in a state of "Sleep and Wakefulness" before take-off which suggests that he was in a state of intoxication! On the other hand the story tells that he ascended to the Seven Heavens with his "Body and Soul" together! It is not out of probability that his soul might have ascended to the space in the dream leaving his body on earth! Muhammad has claimed before that all prophets are paternal bothers! Here in this story he has been addressed as "Son" by Adam and Abraham! It is ok with Adam since he is the "Father" of mankind, but why Abraham? Adam, the most senior among all prophets who Allah created in his own "Image" by his "Both Hands", has been given the lowest heaven, farthest from Allah, probably to punish him for the "Sin" he committed in paradise! Allah has kept Abraham very close to him by giving him the seventh heaven! It may be recalled that Allah has a soft corner for Abraham! He is said to have built the "KABAH" for Allah! It was also Abraham who was tested for his loyalty to Allah through a dreadful "Dream" in which he was asked to sacrifice his beloved toddler in the name of Allah! He passed the "Test" successfully! It is also him who would be the first to receive cloths to cover his nudity after Resurrection! It was also Abraham who took Muhammad on a "TOUR DE PARADISE"! Jesus has been allotted the second heaven probably to prove that Allah is not his "Father"! Otherwise as member of his own family, Jesus could be with Allah in his Palace over seven heavens! This seven heavens have been depicted as a seven storied building and in each one of them, prophets are alive and well! So why it was mentioned in the Quran that they would be resurrected from the earth on the Last Day? When did this miraculous journey happen, before or after the "Revelation"? In a verse it was clearly mentioned by Allah that obligatory prayers are to be performed in the beginning and at the end of the day and sometime at night! So it makes a total of three prayers in one day! However, Muhammad in his own way interpreted it to be five! Why the number "Five" or " Fifty" has not been mentioned in any verse of the Quran? Prophet Moses, who sponsored Judaism, could realize that fifty prayers daily would be a difficult proposition for the followers but neither Mohammad nor All-Knowing Allah could assess the difficulty beforehand! Fascination about that "Lot-Tree" knows no bound! The tree is on the utmost boundary of the seventh heaven beyond which nothing can pass exactly the way nothing can come out of Black Hole! All scientists should know that this expanding universe will come to an end near "Lot-Tree"! Quran says; "Allah, the most gracious rose over the mighty Throne in a manner that suits his Majesty"! For Muhammad, Allah could arrange only a donkey-like animal to take him to Heaven! After reading this story, please read the verse 43 of chapter 53 which says: "AND THAT IT IS ALLAH WHO MAKES LAUGH WHOM HE WILLS, AND MAKES WEEP WHOM HE WILLS"!

Verse-1, Ch-54 states; "THE HOUR HAS DRAWN NEAR, AND THE MOON HAS BEEN CLEFT ASUNDER (THE PEOPLE OF MECCA REQUESTED MUHAMMAD TO SHOW THEM A MIRACLE, SO HE SHOWED THEM THE SPLITTING OF THE MOON)"! What is narrated in the bracket of this verse has been quoted from a Hadith of AL-BUKHARI (Vol. 6, #390)! People of Mecca rejected it saying; "THIS IS CONTINOUS MAGIC"! As per another Hadith (BUKHARI, Vol. 9, #379) Muhammad has denied having sent with any kind of miracle! After being challenged by the pagans Allah bestowed upon him the feat of magic so that he could show the miracle to the people of Mecca by splitting the moon! So far many missions to moon have been made but no rift was visible! Thanks be to Muhammad that he quickly "Repaired" the damage done to the moon! Otherwise the whole of earth would have been adversely impacted by the "Split"! This was a bad move as it could not convince the pagans of Mecca! Allah himself said a number of times that Muhammad is like any other messengers that came before him! Did anyone of those messengers had to show such magic to their people? The "Hour" has not yet reached, though the prediction was made in the Quran more than fourteen hundred years ago! We should not be worried as our solar system is still in its prime. The sun, being five million years old, is still in the middle of its life span! It has enough fuel to survive at least another 500 million years! Let us not be driven by fear when Allah says, "The Hour Has Drawn Near"! It is still millions of years away and the Moon is yet to be driven asunder by religious upheaval! Why the "HOUR" has not yet arrived as predicted by Allah? Anyhow, we have to live a life amidst fear of Hell and torment; deeply concerned with the problem of salvation! Dedicate yourself to "JUSTIFIE THE WAYES OF GOD TO MEN"! "It is not to ring the bell backward" but to do "As the Romans do" and pray for salvation of Galileo in the galilee! Let the religion "Split" the Moon, let it not split the humanity.

Verse-13, Ch-55 says; "THEN WHICH OF THE BLESSINGS OF YOUR LORD WILL YOU BOTH DENY (JINN AND MEN)?" The unique feature of this verse is that, it is the only verse in the entire Quran that has been repeated 31 times in the same chapter called "THE MOST GRACIOUS"! The title of the chapter refers to Allah himself and also signifies how much importance he has attached to this grave question! Another peculiar aspect of this question is that it has been addressed to two different species; the Jinn and the Men, made of two different materials! The Jinn are made of "Fire" whereas the men are made of mud, clay, dust, water, "Despised Water" etc.! Men are visible while the Jinn are invisible! Since the verse poses the serious question to both species, the response should also be given jointly! The only time where they are likely to be together is probably on the "Day of Resurrection"! But we, as humans, cannot deny any of the "Blessings" of the Lord! The Lord also blessed us with "Curses", such as pandemics, calamities, disease, deaths, destructions etc. for not walking the path to paradise! "THEN WHICH OF THE CURSES OF YOUR LORD WILL YOU DENY"? However, the positive side of the Lord is that the "Blessings" and the "Curses" he sends down from heaven on mankind impact believers and non-believers equally! In this respect he behaves secularly! One of the most attractive heavenly "Blessing" from Allah for the pious believers of Islamic monotheism is the "HUR" (Verse 54, chapter 44): "BEAUTIFUL FAIR FEMALES GUARDED IN PAVILIONS. IN BEAUTY THEY ARE LIKE RUBIES AND PEARLS. THEY ARE NOT FROM THE OFFSPRING OF ADAM BUT ESPECIALLY CREATED BY ALLAH. THEY HAVE THEIR HYMENS INTACT SINCE NO MAN OR JINN HAS HAD SEXUALL INTERCOURSE WITH THEM"! Why the question of having sex with "HURS" by any Jinn or man arises if "GUARDED IN PAVILION"? Are they not safe even in paradise? These "HURS" are not offspring of Adam but especially created by Allah himself!

Verse-75, Ch-56 states; "SO I SWEAR BY THE SETTING OF THE STARS"! What does the phrase "SETTING OF THE STARS" mean? Why does Allah, the so-called Lord of the heaven, have to swear by the setting of the stars? Doubt and confusion often arise about the meaning of words of the Quran! Arabic translators and the scholars will come up with an excuse saying that each Arabic word has a wealth of meaning. For example, "MAWAQIL AN-NUJUM" is an Arabic expression related to above verse and according to Islamic scholars it has many interpretations; "IT MAY MEAN THE SETTING OR THE RISING OR THE MANSIONS OF THE STARS, OR THE QURAN AND ITS GRADUAL REVELATION IN STAGES"! Out of tens of thousands of written languages in use all over the world, which language has a single magic word that has the potential to mean "RISING", "SETTING" and "MANSIONS" of a "STAR"? How the word "Star" also mean the "Quran" and its gradual "Revelations"? Does a star "Rise" and "Set" like the sun? Though the sun is also a star but Allah does not accept that definition, rather he says it is a "Lamp"! Allah has created more "Stars" than needed to decorate the first heaven and to use them as missiles to hit the devils! If anyone is yet not satisfied, the translators have referred to another reference book called "TAFSIR-AL-TABARI" for further details! If still not satisfied, one may have to travel to Seven Heavens to look for the actual meaning of the word in the so called "MOTHER BOOK" of the Quran (AL-LAUH-AL-MAHFUZ) which is the ultimate source of all knowledge about the "Universe" and its "Creator"! Since the inception of dogma and doctrines, each one of them has suffered from fragmentation due to misinterpretations given by the cult leaders! In chapter 95 Allah swears by Figs, Olives and Mountains to claim that he is the "Best of Judges"! Does the "Creator of the earth and the Heaven" have to swear by his own "Creations" in order to secure recognition of his achievements? To say the least, it invalidates the very existence of the "Creator"!

Verse-3, Ch-57 states; "HE IS THE FIRST (NOTHING IS BEFORE HIM) AND THE LAST (NOTHING IS AFTER HIM), THE MOST HIGH (NOTHING IS ABOVE HIM) AND THE MOST NEAR (NOTHING IS NEARER THAN HIM)"! This verse appears to be a kind of certification of

Allah's existence as one and only "Creator" by someone other than Allah himself! Why Allah as the "Author" of the Quran could not state of his being boldly; "I AM THE FIRST AND I AM THE LAST, THE MOST HIGH AND THE MOST NEAR"? This verse provides an excellent opportunity for all man of sound understanding to come to a conclusion that nothing can exist in and around "Nothing"! So there was nothing before him! Those who ask "Who created the Creator" should find an answer to their question in this verse! Our creator is either self-created or created out of nothing or he was never created! Did he emerge from a vacuum to create the universe? He is either born out of "Singularity" or he himself is the "Singularity"! Mystery of his creation seems to be hiding behind the darkness of the dark matter! He created everything out of nothing! In his word nothing means everything! In this universe nothing matters except himself! What about us? Do we have a creator? Logically one might say, "My creator has no creator, so do I". Are we than the creation of an "Uncreated Creator? But those who oppose this view would say, "Look at the universe, you will find an answer"! Well, as the saying goes, "Beauty lies in the eyes of the beholder"! In fact the "Truth lies in the eyes of the believer" and the blind! They "See" the "Creator" even when he claims to have created stars to use them as "Missiles" to hit the devils! If an All-Powerful All-Mighty could come to existence when nothing existed before him, why every tiny creature needed a creator? How he came to know that nothing existed before him? And to begin the process of procreation Allah sent only one pair of man and woman (Adam and Eve) and to support their sustenance he sent four kinds of animals only! His creative genius, as a creator, has no match inside or outside the universe! Allah is also the "Last" since he left no room for a second creator! Muhammad was also his last messenger as he did not want any messenger coming after him to corrupt his Book of divine verses! He discredited all other scriptures of the past claiming Quran as the latest revelation from him! Allah being unmarried leaves no offspring, nor even a "Crown Prince" to inherit his vast "Kingdom"! Muhammad followed suit, leaving no inheritor to succeed him! Allah neither took a "Son" himself nor gave one to Muhammad! He has proudly declared that everything will be destroyed including the universe and it is he who would live on forever! It might not feel out of context to say that Jesus was so unlucky to have been rejected by Allah as his son! Otherwise he could inherit the "Kingdom" as the first in line to the "Throne"! Jesus, though had a caring mother, was deprived of the love and affection of a loving "Father"! Adam, the father of the "Mankind" had neither a father nor a mother! Prophet Muhammad, the "Last" messenger, could not leave behind a male child to inherit his legacy! Allah is the "Most High" and nothing is "Above" him for obvious reason that he lives on his "Palace" located over Seventh Heaven near the "Lot-Tree" planted at the outermost boundary of the universe! Yet he is the "Most Near" and nothing is nearer to him than himself! Most likely, his brightness is brighter than a supernova! Its heat was so intense that it reduced the mountain to ashes when Moses went to see his Lord near that mountain! It is for our safety that Allah does not want any of us to go "Near" him! On the 9th day of the Holy month of Hajj and at the third part of every night, Allah comes down to "First heaven" which is more than four light years away from the earth! He keeps his distance for our safety! Muhammad also claims that he is the "Nearest" to the believers and as such they must love him more than their loved ones: Parents and children! He, who has no existence, exists everywhere or exists nowhere! If a Muslim wants to make a confession, he must say: "I testify that the creator of all the universe including the stars, the planets, the sun, the moon, the heavens, the earth with all its known and unknown forms of life, is Allah. He is the organizer and Planner of all its affairs. It is he who gives life and death and he is the Sustainer, and the Giver of security". This confession is for the "Oneness of the Lordship of Allah"! How can anybody testify "Oneness" of the Lord if he is not sure of his existence? I cannot testify in favor of Allah being the "Creator" of everything as he lacks knowledge of the Solar System where we live! In the entire Quran there is no mention of any other planets except the planet earth! Allah always claims to have created stars but not the galaxies, why? I cannot certify or testify that Allah has created the earth and the Heaven in "Six Days", can I? Would it not be ridiculous to testify that the Lord has created the stars to use them as missiles to hit the devils? I, for sure, cannot testify that Allah can create anything just by saying a word "Be"! I cannot testify a Lord that claims to have created Adam with ninety foot in height! I cannot testify a God who takes twenty three years to reveal a book by an angel who is made of light! I cannot testify a divinity who mocks his own creation nor can I accept him as my creator who curses me! I can only testify the Nature, not Allah, as the Giver of Pandemics, Calamities, Destruction, Death and Life! I am my own sustainer! I am the giver of my own security! If any other forms of life on earth do not have to make so-called confession, why should the humans? Have they made any deal with the so-called creator to this effect? Is it possible to make a deal with an "Unseen"? Has any human being asked that "Unseen" to give him life in return for a life-long loyalty to him? Finally, last but not the least, the deity who seeks endorsement or testimony for his existence from his creation in the form of a "Confession", does not deserve to be called a "Creator"! As per "The Uncertainty Principle" of Werner Heisenberg the future state of a particle cannot be determined if its present velocity and state is not known precisely! Similarly we cannot testify the existence of any God if his past, present and future are not known and exists only in imagination!

Verse-22, Ch-57 states; "NO CALAMITY BEFALLS ON THE EARTH OR IN YOURSELF BUT IT IS INSCRIBED IN THE BOOK OF DECREES (AL-LAUH-AL-MAHFUZ) BEFORE WE BRING IT INTO EXISTENCE. VERILY THAT IS EASY FOR ALLAH"! Whatever calamity befalls on the mankind, collectively or individually, is already inscribed in the "Book of Decree" before the creation of the earth! So the "Sin" committed by Adam and his expulsion from paradise including the murder of Abel by Cain were all written beforehand by the Lord in his so-called "Book of Decree"! So it is obvious that Allah wrote the "Book of Decree" before the creation of the earth and the heaven? What is easy for Allah; the creation or the destruction? Who is the author of this so-called "Book of Decree? Undoubtedly the author of this Book is also Allah! We have no idea about the size of that "Book"! In a previous verse Allah claimed that seven seas of "Ink" would be too little to write all the words about him! If we assume that all the words about him and his creation are written in that Book, then the size of that Book would out-weigh our imagination! If human's destiny is already written by Allah in that book before existence, than what is the point asking him for mercy? Allah has kept 99% of the total mercy with him and only 1% he has kindly bestowed upon the entire creation on earth! This disproportionate allocation of mercy is also inscribed in the "Book of Decree" by the Merciful Judge of the "Day of Judgment? Does Allah know the disasters that befall on earth? Was it written in the "Book of Decrees" that Hitler would one day annihilate sixty million Jews? Adolf Hitler definitely sided with Allah since the Jews are their common enemies! Obviously, calamity that befell on Muhammad's life and health were written in that book! Allah has subjected his "ASHRAFUL MUKHLUKAT" (Best of Creations) to suffer from deadly diseases! Our consequences are also inscribed in that Book! What is the point going through this religious ordeal in this world for a predestined mankind?

Verse-21, Ch-58 says; "ALLAH HAS DECREED; VERILY IT IS I AND MY MESSENGERS WHO SHALL BE THE VICTORIOUS. VERILY ALLAH IS ALL-POWERFUL, ALL- MIGHTY"! In this verse Allah has finally found his long-waited singular identity; used "I" instead of frequently used "We" to refer to himself! Allah, like many political leaders on earth, has already declared himself "Victorious" as the victory of the dictators is always sealed or decreed before the ballots are counted! We all, including our "Creator", are engaged in a religious "War" that has no end in sight! The ALL-POWERFUL ALMIGHTY and his messengers are on one side and the mankind and the devils are on the other! Is this not like a cruel King, with a strong army on his side, declaring war against his unarmed citizens? Here the powerful "Creator" has done the same against his own creation! Allah and his host of messengers are sure of their success and will ultimately emerge as the victorious against their enemies! Who are the enemies? The devils, deities and the disbelievers! All of whom are the creations of the creator Allah! How can the "Created" win a war against the mighty "Creator"? As the "LORD HAS DECREED"; so the "VICTORY" goes to him! GLORIFIED BE ALLAH for winning a war over adversaries of his own "Creation"! It would have been more dignified for a "Creator" to claim victory against another "Creator"! Alas, there is none to challenge Allah! A victory brings glory only when fought between equals! Let the mankind wait patiently for "D-Day" or "V-Day" or at least the "Dooms-Day" to come! I earnestly pray to Allah to send Gabriel again on earth to count the number of believers who sincerely have embraced Islamic monotheism and then declare victory for him and his messengers! Claiming "Victory" by "Decree" takes away all reputation from the "Creator"! It does not make sense gathering all messengers for their actions on the Day of Judgment when the "JUDGE" has already made them victorious! What about Muhammad? Did he win hearts of all humans as a messenger to all mankind?

Verse-21, Ch-59 says; "HAD WE SENT DOWN THIS QURAN ON A MOUNTAIN, YOU WOULD SURELY HAVE SEEN IT HUMBLING ITSELF AND RENT ASUNDER BY THE FEAR OF ALLAH. SUCH ARE THE PARABLES WHICH WE PUT FORWARD TO MANKIND THAT THEY MAY REFLECT"! We may recall that "HIRA' is a well-known cave in a mountain near Mecca! When Archangel Gabriel landed on that mountain, carrying messages to Muhammad from Allah, it did not humble or rent itself asunder by the fear of Allah! This is the historical fact not a parable!

So, what do the mankind reflect from Allah's parable? Does a divine author have to use parables, like a story-teller, to make his side of the story believable to the mankind? Allah has demolished a mountain over some disbelievers to crush them to death! Another mountain was burnt to ashes when Moses went to meet him! He also ordered mountains to glorify his praises with Prophet David! Most importantly these mountains are affixed on the surface of the earth to keep it from shaking! Do the mountains have the capacity to react to any kind of fear? Do they possess souls? The purpose behind this parable is to make the mankind humble itself to Allah by fear; not love! We, as human being do hereby reflect that what has been stated in the above verse is either wrong or the Quran was not revealed on a mountain near Mecca as is often claimed! A related Hadith (Al-BUKHARI, Vol. 4, #784), narrates an amazing story: "Prophet Muhammad used to deliver religious speech standing on the ground near a palm tree. A man out of respect built a pulpit for Muhammad away from the tree! When he proceeded towards the pulpit to deliver his Friday sermon, the palm-tree started crying like a child for missing the sermon that it used to listen from Muhammad! Then the prophet embraced the tree to stop it from moaning"! What is the moral of this parable? The mankind should be humbling itself by the fear of Allah? What was the reaction of Muhammad when Gabriel descended with messages unto him? Was he shaken by the fear of Allah?

Verse-6, Ch-61 states; "AND WHEN JESUS, SON OF MARY SAID; O CHILDREN OF ISRAEL! I AM THE MESSENGER OF ALLAH UNTO YOU, CONFIRMING THE TORAH WHICH CAME BEFORE ME AND GIVING GLAD TIDINGS OF A MESSENGER TO COME AFTER ME, WHOSE NAME WILL BE AHMAD. BUT WHEN HE (AHMAD i.e. MUHAMMAD) CAME TO THEM WITH CLEAR PROOFS, THEY SAID; THIS IS PLAIN MAGIC"! Is it not unusual that a messenger forecasting arrival of his successor without even knowing his proper name? The Quran contains hundreds of verses but none has ever mentioned "AHMAD" as another name of prophet Muhammad! Allah himself in many verses addressed him as "O MUHAMMAD"! Even before the so-called revelation, when he was about forty, people of his tribe used to call him "MUHAMMAD"! As per the above verse Jesus claims himself as the messenger of Allah confirming "Torah" which came before him! Did "Torah" contain any verse forecasting arrival of Jesus as the next messenger of Allah for the people of Israel? So it is also clear from the above verse that the Lord or Allah first "Revealed" the Torah, then the Bible and then the Quran! The verses of the Quran are said to have been derived from the "Book of Decree" held with Allah! What about the sources of the Torah and the Bible? When Muhammad arrived with "Clear Proofs", they rejected it as "Plain Magic"! The birth of the 'Son of Mary" or Son of God" is itself a pure magic! These words in the verse are told by Jesus to the children of Israel, but from what source did he get this name "AHMAD" before revelation of the Quran? Is it in the Torah or in the Bible? Was it absolutely necessary to create this controversy by changing the name? Since, according to the Quran, Jesus is ultimately coming back to earth from his "Home" in the second heaven, where he is currently living, to rule over the world as a Muslim ruler! And surprisingly, Jesus himself did not talk about his second coming! Jesus's foremost task will be to convert the entire mankind to Islamic monotheism which Muhammad failed to accomplish for lack of efficacy of his performance! Believe it or not, the plan of action to be undertaken by Jesus is clearly stated by Muhammad in a Hadith (Al-BUKHARI, vol. 3, #425) quoted with this verse; "SURELY, THE SON OF MARY WILL SHORTLY DESCEND AMONGST YOU PEOPLE (MUSLIMS), AND WILL JUDGE MANKIND JUSTLY BY THE LAW OF THE QURAN AND WILL BREAK THE CROSS AND KILL THE PIGS AND ABOLISH THE TAXES TAKEN FROM THE PEOPLE OF SCRIPTURES BY THE MUSLIM GOVERNMENT"! So, earlier Jesus forecasted the arrival of Ahmad (alias Muhammad) to replace him and now Muhammad forecasting the descend of Jesus from heaven to accomplish the mission that he left undone! It also indicates that Muhammad knew beforehand that it would not be possible by him to implement Islamic monotheism all over the world though he claims to have come for the whole of mankind! Did all the messengers predict arrival of their successors in the scriptures that were said to have been revealed by Allah since Adam? This Hadith also says, "Ahmad" literally means "ONE WHO PRAISES ALLAH MORE THAN OTHERS"! One who reads the Quran minutely, will find the fact that it is not "Ahmad" but Allah himself who praises him most! Prophet Muhammad is also quoted to have said that he has a total of five names, they are; Muhammad, Ahmad, Al-MAHI, Al-HASHIR and Al-AQIB! Did Shakespeare say, "What's in a name? Name matters a lot! Allah has ninety nine names and not unusual for his messenger to have only five! So, the second coming of Jesus will provide a golden chance to the mankind to verify whether "AHMAD" is really the "Muhammad" or not! Long ago Jesus was sent to the people of Israel and was rejected by them! Now the same prophet will be sent for the whole of mankind! According to a saying of prophet Muhammad, quotes Dr. MANEH HAMMAD of Saudi Arabia, "Jesus will stay for forty years which is going to be the happiest years of life on this earth"! So it is crystal-clear from the above quotation that Muhammad not only failed to bring about the "Happiest Years" for his followers but also for himself! Why Muhammad is still the most favorite of all messengers to Allah? "All is well that ends well"; Allah does not believe in it! Jesus is indeed the last messenger! Can the Muslims deny it? Besides converting the all mankind into Islamic monotheism, Allah has entrusted Jesus with some important assignments, such as to "BREAK THE CROSS", "KILL THE PIGS" and "ABOLISH THE TAXES"! Why pour vengeance on the lifeless "Cross" since Allah does not believe Jesus was crucified! The Muslims are forbidden to eat pigs and probably for that reason Allah wants those animals killed! Does a "Creator" have to pour his anger on animals and the lifeless Cross? An Anglo-Saxon poet, probably a contemporary of Muhammad, explained in his poem "The Dream of the Rood" how it had to play its part unwillingly in the Crucifixion of Jesus! The unjustified taxes may have been imposed on the people of scriptures by the Muslim governments without any "Decree" from Allah! DR. M.T. AL-HILALI, a professor of Islamic faith, Medina university says, in reference to fourth chapter of Gospel, "That the Devil actually carried the Messiah and took him from place to place"! Then he asks; "How can the Devil carry God"? His aim is to establish Jesus only as a prophet or as a servant of God but not a God! In reply to his question above one can also ask, "How Satan can mislead Adam in paradise in the presence of Allah"? DR. HILALI adds more by saying that "The Devil orders Jesus to prostrate before him and worship him"! He then asks; "How can the Devil even dare such an audacity with God (Jesus)? Probably the Devil wanted to take revenge for being ordered by Allah to prostrate before Adam! Let Jesus arrive on his new mission to heal the wounds created by Muhammad! It appears to me that the Judaism, Christianity and the Islam are indeed three branches of the same tree with little deviation in outlook! All the prophets and the related mythical stories, including the Adam-Eve saga are common elements of these three religions! As a result of being originated at one place, the rivalry is so intense among them!

Verse-11, Surah-62 says; "AND THEY (DEVOTEES) SEE SOME MERCHANDISE OR SOME AMUSEMENT (BEATING OF DRUM etc.) THEY DISPERSE HEADING TO IT, AND LEAVE YOU (MUHAMMAD)

STANDING WHILE DELIVERING FRIDAY SERMON"! Merchandise and musical amusement seemed more amusing than prophet's Friday sermon to the believers and that must have sent a message to the messenger, if he could read their minds properly! Selling of merchandise around the mosque on Friday by hawkers and vendors is still in practice in the Middle Eastern countries but sound of drum beat is not heard nowadays! Probably playing music in public places as a social event was prevalent in those days! It is totally banned now by administrative order! When divine "Decree" fails, royal decree comes into play! Subject of this verse does not seem to have come through divine revelation, rather it could be included in a Hadith! Muhammad narrated a story in a previous Hadith that his Friday lecture made such an impact on a date-tree that it cried like a child when he stopped reciting near that tree! Whereas the so called believers ran away from his religious talks! This is indeed a disrespect not only to the messenger himself but also to his messages! This chapter sixty two of the Quran has been named "Friday" because of the special significance attached to this day by Allah! Even "Good Friday" would have been a better choice as its name! The Muslims all over the world consider it as the most sacred day of the week! Though many Muslims do not regularly attend five obligatory prayers, but they try to attend weekly Friday congregation at the mosques to listen to special sermon and to seek blessings of Allah! In fact the entire mankind should consider the Friday as the holiest day! Because, ABU HURAIRAH, an Islamic theologian quoted Muhammad as saying; 'THE BEST DAY ON WHICH THE SUN RISES IS FRIDAY. ADAM WAS CREATED ON IT, AND ON IT HE WAS ADMITTED INTO PARADISE, ON IT HE WAS CAST OUT OF IT, AND THE HOUR WILL ARRIVE ONLY ON A FRIDAY"! So, Friday is the beginning of the mankind as Adam landed on the earth, after being cast out of paradise on this day! Friday will also be the end of life as the angel called ISRAFEEL will blow his "Horn" to mark the arrival of the Dooms day! Adam was created on Friday in paradise which is located near Seven Heavens! Does the "Sun" appear on every weekdays there in paradise as it does on earth? We always find conflicting relations between science and religion, whereas the nature connects science with sense and sensibility of its behavior! Adam died on this day too! Jesus is also said to have been "Crucified" on "Good Friday"! This earth will come to its "End" also on Friday though it was not created on Friday! It means, if mankind can safely pass a Friday, it can be sure that the "Hour" is not coming until the next Friday! When did mankind learn to read and write? When did they begin naming the "Weekdays"? What significance does it hold for the mankind which day Adam was created or died or ousted from heaven? This might look like a conjecture to many, to say the least, that Muhammad fixed Friday afternoon for his weekly address to the followers at the mosque to ensure a large attendance! He also attached lots of important events to this day! Muhammad was unlucky as he was neither born nor died on Friday! Muslims believe Friday as the best day of the week and whoever dies on Friday is considered lucky! So the "Hour" or the "Dooms Day" will arrive on "Friday" but the mankind is yet left with more confusions as regards to Allah's claim that on the Day of Resurrection he would hold the earth on his "Hand" and he will make the sun rise in the West! At a time of turmoil when the traumatized men and women are on the verge of destruction, which calendar should they follow; Gregorian or the Arabian? The Muslims must prefer Arabian calendar and the Christian should go for the Gregorian! Each nation is to follow its own as the doctrinal divide among mankind will persist until the last "Friday"! Science of Quran says the Dooms Day will happen on "Friday" all over the globe simultaneously!

Verse-3, Ch-66 states; "AND (REMEMBER) WHEN THE PROPHET DISCLOSED A MATTER IN CONFIDENCE TO ONE OF HIS WIVES (HAFSA), THEN SHE TOLD IT TO ANOTHER i.e. (AISHAH). AND ALLAH MADE IT KNOWN TO HIM (MUHAMMAD). ALLAH INFORMED PART THEREOF AND LEFT A PART. THEN WHEN MUHAMMAD TOLD HER (AISHAH) THEREOF, SHE ASKED; WHO TOLD YOU THIS? MUHAMMAD REPLIED; THE ALL-KNOWER, THE ALL-AWARE HAS TOLD ME"! AISHAH and HAFSA were the most prominent among many wives of Muhammad! They were the daughters of Muhammad's trusted friends and his successors ABU BAKR and OMAR respectively who after his death became the first and second Caliph of Islam! Interesting to note that Muhammad married AISHA when she was only six or seven in order to cement the bond of friendship between him and her father, ABU BAKR! Also interesting is the fact, his first wife KHADIJA was fifteen years older than him! Well, as far as the above verse is concerned, Muhammad shared a secret with his wife HAFSA and warned her not to disclose it to his other wives! But she disclosed that to AISHAH, another wife of Muhammad! All-Aware and All-knowing Allah made it known to Muhammad that a breach of confidentiality has taken place between him and his wives! How did Allah know of this secret between him and his wives? It is easy for

Allah since he has deployed angels to inform him daily about all affairs of the earth! Why has Allah spied on Muhammad's family secrets? Allah surely knows eves-dropping is immoral? Why he relayed that back to Muhammad? Does it not tantamount to ethical violation of his own code of conduct? Allah said in verse 12 of chapter 49; "O YOU WHO BELIEVE! AVOID MUCH SUSPICION, INDEED SUSPICIONS ARE SINS. AND SPY NOT, NEITHER BACKBITE ONE ANOTHER"! In the light of this verse of Allah, his own role regarding Muhammad's family secret may be evaluated! Well, by all considerations, it is a trifling family matter not unusual in any human's life! What is unusual is the involvement of Allah, the one and only "Creator" of the universe! In the next verse (4 of Ch. 66) Allah asks two wives of Muhammad to turn in repentance to him and not to help one another against Muhammad though they seem inclined to oppose him! If that happens, then Allah and his angels including Gabriel would provide all help to protect Muhammad! Verse-5 of chapter 66 related to this matter states, if Muhammad decides to divorce them, his Lord will give him wives better than those from amongst the pious Muslims; married or virgins! What was the actual dispute between Muhammad and his wives is not mentioned in the verses! However, we cannot lose sight of the fact that sending verses by Allah to settle Muhammad's family issues is not uncommon! Here Allah has played his role as the headman of a tribe! This testifies how much care and concerns Allah had for Muhammad! What else can you expect from the "Creator" of the Universe? One thing is yet missing from this family episode: how Allah conveyed that disturbing news to Muhammad? Was there a direct communication channel between them? We find no mention of any especial angel in those verses being used as messenger! Even more weird is the fact that how Allah, being the Creator of the earth and the heavens, could engage himself in spying into personal affairs of two ladies! Did they pose any danger to Muhammad's life that warranted Allah's intervention? Being a "Creator" how does he manage time to look into someone's private affairs? Isn't it incredible? The answer lies in in his own words; "ALLAH IS ABLE TO DO ALL THINGS AT HIS WILL"! There are a number of verses in the Quran that shed light on Muhammad's family life and the picture they present is one of disappointment! Most of his conjugal unhappiness took place was due to his indiscriminate marriages with women of disproportionate ages and that also impacted his performance as a messenger! As a result disbelievers are much higher in numbers than the believers in Islam!

Verily, this story throws doubt upon the "Existence" of Allah and his "Revelations"!

Verse-3, Ch-67 states, "WHO HAS CREATED THE SEVEN HEAVENS ONE ABOVE ANOTHER, YOU CAN SEE NO FAULT IN THE CREATION OF THE MOST GRACIOUS. THEN LOOK AGAIN; CAN YOU SEE ANY RIFTS"? We don't see "SEVEN HEAVENS" built one over another! Do they really exist? What we see with Hubble telescope is part of a universe filled with billions of galaxies, stars and extra-terrestrial objects! So far we have not been able to go near the nearest star! However, astronauts have travelled to the moon but found no rift due to splitting of the moon by Muhammad! James Webb Telescope might be able to unfold some of the mystery of creation! How can humans see any faults in the "Creation" of the "Most Gracious" since he has deprived them of power of vision as strong as to see the "Rifts"! Though human beings are called "ASHRAFU MUKLUKAT", yet Allah, the creator, has not been able to create a single human being who could lead a life in this "Resting House" without suffering from diseases and discomforts? All men he creates are "Faulty", either physically or mentally, and succumb to gradual decay unto death! So, how that "Creator" could create "Seven Heavens" without "Fault"? The miracles of science and engineering excellence, the "Creator" has used to build "Seven Heavens" placing one over the other, is of course an example of marvelous creation? Probably some scribe of Muhammad might have borrowed the idea of a "Seven Heavens" from the cosmological model of Ptolemy, an astrophysicist of 2nd century A.D.! His model included the then known five planets besides the Sun and the Moon! He had drawn seven rings above the Earth one each for the Moon, Mercury, Venus, Sun, Mars, Jupiter and Saturn! Above them was the sky! Probably these seven rings have been projected as the "Seven Heavens" that Allah claims to have created! The defenders of Islam say that humans are incapable of understanding the science of Allah with their limited knowledge! Einstein never attempted to explain "Theory of Relativity" to elementary students!

Verse-4, Ch-70 says; "THE ANGELS AND THE RUH (GABRIEL) ASCEND TO ALLAH IN A DAY, THE MEASURE WHEREOF IS FIFTY THOUSAND YEARS"! Now let's recall that so-called "MIRAJ" (ascend of Muhammad to heavens)! In that the same angel Gabriel took prophet Muhammad to space at night riding on a donkey-like animal called BURAQ and came back next morning before sunrise! How much time that journey took according to world's standard time? Whereas in verse 5 of Surah-32 Allah says; "HE (ALLAH) MANAGES AND REGULATES EVERY AFFAIR FROM THE HEAVENS TO THE EARTH, THEN IT (AFFAIR) WILL GO UP TO HIM IN ONE DAY, THE SPACE WHEREOF IS A THOUSAND YEARS OF YOUR RECKONING (i.e. RECKONING OF PRESENT WORLD'S TIME)"! When the "Affair" goes to Allah, it takes "One Day" which is equal to "A Thousand" years of our time! How does the affair go to Allah? Do they go by themselves? No! Allah has employed many angels to report every affair of the earth to him on a daily basis! According to the other verse the angels and Gabriel also take "One Day" to reach Allah, but that one day is equal to "Fifty Thousand Years" on universal time-scale! To take the information to Allah who lives over "Seven Heavens" at the edge of the universe, the angels must fly at a speed many, many times faster than light! Whereas Einstein has imposed a limit on speed by his famous equation E=MC(squared)! Verily, this equation does not apply to angels! Probably Einstein being a Jew did not read the Quran and as such he had no knowledge of Muhammad's space mission to "Seven Heavens" which he completed in less than twenty four hours! These two verses were revealed in Mecca but while sending them to Muhammad, Allah may have been staying at different heavens of the Seven Heavens located at different time-zones! It may be recalled that the same Gabriel was deployed to carry messages of the Quran from Allah to Muhammad and he is said to have taken "Twenty Three" years of world standard time to complete the entire revelations! The five obligatory prayers and the beginning and breaking of fast in Ramadan are regulated by the hours and minutes! Now make a comparison of these events with respect to time! A Hadith (AL-BUKHARI, Vol. 6, #351) quoted with verse 24 of chapter 45 says; "I AM 'AD-DAHR' MEANS I AM THE CREATOR OF TIME AND I MANAGE THE AFFAIRS OF ALL CREATIONS INCLUDING TIME"! Albert Einstein`s concept of "Space-Time" is somewhat hard to understand by ordinary people as he combined time as the fourth dimension with other three spatial dimensions of the space! But Allah's concept of "Time" is even harder than that! If Allah wants to accomplish anything in no time taken, he only needs to say "Be"! Allah is not only the creator of "Time", he is also a time-manipulator! Convergence or divergence of time, like a piece of rubber, is all in his hands! Stephen Hawking says that the thermo-dynamic, psychological and cosmological "Arrows of Time" are all moving in the same direction! Perhaps he did not know that Allah, the "Creator" of the

Time and the Universe can change the direction as and when he "Wills"! With so many contradictions and confusions about the "Time", the "Time-Creator" wants us to have complete faith in him for everything he says, everything he does! In the beginning of the chapter 76 Allah says; "HAS THERE NOT BEEN OVER MAN A PERIOD OF TIME, WHEN HE WAS NOT A THING WORTH MENTIONING? VERILY, WE HAVE CREATED MAN FROM DROPS OF MIXED SEMEN (DESPISED WATER) IN ORDER TO TRY HIM"! The same is true for the Universe and its "Creator"! There has been "A PERIODE OF TIME" over the "Universe" and its "Creator" when they were not a thing worth mentioning! No "Arrow of Time" points towards a "Creator"! Men created from drops of semen do not agree with their "Creator" on matters relating to "Time"! Allah's "Day" is flexible; it extends from "A Thousand Years" to "Fifty Thousand Years"! Time is reduced to nothing when Allah utters the word "Be"! The "Time-Creator" now claims to have created man "In order to try him"! Time-Travellers may be able to tell the "Truth" in future!

Verses-40 & 41, Ch-70 state; "SO I SWEAR BY THE LORD OF ALL THE (THREE HUNDRED AND SIXTY FIVE) POINTS OF SUNRISE AND SUNSET IN THE EAST AND THE WEST THAT SURELY WE ARE ABLE TO REPLACE THEM (DISVELIEVERS) BY OTHERS BETTER THAN THEM; WE ARE NOT TO BE OUTRUN"! Please note who is being denoted by three nominatives i.e. "I ", "WE" and "Lord" in this verse? Do all three stand for Allah? "I" is the subject in this verse and that "I" is swearing by the "LORD"! Who is this "I"? This verse may be summarized as "Allah is swearing by the Lord to say that he is able to replace the disbelievers by others better than them"! The truth of the matter is that the Lord is running out of time and the disbelievers are growing at a rate faster than anticipated! At present the "Muslims by name" may account for nearly twenty percent of the world population and the number of "Muslims by deed" is a fraction of that! We are sure that the Lord has no plans to create a new Adam better than the old one! Scientifically speaking, the sun never rises in the east nor sets in the west! We are familiar with 365 days of the year as the Earth takes 365 days to complete one revolution around the sun! But we are not convinced why Allah, the "Creator" of the Heavens and Earth, has to swear by "365 POINTS OF SUNRISE AND SUNSET IN THE EAST AND THE WEST"? When Allah says, "I SWEAR BY THE LORD", we just cannot understand which "Lord" he is talking about? When it comes to replacing the disbelievers by believers, Allah says, "WE ARE NOT TO

BE OUTRUN! But in essence he is yet to replace "Bad" people by "Good" people! What Allah said has not happened yet, as the number of people disloyal to him is rising at an alarming rate! This trend is vividly going ahead and seems unstoppable until resurrection! In this respect prophet Noah raised the alarm and cautioned Allah by addressing him directly in verses 26 & 27 of chapter-71; "MY LORD! LEAVE NOT ONE OF THE DISBELIEVERS ON THE EARTH! IF YOU LEAVE THEM, THEY WILL BEGET NONE BUT WICKED DISBELIEVERS"! Though his son was one of the wicked disbelievers, yet Noah rightly predicted the future outcome but Allah did not pay heed to his advice and the "Wicked Disbelievers" have multiplied many folds since then! If an impartial survey is conducted by a group of angels under the leadership of Archangel Gabriel to ascertain the number of "Good" people Allah has made, he will be utterly disappointed after receiving the reports! If he wants to replace the "Bad" people by one better than this, he will have to overhaul his creative genius from the start to the end! We know the Creator Allah has the habit of creating and destroying generations after generations! It remains to be seen whether Allah will be able to replace disbelievers by believers before the Resurrection! Noah himself, knowingly or unknowingly, made mistakes by allowing some "Wicked Disbelievers" to embark on his "Boat" of salvation which was constructed on Allah's order to rescue his troubled believers! Allah seemingly failed to get rid of disbelievers by inundating the earth with mountain-high tidal waves! The All-Knowing Allah failed to realize the reality what Noah predicted thousands of years ago! He could have easily avoided sending Jesus back to earth again with a new mission to convert all human beings to Islamic monotheism! In verse 27 of chapter 7 Allah says; "O CHILDREN OF ADAM! LET NOT SATAN DECEIVE YOU, AS HE GOT YOUR PARENTS (ADAM AND EVE) OUT OF PARADISE, STRIPPING THEM OF THEIR RAIMENTS TO SHOW THEM THEIR PRIVATE PARTS"! What a shame! They came down from paradise to earth in naked state? No problem! Nudity is natural! We are born naked and will be raised naked! It proves how helpless was the "Creator" of the Universe in controlling Satan! How is he going to "Replace" billions of disbelievers on this earth "BY OTHERS BETTER THAN THEM"? Jesus's second coming is his last hope! DR. AL-JOHANI quotes Muhammad as saying; "Jesus's forty years of rule before Resurrection is going to be the happiest years on earth"! The Jews and the Christians may not accept Allah's plan to send Jesus again to rule over the world as a "Muslim Ruler"!

Verses 1-3, Ch-72: SAY (O MUHAMMAD), "IT HAS BEEN REVEALED TO ME THAT A GROUP OF JINN LISTENED TO THIS QURAN. THEY SAID VERILY WE HAVE HEARD A WONDERFUL RECITATION. IT GUIDES TO THE RIGHT PATH AND WE HAVE BELIEVED THEREIN AND WE SHALL NEVER JOIN ANYTHING WITH OUR LORD. HE, EXALTED BE THE MAJESTY OF OUR LORD, HAS TAKEN NEITHER A WIFE NOR A SON"! The title of this chapter is "The Jinn"! We may recall an aforesaid Hadith in which Muhammad claimed that he is the only prophet who has been sent as the messenger for the mankind! I think this statement is partially true; he has been sent as messenger to the Jinn as well! Otherwise why Allah should send so many verses for Jinn to Muhammad? Question obviously arises about the Jinn? Just to remind the readers again I may quote that the Jinn "IS A CREATION, CREATED BY ALLAH FROM FIRE"! This definition about the Jinn is also not entirely correct as Allah says he has created the Jinn from "SMOKELESS FLAME OF FIRE" (Verse 27 of Ch. 15)! Why Allah created Jinn? Allah says in his own words (Verse 112 of chapter 6) "WE HAVE APPOINTED FOR EVERY PROPHET ENEMIES—DEVILS AMONG MANKIND AND JINN, INSPIRING ONE ANOTHER WITH ADORNED SPEECH AS A DELUSION"! After listening to the "Wonderful "Recitation" of the Quran, the Jinn endorses it as the "RIGHT PATH" and promises not to join anything with their "Lord"! Did the Jinn keep their promise? The Jinn did a favor to "THE MAJESTY, THE LORD" by certifying that "HE HAS TAKEN NEITHER A WIFE NOR A SON"! Allah, the "Creator" of the earth and the heaven, is indeed in need of an endorsement from the Jinn since they have a common feature; both are invisible! For what purpose he created man and Jinn together is hard to comprehend! What business do the mankind have with Jinn who have been kept beyond our visible spectrum? Allah said he created everything, including the Jinn, with some "PURPOSE"? What "Purpose" do the Jinn serve in implementing Allah's Monotheism?

Verses 3&4, Ch-75 state; "DOES MAN (DISBELIEVER) THINK THAT WE SHALL NOT ASSEMBLE HIS BONES? YES, WE ARE ABLE TO PUT TOGETHER IN PERFECT ORDER THE TIPS OF HIS FINGERS"! Yes my Lord, many skeptics do have doubts whether men would be resurrected to life with souls implanted back into their skeletons! To magnify the greatness of the "Creator", the translators in a footnote added; "EACH HUMAN BEING HAS HIS OR HER SPECAL FINGER PRINTS NOT RESEMBLING ANYONE ELSE, INDICATING THAT OUR LORD IS THE MOST SUPERIOR

CREATOR OF EVERYTHING"! Indeed "THE MOST SUPERIOR CREATOR OF EVERYTHING" has printed finger tips of all human being with unique signature and at the same time he has infected each and every human being, including Muhammad, with numerous communicable and non-communicable diseases so that no one dies healthy! What about the rest of the creatures? Do all of them have their fingers printed with unique signatures? Many of whom are even "Handless"! Allah wants all creatures to assemble before him on the Day of Judgment! What will establish their individual identification before their "Creator"? Surprisingly there is an exception; out of many millions of species, only the koalas have their finger prints like humans! Lord's creative strategy is not free of exceptions! The finger printing is not a rocket science, it is a mere identification mark! The humans have gone past that technology long ago! What the "Author" of the Quran and "The Most Superior Creator" did not know is that it is the DNA that holds the most unique signature for all living creatures bestowed upon by the Nature! What will happen if hands or the fingers are cut off from the body? As an alternative to finger-tips, eye-balls can also be used for identification! Can the finger prints identify a believer from disbelievers? May I request the Islamic thinkers to compare DNA tests with finger prints! Which test seems superior; the one devised by the "Most Superior Creator" or the one developed by the "Ingrate Humans"? Oh Lord! Let the believers see the truth!

Verse-9, Ch-75 states; "AND THE SUN AND MOON WILL BE JOINED TOGETHER" as a sign of the "Day of Resurrection" but Allah has not explained how they will be joined together! A Hadith (Al-BUKHARI, Vol. 4,#422), quotes Prophet Muhammad as saying that the sun and the moon will be joined "BY GOING ONE INTO THE OTHER OR FOLDED UP OR DEPRIVED OF THEIR LIGHT"! A previous verse stated that "THE SUN WOULD RISE IN THE WEST ON THE DAY OF RESURRECTION"! It seems that Allah, living in his "THRONE" over Seventh Heavens, is yet to decide what to do with the sun and the moon on the Dooms Day! Will the sun rise in the west with the moon folded into it? If so, Allah will have to dislodge the moon from its orbit around the Earth! On the Day of Judgment he will have to "Hold" the "Earth" on his "Hand" without the moon circling around it! In comparison with the size of the sun, the moon is like a drop in the ocean! The sun has a diameter of 864000 miles and about ten millions earth cam be holed up inside the sun and the moon is much smaller than the earth! Joining moon with the sun would mean throwing a tiny pebble into a huge nuclear furnace! Now make an assessment of Allah's plan to fold up sun and the moon together! Will it be possible to fold them or joined them together? The one way that can be done is to keep the moon at a safe distance from the sun lest it should get burnt to ashes! With the passage of time the sun may gain infinite density and turn into a Black Hole due to catastrophic gravitational collapse! It may pull entire solar system with all eight planets and their moons inside it! Why Allah is so worried about only one planet and its only moon? Allah and his messenger seem to have no idea from where the moon gets its light! But the Pope in the Middle ages who wanted to be "World Pope" and "World King", argued that their earthly jurisdiction comes from the "Supreme Spiritual Authority" just as the "Moon derives its light from the Sun"! Thanks to those popes that they at least knew one scientific fact! Papal authority in late twentieth century even expressed their regrets and remorse for the injustice they did to Galileo! Popes are gradually trying to come to terms with science and the truth but the Islamic Gurus are still adamant and blind to the reality! If Allah wants to plunge both sun and the moon into darkness together, he needs to put an end to the nuclear fission of the sun only! By doing that, instead of destroying "Generation after Generation", he can destroy all creatures including the mankind in one go! Allah has not mentioned anything of his plan about other planets of the solar system! If Allah can delay the arrival of the Day of Judgment for at least five hundred million years from now, chances are there that this sun at the end of its life-cycle might become a Black Hole or might die out for lack of fuel! If Allah insists making the sun rise in the west as a sign of the Dooms Day, then he may have to bring forward the Day of Resurrection before the sun gets too old! Muhammad or the "Author" of the Quran has time and again proved that he has no knowledge about the functioning of the Solar System at all! He says the sun and the moon will be joined together "BY GOING ONE INTO THE OTHER"! The moon might go into the sun but the sun can never go into the moon! An alternative to this suggest that they may also be "FOLDED UP"! How can anyone think of folding two objects when one is tens of millions of times greater than the other? The third option says they may be "DEPRIVED OF THEIR LIGHT"! Allah created the sun as a "Lamp"! He sure knows how the sun gives off light! He can easily put an end to all kinds of radioactivity inside the sun! Thereby it will not only deprive the moon of its light but the entire solar system will plunge into darkness! Otherwise death is destined to come to it in a natural way around five hundred million years from now! Its fuel, which is generated by converting Hydrogen into Helium, may not last more than that! Allah wants to join "THE SUN AND THE MOON TOGETHER", but he did not forecast his plans for other planets! Astrophysicists are looking for new habitable planets for mankind; the best would be the one without a God!

Verses-26 & 27, Ch-75 state; "NAY! WHEN THE SOUL REACHES TO THE COLLAR BONE (UP TO THE THROAT IN ITS EXIT), AND IT WILL BE SAID 'WHO CAN CURE HIM AND SAVE HIM FROM DEATH'? So the soul will exit through the mouth of the body? We were under the impression that the soul has no solid state and it is invisible! Probably this is why the ancient Egyptians preserved the bodies of their Kings and the Queens inside the Pyramids hoping the souls might one day return to their abodes! We may also recollect that Muhammad travelled to heaven to meet with Allah with his "Body and Soul"! Where does it stay in the body and in what form? According to above verse, the soul uses mouth as its exit to leave the dead body! Is that the high time, when the soul reaches the collar bone, to ask that "Million Dollar Question"; "Who can cure him and save him from death"? The answer is plain and obvious! The "One" who brought the soul up to the collar bone is the one who can return it back to where it was! In the history of human inception that has never happened with any of the human beings including Muhammad! What would happen if the mouth of the dying is sealed? In that case the soul will definitely look for an alternative exit! So, before the body is either buried or burned, the soul goes back to its originator in the heaven? When the two angels arrive for questioning soon after "The Burial of the Dead", the soul probably enters the body again? Once the Q&A session is over, the soul will have to leave the body for the second time since it will not like to stay in the grave until Resurrection! The body and the soul will reunite on the Day of Judgment to face the "Grand Trial"! Having finished the creation of Adam from "Dried Sounding Clay", Allah says (Verse 29 of chapter 15); "I HAVE FASHIONED HIM COMPLETELY AND BREATHED INTO HIM THE SOUL WHICH I CREATED FOR HIM"! Allah had "Breathed" the "Soul" into Adam's body through his mouth and then uttered the word "Be"! So the soul that has gone in through mouth, must exit through it, says the Lord!

Verse-29, Ch-75 says; "AND ONE LEG WILL BE JOINED WITH ANOTHER (SHROUDED)! The plain meaning of this verse is that when the soul reaches the collar bone, the two legs of the person dying will be joined together! But a footnote (TAFSIR-AL-TABARI) attached to this verse has complicated the meaning by saying; "OR IT MAY MEAN HARDSHIP AND DISTRESS WILL BE JOINED WITH ANOTHER HARDSHIP AND DISTRESS (DISTRESS OF DEATH AND OF THE THOUGHT AS TO WHAT IS GOING TO HAPPEN TO HIM IN THE HEREAFTER")! What is the point using two legs to represent "DISTRESS AND HARDSHIP" of the life hereafter? Sixteenth century English poet John Donne had used such metaphysical conceits of highly intellectual nature in his poems! Well done! Amidst threats of death, distress and destructions, the Hadith has poured some literary flavor on the "Divine" verses! This kind of dreadful interpretation of the verses of the "Plain Book" is done in order to mislead the readers! Generating fears and frustration among the people to extract obedience has always been one of the psychological warfare adopted by the cruel dictators and the oppressors in this world which they learned from the divine deities! Death has been the weakest link in the chain of generations of people who have come and gone from time immemorial! Words such as stated in the above verse; "Distress of death and of the thought as to what is going to happen to him in the hereafter" have played a key role in generating fears and the sponsors of religions have taken full advantage of it to establish their doctrines! The "God of Death" has used death to its full potential to terrorize humans! Why an All-Merciful "Creator" chose to use such an abominable threat for his "Creation"? The "King of the Universe" has used death as a tool to his advantage! "A BEARDLESS BOY HAS DISAPPOINTED THE KING'S PURPOSE"! Who has the guts to oppose his "Will" and bear the wrath of the monarch? A "Beardless Boy" is a rare find in Allah's "Kingdom" who can frustrate his "Divine Purpose"! Long live the "KING"!

Verse-5, Ch-76: state; "VERILY THE PIOUS AND RIGHTEOUS SHALL DRINK A CUP OF WINE MIXED WITH WATER FROM A SPRING IN PARADISE CALLED 'KAFUR'." The disbelievers on earth mix wine with ice cubes made from normal water as they have no such spring like the one in paradise! However, the process is similar but they often get drunk! Allah assures those in paradise shall never get drunk! Allah said that he had created a river of wine in paradise! Do they have to mix that wine with spring-water? Allah continues describing paradise in detail for the dwellers in this chapter from verses 13 to 21: "RECLINING THEREIN ON RAISED THRONES, THEY WILL SEE THERE NEITHER THE EXCESSIVE HEAT OF THE SUN, NOR THE EXCESSIVE BITTER

COLD. AND THE SHADE THEREOF IS CLOSE UPON THEM, AND THE BUNCHES OF THE FRUIT THEREOF WILL HANG LOW WITHIN THEIR REACH. AND AMONGST THEM WILL BE PASSED ROUND VESSELS OF SILVER AND CUPS OF CRYSTAL. AND THEY WILL BE GIVEN TO DRINK THERE A CUP OF WINE MIXED WITH GINGER FROM A SPRING THERE CALLED 'SALSABIL'. AND ROUND ABOUT THEM WILL (SERVE) BOYS OF EVERLASTING YOUTH. IF YOU SEE THEM, YOU WOULD THINK THEM SCATTERED PEARLS. AND WHEN YOU LOOK THERE (IN PARADISE), YOU WILL SEE A DELIGHT THAT CANNOT BE IMAGINED, AND A GREAT DOMINION. THEIR GARMENTS WILL BE OF FINE GREEN SILK, AND GOLD EMBRODERY. THEY WILL BE ADORNED WITH BRACELETS OF SILVER, AND THEIR LORD WILL GIVE THEM A PURE DRINK"! Allah said he would fold up the sun! Will the sun rise and set in paradise located over Seven Heavens? Bunches of fruits will hang within reach! Wine will be served in crystal cups from silver vessels, mixed with ginger from a special spring by the boys of everlasting youth! They will wear green silk embroidered in gold! Lastly, the Lord himself will entertain the dwellers with a pure drink! What is so "Unique" in paradise? Man in this world can afford better entertainment than what has been described in the above verse!

Verses 31-34, Ch-78 state; "VERILY, FOR THE 'MUTTAQUN' (PIOUS BELIEVER OF ISLAMIC MONOTHEISM WHO FEAR AND LOVE ALLAH MUCH)THERE WILL BE A SUCCESS (PARADISE); GARDENS AND VINEYEARDS. AND YOUNG FULL-BREASTED (MATURE) MAIDENS OF EQUAL AGE AND A FULL CUP OF WINE"! In a previous chapter Allah gave in details all entertainments and luxuries of life in paradise! We are already familiar with excessively beautiful HURS created (not from the offspring of Adam) whose bone marrow is visible from outside through their flesh! What is noteworthy addition to this verse is the most attractive "YOUNG FULL-BREASTED MAIDENS"! But one thing is not clear why they got to be of "EQUAL AGE"? Those who died at old age may not like the "Full Breasted Maidens" of same age! Muhammad died at sixty three and Abraham at around hundred! Noah is said have lived amongst his people for more than nine hundred years! How old would be their mates in paradise? For Muhammad it may not be a problem since he married both young and old alike in this world! He married his first wife who was fifteen years older than him! After her demise he married Aisha who was only seven! Believe it or not, he even married an old lady of seventy! Abraham's wife Sara gave birth to Isaac, by the leave of Allah, when she was ninety nine! These prophets and messengers might reject these offer of "FULL-BREASTED MAIDENS OF EQUAL AGE"! They deserve a lot better and young maidens! What is conspicuously missing is the rewards for the women who would qualify for an eternal life in paradise! Would they not ask for equal treatment in paradise like the male dwellers? Allah has not spelled out their recompense for reasons best known to him! However, after reading the Quran right from its beginning to the end, one cannot lose sight of the fact that the All-Mighty Lord is male and he is male-friendly too! How can we expect such biased judgment from the "Best of Judges"? Women are subject to discrimination even in paradise!

Verse 1-5, Ch-81 says; "WHEN THE SUN IS WOUND ROUND AND ITS LIGHT IS LOST AND IS OVERTHROWN. AND WHEN THE STARS FALL. AND WHEN THE MOUNTAINS ARE MADE TO PASS AWAY. AND WHEN THE PREGNANT SHE-CAMELS ARE NEGLECTED. AND WHEN THE WILD BEASTS ARE GATHERED TOGETHER"! First thing first. Let's begin with the first verse which says that the sun will be wound round, its light will be lost and overthrown! In a previous verse Allah said he would join or fold up the sun and the moon together! Why can't the "Creator" see from his palace over "Seven Heaven" that the sun is round which he claims to have created as a "Lamp" for the mankind? Time will put the sun to death which might happen in less than five hundred million years! If Allah wants to extinguish the sun before that, then he will have to stop the ongoing nuclear activities at the core of the sun! If the sun is overthrown, the entire solar system will disintegrate into pieces in the twinkling of an eye! All planets along with their moons will be dislodged from their orbits and will slip out of the "Grasp" of their "Creator"! Those celestial bodies drifting with the Space-Time might berth at the edge of the universe near the "Lot-tree"! Allah will not have to worry about what to do with the earth and the moon! All problems will be resolved in one go! Now let's talk about the fall of stars! Where would they fall? On this earth? Out of trillions of stars, just one would be more than enough to smash this "Resting Place" into dust in a fraction of second! Then comes the death to mountains as they will be made to "Pass Away"! Please don't get confused! If the mountains can be made to "Glorify" the All-Mighty, why can't they be made to pass away? During that catastrophic destruction who would venture his life to take care of the pregnant she-camels? And lastly all the "Wild Beasts" will be gathered together! Will the dinosaurs be resurrected?

These so-called revealed verses provide enough food for thoughts to man of understanding! Will it be so difficult to assess the intentions and the sources of their origin?

Verses 1-5, Ch-82: state; "WHEN THE HEAVEN IS CLEFT ASUNDER. AND WHEN THE STARS HAVE FALLEN AND SCATTERED. WHEN THE SEAS ARE BURST FORTH. WHEN THE GRAVES ARE TURNED UPSIDE DOWN AND BRING OUT THEIR CONTENTS. THEN A PERSON WILL KNOW WHAT HE HAS SENT FORWARD AND WHAT HE HAS LEFT BEHIND OF GOOD AND BAD DEEDS"! When a tree is violently shaken, its fruits and flowers fall down scattered all over the ground below it! Same will be the scenario before the Doomsday when Allah will cleave the heaven (Universe?) into pieces; all stars will fall down from the "First Heaven"! Since Allah said that, out of Seven Heavens, he decorated only the First heaven with stars! Where would they fall? On earth? No way! Each star is at least million times bigger than the earth! In space? That's a possibility! But the stars are already scattered all over the space clustered around their galaxies! If the seas are burst forth before the graves are turned upside down, then Allah will have hard time finding the contents at one place! Will the fossils stay intact until resurrection? MR. SHAIKH MOHAMED CHAIRI, an Islamic scholar who wrote an article on "The Last Day" in a periodical called "Islamic Relief" published from California, claims that "Allah places in every human being a bone which the earth can never consume and from which creatures will be reconstructed on the Day of Resurrection. It is the coccygeal tip"! I am not in a position to say whether this is scientifically true or not! But religiously one must believe in it to avoid being enlisted as disbeliever! After resurrection, will it be of any consequence for any human being to know what he sent forward or left behind? Allah has declared that even an earth full of gold will not be accepted as ransom from an evil doer! Who goes to Hell or who goes to Heaven is decreed in Allah's "Book of Decree"! "IT IS NOT FOR ANY PERSON TO BELIEVE, EXCEPT BY LEAVE OF ALLAH" (Verse 100 of chapter 10)! So, majority of the mankind could not have become "Disbelievers" except by the "LEAVE OF ALLAH"!

Verses, 22-28, Ch-83: state; "VERILY, THE PIOUS AND RIGHTEOUS WILL BE IN DELIGH IN PARADISE ON THRONES. YOU WILL RECOGNISE IN THEIR FACES THE BRIGHTNESS OF DELIGHT. THEY WILL BE GIVEN TO DRINK OF PURE SEALED WINE. THE LAST

THEREOF (THAT WINE) WILL BE THE SMELL OF MUSK. THE WINE WILL BE MIXED WITH WATER FROM A SPRING CALLED 'TASNIM'. A SPRING WHEREOF DRINK THOSE NEAREST TO ALLAH"! As in a wine shop, Allah's paradise has a variety of drinks available for the dwellers! Allah being the All-Knower knows well that Adam's offspring are very fond of wine and alcoholic drinks! However, Allah has assured his believers that the drinks in paradise will not make them drunk since those will be free of intoxications! Allah has created a "Rivers of Wine" (Verse 15 of Ch. 47) in paradise so that his loyal believers will not have to face severe shortage of drinks as they did in the deserts! Among many brands of wine there is a type "White and delicious" (Verse 46 of Ch. 37)! There is another brand which the Lord will give them as a "Pure Drink" (Verse 21 of Ch. 76)! The Lord has made available "Sealed Wine" for the believers! Old "Sealed Wines" are really tasty and costly! There are "Vineyards" in paradise so that fresh wine can be brewed out of grapes for the drinkers! Each one of the dwellers will be also be given "A CUP OF WINE MIXED WITH GINGER FROM A SPRING THERE CALLED 'SALSABIL' (Verse 18 of Ch. 76)"! The same verse mentions that another type of wine will be served in paradise mixed with water from a spring called 'KAFUR"! Besides, the wine will be preserved in large silver vessels and will be served in gold and silver cups! Who will serve these wines to the dwellers? They are boys of everlasting youth who would look like "Pearls"! These wines will substantially differ in taste from one another since they will be mixed with water from different springs in paradise, namely; the "TASNIM", "SALSABIL", "KAFUR" Those drinks will be made exclusively for those who are "NEAREST TO ALLAH"!

Verses 6-11, Ch-84: state; "O MAN! VERILY, YOU ARE RETURNING TOWARDS YOUR LORD WITH YOUR DEEDS AND ACTIONS (GOOD OR BAD), A SURE RETURNING, AND YOU WILL MEET THE RESULTS OF YOUR DEED WHICH YOU DID. THEN AS FOR HIM WHO WILL BE GIVEN HIS RECORD IN HIS RIGHT HAND, HE SURELY WILL RECEIVE AN EASY RECHONING. AND WILL RETURN TO HIS FAMILY IN JOY! BUT WHOEVER IS GIVEN HIS RECORD BEHIND HIS BACK, HE WILL INVOKE HIS DESTRUCTION!" What a glad tiding from the Lord! Our family will be waiting to receive us in the paradise! Muhammad will be reunited with all of his wives! We are not sure of a "Sure Returning" but sure of a Death! As of now none except Jesus could skip death! We are not able to predict what would happen to him after his "Second Coming" to this world! Will he be raised alive by Allah again to save him from "Second Crucifixion"? It all depends on Allah's Will! Let's assume that "Sure Returning" does happen and the pious gets his "Records" in his "Right Hand" and as a result this guy will be blessed with a happy reunion with his family in joy! Where would this family reunion take place? Obviously in the paradise? What if other members of his family do not qualify for an eternal life in paradise? Imam Al-QURTUBI, an authority on Islamic affairs says; "After resurrection, people will stand barefoot and naked and the angels will bring the Book of Records of each person! Who gets his book in his right hand is a happy one, and a person who gets it with his left is a wretched one"! Allah might decide to hand-over the records of the wretched one behind his back! Can Muhammad have family reunion with his uncle, ABU TALIB, who died as a non-believer? A quote from "ISLAMIC RELIEF" says; Muhammad's request to have his uncle's punishment reduced will be rejected as: "Allah will get him away from the middle of the blaze of fire to a shoal of fire that will cover his feet, making his brain boil"! Because Allah wanted to see his brain blown out as he did not succumb to brain-washing!

Verses 1-3, Ch-85: state; "BY THE HEAVEN HOLDING THE STARS. AND BY THE PROMISED DAY (i.e. THE DAY OF RESURRECTION). AND BY THE WITNESSING DAY (i.e. FRIDAY) AND BY THE WITNESSED DAY (i.e. THE DAY OF ARAFAT OR THE NINTH DAY OF THE MONTH OF HAJJ). Allah begins writing this surah swearing by the "Heaven" holding the stars! The word "Heaven" in Allah's dictionary has a lot of meanings which might confuse the readers! It may mean "Seven Heavens", "The First Heaven", and in some cases it stand for the "Universe"! When Allah claims that he is the "Creator" of the Earth and the Heaven, one gets even more confused over the word "Heaven"! How a Creator of an endless Universe takes credit for creating a tiny object like the earth? We lose faith in Allah when he says he decorated the "First Heaven" with stars as if his other six heavens are devoid of stars! Then Allah swears by the Day of Resurrection which is still behind the clouds of doubt and hangs in the balance! It has little significance to the mankind except the believers! Then comes the Friday, the so-called witnessing day? What does Allah mean by "Witnessing Day"? Friday is important to Allah! Muhammad claims "The best day on which the sun rises is Friday. On Friday Adam was created, on it he was admitted into paradise, on it he was cast out of it, and the Hour will arrive only on a Friday"! Allah deprived Muhammad of this sacred

Friday! He neither died nor was born on Friday! Then Allah swears by the "Day of Arafat" which happens once in a year and is attended by a handful of affluent Muslims who can afford to bear the expenses of performing the Hajj! Why this Day of Arafat is so important to Allah? Because on this day he comes down to "First Heaven" over Arafat, a place near Mecca, to see for himself the number of "Guests" (Pilgrims are known as Allah's guests) who have come to receive his blessings! However, Allah is witness to all statements, true or false, he made in his "Book of Miracle"; he swears by many things, both dead and alive, yet most of the people are not convinced of his promises!

Verse-4, Ch-86 states; "THERE IS NO HUMAN BEING BUT HAS A PROTECTOR OVER HIM OR HER (i.e. ANGEL INCHARGE OF EACH HUMAN BEING GUARDING HIM, WRITING HIS GOOD AND BAD DEEDS)"! It is the Lord who makes you laugh or cry as and when he "Wills" (Verse 43 of chapter 53)! So, this verse clearly says that every human being irrespective of his cast, creed and color is protected and guarded by an invisible angel! Plain meaning of this plain verse is that even Adam, Cain, Hitler, Saddam, Osama, etc. had angels guarding them as protectors; writing their good and bad deeds! And all the disbelievers who do not believe in Islam also come under this angelic protection from Allah unconditionally! But the "Protection" is not that easy to come by! The Islamic scholars while explaining this verse have set conditions to receive this protection! Under what spiritual authority they created the barriers to receive this heavenly protection is not stated! However, "IMAM IBNUL-QAYYIM", a contributor to an Islamic periodical called "Islamic Relief" published from CA, U.S.A. says; "When the "Servant" wakes up in the morning, both Satan and the angel rush to him. When he remembers Allah, praises him and thanks him, the angel drives Satan away and sets himself in charge of his protection. However, if he begins the day with other than that, the angel leaves him and Satan sets himself in charge of him"! What has not been clearly stated in the verse is the nature of protection! Does this protection include protection from devils, disease and destruction? The mankind is living a life on this planet under severe onslaught of various calamities! The global climate change has worsened the situation to a point no return! Who is responsible for this? Man, Nature or the "Creator"? Divine "Protection" has never been able to safeguard humanity from death and destruction! The visibility is so poor that it does not allow humans to see the "Protection" coming from the invisible angels! Why Adam could not be protected from the "Sin" he committed in paradise? Probably the angel who was entrusted with the task to protect Adam was overpowered by the Satan! His angel in-charge could not drive Satan away! The next who was left unprotected is Adam's son Abel! The first "Brother" of mankind was killed by the second due to utter negligence of the angel responsible to protect him! Or it may be the reason, according to the Hadith quoted above, that the angels in charge of their protection left them as they were not remembering Allah when they woke up in the morning and the Satan set himself in charge of them! If the first man of the mankind could not be "Protected" against sin, then how can rest of the mankind believe in the protection Allah promised to provide? Is this not a hypocritical approach to grant "Respite" to Satan and his associates to mislead humans and then deploying angels to protect them? As a matter of fact, entire infrastructure of faiths and religions is built upon a kind of invisible veil erected between light and darkness; truth and untruth! Why can't a religion of that magnitude is not forth coming from the heaven at this juncture of science and civilization? Because the darkness which acted as a launching pad for those faiths is missing now! At present no emerging messenger or prophet will be able to make as much noise as Jesus and Muhammad did during that period of darkness! In this regard Allah states; "AS FOR THOSE WHO SAY OUR LORD IS ALLAH AND THEN REMAIN STEADFAST, THE ANGELS DESCEND ON THEM SAYING; FEAR YOU NOT, NOR GRIEVE; AND REJOICE IN THE GARDEN THAT YOU WERE PROMISED" (Verse 30 of chapter 41)! Explaining the relationship between the servant and the angels, Mr. IMAM-IBNUL adds more, saying; "When the angel becomes his friend and protector, he has in fact won the company of the best counselor to him ever"! Oh Lord! All disbelievers in Islam solemnly testify that most of the devils have set themselves in-charge of them and angels protecting them have been sent back to where they belong! The outcome is obvious; disbelievers have outnumbered the believers in Islam by a large margin!

Verse-17, Ch-88 says; "DO THEY NOT LOOK AT THE CAMELS, HOW THEY ARE CREATED"? In the beginning of this chapter Allah described his wonderfully created paradise in seven short verses! But all of a sudden he changed the subject which is one of the usual features of the Quran! In the next four verses, Allah asks the disbelievers to focus their attention to "Look" how "Camels" are created, the "Heaven" is raised, the "Mountains" are rooted and the "Earth" is outspread? The creator Allah has described how he created Adam, Eve, Jesus and the rest of the mankind but he never said anything about how he himself was created! It would have been more interesting and realistic if Allah had asked, "DO THEY NOT LOOK AT THE MAN HOW THEY EVOLVED OUT OF MONKEYS"? Camel is a mere beast of burden also known as the "Ship of the Desert"! They are very useful animals for the people of desert since besides carrying goods they also provide milk and meat for them! These camels also played a very crucial role in exporting Muhammad's view of Islamic monotheism in and around the peninsula! Camels are one of four most important animals sent by Allah, along with Goats, Oxen and Sheep on earth as sustenance for the offspring of Adam! These camels should be thankful to their creator as they have been specially mentioned in the Quran as one of his creative marvels! But why the Quran is silent about the dinosaurs? Yet the disbelievers prefer pre-historic dinosaurs over the camels as a marvel of "Creation" and Extinction! Right now men are busy looking into their fossils to unfold the mystery! Then Allah asks skeptics to look how he "Raised" heavens! After creating the earth he ascended towards the heaven when it was all smoke! And out of that smoke he created "Seven Heavens" one over the other without "Pillars"! Finally he rose over the "Throne" at his palace located on top of the Seventh Heaven! Lastly Allah wants us to look at the Earth how he "Outspread" it and affixed mountains over it to stop it from shaking! Yet the earth shakes!

Verses 18-20, Ch-90 state; "THEY ARE THOSE ON THE 'RIGHT HAND' (i.e. THE DWELLERS OF PARADISE). BUT THOSE WHO DISBELIEVED IN OUR PROOFS, EVIDENCES, VERSES LESSONS, SIGNS, REVELATIONS etc., THEY ARE THOSE ON THE 'LEFT HAND' (THE DWELLERS OF HELL). THE FIRE WILL BE SHUT OVER THEM (i.e. THEY WILL BE ENVELOPED BY THE FIRE WITHOUT ANY OPENING OR WINDOW OR OUTLET"! The same retributions are reverberated in verse 100 of chapter 21 which says; "THEREIN BREATHING OUT WITH DEEP SIGHS AND ROARING WILL BE THEIR PORTION, AND THEREIN THEY WILL HEAR NOT"! IBN MASUD, a contemporary of Muhammad, gave his explanation after reciting this verse: "When those (who are destined to remain in the hellfire forever) will be thrown in the hellfire, each of them will be put in a separate box of fire, so that he will not see anyone punished in the hellfire except he himself"! Verses 104 to 108 of chapter 23 present a scenario in the form of a dialogue between Allah and the dwellers of the hell; "THE FIRE WILL BURN THEIR FACES, AND THEY WILL GRIN WITH DISPLACED LIPS (DISFIGURED)" Then it will be said to them by Allah; "WERE NOT MY VERSES RECITED TO YOU AND THEN YOU USED TO DENY THEM"? They will say; "OUR LORD! OUR WRETCHEDNESS OVERCAME US AND WE WERE AN ERRING PEOPLE. OUR LORD! BRING US OUT OF THIS, IF WE EVER RETURN TO EVIL THEN INDEED WE SHALL BE WRONGDOERS"! Allah will then say to them; "REMAIN YOU IN IT WITH IGNOMINY! AND SPEAK YOU NOT TO ME"! So to speak, Allah is not on speaking terms with the dwellers of the Hell anymore! Their "wretchedness" prevented them to act on the verses sent by him! Allah is genuinely annoyed with them! At this point of time they cannot ask for "Freedom of Speech"! Where is Satan who misled them into this misery? Muhammad will intercede with Allah on the Day of Judgment saying, "Lord, my nation! My nation"! This proves that he did not come for the whole of mankind! Let all other nations go to Hell except his!

Verses 1-6, Ch-91 state; "BY THE SUN AND ITS BRIGHTNESS. BY THE MOON AS IT FOLLOWS IT (THE SUN). BY THE DAY AS IT SHOWS UP (THE SUN'S BRIGTNESS). BY THE NIGHT AS IT CONCEALS IT (THE SUN). BY THE HEAVEN AND HIM WHO BUILT IT. BY THE EARTH AND HIM WHO SPREAD IT"! There are many faiths and dogmas which allow their followers to worship the sun or the moon besides various types of animals like cows, monkeys, elephants, snakes etc. as their deities! But in Islam it is totally forbidden for the followers to worship the sun or the moon or any other objects or animals! It really seems unusual for Allah to swear by such objects as the sun, moon, day, night, evening etc.! Will it be acceptable to Allah if any Muslim swears by the sun and moon? Probably there would be a lot of hue and cry among the Hadith experts! They will, as usual, never agree on such Islamic affairs citing contrasting and conflicting views of their own making! What is the thin line of separation between the worshipping and the swearing? Muslims are allowed to swear by Allah only! Surprising to note that Allah is not only swearing by the earth and the heaven but also by "HIM WHO BUILT THEM"! We already know that the builder has made the heaven as "Seven Heavens" like a seven-storied building one over the other and then he spread out the earth! Unscientific statements such as "Day shows the brightness of the sun" and the "Night conceals it" actually show the ignorance of the "Author"! Does he know how day and night alternates in a twenty four hour cycle? The same futile attempt is repeated in the next chapter 92: "BY THE NIGHT AS IT ENVELOPES. BY THE DAY AS IT APPEARS IN BRIGHTNESS. BY

HIM WHO CREATED MALE AND FEMALE"! What is the identity of the swearer who is swearing by "HIM", the creator of male and female? If the creator is Allah, then why he has to swear by himself? Does this swearing have any significance as far as believing in the unseen is concerned? It sure does! At least for those who have their conscience "Enveloped" by the darkness of the "NIGHT"!

Verses 1-5, Ch-93 state; "BY THE FORENOON (AFTER SUNRISE). BY THE NIGHT WHEN IT DARKENS (AND STAND STILL)! YOUR LORD (O MUHAMMAD) HAS NEITHER FORSAKEN YOU NOR HATES YOU! AND INDEED THE HEREAFTER IS BETTER FOR YOU THAT THE PRESENT (LIFE OF THIS WORLD). AND VERILY, YOUR LORD WILL GIVE YOU (ALL GOOD) SO THAT YOU SHALL BE WELL PLEASED". This surah, containing eleven verses, is entirely dedicated to the prophet Muhammad reminding him of the hardship of his present life and the "ALL GOOD" life he is going to have hereafter! So far we have not encountered any night that stands still! It can only happen if the earth stops rotating around its axis! Legend has that Joshua did stop the sun? If so, than it is not impossible for Allah, the creator of the heaven and the earth to make the night stand still! In the subsequent verses Allah reminds Muhammad that he was an orphan and he provided him a refuge! Muhammad got his refuge with his uncle who, until the last breath, refused to embrace Islam! Allah than reminds him that he was poor and Allah made him rich! But how? It is said that Muhammad married a rich and wealthy woman, named Khadija, who was fifteen years older than him! Allah than assures Muhammad that he has neither "Forsaken" nor "Hates" him! This surah belongs to the last part of the Quran! Is it the right time, in Creator's consideration, to console his messenger? Allah has already said that his past and future sins have been forgiven! He was raised to space on a trip to "Tour de Paradise"! There in paradise Allah rewarded his guest with the most beautiful river "AL-KAUTHAR! Allah has specially made a home for Muhammad called "MAQAM-MAHMUD", the highest place in paradise which will be granted to prophet Muhammad, and none else! After repeated assurances, Allah still felt it necessary to say to Muhammad; "I Love You"! Muhammad's prolong illness, conjugal unrest, and relentless struggle against disbelievers may have prompted Allah to send some consolatory verses before his death!

Verses 1-4, Ch-94 state; "HAVE WE NOT OPENED YOUR BREAST FOR YOU (O MUHAMMAD)? AND REMOVED FROM YOU YOUR

BURDEN WHICH WEIGHED DOWN YOUR BACK? AND HAVE WE NOT RAISED HIGH YOUR FAME? If we take the plain meaning of the above statement of Allah as it stands, at some point of time he carried out an open heart surgery of Muhammad to remove his "Burden" that weighed down his back! When did Allah opened Muhammad's breast? Where and how? There is no trustworthy explanation of this verse! Many Hadith experts have tried to give various interpretation in their own way but all ended up as nothing but guess-works! The only instance, prior to his miraculous voyage to Heaven, in which Muhammad states that "A golden tray full of wisdom and belief was brought to me and my body was cut open from the throat to the lower part of the abdomen and then my abdomen was washed with ZAMZAM water and my heart was filled with wisdom and belief"! Why at this stage, when the so-called revelation of the Quran was coming to a close, Allah raised these questions about Muhammad? Did any misunderstanding between Allah and Muhammad develop? How Allah claims to have raised Muhammad's fame in his life time? The pagans used to call him a madman! He was driven away from Mecca and that forced him to take shelter in Medina! He was all along busy fighting his enemies! He is said to have come for the whole of mankind but what was the state of mankind when he left it? Why his followers were divided into 73 factions while he was still alive? If Allah had raised him to fame, why he could not grant him few more years to compile the "Book" to keep his name and fame above controversy? At the end of this chapter (Verse 7&8), Allah advises Muhammad: "WHEN YOU HAVE FINISHED (YOUR OCCUPATION), DEVOTE YOURSELF IN ALLAH'S WORSHIP AND TO YOUR LORD (ALONE) TURN ALL YOUR INTENTIONS AND HOPES"! Does it not look weird that at the end of his life, the Messenger to Mankind needs such counseling from his Lord?

Chapter 95: It is composed of only eight small verses and together they state; "BY THE FIG AND THE OLIVE. BY MOUNT SINAI. BY THE CITY OF SECURITY (MECCA). VERILY, WE CREATED MAN IN THE BEST STATURE (MOULD). THEN WE REDUCED HIM TO THE LOWEST OF THE LOW SAVE THOSE WHO BELIEVE IN THE ISLAMIC MONOTHEISM. THEN WHAT CAUSES YOU TO DENY THE RECOMPENSE? IS NOT ALLAH THE BEST OF JUDGES"? Allah, the "Creator" of the universe, is swearing "BY THE FIG, OLIVE, MOUNT SINAI AND THE CITY OF MECCA" to say that he created humans in the best stature but later reduced them to the "Lowest" of the low save the believers and he concludes the chapter by asking "IS NOT ALLAH THE BEST OF JUDGES"? Why our "Creator" is swearing by the Figs? The Olive however is a useful fruit! Mount Sinai and the City of Mecca are religiously linked to Islam! Is Fig the best of fruits to the best of Judges? I don't know what prompted Eliot, the prophet-like poet to compare "Bellied Window" with Fig in his poem the "Ash Wednesday"! It may have been a mere co-incidence! Allah often swears by sun, moon, heavens, mountains, day, night, evening, what and what not! But for what reasons these ordinary fruits as Figs and olives have drawn Allah's attention that he decided to swear by them? Even an ordinary person would at least think twice to swear by the Figs or the Olives! Does the sublime Lord of the universe need endorsement from Figs and Olives to declare him as the best of judges? Among the fruits, the Dates could have been the best choice to swear by, in order to show some respect to the fruit as it acted as one of the major sources of energy for the believers of Islam and others in the infertile deserts of the Middle East from time immemorial. The Sinai is now one of the best hideouts for the "Islamists" from where they plan their killing mission to attack "Enemies" of Allah! The city of security (MECCA) has come under attack by the coronavirus and rendered it insecure for the worshippers! Allah, the "WALI", (protector) has failed to protect the so-called city of security from virus where his own house "KABAH" is also located! The divine ordinance has failed and forced the "Custodians" of the two holy mosques of Mecca and Medina to seek security and protection from those disbelievers who Allah has "REDUCED TO THE LOWEST OF THE LOW" since they can no longer rely on spiritual pledges anymore! Allah has created man in the "Best Stature" but while doing so, probably he himself was not in his best frame of mind! The "Creator" has downgraded his own "Stature" by choosing to swear by the Figs and the Olives! Taking factual realities into considerations, the disbelievers possess the better stature than the believers in Allah on this earth in terms of height, color, physique, appearance, intellect, morality, truthfulness etc.! Their average life expectancy is also much higher than those of the believers! This observation may be verified through angelic reports! Besides the dates, the Figs and the Olives are very popular in the Middle Eastern countries! Those who have been termed as the "Lowest of the Low" are now in the driving seat in every affairs of the world! Considering the expressions in the verses, Allah doesn't appear to be the "Best of Judges"! These substandard expressions made considerable damage to the greatness of the All-Powerful "Creator"! Our state of mind as human beings got to be reshaped to accept the fact that the "Creator" of the universe is swearing by Figs and Olives to justify his claim as the "Best of Judges"! It seems that the writer of the divine verses were intellectually less competent than those of Hadith writers! In the fourth verse Allah says; "VERILY, WE CREATED MAN IN THE BEST STATURE (MOULD)"! Adam, the father of the mankind was created ninety foot in height and then Allah kept reducing his offspring down to around six foot! Adam was created from ordinary "DRIED SOUNDING CLAY" who was outwitted by the Satan in paradise and on the earth he has successfully misled majority of mankind to his side! Today the disbelievers are in "THE BEST STATURE" and the believers in Islamic monotheism are "THE LOWEST OF THE LOW"!

Verses 1-4, Ch-96 state; "READ! IN THE NAME OF YOUR LORD WHO HAS CREATED (ALL THAT EXISTS). HE HAS CREATED MAN FROM A CLOT (A PIECE OF THICK COAGULATED BLOOD). READ! AND YOUR LORD IS THE MOST GENEROUS WHO HAS TAUGHT (THE WRITNG) BY THE PEN"! Chaos and controversy has engulfed the Quran right from day one of its revelation, when Muhammad was alive, and continued until compilation after his death! Some composers of the Hadith claim that this is the chapter (96) which was revealed first! Some say chapter #74 was the first that has been revealed! Another group claim surah FATIHAH is the first and presently it is the one compiled as the first surah of the Quran! To escape from this differences of opinion, the Muslim scholars say that the order of the chapters is not necessary for recitation! How can you call it a complete book or a "Complete code of life" when it is not judiciously and logically compiled? Why was it not possible for so many people involved, from revelation to collection of the manuscript, to maintain the chronological order? It is also claimed that Muhammad, before his death dictated the order of the surah and the verses! Why then controversy arises? Allah says (Verse 106 of Ch. 17) "WE HAVE REVEALED QURAN BY STAGES IN 23 YEARS"! Was that time not enough to maintain the time and dates of revelation? In another verse (Verse 106 of Ch. 2) he claims: "WHATEVER A VERSE (REVELATION) DO WE ABROGATE OR CAUSE TO BE FORGOTTEN, WE BRING A BETTER ONE OR SIMILAR TO IT"! So, Allah abrogates his verses during revelation and at the same time causes to be forgotten? What does this indicate? Is it the "Creator of the universe" speaking? He is so generous that he has created us from a "Clot"; a piece of thick coagulated blood; semen; a drop of despised water;

mud; altered sounding clay etc.! Then Allah says; "YOUR LORD IS THE MOST GENEROUS WHO HAS TAUGHT THE WRITING BY PEN"! Yet Allah has chosen an illiterate as the "Messenger for Mankind" who could neither read nor write!

Chapter 97: This chapter contains only five small verses and states; "VERILY, WE HAVE SENT DOWN THE QURAN IN THE NIGHT OF AL-QADIR (DECREE). THIS NIGHT IS BETTER THAN A THOUSAND MONTHS IN TERMS OF WORSHIPPING ALLAH. THEREIN DISCEND THE ANGELS AND GABRIEL BY ALLAH`S PERMISSION WITH ALL DECREES. ALL THAT NIGHT, THERE IS PEACE UNTIL THE APPEARANCE OF DAWN"! Verses 3 & 4 of chapter 44 is also about the same subject and state; "WE SENT THE QURAN DOWN ON THE BLESSED NIGHT OF AL-QADIR! THEREIN (THAT NIGHT) IS DECREED EVERY MATTER OF ORDAINMENTS"! This is another feature of Allah's authorship that he often repeats verses on similar subject! If he could avoid such repeats, the size of the Quran would have been much smaller than what it is now! Also the Archangel Gabriel could reduce the number of trips he had to make between the Earth and the Heavens! Most importantly Allah could bring down the time for revelation much less than twenty three years! A footnote attached to this verse explains the significance of this night in greater details; "THE MATTERS OF DEATHS, BIRTHS, PROVISIONS, CALAMITIES FOR THE WHOLE COMING YEAR AS DECREED BY ALLAH"! So no one can avert his death nor can anyone control birth rate against Allah's "Decree"! It is to be noted in practical terms that the rate of births and deaths are much higher in low-income countries whereas they get lower share of the "Provisions"! Calamities are secular in nature and make no distinction between believers and disbelievers! The characteristics of Allah's annual budget allocation in matters of births, deaths, provisions and calamities have seen no changes ever since the mankind came into existence! Those who spend more time in worshipping and reading scriptures get less provisions than those who spend more times in Labs and read Science! Another Hadith (Al-BUKHARI, Vol. 3, #234) quotes Allah's messenger (Muhammad) as saying; "SEARCH FOR THE NIGHT OF QADIR IN THE ODD NIGHTS OF THE LAST TEN NIGHTS OF RAMADAN"! The Lord has named this night as the "NIGHT OF DECREE" for revealing his messages for mankind to Muhammad! If he could kindly come down to Earth in person, then lot of chaos and confusion could have been avoided! However, while the revelations, peace, blessings and decrees come down in full swing in the "Night of Decree" in the East, people in the West bask in the warm sunshine! May be Allah will move to the western hemisphere when the nightfall descend there! Whoever spends this whole night worshiping Allah, would be rewarded as much as he could otherwise earn in a thousand months which is more than eighty three years! So, who can afford to miss this "Night of Fortune"? Gabriel accompanied by other angels come down in the month of holy Ramadan with all decrees and every matters of ordainments with Allah's permission! This night is also unique for the reason that Allah keeps pouring "Peace" until dawn! It is also by the "Decree" of Allah that the "Dawn" does not appear all over the world simultaneously despite Allah swearing upon the "Lord" of the 365 points of sunrise in the East and 365 points of the sunset in the West! Muhammad advised his followers to search for the "NIGHT OF QADIR" in the "Odd" nights of the last ten nights of Ramadan! Allah favors "Odd" numbers more than the "Even"! Allah himself is "One" and has "Ninety Nine" names! He has kept "Ninety Nine" percent of the total mercy with him! He has created just "One" mankind to glorify him "Five" times a day! Besides, he has created "One" earth, "One" moon, "One" sun and "Seven Heavens"! And also he has selected only "One" "Night of Decree" out of "365"! He has appointed only "One" messenger for the mankind and given him "Five" names with 63 years of lifespan! Also note that Allah prefers "Night" over "Day"! He allocates his annual provision for the coming year at "Night"! He took Muhammad for a visit to Jerusalem at "Night"! His visit to paradise also took place at "Night"! Allah comes down from "Seventh Heaven" to the "First Heaven" at the third quarter of each "Night"!

Verse-6, surah-100 states; "VERILY, MAN (DISBELIEVER) IS UNGRATEFUL TO HIS LORD". Who put the word "Disbeliever" in the bracket of this verse? Is it in the original text of the verse? If the word "MAN" stands only for the "Disbelievers", then Allah does not have to be so worried since all kinds of disbelievers have their own Lords to whom they are surely grateful! Why do I raise this question? Because in another verse (67 of chapter 17) Allah says "MAN IS EVER UNGRATEFUL"! Here again the word "MAN" is misleading! Adam and his offspring including all of the prophets and messengers are "Man"! They are not expected to be "UNGRATEFUL" forever! Even if they are, who created them as such? Allah created the Satan and then granted him "Respite" and lastly "ALLAH CURSED HIM. AND THE SATAN SAID 'I WILL TAKE AN APPOINTED PORTION OF YOUR SLAVES" (Verse 118 of Ch. 4)! So it is Allah who let

Satan lose in order to go after his creation and he also says "ALLAH DOES WHAT HE WILLS"! The consequence of his erroneous strategy, with regards to creation of the human beings, has been exposed in his own words: "SO WHEN THEY EXCEEDED THE LIMITS OF WHAT THEY WERE PROHIBITED, WE SAID TO THEM 'BE YOU MONKEYS, DESPISED AND REJECTED" (Verse 166 of chapter 7)! This rejection has come too late as most of the "Ungrateful" men of his own creation have already rejected his "Islamic Monotheism" and began practicing other options! For the minority of the mankind who are still with Allah, comes the consolation in the verse (Verse 111 of Ch. 9); "VERILY, ALLAH HAS PURCHASED OF THE BELIEVERS OF THEIR LIVES AND THEIR PROPERTIES FOR (THE PRICE) THAT THEIRS SHALL BE THE PARADISE"! Allah's messenger gives his affirmation saying; "Allah guarantees him who strives in His Cause and whose motivation for going out is nothing but Jihad in His Cause and belief in His words (Islamic Monotheism) that He will admit him into paradise" (BUKHARI, Vol. 4, #352)! Let those "Ungrateful", unwilling to take part in "Jihad" go to Hell!

Verses 1-5, Ch-101 state; "THE STRIKING HOUR i.e. DAY OF RESURRECTION. WHAT IS THE STRIKING HOUR? AND WHAT WILL MAKE YOU KNOW WHAT THE STRIKING HOUR IS? IT IS A DAY WHEREON MANKIND WILL BE LIKE MOTHS SCATTERED ABOUT. AND THE MOUNTAINS WILL BE LIKE CARDED WOOL"! The striking hour or the Day of Resurrection has many names! Some of those have been mentioned in the "Islamic Relief" (an Islamic magazine), they are; "The Last Day", "The Day of Rebirth", "The Day of Recompense", "The Day of Regret", "The Day of Eternity". "The Day of Collecting Together", "The Day of Meeting", "The Day of Judgment" etc.! What will make you know the Striking Hour? The magazine says; "Earth trembles as ground rips apart. The tempest of horror pulses tears surge, as the dark locks of babes fall ashen running, petrified, scattered and numb, The day of Judgment has arrived, The Last day is come"! Either you got to be tempted by the fair ladies and the pure wine or you must be terrified by the horrors of the Hour! Allah, the "Creator" of the universe has chosen terror and temptation as the two most effective tools to secure love and loyalty of his creation towards him and his religion! Let the mountains go to hell, who cares? What about the mankind? They will be like moths scattered nude, barefoot and uncircumcised! After Allah destroys this universe, and everything other than Allah perishes, he will bring people back to life for the Day of Return! The first to emerge from the cracking grave will be the prophet Muhammad and he will say, "I am the master of Adam's offspring on the Day of Resurrection"! It is not the "Master of Adam's offspring" but Allah's intimate friend Abraham who will be the first to get covered with cloths to hide his nudity! Moreover, kin relations will be severed. No son will enquire about his parents, no mother about her children! "People will be gathered on the Day of Resurrection on a purely white earth, like a loaf of pure wheat! What a grisly picture! What a steep climb! A perilous path to the ultimate destination of mankind!

Verse-8, Ch. 102 states; "THEN ON THAT DAY YOU SHALL BE ASKED ABOUT THE DELIGHTS YOU INDULGED IN, IN THIS WORLD"! This verse begins with a warning that the mutual rivalry for piling up of worldly things diverts man until he reaches the grave! Islam or Allah has not set a limit on worldly things that a man can acquire? Allah is an absolute dictator and a capitalist; not a socialist! When Muhammad was poor, Allah made him reach! All kings of the Muslim world, who are expected to safeguard Islamic principles, have set example of accumulating unlimited wealth for themselves! When the followers of Muhammad and his succeeding generations in Arabian peninsula were facing severe shortage of food and drinks, Allah sent Americans, instead of angels, with the message of the "Liquid Gold" lying underneath the desert and made them rich in worldly things! Their "Delights" know no bound! Dark nights in the deserts are illuminated and the guests enjoy enchanting belly-dances by the Fair Ladies! Days of the dates and droughts have vanished into oblivion! To highlight the hardship of Muhammad's life, a Hadith (Muslim, Vol. 6, ch-20) related to this verse narrates a story: "Once Muhammad came out of his house and met his friends ABU BAKR and UMAR (later they became his successors and Father-in-Laws)! Coincidently all of them were hungry and looking for food! Muhammad took them to a neighbor's house who entertained them with date-fruits! Later the neighbor slaughtered a sheep to give his respected guests a feast to their satisfaction! After the meal Muhammad said, "By him in whose hand my soul is, you will be asked about this treat on the Day of Resurrection. Allah brought you out of your homes with hunger and you are not returning to your homes till you have been blessed with this treat"! Does this story paint a realistic picture? Muslims in millions did die of hunger across the globe! Upon Resurrection on the day of Judgment, these hungry millions will say Oh Lord; we stand naked, hungry and barefoot before you!

Verses 1-5, Ch-105 state; "HAVE YOU (O MUHAMMAD) NOT SEEN HOW YOUR LORD DEALT WITH THE OWNERS OF ELEPHANT? {THE ELEPHANT ARMY WHICH CAME FROM YEMEN INTENDING TO DESTROY THE KABAH AT MECCA}. DID HE NOT MAKE THEIR PLOT GO ASTRAY? AND HE SENT AGAINST THEM BIRDS, IN FLOCKS, STRIKING THEM WITH STONES OF BACKED CLAY. AND HE MADE THEM LIKE STALKS (OF WHICH THE CORN HAS BEEN EATEN UP BY CATTLE"! This chapter is about an army of elephants that came from Yemen to destroy KABAH at Mecca in the year Muhammad was born! Before narrating the story, I would like to point out how Allah asks Muhammad, who was then a new-born baby; "HAVE YOU (MUHAMMAD) NOT SEEN HOW YOUR LORD DEALT WITH THE OWNERS OF THE ELEPHANTS"? Moreover, prophet Muhammad was an illiterate messenger who could neither read nor write! It would have been more appropriate for the "Author" to have asked him; "HAVE YOU NOT HEARD (O MUHAMMAD)"? However, Allah knows better! The story says that the King of Ethiopia asked governor of Yemen (which was then a part of Ethiopian kingdom) to send an army to destroy KABAH! The army came riding on thirteen elephants led by ABRAHAH, the governor of Yemen to demolish KABAH! Because he wanted to build a house like KABAH in Sana and call the Arabs to perform the pilgrimage there! His main intention was to divert trade and benefits from Mecca to Yemen! When the army of elephants reached on a valley near Mecca, suddenly it was overtaken by flocks of birds throwing small stones at them! The stone dissolved their flash and burst into pieces! So they perished with a total destruction! Such was the victory and protection Allah provided to his house KABAH in Mecca! But Allah could not protect KABAH from Virus attack! Why Allah used "Stones of Backed Clay" to destroy an army of elephants when he had billions of "Stars" ready to be used as missiles? Truly, bizarre are the ways of the "God of Creation and Destruction"!

Verses 1-3, Ch. 108: This chapter is composed of only three verses and states; "VERILY, WE HAVE GRANTED YOU (MUHAMMAD) AL-KAUTHAR (A RIVER IN PARADISE). THEREFORE TURN IN PRAYER TO YOUR LORD AND SACRIFICE (TO HIM ONLY). FOR HE WHO HATES YOU (MUHAMMAD) HE WILL BE CUT OFF (FROM PROSPERITY AND EVERY GOOD THING IN THIS WORLD AND IN THE HEREAFTER". This is the smallest Surah of the Quran and it can be recited just in one breath! The longest surah has 286 verses and would take five to six hours to finish its reading! I have mentioned this unique feature of the Quran to highlight Allah's writing skill! Allah gifted the best of rivers in paradise called the Al-KAUTHAR to Muhammad when he paid a visit to him over Seven Heavens! Yet Allah is said to have instructed Muhammad to say to his followers: "I DO NOT KNOW WHAT WILL BE DONE WITH ME OR WITH YOU IN THE HEREAFTER" (Verse 9 of Ch. 46)! Muhammad's mission to space is known as "MIRAJ" in Arabic, meaning ascend to heaven! He rose to space without using any kind of spaceship! However, Allah sent Gabriel with a horse-like animal and that animal took them to heaven! Al-KAUTHAR is a special river in paradise! Its banks are made of tents of hollow pearls! In "The Fire Sermon" while talking of the Sweet Thames T.S. Elliot began by saying, "The river's tent is broken"! This is the big difference between AL-HAUTHAR and the Thames! Rivers have great significance in the life of those who are born and raised in the desert amidst constant scarcity of water! Perhaps for this reason Allah decided to reward his "Guest" with such a precious gift! So, in gratitude Muhammad is obliged to turn in "Prayer" and make "Sacrifice" to his Lord only! But the Lord has not kept his promises to "Cut Off" those who "Hate" Muhammad in this world! He rather did exactly the opposite to what has been said in this verse! The "Haters" who make up the majority of the mankind are indeed leading their lives with greater prosperity and dignity than those who "Love" Muhammad! They are also enjoying "EVERY GOOD THING IN THIS WORLD"! But they may be "Cut Off" from prosperity in the hereafter! The irony is that they care less about life "HRERAFTER"! Most people believe that a penny in hand is worth more than a treasure buried in sand! A Hadith (Al- BUKHARI, Vol. 1, #14), supplementing this surah, quotes Muhammad as saying: "NONE OF YOU WILL HAVE FAITH TILL HE LOVES ME MORE THAN HIS FATHER, HIS CHILDREN AND ALL MANKIND"! Allah, the "Creator" has never demanded such "Love" from "All Mankind" that he claims to have created! I feel it is Adam, who, as the Father of mankind, deserves to be loved by all mankind! Though Allah said that Muhammad is not father of man but he demanded his wives to be regarded as their "Mothers" by the faithful! And as such Allah has forbidden others to marry Muhammad's widows after his death! Earlier Allah had drawn a red line for Muhammad at which to stop by warning him that he was a mere warner like any other messengers before him! Here Muhammad may have crossed the red line! Yet thanks be to him that he has not specifically included mothers and wives along with fathers and children in the list of "Lovers"! However, Muhammad has included them in "All mankind" who must love him to impart validity to their faith in Islam! Writing about Muhammad, Dr. M.H. DURRANI an Islamic scholar from Pakistan described him as a "God-like Character"! He added more by saying that "The Holy prophet being very close to the Almighty, learnt those attributes and this is the character of God yet he was a human being"! Muhammad himself claimed that any Muslim who bypasses him will not have his or her faith complete! Christians, Jews and other disbelievers who did not recognize him as the messenger of God will not be admitted into paradise! Besides this, he claims that this earth has been created for him and his follower to pray! Allah "Created' Adam in his own "Image" by his "Both Hands" and now we find all attributes of Allah in Muhammad! Had he lived for few more years, probably he would have claimed himself a Godhead! Clearly Muhammad crossed the Red Line and finally Allah decided to take him before schedule! So, from the above outline we may imagine and construct a "Figure" of Allah and be loyal to him to receive his bounties and blessings in paradise! Bit by bit we are coming close to unfolding the real identity of the "Author" of the Quran! The truth of the matter is that the total number of disbelievers who "Hate" Muhammad is much greater than those who "Love" him! Oh Lord, please look into the daily reports, the angels submit to you to verify the truth about the actual number of "Lovers" Muhammad has in this world! This Hadith of prophet Muhammad may have played a detrimental role against the implementation of the Islamic monotheism! Hadith writers and the Islamic scholars have exceeded all associates of Muhammad in projecting Islam as way of life here and hereafter! Dictators of the ancient era like Alexander the great or the rulers of Tang Dynasty, never demanded such conditional love and loyalty from their subjects as did Muhammad as a messenger! The Lord tested prophet Abraham by asking him to sacrifice his minor child in the "Dream" in order to show his love for Allah! Whereas Muhammad's demand for love from his followers is a real-life episode! Allah being the "Creator" did not ask his creation to love him more than their loved ones! Muslim scholars on Islam need to think minutely if a messenger's demand for such mandatory "Love" constitutes a "SHIRK" that implies worshiping or glorifying someone besides Allah! They may also look into the fact how many of the believers do really "Love" Muhammad more than their "Father" and "Children"? And from that real perspective it would be unambiguously understood how much of the Islamic Monotheism has been accepted by the mankind! Yet Allah assured Muhammad; "YOUR LORD HAS NEITHER FORSAKEN YOU NOR HE HATES YOU" (Chapter 93)! Believers in religions, both literate and illiterate, lack moral courage to come to terms with the facts and reality on the ground!

Verses 1-6, Ch. 109: This chapter is composed of six short verses, which states; "SAY, (MUHAMMAD) TO AL-KAFIRUN (DISBELIEVERS), I WORSHIP NOT THAT YOU WORSHIP, NOR WILL YOU WORSHIP THAT WHICH I WORSHIP. TO YOU BE YOUR RELIGION, AND TO ME MY RELIGION (ISLAMIC MONOTHEISM)". The Lord, giving up all hopes and out of frustration, is asking Muhammad to say these words! Muhammad's failure to convince people of opposite views on faith may have induced the "Creator" to reveal his anguish by asking each party to go its own way! Muhammad as the last messenger must have been disappointed by such discouraging words from the "King" of the universe who sent him with high hope to implement Islamic monotheism! His "Decree" to kill all disbelievers through Jihad has also failed! The disbelievers were pushed to a point of no return but the last verse of this chapter brought a sigh of relief for them when Muhammad was asked by his Lord to say to them, "TO YOU BE YOUR RELIGION, AND TO ME MY RELIGION"! These words reflect a reconciliatory attitude that might help establish peace on earth! Please compare the differences in wordings and the tone of these two translations and judge for yourself what Allah said to prophet Muhammad and how his followers responded! If what is said in the original verse is followed by the Islamic fanatics, the world will instantly become a planet of peace! If we look at the verse from a different angle, it reflects a change in tone that rings a message of "Peace" and "Tolerance" for every individual of the mankind, accepting the right to practice religion of one's own choice! But Islam as a religion opted to follow extremism and intolerance abandoning the path of peace through reconciliation! Instead it resorted to Jihad, war and bloodshed! Because Allah says (Verse 293 of Ch. 2); "AND FIGHT THEM UNTIL THERE IS NO MORE FITNAH (DISBELIEF AND POLYTHEISM)"? Believers are faithfully "Blind"; they don't see contradictions in the Quran! They are sure of their entry into paradise over Seven heavens!

Verses 1-5, Ch. 111 state; "PERISH THE TWO HANDS OF ABU LAHAB (AN UNCLE OF THE PROPHET) AND PERISH HE! HIS WEALTH AND HIS CHILDREN WILL NOT BENEFIT HIM! HE WILL BE BURNT IN A FIRE OF BLAZING FLAMES! AND HIS WIFE, TOO, WHO CARRIES

THORNS TO PUT ON THE WAY OF THE PROPHET OR TO SLANDER HIM! IN HER NECK IS A TWISTED ROPE OF PALM FIBRE"! How and when this verse was revealed? Once after being dictated by verse 214 of Ch. 26, Muhammad ascended a mountain to address people of his tribe to tell them of this new revelation saying; "I AM A PLAIN WARNER TO YOU OF A COMING SEVERE PUNISHMENT"! Among the audience his uncle ABU LAHAB was also present and after listening to Muhammad he commented that "MAY YOU PERISH"! And soon after that Allah revealed this chapter (111)! ABU LAHAB means "Father of Flame"! Allah is cursing ABU LAHAB to perish with his two hands! Why Allah could not kill or destroy him with a missile fired from the "First Heaven"? It is also a fact of the history that his uncle looked after Muhammad since he lost his both parents in his infancy! Despite being All-Knower, Allah bestowed his enemy ABU LAHAB with children and wealth! Wife of his uncle was in a habit collecting thorny wood from jungle to put on the way of Muhammad in order to prevent him from preaching his religion! There is again difference of opinion about putting thorns! As per Hadith (BUKHARI. Vol. 6, Ch. 356), carrying the woods with thorns means that she used to slander the prophet and goes about with calumnies! The same hadith also says; "In her neck is a twisted rope of palm-fiber" means the chain which is in the Fire of Hell! The fact is neither ABU LAHAB nor his wife perished after the revelation! Muhammad, On the Day of Resurrection, will pray to Allah to have his uncle's punishment reduced! However, this reduction will be as such that "Fire will cover his feet, making his brain boil"! Whereas Allah promised to accept all requests of Muhammad on the Day of Judgment!

Verses 1-4, Ch. 112 states; This chapter has only four verses which state; "SAY (MUHAMMAD); HE IS ALLAH, THE ONE AND ONLY. ALLAH THE SELF-SUFFICIENT MASTER, WHOM ALL CREATURES NEED, (HE NEITHER EATS NOT DRINKS). HE BEGETS NOT, NOR WAS HE BEGOTTEN AND THERE IS NONE CO-EQUAL OR COMPARABLE UNTO HIM". This proclamation that the Allah is "THE ONE AND ONLY" has been made over and over again in the Quran! This book of religion has a unique position among all the scriptures for being loaded with unnecessary repetitions and appreciations of its "Author"! Allah is self-sufficient as he needs no sleep, no food, no drinks! He did not even marry to have children! On the contrary he has created all creatures, making all those needs essential for survival! Even in paradise he made life dependent on food and drinks! A diet-free life he has chosen only for himself! We are indeed needy as we have been made to be! Animal and human existence is closely linked to drinking and as such Allah created many rivers on the earth and in the heaven! He was neither "Created" nor "Begotten"! Generally, common sense dictates that a "Creator" precedes his "Creation". Both cannot be created simultaneously at any point of time! Again Allah is also the "Creator" of "Time"! So, Allah was already in existence before the creation of the "Universe and Time"! After being self-created, Allah may have conceived the idea of creating a universe, since self-created universe, at least to him, was not an option! His universe consists of an earth and a heaven which took him "Six Days" to complete its creation despite having a creative word "Be", immensely powerful as the Big Bang! This "Word" symbolizes the power of creation of Allah to make or unmake anything as he wills! But in the creation of the earth and the heaven he did not use it for some mysterious reasons! Before the creation of the universe and in the absence of his "Palace" and the "Throne" over seventh heaven, how and where Allah resided is of course a matter of great mystery! What has been said about Allah in the Quran, makes him unparalleled in the true sense of the word and "THERE IS NONE CO-EQUAL OR COMPARABLE UNTO HIM'! Comparison cannot take place in the absence of co-equals! If Muhammad had been destined, like Jesus, to come again on earth, he could have surely created another "Allah" of his own choice out of his imagination so that a comparison could be made between the two! Muhammad in a related Hadith (Al-BUKHARI, Vol. 9, #470) said, Allah has a "Right" upon his slaves which is; "TO WORSHIP ALLAH ALONE AND TO JOIN NONE IN WORSHIP WITH HIM"! Allah seems quite alive to his "Rights" upon his "Slaves" but cares less about "HUMAN RIGHTS" that are constantly violated in his name by his believers, particularly the Jihadists, all over the world! Millions and millions have died of hunger and calamities that Merciful All-Mighty bestowed upon mankind! Didn't they have right upon their "Creator"? Allah claims to have created Adam in his own "Image" but he was not made "Self-sufficient"! Allah is "Self-Sufficient" as he neither "Eats nor Drinks" but why he failed to create a single living being, either on Earth or in the Heaven, who could live its life without food and drinks? This verse also states that all creatures "Need Allah" but as far as Adam is concerned it was Allah who needed him more than he needed Allah! As Allah needed Adam to set forth the scheme for the spiritual progress of mankind from the day of his birth to the "Day of Judgment"! Can Allah deny being a "Begetter"? He is the "Begetter" of the earth and the heaven and the mankind including Adam and Jesus! A creator, who is neither "Begotten" or "Created" does not possess the right to exist at all! There are many among the begotten who feel "Orphaned", "Abandoned" and "Forgotten" in the absence of a "Begetter"! So, let a "SELF-SUFFICIENT MASTER" exist at least in their imagination who are driven by devotions! But why Allah is so scared of "CO-EQUAL COMPARABLE" unto him? Rest of the Gods and deities who also claim their share in the "Creation", are bound to burn with their followers in the Hellfire forever!

Verses 1-5, Ch. 113: Five short verses of this surah state; "SAY; I SEEK REFUGE WITH ALLAH, THE LORD OF THE DAY BREAK. FROM THE EVIL OF WHAT HE HAS CREATED AND FROM THE EVIL OF THE DARKENING NIGHT AS IT COMES WITH ITS DARKNESS. AND FROM THE EVIL OF THOSE WHO PRACTICE WITCHCRAFT WHEN THEY BLOW IN THE KNOTS. AND FROM THE EVIL OF THE ENVIER WHEN HE ENVIES". The universe is made of both positive and negative energy of equal amount and they cancel each other leaving it with zero force! The Lord of the Day Break has created "Good" and "Evil" in equal proportion! So, what is the net outcome? Many people believe the Sun as the Lord of the day break and they express their gratitude to it through worship! Mankind is convinced that the Sun is not just a "Lamp" rather it is the indispensable source of energy for all living creatures on earth! They see no other Lord hiding behind that "Lamp"! So, most of what Allah creates comes with evils! It is our duty to seek refuge with Allah to stay safe from those evils created by him, the All-Mighty and the WALI (Protector)! When it became clear to the mankind that there is indeed no "Protector" to protect them in need, they began to practice witchcraft by blowing in the knots! Blowing with saliva on a sick person after reciting verses from the Quran, an Islamic medical therapy known as "AR-RUKYAH", is equally harmful as the witchcraft! So, what is the way out? The futility of this "Therapy" is enough to invalidate the whole concept of Islam considering its harmful effects in the context of contagious diseases! Surprisingly, the positive aspect of the coronavirus is that it does not discriminate between religion, cast or creed! This virus is truly secular in nature unlike Allah! Allah also advises his followers to seek refuge from enviers! The believers indeed envy the disbelievers as they are lacking behind in every aspects of life! Allah says every human being is protected by an angels! Why can't they protect mankind entangled in the "THE KNOTS" of witchcraft! A God in need is a God Indeed!

Verses 1-6, Ch. 114: This is the last chapter of the Quran but it has failed to make a lasting impression! Unfortunately it is the repetitions of old things as if old wine poured into a new bottle! It says; " SAY, I SEEK REFUGE WITH ALLAH, THE LORD OF THE MANKIND, THE KING OF THE MANKIND, THE GOD OF MANKIND. FROM THE EVIL OF THE WHISPERERS (DEVILS) WHO WITHDRAWS. WHO WHISPERS IN THE BREASTS OF MANKIND, OF JINN AND MEN". All creatures must seek refuge with Allah; the Lord of the Mankind; the God of the Mankind; the King of the Mankind; the Creator of the Mankind; the Protector of the Mankind; the Originator of the Mankind; the Sustainer of the Mankind! In the previous chapter Allah also proclaimed himself as the "Lord of the Day Break"! We have no knowledge how the Jinn have been affected but the mankind have been heavily impacted by the evils of the devils much beyond the expectation of the "Creator"! Devils have taken full advantage of the "Respite" Allah granted to their leader, the Satan! How these two terms "Mankind" and "Men" differ in meaning? Evils that include drinking, dancing, singing, illegal sex, killing, radicalization, extortion, usury etc. are surely the works of Satan and his associates! Here we cannot play the blame game, since the Lord has already declared in clear terms that whatever good happens to mankind is from him and whatever bad things happen to them is from themselves! Oh Lord of the mankind! We have learnt to live with these evils and hopefully there will be no recess until resurrection! Did Allah create Satan and the devils with evil intentions? If so, let them do their job! Satan began doing evil things in paradise in the presence of the Omnipotent and his first victim was Adam, the "Father" of mankind and also the "First" man Allah created in his own "Image" by his "Both Hands"! Allah claims to have taught Adam all names of the things he created but forgot to teach him how to seek refuge from evils of devils! It is indeed hard to believe that All-Knowing Allah did not know when Satan was whispering his evil design into Adam and Eve's breasts! All human beings should be thankful to Satan for his ploy that ultimately ousted Adam from paradise to this earth and as a result we are able to lead a busy life looking for the "Creator" in many different ways and means! What is conflicting about the divine justice is the fact that the victim has been punished for his "Sin" and the perpetrator has been granted indemnity; "Respite" with respect until resurrection! The second verse of this chapter has special significance and relates to a statement of Allah; "I AM THE KING OF MANKIND"! This statement has been further amplified by Muhammad in a related Hadith

(Al-BUKHARI, Vol. 9, # 479); "ON THE DAY OF RESURRECTION ALLAH WILL GRASP THE WHOLE PLANET OF EARTH BY HIS HAND AND SHALL ROLL UP THE HEAVEN WITH HIS RIGHT HAND AND SAY; I AM THE KING, WHERE ARE THE KINGS OF THE EARTH?" Ok, let the planet earth rest on his hand but what would happen to his palace "AL-BAIT-UL-MAMUR" over Seventh Heaven if he "ROLLS UP THE HEAVEN WITH HIS RIGHT HAND? Where would he stay? With respect this verse, another Hadith (Al-BUKHARI, Vol. 8, #494) is quoted to state; "WHAT LEADS TO HELL IS EASY TO DO WHILE WHAT LEADS TO PARADISE IS DIFFICULT TO DO"! So, "The Silk Road" to paradise is not as smooth as the silk itself! Allah gave green signal to Satan to mislead mankind to make the path to hell easier than that of the paradise! Angels appointed, one each for every human being, by Allah have proved to be less efficient than the devils! It was Allah's earnest desire to fill the hell with Jinn and Men and the Satan will help Allah fulfill his dream! Satan has done his job well! He made the passage to hell easier for the disbelievers! Whereas the angels and the prophets together made the path to paradise difficult and dangerous for the believers! So, it seems obvious that after Resurrection Allah will find fewer followers who could be granted a permanent residence in paradise! Out of one hundred divisions of the luxurious paradise, many might remain absolutely vacant for lack of qualified occupants unless the "Best of Judges" declares a general amnesty for the disbelievers! Here we may recall Muhammad's claim that Allah has made this earth only for him and his followers to worship! If we take this claim in its face value, we can definitely say Allah could have made a much smaller earth for them! All-knowing Allah surely knew in advance how many of men and Jinn would embrace Islam! In another Hadith Muhammad said his followers would be divided into 73 groups and only one group will remain loyal to him and they are the ones who will enter paradise with him! So the responsibility for this shortfall in number of believers squarely lies on the shoulders of those angels, prophets and the messengers who were entrusted with the task of implementing Islamic monotheism on behalf of Allah! Leave the Lord alone, why should he take the blame? Remember the thunderous announcement Allah will make on the Day of resurrection; "I AM THE KING, WHERE ARE THE KINGS OF THE EARTH"? Allah will summon all the kings of the earth without discriminating against their origin or faiths to take stock of what they did to their subjects! On the Day of Judgment, first of all Allah will surely hold all Kings of the Middle Eastern countries accountable for taking Christians as their protectors and making friends with the Jews for doing business with them! Allah has time and again warned Muslims not to trust those disbelievers as they are "Enemies" to him and the Muslims! Probably these Muslim kings have lost faith in their heavenly "WALI"; the divine protector! Oh Lord; the "King" of the Day of Judgment: Are you not going to summon the Queens? There are quite a few of them who led an unholy life on earth! At least, Cleopatra, the most glamorous Queen of Egypt, should be summoned on the Day of Judgment for her illegal, amorous relationship with her lovers! But she might escape punishment by pleading not guilty since neither Jesus nor Muhammad came with their messages during her rule in Egypt! Moreover she was "Green in judgment and cold in blood"! But Allah claims the "Revelation" begun with Adam! No problem, our Lord is the "Best of Judges" and has the habit of making judgment before trial! Cleopatra, in her defense, has a strong point to make; it was Mark Antony who induced her saying she must "Find out New Heaven, New Earth" for love! Otherwise, she could be as chaste as the Mother Mary! Cleopatra's life had gone through a striking resemblance with divine ordinance! History recorded that out of Royal Necessity she married her own brothers! Accordingly, out of divine necessity, Adam's daughters had to marry their brothers! Necessity is negotiable! Chances are there that Cleopatra might get away with a "Respite" from the Merciful Lord! Antony, the greatest soldier of the world was her "Man of Men"! So what? Let him live a life alone in Hell where even death is undone as an escape!

In chapter twenty three of the Quran, Almighty Allah, the "Creator" of the universe summed up all arguments: When the trumpet is blown, no kinship will be shown among them! With their faces burnt and lips disfigured, they will say; our Lord, bring us out of this! The Merciful Lord would ragingly reply; "SPEAK NOT TO ME! REMAIN YOU IN IT WITH IGNOMINY! WERE NOT MY "VERSES" RECITED TO YOU"?

HELIX OF HADITHS

(Sayings of Muhammad)

Quranic verses are said to have been sent down to earth by the Lord of the heavens through Revelation but Hadiths are homegrown! What is a Hadith? Commonly it is understood as the sayings, deeds and approvals of Prophet Muhammad narrated and described by a number of recognized Islamic scholars! It also includes the legal ways, orders, acts of worship and statements of Muhammad that have become models to be followed by the Muslims! In many of his sayings Muhammad crossed his limits set by the Lord! As such a great number of his followers often regard him as a "Second God". Allegiance to his teachings and prophethood is a mandatory precondition for every Muslim. Whoever fails to "love" Muhammad more than his parents and children will not qualify for an entry into paradise! Some even prefer Hadiths of Muhammad over Verses of the Quran! Allah warned Muhammad not to transgress limits as he is only a warner and a messenger like one of those who preceded him! As is the case with the so-called revealed verses, Hadiths are also not above controversy though in many cases they are said to have been narrated by trusted companions of Muhammad! Hadiths are originated from different sources, known as "Schools of Hadiths" led by scholars such as AL-BUKHARI, MUSLIMS, THIRMITHI, KATHIR, TABARI, QURTUBI etc.! Out of all AL-BUKHARI is regarded as the leading source of Hadiths! If all the Hadiths are compiled into one volume, that would be at least a thousand times larger than the Quran itself! To verify their contents, I would present a few of those Hadiths for the readers to evaluate them against a scientific perspective keeping in mind that those have not been revealed from Heaven! Muhammad claims that he is the only prophet who has been affiliated to act as the "Messenger for all Mankind" by his Lord! But Allah, in verse 7 of chapter 42, belies his claim saying; "THUS WE HAVE REVEALED TO YOU (MUHAMMAD) A QURAN IN ARABIC, SO THAT YOU MAY WARN THE MOTHER OF THE TOWN (MECCA) AND ALL AROUND IT"! This verse has surely narrowed down Muhammad's role as the only messenger for all of mankind and shrunk his domain of religious influence in and around the City of Mecca! If the so-called revealed verses are not consistent in terms of their contents, then how people can rely on him and his Hadiths? These Hadiths themselves, being subject to whimsical interpretations by different quarters, are also responsible for creating many radical factions in Islam in the name of Allah, the so-called Creator of the Seven Heavens! Whether these Hadiths united the Muslims or divided them is a million dollar question and need to be assessed in the light of other evidences of divine history!

1.   "All of the prophets before were given miracles because of which people had belief, but what I have been given is the Divine Revelation which Allah has revealed to me. So I hope that my followers will be more than those of any other prophets on the Day of Resurrection"! (BUKHARI, Vol. 9, #379).

2.   "Both in this world and in the hereafter, I am the nearest of all the people of Jesus, the son of Mary. The prophets are paternal brothers, their mothers are different, but their religion is one i.e. Islamic Monotheism"! (BUKHARI, Vol. 4 #652).

3.   "By him (Allah) in whose hand my soul is, there is none from amongst the Jews and the Christians who hears about me and then dies without believing in the message with which I have been sent (Islamic Monotheism), but he will be from the dwellers of Hellfire"! (MUSLIM, Vol. 1, #4).

4.   "Order your children for prayers at seven and beat them at ten! Chief of a family, town, tribe and the Muslim rulers are held responsible in case of non-fulfillment of this obligation by the Muslims under their authority"! (BUKHARI, Vol. 1, #702).

5.   "Zakat, a certain fixed proportion of the wealth must be paid by all Muslims to the poor in the Muslim community only"! (BUKHARI, Vol. 2 #24).

6.   "In order of gravity, the three sins are: a) Setting up a rival to Allah, b) Killing your son lest he should share your food with you, c) Committing sexual intercourse with the wife of your neighbor"! (BUKHARI, Vol. 6, # 4).

7. "HANIF", not Islam, was the name of prophet Abraham's religion! He was neither a Jew nor a Christian but a Muslim"! (BUKHARI, Vol. 5, #169).

8. "The person who severs the bond of kinship will not enter paradise"! (BUKHARI, Vol. 6, #13).

9. "The best among you are those who learn Quran and teach it" (AL-BUKHARI).

10. "The Muslim is the person whose tongue and hand do not harm others" (Muhammad).

11. "The best day is Friday. On Friday Adam was created, on it he was admitted into paradise, on it he was cast out of it, and the Hour will arrive only on a Friday"! (ABU HURAIRAH).

12. "Allah, the most glorious and sublime, places in every human being a bone which the earth can never consume and from which creatures will be reconstructed on the Day of Resurrection. It is the coccygeal tip"! (BUKHARI and MUSLIM).

13. "I am the master of Adam's offspring on the Day of Resurrection; the first for whom the tomb cracks"! (TIRMITHI).

14. "When they are gathered, all people will be barefoot, nude and uncircumcised. When Muhammad's wife Aisha heard him say that, she asked; will all men and women be looking at each other? He replied; "The situation is too serious for them to look at each other"! (IBN ABBAS).

15. "The same source adds that the first person to get covered with cloths will be Allah's intimate friend Abraham, and next will be Muhammad"!

16. "People will be gathered on the Day of Resurrection on a purely white earth, like a loaf of pure wheat"! (SAHL-IBN-SA'D).

17. "The earth will be replaced by an earth like silver, no forbidden blood having been shed on it and no sin having been committed"! (IBN MASOUD).

18. "When people are resurrected from their tombs and brought to the site, stand there, barefoot and nude, and the time of accounting arrives, order will be given for the records made by angels to be brought, and they will be handed out. A person who gets his book in

his right hand is a happy one, and a person who gets it with his left is a wretched"! (IMAM AL-QURTUBI).

19. "On the Day of Resurrection I will praise Allah and fall prostrate. I will be told, Muhammad, lift your head and speak, and you will be listened to. Ask, and you will be given. Intercede, and your intercession will be granted"! (ABU HURAIRAH).

20. "The son of Mary will shortly descend amongst you (Muslims) and will judge mankind justly by the Law of the Quran! He will stay for forty years which is going to be the happiest years of his life on earth"! (Prophet Muhammad).

21. "Every newborn child is born on the innate nature (Islam, complete surrender to Allah). Then his parents change him into Judaism, Christianity etc."! (prophet Muhammad).

22. "Allah will not let Muhammad die till he makes straight the crooked people by making them say none has the right to be worshipped but Allah, by which 'blind eyes, deaf ears and closed hearts' will be opened"! (ATA BIN YASAR).

23. "Jews, Christians and Pagans say: Allah has begotten a son. The son of Adam tells lies against me. No! Glorified be me! I am far from taking a wife or a son"! (BUKHARI, Vol. 6, #9).

24. "A dog was about to die of thirst. An Israeli prostitute saw it and took off her shoes and watered it. So Allah forgave her because of that good deed"! (BUKHARI, Vol. 4, #673).

25. "Allah says if a believer comes one span nearer to me, I go one cubit nearer to him, and if he comes one cubit nearer to me, I go a distance of two arms nearer to him, and if he comes to me walking, I go to him running"! (BUKHARI, Vol. 9, #502).

26. "Smell coming out from the mouth of a fasting man is better with Allah than the smell of musk"! (BUKHARI, Vol. 3, #118).

27. "I have been ordered by Allah to fight against the people till they testify that "None has the right to be worshipped but Allah"! (BUKHARI, Vol. 1, #24).

28. "Whoever drinks alcoholic drinks in this world, will be deprived of it in the hereafter"! (BUKHARI, Vol. 7, #481)

29. "Portents of the Hour: Men will decrease and women will increase so much so that for every fifty women there will be one man to look after them"! (BUKHARI, Vol. 7, #483).

30. The prophet said " I have been given five things which were not given to any prophet before me: a) Allah made me victorious by frightening my enemies. b) The earth has been made for me (and for my followers) a place for praying and a thing to purify. c) The war booty has been made HALAL or lawful to me yet it was not lawful to anyone else before me. d) I have been given the right of intercession on the Day of Resurrection. e) Every prophet used to be sent to his nation only, but I have been sent to all mankind"! (BUKHARI, Vol. 1, #331).

31. "Aisha, wife of Muhammad, narrated that Allah's messenger, while on his death bed, said; "May Allah's curse be on the Jews and the Christians for they built places of worship at the graves of their prophet"! (BUKHARI, Vol. 4, #660).

32. "The Jews and Christians were divided into seventy one or seventy two religious sects, and this nation (Muslims) will be divided into seventy three religious sects---all in Hell except one, and that one is the one on which I and my companions are today"! (AL-TIRMIDHI).

33. "The prophet said, "Allah wonders at those people who will enter paradise in chains"! The people referred to here may be the prisoners of war who were captured and chained by the Muslims and their imprisonment was the cause of their conversion to Islam. So it is as if their chains were the means of winning paradise"! (BUKHARI, Vol. 4, #254).

34. "Do not exaggerate in praising me as the Christian praised the son of Mary, for I am only a slave. So call me the slave of Allah and his messenger. The Christian overpraised Jesus till they took him as a God besides Allah"! (BUKHARI, Vol. 4, #654).

35. "The first group of people who will enter paradise will be glittering like the moon on a full-blown night. They will neither spit therein, nor blow their noses therein nor relieve nature. Everyone one of them will have two wives; the marrow of the bones of the wives' leg will be seen through the flesh. They will have no menses, urine or stool"! (BUKHARI, Vol. 4, #468).

36. Someone asked the prophet when will the Hour be established? Muhammad replied, "The answerer has no better knowledge than the questioner". (BUKHARI, Vol. 1, #47).

37. "All my followers will enter paradise except those who refuse and whoever disobeys me is the one who refuses to enter into paradise"! (BUKHARI, Vol. 9, #384).

38. "Paradise has one hundred grades which Allah has reserved for those who fight in his cause, and the distance between each of two grades is like the distance between the heaven and the earth"! (BUKHARI, Vol. 4, #48)

39. "Muhammad said that once a prophet carried out a military expedition. He reached the town at a time when it was almost time for Afternoon prayer. Then that prophet said to the sun, 'O sun! You are under Allah's order and I am under Allah's order. O Allah! Stop the sun from setting. It was stopped till Allah made him victorious"! (BUKHARI, Vol. 4, #353).

40. "The Jews were ordered in the Torah and the Christians in the Gospel to follow Muhammad when he comes as a messenger of Allah to all mankind. Jews refused to believe in the message of Jesus, so all their work was annulled. The Christians refused to accept the message of Muhammad and their work was annulled too! On the other hand, Muslims accepted and believed in all three messengers and deserved a full reward for their complete surrender to Allah"! (AL-QASTALANI, Vol. 4, Page-133).

41. "No human being is killed or murdered, but a part of responsibility for the crime is laid on the first son of Adam who invented the tradition of killing"! (BUKHARI, Vol. 9,#6).

42. Muhammad said, after my death don't become disbelievers by cutting the necks of one another! (BUKHARI, Vol. 9, #7).

43. The prophet also said, "Know that paradise is under the shades (blades) of swords" (in Jihad)! (BUKHARI, Vol. 4, #73).

44. Allah's messenger said; "By him (Allah) in whose hands my soul is, the Day of Resurrection will not be established till beasts of pray speak to the human beings"! (BUKHARI, Vol. 5, #15).

45. Allah's messenger said; "The Hour will not be established until the sun rises from the west"! (BUKHARI, Vol. 6, #159).

46. "The people of Mecca (Pagans) requested Allah's messenger to show them a miracle, and so he showed them the splitting of the moon"! (BUKHARI, Vol. 4, #831).

47. Muhammad says; "The Hour will not be established until you fight against the Jews. The stone, behind which a Jew will be hiding, will say; O Muslim, there is a Jew hiding behind me, so kill him"! (BUKHARI, Vol. 4,#177).

48. "Whoever had camels or cows or sheep and did not pay their Zakat (a kind of tax to be paid to the poor Muslims), those animals will be brought on the Day of Resurrection far bigger and fatter than before and they will tread him under their hooves and will butt him with their horns until Allah finished the judgments among the people"! (BIKHARI, Vol. 2, #539).

49. The prophet also said; "Allah has ninety nine names and whoever believes in their meaning and acts accordingly, will enter paradise"! (BUKHAI, Vol. 8, #419).

50. "A true believer in Allah and Muhammad who goes out for Jihad and is martyred, that is not a death but an eternal life in paradise forever"! (BUKHARI, Vol. 8, #381).

51. Muhammad said, "Jesus will judge mankind justly by the law of the Quran as a Muslim ruler and will break the cross and kill the pigs and abolish the taxes from the Jews and Christians imposed by the Muslim government "! (BUKHARI, Vol. 3, #425).

52. In reference to Verse 73:8 Muhammad said; "There shall not be more than one KHALIFAH (a chief Muslim ruler) for the whole Muslim world. Otherwise there will be a great mischief and evil amongst the Muslims"! (TAFSIR AL-TABARI).

53. Allah's messenger says; "Whoever can guarantee the chastity of what is between his two jaw-bones and what is between his legs (private parts)", I can guarantee paradise for him! (BUKHARI, Vol. 8, #481).

54. "Verily Allah created mercy. Then he made it into one hundred parts. He withheld with him ninety-nine parts, and sent its one part to all of his creations"! (BUKHARI, Vol. 8,#476).

55. Muhammad said. "I was shown the Hell-fire and that the majority of its dwellers were women who were disbelievers and ungrateful to their husbands"! (BUKHARI, Vol. 1, #26).

56. "If the people of a town indulge in illegal sexual intercourse and practice RIBA (usury of all kinds), Allah permits its destruction"! (TAFSIR AL-QURTUBI).

57. The prophet said, "Don't you trust me though I am the trustworthy man of the One in the Heavens and I receive the news of heavens (Divine Revelation) both in the morning and in the evening"? (BUKHARI, Vol. 5, #638).

58. Allah's messenger said, "Whoever performs Hajj to this house of HABAH and does not approach his wife for sexual relations nor commits sins while performing Hajj, he will come out as sinless as a newly-born child"! (BUKHARI, Vol. 3, #45).

59. The prophet said, "Allah does not listen to anything as he listens to the prophet reciting the Quran in a nice, loud and pleasant tone"! (BUKHARI, Vol. 6, #542).

60. "From among my followers there will be some people who will consider illegal sexual intercourse, the wearing of silk, the drinking of alcoholic drinks, and the use of musical instruments as lawful"! (BUKHARI, Vol. 7, #494B).

61. "On the Day of Resurrection Allah will grasp the whole planet of earth by his hand, and roll all the heavens up with his Right Hand, and then he will say, I am the King, where are the kings of the earth"? (BUKHARI, Vol. 9, #479).

62. Allah's messenger said, "People are just like camels; out of one hundred, one can hardly find a single camel suitable to ride"! (BUKHARI, Vol. 8, #505).

63. Muhammad said, "People will be thrown into the Hellfire and it will say, 'Are there any more to come? Till Allah put his foot over it and it will say "Enough'!" (BUKHARI, Vol. 6, #371).

64. "Allah has prepared for his pious slaves things which have never been seen by an eye, nor heard by an ear or even imagined by a human being"! (BUKHARI, Vol. 4, #467).

65. The prophet said, "I have five names: I am MUHAMMAD and AHMAD; I am AL-MAHI (who eliminates infidelity or disbelief in Islam); I am AL-HASHIR (who will be the first to be resurrected); I am also AL-AQIB (the last prophet)"! (BUKHARI, Vol. 4, #732).

66. The messenger said, "The sun and the moon will be folded up (joined together or deprived of their light) on the Day of Resurrection"! (BUKHARI, Vol. 4, #422).

67. The prophet said, "Allah ordered the angels appointed over you that the good and the bad deeds be written, and he then showed them the way how to write"! (BUKHARI, Vol. 8, #498).

68. The creation of the stars is for three purposes; i.e. as decoration of the heaven, as missiles to hit the devils and as signs to guide travellers. So, if anybody tries to find a different interpretation, he is mistaken and just wastes his efforts, and troubles himself with what is beyond his limited knowledge"! (BUKHARI, Vol. 4, Ch. 3).

69. "Allah is more pleased with the repentance of his slave than anyone of you is pleased with finding the camel which he had lost in a desert" (BUKHARI, Vol. 8, #321)!

70. The messenger for all of mankind said, "None of you will have faith till he loves me more than his father, his children and all mankind"! (BUKHARI, Vol. 1, #14)!

71. In the hellfire, each and every one of the disbelievers will be put in a separate 'Box of Fire', so that he will not see anyone punished except he himself! (TAFSIR IBN KATHIR)!

72. It is obligatory to have belief in the message (Islamic Monotheism) of Muhammad! Those who belie him are on the road to hellfire! (SAHIH MUSLIM Ch.# 240)!

73. If a person commits a sin, a black dot is dotted on his heart. If he repents or asks forgiveness from Allah, his heart is cleared. If he repeats the sin, his heart is completely covered with black dots. (AL-TIRMIDHI, Vol. 5, #3334)!

74. Allah's messenger said; I have been ordered to fight the people till they say "None has the right to be worshipped but Allah"! (BUKHARI, Vol. 1, #387).

75. Each human being has his own special finger prints not resembling anyone else, indicating that our Lord (Allah) is the 'Most Superior Creator' of everything. (BUKHARI, Vol. 9, #532B)

76. The prophet said; "On the Day of Judgment, Allah will lay bare his shin and then all the believers, men and women, will prostrate themselves before Him and those who used to prostrate in the world for showing off and gaining reputation, will have their back bones stiffen so that they will not be able to prostrate even if they want to"! (BUKHARI, Vol. 6, #441).

77. When Muhammad was asked by associates; "Shall we see our Lord on the Day of Resurrection? He replied; "Do you have any difficulty in seeing the sun and the moon when the sky is clear? (BUKHARI, Vol. 9, #532B).

78. On the Day of Judgment it will be announced; "Let every nation follow what they used to worship"! The people of the Cross will follow their Cross! Other idolaters will follow their idols save the followers of Islam! Then the Jews will be asked what they used to worship? They will reply; we used to worship Ezra, the Son of Allah! This reply will make Allah angry and he will dismiss their claim saying; "You are liars, for Allah has neither a wife nor a son"! (BUKHARI, Vol. 9, #532B).

79. Allah's messenger said; "Many amongst men reached the level of perfection but none amongst the women reached this level except Aisha (one of the wives of Muhammad), Pharaoh's wife, and Mary! But the superiority of Aisha to other women is like the superiority of "THARID" (a meal and bread dish to other meals)! (BUKHARI, Vol. 4, #623).

80. Every day two angels come down from heaven and one of them says, "O Allah! Compensate every person who spends in your cause, and the other angel says, "O Allah! Destroy every miser"! (BUKHARI, Vol. 2, #522).

81. Muhammad used to deliver Friday Sermon standing near a date tree. A man or woman built a pulpit for him to read out his religious talks! The tree begun crying like a child for missing out the recital by Muhammad and continued crying even when he embraced the tree! But why? Because the tree was deprived of "religious knowledge given near it"! (BUKHARI, Vol. 4, #784).

82. "Allah curses those ladies who practice tattooing and those who get themselves tattooed, and those ladies who get their hair removed from their eyebrows and faces except the beard and moustache, and those who make artificial spaces between their teeth in order to look more beautiful! He also curses those ladies who use false hair whereby they change Allah's creation"! (BUKHARI, Vol. 6, # 409).

83. "If any man of the Scriptures (Jews or Christians) believes in his own prophet and then believes in me (Muhammad)too, he will get a double reward"! (BUKHARI, Vol. 7, #20).

84. "The people of Mecca asked the prophet to show them a sign (Miracle). So he showed them the cleaving of the moon"! (BUKHARI, Vol. 6, #390).

85. Allah will ask a person who gets the least punishment in hell; "If you had everything on earth, would you give it as a ransom to free yourself from Hellfire? He would say "Yes"! Then Allah will say; "When you were in the backbone of Adam, I asked you much less than this, but you insisted on worshipping others besides me"! (BUKHARI, Vol. 4 #551).

86. Once Muhammad saw two persons being tortured inside their graves: One for not cleaning himself after urination and the other used to go about with calumnies! Muhammad picked a green branch of a date-tree; split it into two pieces and planted one on each grave and said "Their punishments may be abated till the branches get dried"! (BUKHARI, Vol. 8, #78).

87. The believers will be stopped at a bridge between Paradise and Hell and mutual retaliation will take place among them about their wrong doings! After being cleansed and purified, they will be admitted into paradise"! (BUKHARI, Vol. 8, #542).

88. "There are many prophets and messengers of Allah, about twenty-five of them are mentioned in the Quran. Only five of them are of strong will, namely; Muhammad, Noah, Abraham, Moses and Jesus"! (Ref. V. 35:46).

89. During burial of the dead, his relatives, properties and his deeds follow him to the grave! All return but his deeds remain with him! (BUKHARI, Vol. 8, #521).

90. The prophet said; "I seek refuge with you (Allah), the most honorable and powerful, who does not die, while the Jinn and the human beings die"! (BUKHARI, Vol. 9, #480).

91. Prophet Muhammad says, Allah is annoyed by the "Sons of Adam" as they abuse "AD-DAHR" (Time)! Allah himself is AD-DAHR! He causes the revolution of the day and night while keeping the earth fixed, flat and floating in space without pillars! (BUKHARI, Vol. 6 #351).

92. "The place on which a believer (Muslim) used to prostrate on earth and the gate of the heaven through which his good deeds used to enter will both weep when he dies, while they do not do so for the disbelievers"! (TAFSIR AL-TABARI).

93. Someone asked prophet Muhammad; "Will Allah gather a disbeliever prone on his face on the Day of Resurrection? Muhammad replied; "The One, who made the disbeliever walk on his feet in this world, will also be able to make him walk on his face on the Day of Resurrection. Such is the power of our Lord"! (BUKHARI, Vol. 6,#283).

94. The prophet said; "I will be the first to raise my head after the second blowing of the Trumpet and will see Moses clinging to the Throne" (BUKHARI, Vol. 6, #337).

95. The prophet said; " Everything of a human body will waste away, perish or decay except the last coccyx bone (of the tail) and from that bone Allah will again reconstruct the whole body"! (BUKHARI, Vol. 6 #338).

96. The sun has approx. 365 points for its rising and 365 points for its setting! Every day it rises and sets in a new point. After a year it comes back to the same point from where it started! (TAFSI AL-KURTUBI). However, the Hadith did not mention how many times the sun rises and sets in the polar regions in a year?

97. Once UMAR- BIN-KHATTAB (who later became the second Caliph to succeed Muhammad) said; "O Allah's Messenger! You are dearer to me than everything except myself! Muhammad was not so pleased and said; "No, you will not have complete faith till I am dearer to you than your own self"! Umar then said; "Now you are dearer to me than myself! Muhammad then said; "Now you are a believer"! (BUKHARI, Vol. 8, #628).

98. Allah claims to have created the Earth and the Heavens in "Six Days"!
How he spent these "Six days" has been explained by an Islamic
expert (SAYEED BIN ZUBAYAR) saying that: Allah began creation
of the Earth on Sunday and finished on Monday! On Tuesday and
Wednesday he created all materials including the mountains, roads
and the rivers for the Earth! He spent Thursday and Friday creating
the Seven heavens including the stars, the Sun and the Moon etc.!
Saturday was his "Day off"!

MUHAMMAD'S MISSION TO SPACE

"MIRAJ" is an Arabic word which literarily means the ascent of Prophet Muhammad to the Heavens (by soul and body)! People of his time, particularly the pagans, already had mistrust on his claim that he had been sent by Allah as the last and the only messenger for all of mankind! People of his own tribe including his uncle did not believe in the revelation he claimed to have received from Allah through Gabriel! They even branded him as a "madman" and also alleged that he and his loyal associates fabricated the Quran themselves! When challenged by the Arab pagans, Muhammad is said to have split the moon to gain their trust in him as the messenger of Allah! Unconvinced and unmoved by this miracle, Pagans dubbed him a "Magician"!

Before going into describing the MIRAJ, I would like to briefly narrate another story of almost similar in nature which took place on earth, much down below the heaven! This is known as "THE JOURNEY BY NIGHT" described in the 17th chapter of the Quran! This unbelievable journey took place from AL-MASJID-AL-HARAM at Mecca to AL-MASJID AL-AQSA in Jerusalem! But why? Because Allah wanted prophet Muhammad to see for himself what the Lord has blessed in and around the neighborhood of Jerusalem; his proofs, evidences, lessons, signs etc.! After having accomplished the journey by night, the prophet was still not out of the woods! The pagans did not believe that story to say the least! The most mysterious part of this story was narrated by none other than the most famous among all the Hadith Composers, AL-BUKHARI! In Hadith #226 of vol. 5 he quoted Muhammad as saying; "When the people of QURAISH (his own tribe) did not believe me (i.e. story of his journey to Jerusalem), I stood up at a compound near KABAH and Allah displayed Jerusalem in front of me, and I began describing it to them while I was looking at it"! Probably this was the first ever virtual digital display on a video screen in the history of mankind! Otherwise this display could not have taken place since Jerusalem is about a thousand km away from Mecca! However, everything is possible in domain of divinity! Another important piece of information is missing from the story; what means of transportation was used by Allah to take his slave (Muhammad) to Jerusalem by night? Quite a number of times the Quran mentioned that Allah rose to his Throne over seven heavens "Really in a manner that suits His Majesty"! In what manner Jesus was raised unto Allah is also not mentioned in the Quran! This short story of Muhammad's "Journey by Night" to Jerusalem might help readers understand the credibility of AL-MIRAJ; the ascent of Prophet Muhammad to heavens where he is said to have met with Allah at his palace!

This story of Muhammad's space travel is related to verse #12 of Chapter 53 titled "AN-NAJM" or The Star! The Chapter begins with the verse: "BY THE STAR WHEN IT GOES DOWN (OR VANISHES)! The story is narrated by MALIK BIN SASA'AH in reference to Hadith of AL-BUKHARI, Vol. 4, #429! The narrator quotes the Prophet as having told the story in his own words! Allah wanted Muhammad to see the greatest signs of his creation; "SIDRAT-UL- MUNTAHA", a lot tree of the outmost boundary of the universe over the seventh heaven beyond which none can pass and near it is the Paradise of Abode! For your recollection I may quote verse 3 of chapter 67 again in which Allah says; "HE HAS CREATED THE SEVEN HEAVENS ONE ABOVE ANOTHER; YOU CAN SEE NO FAULT IN THE CREATION OF THE MOST GRACIOUS"!

Before the journey begun, Muhammad in his own words says, "I was at the house in a state midway between sleep and wakefulness"! As part of preparation for the space travel Allah created an animal called AL-BURAQ! Its color was white and as for its size, it was smaller than a mule and bigger than a donkey! An angel recognized Muhammad as he was lying between two of his companions! A golden tray full of "Wisdom and Belief" was brought to him and his body was cut open from the throat to the lower part of the abdomen! Then his abdomen was washed with water from ZAMZAM (a sacred well near KHABA) and finally his heart was filled with that new wisdom and belief brought by the angels! As usual Arch-angel Gabriel was appointed in-charge of the mission and also as guide to Muhammad! Since Muhammad was going to meet with his Lord, he cannot go there with his abdomen filled with dirty and stinky wastes! So it was washed and cleaned with purified water of the Holy ZAMZAM! His heart was filled with innovated wisdom and belief which were brought upon a golden tray from heaven! After going through the overhauling process of his heart and body, Muhammad must have become a New Man, worthy of meeting his Lord in person! Riding on that animal (BURAQ) Muhammad and Gabriel took off and reached at the gate of the First Heaven! Gabriel asked the Gate keeper to open the gate! But the gate keeper wanted to know the identity of the guest asking "Who is accompanying you"? Gabriel introduced the guest as Muhammad. Then the keeper again asked whether he is wanted here or not? Gabriel assured him that he is an invited guest and then the gate keeper let them in saying ' you are welcome'; what a wonderful visitor he is'! When the gate of the first heaven was opened, therein Muhammad met with Adam who received him saying, 'you are welcome, O son and a prophet'! From there they ascended to the second heaven and again Gabriel had to introduce himself and his guest to the gate keeper! In the second heaven Muhammad met with Jesus and John who said, 'you are welcome, O brother and a prophet'! Then they ascended to the third heaven! After formal identity checks at the check-post, they were allowed into the third heaven where Muhammad met Prophet Joseph who greeted him saying, 'you are welcome, O brother and a prophet'. Then they ascended to the forth heaven and after having finished the checking at the gate, Muhammad was allowed to meet with prophet Enoch, who welcomed him saying, 'You are welcome, O brother and Prophet'. Obviously their next destination was fifth heaven and again same questions were asked by the gate keeper. There Muhammad met and greeted Aeron who in return welcomed him saying, 'You are welcome, O brother and a prophet'. Now their next destination is sixth heaven and after the checks they were allowed to get in and Muhammad met Moses who also greeted in the same language saying. 'You are welcome, O brother and a prophet'. When Muhammad proceeded on his way to the last heaven, Moses started weeping and on being asked why he was weeping, he said, "O Lord! Followers of this youth (Muhammad), who was sent after me, will enter paradise in greater number than my followers"! Then Muhammad ascended to the seventh heaven and at the gate similar questions and answers were exchanged as in the previous heavens! There Muhammad came across Allah's most intimate friend Abraham and greeted him! Abraham has been lodged in the heaven nearest to Allah himself! It may be mentioned that Abraham would be the first to be clothed on the Day of Resurrection! It is also he who built the KABAH at Mecca for Allah! Abraham greeted his guest saying; 'you are welcome, O son and a prophet'! All prophets greeted Muhammad calling him 'O brother" except Adam and Abraham! Muhammad claimed in a Hadith that "All prophets are paternal brothers" (BUKHARI, Vol. 4,#652)! Most probably Adam and Abraham did not like to address Muhammad as brother! Then Muhammad was taken to visit the most beautiful and luxurious house of the universe, i.e. the house of Allah, "AL-BAIT AL-MAMUR"! Gabriel when asked by Muhammad said, this is the house of Allah where 70,000 angels perform prayers daily and when they leave, a fresh batch of angels take their place! After that the Prophet was shown the "SIDRAT-UL-MUNTAHA", i.e. the LOTE-TREE of the utmost boundary over the seventh heaven! He saw its fruits which resembled the clay jugs and its leaves were like the ears of elephants! The "Tree" is indispensable as it marks the edge of the universe! Besides, four remarkable rivers are originated at its roots; two of them are apparent and two are hidden! When Muhammad asked Gabriel about those rivers, he said; "The two hidden rivers are in paradise and the apparent ones are the Nile and the Euphrates"! It is indeed a good news from paradise for the people who live on the banks of these two rivers! After meeting the Lord, he begun descending but came across Moses at sixth heaven and told him that Allah has ordained "Fifty Obligatory Prayers " to be performed daily by him and his followers! Apparently Moses was displeased and said; " I know the people better than you, because I had the hardest experience to bring people of Israel into obedience. Your followers cannot put up with such obligation. So, go back to your Lord and request him to reduce the number of prayers. Muhammad returned to his Lord and requested him to reduce the number of prayers. Upon his request Allah reduced it to forty! Moses, yet not satisfied, sent Muhammad again and again (a total of four times) back to his Lord until he reduced the number from forty to thirty, from thirty to twenty, from twenty to ten and finally it was fixed at five! Moses even advised Muhammad to go back again for further reduction but Muhammad declined saying; "I have surrendered to Allah's final order"! At the end of the journey, Allah is said to have addressed his messenger saying; " I HAVE DECREED MY OBLIGATION AND HAVE REDUCED THE BURDEN ON MY SLAVES"! But the "Master" could not perceive that his "Slaves" would not be able to attend congregational prayers fifty times in twenty four hours! Now the question arises about the timing of his journey to the heaven? In twenty three years of "Revelation" period, at what stage did the mission take place is not clear! What was the number of obligatory prayers before his ascent to heaven? In verse 39 of chapter 50 Allah also says addressing Muhammad that "GLORIFY THE PRAISES OF YOUR LORD, BEFOR THE RISING OF THE SUN AND BEFORE ITS SETTING AND DURING A PART OF THE NIGHT"! Allah also claims to be the Lord of the 365 points of the sunrise and sunset! Why he has to be worshipped at a fixed time and number? What would be your reactions after reading this story? That also depends on Allah! Verse 43 of Chapter 53 states: "AND THAT IT IS HE (ALLAH) WHO MAKES (WHOM HE WILLS) LAUGH, AND MAKES (WHOM HE WILLS) WEEP"! Indeed there are a lot of believers who weep after listening to this kind of religious myths but those who laugh, outnumber them by a large margin! Miracle of this nature can only happen to people in a drunken state who sometimes become a victim of hallucination! Do we still have to believe in the name of any deity, at this juncture of time, that a donkey-like animal can fly to heavens and come back safely next morning? Those who may have been frightened by the colossal torment of hellfire described in the Quran or may have confronted a near-death situation, might believe in such miracles!

There is not a single verse in the Quran that says all believers in Islam must say five compulsory prayers every day! If Allah could reveal all verses through Gabriel, why he had to take Muhammad to heaven to fix the number of prayers? Can any one of the Islamic Scientists prove that the Nile and the Euphrates are originated from the "Lot Tree" located at the outer most boundary of the heaven?

MUHAMMAD'S CONJUGAL LIFE

Divine Revelations played an important part in the life of the prophet Muhammad when his marital life became chaotic! Allah not only revealed the Quran to Muhammad for the whole of mankind but in it he had to dedicate quite a number of verses exclusively for the wives of the prophet in order to fix the problems he was facing about his conjugal life! In fact his marital debacle begun long before the so-called revelation when he first decided to marry a woman about fifteen years older than him! Her name was KHADIJA, a wealthy, twice widowed woman of his time! Question remains unanswered as regards to his first marriage whether it was lawful or not from Islamic perspective as it took place before the revelation of the Quran! Was that marriage solemnized under Muslim marriage Laws? However by Allah's leave he became rich because of that marriage! He took more than a dozen wives aged between six to seventy giving unconvincing reasons! Among his wives, AYASHA and HAFSA were the daughters of his trusted friends and successors ABU BAKR and UMAR! When he married AYSHA, she was only six and obviously an underage girl! On the contrary he married SAUDA who was about seventy years old! According to DR. M.H. DURRANI, an Islamic expert from Pakistan; "The circumstances compelled the prophet to take this old lady in marriage, because he did not want a woman to stay in his house without marriage"! What circumstances compelled Muhammad to marry an old lady of his mother's age? Because she was one of the early converts to Islam and her husband died in Jihad! An old lady of seventy could easily be given shelter as an elder sister since Muhammad is said to have had no intention of having physical relations with her and AYSHA being a minor could be adopted and looked after as his own daughter! It does not matter whether the Messenger was right or wrong about his marriages as long as he received the blessings from his Lord!

Allah often leveled Muhammad as a warner like many of his predecessors! This assessment of Allah about Muhammad does not commensurate with the uniqueness he bestowed upon him! Muhammad is the only messenger sent for all of mankind; he will be the first to be resurrected; he is the one given the right to intercede with Allah on the Day of Resurrection; he is the one who had met Allah in paradise in his lifetime; he is the one for whom Allah has made a special home in paradise; he is the one whose past and future sins have been forgiven; he is the one who was given the magical power to split the moon and so and so forth! As for the number of wives, probably he had exceeded all of his predecessors and in this respect Allah aided him with an open mind!

Out of numerous verses about Muhammad's marriage and his wives, let us begin with verse 50 of chapter 33! In it Allah said; "O PROPHET! VERILY WE HAVE MADE LAWFUL TO YOU YOUR WIVES, TO WHOM YOU HAVE PAID YOUR BRIDAL MONEY AND THOSE SLAVES WHOM YOUR "RIGHT HAND" POSSESS, WHOM ALLAH HAS GIVEN TO YOU, AND THE DAUGHTERS OF YOUR PATERNAL UNCLE, AND PATERNAL AUNTS, AND DAUGHTERS OF YOUR MATERNAL UNCLES AND MATERNAL AUNTS WHO MIGRATED FROM MECCA WITH YOU, AND ANY BELIEVING WOMEN IF SHE WISHES TO MARRY YOU, A PRIVILEGE FOR YOU ONLY, NOT FOR THE REST OF THE BELIEVERS"!

Another verse of the same chapter is a bit more interesting as it unfolds Muhammad's hidden desire to marry wife of his adopted son! Allah being the All-Knower came to know what his messenger had in his mind and accordingly he revealed the verse to facilitate him fulfill his desire! The prophet had a slave whose name was ZAID-BIN-HARITHAH and he later converted to Islam and Muhammad adopted him as his son after manumitting him! In the backdrop of this scenario, Allah revealed his approval and blessings for the prophet in verse 37 of chapter 33 which states; "WHEN YOU SAID TO YOUR FREED-SLAVE, 'KEEP YOUR WIFE TO YOURSELF AND FEAR ALLAH'. BUT YOU DID HIDE IN YOURSELF WHAT HAS ALLAH ALREADY MADE KNOWN TO YOU THAT HE WILL GIVE HER TO YOU IN MARRIAGE! BUT YOU DID FEAR THE PEOPLE, LEST THEY SAY MUHAMMAD MARRIED THE DIVORCED WIFE OF HIS ADOPTED SON"! Probably the manumitted slave also came to know of his adopted father's weakness towards his wife and he was under pressure to divorce her! The verse continues to state, "SO WHEN ZAID ACCOMPLISHED HIS DESIRE ON HER (DIVORCED HER), WE GAVE HER TO YOU IN MARRIAGE SO THAT IN FUTURE THERE MAY BE NO DIFFICULTY TO THE BELIEVERS TO MARRY DIVORCED WIVES OF THEIR ADOPTED SONS"! Though Muhammad and Allah have jointly set an example, yet there would be very few people who would like to marry wives (even after divorce) of their adopted sons! In the next verse (V.#38) of the same chapter Allah assures his messenger saying; "THERE IS NO BLAME ON THE PROPHET IN THAT WHICH ALLAH HAS MADE LEGAL FOR HIM"! Muhammad's hidden desires and Allah's actions have matched perfectly!

Allah also revealed verses in the Quran for Muhammad advising him how to schedule sexual relations and conduct his conjugal life with his multiple wives! Verse 51 of chapter 33 dictates; "YOU (O MUHAMMAD) CAN POSTPONE THE TURN OF WHOM YOU WILL OF YOUR WIVES AND YOU MAY RECEIVE WHOM YOU WILL. AND WHOSOEVER YOU DESIRE OF THOSE WHOM YOU HAVE SET ASIDE HER TURN TEMPORARILY, IT IS NO SIN ON YOU TO RECEIVE HER AGAIN: THAT IS BETTER THAT THEY MAY BE COMFORTED AND NOT GRIEVED, AND MAY ALL BE PLEASED WITH WHAT YOU GIVE THEM. ALLAH KNOWS WHAT IS IN YOUR HEART"! Then comes the warning for his wives in verses 30, 31 & 32 of the same chapter: "O WIVES OF THE PROPHET! WHOEVER OF YOU COMMITS AN OPEN ILLEGAL SEXUAL INTERCOURSE, THE TORMENT FOR HER WILL BE DOUBLED, AND THAT IS VERY EASY FOR ALLAH. AND WHOEVER OF YOU IS OBEDIENT TO ALLAH AND HIS MESSENGER, WE SHALL GIVE HER, HER REWARD TWICE OVER. YOU ARE NOT LIKE ANY OTHER WOMEN. IF YOU KEEP YOUR DUTY TO ALLAH, THEN BE NOT SOFT IN SPEECH LEST HE IN WHOSE HEART IS DISEASE OF HYPOCRACY OR EVIL DESIRE FOR ADULTRY SHOULD BE MOVED WITH DESIRE"!

There is also a code of conduct formulated by the Lord of the heaven for the visitors to prophet's house in verse 53 of the chapter 33: "O YOU WHO BELIEVE! ENTER NOT THE PROPHET'S HOUSE, UNLESS PERMISSION IS GIVEN TO YOU FOR A MEAL. BUT WHEN YOU ARE INVITED, ENTER, AND WHEN YOU HAVE TAKEN YOUR MEAL, DISPERSE WITHOUT SITTING FOR A TALK. VERILY, SUCH BEHAVIOUR ANNOYS THE PROPHET, AND HE IS SHY OF ASKING YOU TO GO, BUT ALLAH IS NOT SHY OF TELLING YOU THE TRUTH. AND WHEN YOU ASK HIS WIVES FOR ANYTHING YOU WANT, ASK THEM FROM BEHIND A SCREEN. AND IT IS NOT RIGHT FOR YOU TO ANNOY ALLA'S MESSENGER, NOR THAT YOU SHOULD EVER MARRY HIS WIVES AFTER HIS DEATH"! Allah has truly read what was going on in the mind of his messenger about his own conjugal life and accordingly he reveled those verses for the messenger of the whole of mankind! In the first verse of chapter 66 Allah again reminds his messenger saying; "O PROPHET! WHY DO YOU FORBID FOR YOURSELF THAT WHICH ALLAH HAS ALLOWED TO YOU; SEEKING TO PLEASE YOUR WIVES?"

There is a short story that tells us of a breach of trust which took place between Muhammad and two of his most beloved wives; HAFSA and AYSHA! Allah became the witness to it! The story is briefly narrated in verse 3 of chapter 66 and it states; "Once the prophet disclosed a confidential matter to his wife HAFSA and cautioned her to treat the matter as secret but defying the confidentiality she shared the matter with AYSHA, another wife of Muhammad! As Allah is aware of every affairs on earth, he came to know that HAFSA did not keep the secret to herself! So Allah made it known a part thereof to Muhammad and kept a part with him! When Muhammad inquired about the matter from HAFSA, she then asked, 'who told you this'? Muhammad's reply was; "THE ALL-KNOWER, THE ALL AWARE (ALLAH) HAS TOLD ME"! Then came the warning from the Lord to the offenders: Allah revealed two verses (4&5 of chapter 66) which state; "IF YOU TWO (WIVES OF THE PROPHET: AYSHA and HAFSA) TURN IN REPENTANCE TO ALLAH, IT WILL BE BETTER FOR YOU, YOUR HEARTS ARE INDEED SO INCLINED TO OPPOSE WHAT THE PROPHET LIKES! BUT IF YOU HELP ONE ANOTHER AGAINST HIM, THEN VERILY ALLAH IS HIS PROTECTOR, AND GABRIEL, BELIEVERS AND ANGELS ARE HIS HELPERS! IT MAY BE IF HE (MUHAMMAD) DIVORCED YOU ALL, HIS LORD WILL GIVE HIM WIVES BETTER THAN YOU"! From this story it has become apparent that these two wives of the prophet were inclined to oppose and hurt their husband with their actions!

DR. M.H. DURRANI while commenting about the prophet said; "There is no evidence of the prophet having been content with one wife and turning suddenly to lust and passion in his old age"! If so, why then Allah warns Muhammad in verse 52 of chapter 33 saying; "IT IS NOT LAWFUL FOR YOU TO MARRY OTHER WOMEN AFTER THIS, NOT TO CHANGE THEM FOR OTHER WIVES EVEN THOUGH THEIR BEAUTY ATTRACTS YOU EXCEPT THE SLAVES THAT YOUR RIGHT HAND POSSESS"! Yet Muhammad has been allowed to satiate his "Lust and

Passion" with those slaves whom his "Right Hand" possessed and whose beauty attracted him!

Allah has created HURS (Fair-skin ladies) two for each of the dwellers of paradise, using special material, not mud or clay as was used for Adam's offspring! Muhammad has been allowed on earth to take dozens of wives including many slaves that his "Right Hand" possessed! But why the Lord refrained from mentioning the number of HURS or special mates that he has created for his dearest messenger Muhammad? Is he going to stay alone and lead a lonely eternal life In his MAQAM-MAHMUD in paradise?

To highlight the reasons for Muhammad's many marriages, I would like to mention only one instance quoting DR. DURRANI again, who says; "The reason why the prophet married AYSHA (an underage daughter of his close friend and first successor to him, ABU BAKR) is simple (?)! ABU BAKR was the first man to embrace Islam and he spent all his fortune in the way of God, who severed all connections with his relatives because of his faith and left Mecca with the prophet sharing his dangerous journey to Medina, exposing himself to death and a terrible end. If the prophet wished to honor him and cement their friendship, it would be quite reasonable to give this as the true explanation for this marriage"! What a noble example of honoring a friend set by the "Only Messenger for mankind"! How come a prophet decides to marry an underage girl of six in order to honor his friend? This is an example how the Islamic intellectuals all around the world go out of their way to defend Allah and Muhammad!

It would be easier for the readers to keep in mind the vastness of the universe and the greatness of its creator, if it has one, in order to understand the credibility of the stories above! Let all of us be thankful and glorify the "Creator of Everything" who had dedicated so much time and energy to look into the marital affairs of his messenger!

NATURAL SCIENCE VS. MIRACLES OF THE QURAN

There are hundreds of verses in the Quran on the creation of life, heavens, stars, sun, moon, earth, etc. These verses not only contradict natural sciences but also do not conform to the norms of common sense! Islamic scholars claim that those verses should not be misinterpreted by human beings with their limited knowledge! Question naturally arises why the "All-Knowing Allah" sent these verses to the mankind who are incapable of understanding his science of "Creation"? Allah repeatedly says in the Quran that he has spread out the "Earth" and "affixed" mountains so that it does not shake or move! Our earth is a rotating sphere while that of Allah is flat and fixed! Allah's revealed verses themselves invariably put his existence in doubt! The Revelation through an angel was outright rejected even by the ordinary pagans of that time! An imaginary sketch of Allah depicted in the Quran has failed to generate trust in him as the "Creator" of the earth and the heavens! People in general have adapted the notion that they have to have a religion as a way to the God to whom they must return! Narration and the contents of many of these verses are so cheap that those cannot be attributed to the creator of the universe even if he exists! Rather those verses exemplify their author as persons with poor intellectual background having no knowledge of astrophysical composition of the cosmos or the universe! The author claims in the verse #37 of chapter 10 that, "THIS QURAN IS NOT SUCH AS COULD EVER BE PRODUCED BY OTHER THAN ALLAH"! The Lord also says in his Glorious Book, "THERE HAS COME TO YOU FROM ALLAH A LIGHT AND A PLAIN BOOK"! Soon after that the author says, "THE NOBLE QURAN IS A MIRACLE FROM ALLAH TO PROPHET MUHAMMAD"! Contents of the verses below may be projected on a mirror of science to see what a hazy picture it reflects!

1. ALIF-LAM-MIM: These Arabic letters are miracles of the Quran and none but Allah knows their meanings! (Ch. 2:V.1).

2. Allah has made the earth a resting place for you, and the sky as its canopy! (Ch. 2:V22).

3. Allah taught Adam names of everything! (Ch. 2:V31).

4. Allah is the originator of the heavens and the earth. When he decrees a matter, he only says to it "Be" and it is! (Ch. 2:V117).

5. Allah shapes you in the wombs as he wills! (Ch. 3:V6).

6. For the pious, there are gardens (paradise) with their Lord, under which rivers flow. Therein is their eternal home with purified mates or wives who will have no menses, urines or stools! (Ch. 3:V15).

7. Allah makes the night to enter into the day, and he makes the day enter into the night! (Ch. 3:V.27).

8. Jesus will speak to the people in the cradle! (Ch. 3:V.46).

9. And no person can ever die except by Allah's leave and at an appointed term decided by Allah at his will! (Ch. 3:V145).

10. Allah sent a crow who scratched the ground to show Cane, killer of Abel, how to bury the dead body of his brother! He said, "Woe to me! Am I even not able to be as this crow"? (Ch. 5:V.31).

11. He (Allah) it is who has created you from clay and then decreed a term for you to die! (Ch. 6:V.2).

12. It is Allah who takes your souls by night when you are asleep! (Ch. 6:V.60).

13. He is the cleaver of the daybreak. He has appointed the night for resting, and the sun and moon for reckoning! (Ch. 6:V96).

14. Allah is the originator of the heavens and the earth. How can he have children when he has no wife? (Ch. 6:V.101).

15. Surely, your Lord is Allah who created the heavens and the earth in six days and then rose over the Throne really in a manner that suits His Majesty! (Ch. 10:V.3).

16. It is he who has made the sun a shining thing and the moon as a light and measured out for it stages that you might know the number of years and the reckoning! (Ch. 10:V.5).

17. He it is who has created the heavens and the earth in six days and his Throne was on the water! (Ch. 11:V.7).

18. Allah said to Noah: "And construct the ship under our eyes and with Our Revelation! (Ch. 11:V.37).

19. When Allah's dream was fulfilled (i.e. destruction of the people of Noah), he said, "O earth! Swallow up your water, and O sky! Withhold your rain"! (Ch. 11:V.44).

20. I shall fill Hell with Jinn and men all together! Except him whom your Lord has bestowed his mercy (Ch. 11:V.119).

21. Allah is he who raised the heavens without any pillars that you can see. Then he rose above the Throne. He has subjected the sun and the moon (to continue going round), each running its course for a term appointed! (Ch. 13:V.2).

22. On the Day when the earth will be changed to another earth and so will be the heavens and they (all creatures) will appear before Allah, the One, the irresistible! (Ch. 14:V.48).

23. And the earth We (Allah) have spread out, and have placed therein firm mountains, and caused to grow therein all kinds of things in due proportion! (Ch. 15:V.19).

24. And indeed, We (Allah) created man from dried (sounding) clay of altered mud! (Ch. 15:V.26).

25. And the Jinn, We (Allah) created aforetime from the smokeless flame of fire! (Ch. 15:V.27).

26. And he has affixed into the earth mountains standing firm, lest it should shake with you, and rivers and roads, that you may guide yourselves! (Ch. 16:V.15).

27. Verily, Our word unto a thing when We intend it, is only that We say unto it "Be"---and it is! (Ch. 16:V.40).

28. Do they not see the birds held flying in the midst of the sky? None holds them but Allah! (Ch. 16:V.79).

29. The seven heavens and the earth and all that is therein, glorify Allah and there is not a thing but glorifies his praise. But you understand not their glorification! (Ch. 17:V.44).

30. On the Day of Resurrection the Book of one's Record will be placed in the right hand for a believer and in the left for a disbeliever! (Ch. 18:V.49).

31. Mary asked Gabriel, who appeared before her in the form of a man; "How can I have a son, when no man has touched me, nor am I unchaste?" He said, "So it will be, your Lord said: "That is easy for Me (Allah)! (Ch. 19:V.21).

32. And indeed We made a covenant with Adam before, but he forgot, and We found on his part no will-power! (Ch. 20:V.115).

33. Had We intended to take a pastime (i.e. a wife or a son), We could surely have taken it from Us! (Ch. 21:V.17).

34. When the pagans put Abraham into fire, Allah said; "O fire! Be you coolness and safety for Abraham! (Ch. 21:V.69).

35. And indeed We have created above you seven heavens (one over the other)! (Ch. 23:V.17).

36. And We sent down from the sky water (rain) in (due) measure! (Ch. 23:V.18).

37. On the Day their (wrong doers) tongues, their hands, and their legs will bear witness against them as to what they used to do! (Ch. 24:V.24).

38. Allah is the Light of the Heavens and the Earth! (Ch. 24:V.35).

39. Is not He (Allah) better than your gods who has made the earth as a fixed abode, and has placed rivers in its midst, and has placed firm mountains therein, and has set a barrier between the two seas of salt and sweet water? (Ch. 27:V61).

40. He brings out the living from the dead and brings out the dead from the living. And he revives the earth after its death. And thus shall you be Resurrected! (Ch. 30:V.19).

41. And among his signs is this, that he created you (Adam) from dust, and then Eve from Adam's rib, and then his offspring from the semen (despised water)! (Ch. 30:V.20)

42. And among his signs is the creation of the heavens and the earth, and the difference of your language and colors. In that are indeed signs for men of sound understanding! (V. 30:22).

43. And among his signs is that the heaven and the earth stand by his command! (Ch. 30:V.25).

44. Allah created the heavens without any pillars and has set on the earth firm mountains lest it should shake with you! (Ch. 31:V.10).

45. If all the trees on the earth were pens and the sea (were ink wherewith to write) with seven seas behind it to add to its supply, yet the Words of Allah would not be exhausted! Verily Allah is All-Mighty, All-Wise! (Ch. 31:V.27).

46. Allah manages and regulates every affair from the heavens to the earth, then the affair will go up to him in one Day, the space whereof is a thousand years of your reckoning (i.e. reckoning of present world's time)! (Ch. 32:V.5).

47. The prophet is closer to the believers than his own self, and his wives are their mothers! (Ch. 33:V.6).

48. All the praises and thanks be to Allah, the Originator of the heavens and the earth, Who made the angels messengers with wings, two or three or four! (Ch. 35:V.1).

49. And the two seas (kinds of water) are not alike: this is palatable, sweet and pleasant to drink, and that is salt and bitter! (Ch. 35:V.12).

50. Eden of paradise (everlasting gardens) will they enter, therein will they be adorned with bracelets of gold and pearls, and their garments therein will be of silk! (Ch. 35:V.33).

51. Verily, Allah grasps the heaven and the earth lest they should move away from their places, and if they were to move away from their places, there is not one that could grasp them after Him! (Ch. 35:V.41).

52. It is not for the sun to overtake the moon, nor does the night outstrip the day. They all float, each in an orbit! (Ch. 36:V.40).

53. Abraham said to his child, still a minor, "O my son! I have seen in a dream that I am slaughtering you in sacrifice to Allah. So what you say? O my father! "Do that what you are commanded", replied the boy! (Ch. 37:V.102)

54. Verily, We made the mountains to glorify Our praises with David after the mid-day till sunset and after the sunset till mid-day! (Ch. 38:V.18).

55. Allah created you all from a single person (Adam); then he made from him his wife (Eve). And he has sent down for you of cattle eight pairs: Of the sheep two male and female, of the goats two male and female, of the oxen two male and female, of the camels two male and female! (Ch. 39:V.6).

56. It is Allah who takes away the souls at the time of their death, and those who die not during their sleep. He keeps those souls for which he has ordained death and sends back the rest for a term appointed! (Ch. 39:V.42).

57. And the earth will shine with the light of its Lord (Allah) when he will come to judge among men! (Ch. 39:V.69).

58. And you will see the angels surrounding the Throne of Allah from all around, glorifying the praises of their Lord. All creatures will be judged with truth! (Ch. 39:V.75).

59. The creation of the heavens and the earth is indeed greater than the creation of mankind! (Ch. 40:V.57).

60. Allah, is he who has made the night for you that you may rest therein and the day for you to see! (Ch. 40:V.61).

61. When iron collars will be rounded over their necks, and the chains, they shall be dragged along in the boiling water, then they will be burned in the Fire! (Ch. 40:V.71&72).

62. Say (O Muhammad), "Do you verily disbelieve in Him Who created the earth in two Days?" (Ch. 41:V.9).

63. He placed therein (the earth) firm mountains from above it, and He blessed it, and measured therein its sustenance for its dwellers in four Days equal! (Ch. 41:V.10).

64. Then He completed and finished from their creation (as) seven heavens in two Days and He made in each heaven its affair. And We adorned the nearest heaven with lamps (stars) to be an adornment as well as to guard from devils by using them as missiles against the devils. Such is the decree of Allah, the All-Mighty, the All-Knower! (Ch. 41:V.12).

65. And when they reach Hellfire, their ears, eyes and skins will testify against them as to what they used to do! (Ch. 41:V.20).

66. And they will say to their skins; "Why do you testify against us"? They will say; "Allah has caused us to speak---He causes all things to speak! (Ch. 41:V.21).

67. And among his Signs are the ships in the sea like mountains! (Ch. 42:V.32).

68. Allah bestows male or female, or both males and females (offspring) upon whom He wills. He also renders barren whom He wills! (Ch. 42:V.49&50).

69. If it were Our Will, We would have destroyed all mankind and made angels to replace you on earth! (Ch. 43:V.60).

70. Say (O Muhammad) "I am not a new thing or the first among the messengers nor do I know what will be done with me or with you"! (Ch. 46:V.9)

71. Allah sent Muhammad with guidance and religion of truth, that he may make Islam superior to all religions! (Ch. 48:V.28).

72. Have they not looked at the heaven, how We (Allah) have made it and adorned it, and there are no rifts in it? (Ch. 50:V.6).

73. Remember, two angels record his or her actions sitting one on the right and one on the left of each human! (Ch. 50:V.17).

74. And We (Allah) have spread out the earth: how Excellent Spreader are We! (Ch. 51:V.48).

75. I (Allah) seek not any provision from them nor do I ask that they should feed Me! (Ch. 51:V.57).

76. And that it is He (Allah) Who makes (whom He wills) laugh, and makes (whom He wills) weep! (Ch. 53:V.43).

77. The Hour has drawn near, and the moon has been cleft asunder (Because of the miraculous splitting of the moon by Muhammad as requested by the people of Mecca)! (Ch. 54:V.1).

78. Allah has created all things with Divine Preordainments as written in the Book of Decrees (AL-LAUH-AL-MAHFUZ); the mother Book of the Quran, held with Allah in his Throne over Seven Heavens! (Ch. 54:V.49).

79. The sun and the moon run on their fixed courses exactly calculated with measured out stages for reckoning! (Ch. 55:V.5).

80. And the herbs (or stars) and the trees both prostrate themselves to Allah! (Ch. 55:V.6).

81. Allah created man (Adam) from sounding clay like the clay of pottery! (Ch. 55:V.14).

82. "Then which of the blessings of your Lord will you both (Jinn and Men) deny"? (Ch. 55:V.16). (It may be mentioned that Allah has repeated this question 31 times in this chapter alone).

83. He has let loose the two seas (the salt and fresh water) meeting together. Between them is a barrier which none of them can transgress! (Ch. 55:V.19&20).

84. In paradise the believers will be with chaste fair females (in beauty they are like rubies and corals) with whom no man or Jinn has had TAMITH (opening their hymens with sexual intercourse)! (Ch. 55:V.56).

85. If We willed, We could make water salt and undrinkable. Why then do you not give thanks to Allah? (Ch. 56:V.70).

86. "So I swear by the setting of the stars"! This word, according to Islamic experts, has many interpretations: It may mean the setting or the rising or the mansions of the stars, or the Quran and its gradual revelation in stages! (Ch. 56:V.75).

87. No calamity befalls on the earth or in yourselves but it is inscribed in the Book of Decrees (AL-LAUH-AL-MAHFUZ held with Allah) before We bring it into existence! (Ch. 57:V.22).

88. Had we sent down this Quran on a mountain, you would surely have seen it humbling itself and rent asunder by the fear of Allah! (Ch. 59:V.21).

89. Whatsoever is in the heavens and the earth glorifies Allah, King of everything, the Holy, All-Mighty, All-Wise! (Ch. 62:V.1).

90. Then when the Trumpet will be blown, with one blowing, the earth and the mountains shall be removed from their places and crushed with a single crushing! (Ch. 69:V.13&14).

91. On that Day heaven will be rent asunder, it will be frail and torn up. Angels will be on its sides and eight angels will bear the Throne of your Lord above them! (Ch. 69:V.16&17).

92. The angels including the Archangel Gabriel ascend to All-Mighty Allah in a Day, the measure whereof is fifty thousand years of world standard time! (Ch. 70:V.4).

93. Does a disbeliever think that We shall not assemble his bones? We are Able to put together in perfect order the tips of his fingers! (Ch. 75:V.3&4).

94. Sun and the moon will be joined together, going one into the other or folded up or deprived of their light! (Ch. 75:V.9).

95. For believers there will be gardens and vineyards and young full-breasted mature maidens of equal age! (Ch. 78:V.33).

96. Allah, swearing by the Figs, Olives, Mount Sinai and City of Mecca says that he created man in the best stature but then reduced him to the lowest of the low save those who believe in Islamic monotheism. Then he asks; Is not Allah the best of Judges? (Ch. 95:V.1-8).

97. Verily, the Jews and the Christians who disbelieve in the religion of Islam will abide in the Fire of Hell. They are the worst of creatures! (Ch. 98:V.6).

THE QURAN: REVELATION TO COMPILATION

It is obvious that the Islamic believers will not like the word "Scripted" as they ardently believe this Quran is "Authored" by none other than Allah who " Revealed" it to Muhammad thru angel Gabriel! The Quran is also said to have been derived from its "Mother Book" known as "AL-LAUH-AL MAHFUZ" held under Allah's custody at his throne over Seven Heavens! The Quran has taken twenty three years to be revealed as Allah decided sent it in stages to facilitate prophet Muhammad to remember its contents so that he could relay the messages to his associates and scribes! It was revealed in QURAISH dialect since Muhammad was not conversant with the modern Arabic language! So it is apparent that Allah, Gabriel, Muhammad and his companions were fluent in Quraish dialect! But in a number of verses, Allah called it an "Arabic Quran"! The "Author" also claims that he sent all the revelations in Arabic to the one and only "Messenger of Mankind", so that all of mankind can "Understand" his messages! The Quran is also called a "Miracle" from Allah; a "Plain Book" and a "Plain Statement" that has no crookedness in it! Allah, the author of the Quran, has openly challenged that no human being will be able to write a "Surah" or a Chapter like the one in his Book!

HASSEN A. LAIDI, an expert in the "Science of the Quran" and a contributor to the "Islamic Relief" published from California, U.S.A. said; "ZAID, a close companion of Muhammad, accepted the honor of being the person responsible for the first compilation of the Quran"!

To help him in the process of collecting the fragmentary pieces of the Quran, UMAR IBNUL KHATTAB, who was the Father-in-Law and second successor to Muhammad, announced in the mosque that "Whoever has any part of the Quran which he or she learned from the Prophet, then let him bring it forth"! Following this announcement, people hastened to ZAID whatever craps on which they recorded part of the revelation or any verses of the Quran! He gathered these divine verses of the "King of the Heaven" from parchments, scapula, leaf-stalks of the date trees and from "Memories" of those who knew it by heart! Mr. LAIDI adds more by saying that ZAID could have written the Quran all by himself since he "Memorized" it! But ZAID, who also acted as one of the scribes of the prophet, needed two more memorizers and a written copy of the verses, to ensure the "Authenticity" of the Quran! Now a legitimate question arises how a memorizer can ensure authenticity of the Quran when the "Receiver of the Revelation" himself is dead? While sending these verses to Muhammad directly thru Gabriel Allah never asked that a memorizer or a witness to revelation to be present with the prophet! ZAID reported; "The manuscript on which the Quran was collected remained with ABU BAKR (The first successor to Muhammad, his friend and Father-in-Law) till Allah took him unto him, and then with UMAR (the second Caliph and another Father-in-Law of Muhammad), till Allah took him unto him, and finally it remained with HAFSA (another wife of Muhammad). She kept this manuscript in her house in Medina, allowing people to make copies of it to make sure they had memorized it correctly! Another tempering of the original manuscript of ZAID happened during the rule of ABU BAKR! It is said that "The first compilation of ZAID was written according to seven AHRUF or modes in which the Quran was originally revealed! These AHRUF or the modes were the most common Arabic dialects in which Allah permitted the prophet to recite the Quran"!

Prof. M.M. AL-AZAMI of UK Islamic Academy was more explicit about the so-called first compiler of the Quran! He introduced him as ZEYD-IBN-THABIT! The Professor claims that ZEYD or ZAID was personally present and attended "The Archangel Gabriel's recitation of the Quran with the prophet during revelation in the month of Ramadan"! Professor further adds that a total of 65 companions of the prophet Muhammad functioned as scribes at one time or the other! The parchments and other materials on which the prophet's scribes wrote were, however, not bound in the form of a book during his lifetime! But why? Because, as the professor claims, Allah kept sending revelations continuously! It had to wait until prophet's mission was completed! Did he really complete his mission? The obvious reason for his premature death was that the prophet's health brook down and Allah could not cure him! Allah, who is the giver of life and death, took prophet's life at a time long before the collection and compilation of the Quran! Islamic historians claim that the manuscript of the Quran was compiled months after the death of the prophet in Medina! It is also not convincing as to why Muhammad did not call upon his trusted companions to verify the authenticity of contents of the Quran when he was laying in his death bed for a long period of time? Did he not hear the bell ringing of his imminent death?

What ABU BAKR, the first successor to Muhammad, did was to collect all written texts from parchments into a master volume! He is also said to have verified the accuracy against what was written by others and memorized by the prophet's companions! The pronunciation of the words of the Quran continued to be in the various dialects because the prophet had allowed the people, out of necessity, to recite the Quran in their own dialects! Whereas, at present no nation on earth is allowed to recite the Quran in their own dialects, except Arabic, during prayers!

More than a decade after the death of Muhammad it was UTHMAN, the third successor to his legacy, who is said to have made contribution to standardize the pronunciation in QURAISH dialect! For this purpose he obtained the manuscript from HAFSA and appointed a committee of twelve persons who were sent to different provinces along with official reciters! Several copies of the Quran were made but again there is difference of opinion as to the exact number of copies made! In a bid to improvise the text of the Quran a number of reading aids have been added! Every Surah or Chapter, with the exception of chapter nine, begins with "BISMILLAH" which means in the name of Allah! No reason has been assigned by Allah or prophet Muhammad as to the fact why chapter nine has not begun in the name of Allah! Was it not reveled from heaven? whereas it is claimed that the entire Quran was written by Allah in his own name! Every chapter of the Quran has been given a title! In the beginning the entire text of the Quran was divided into seven parts and after about a century it was again divided into thirty! Later some punctuations were also added! Nowhere it is mentioned who, under what divine or spiritual authority made these changes? Allah clearly said that Muhammad had been sent as Messenger for all mankind and Jinn! It is only the Muslims, a fraction of the mankind, who are busy manufacturing stories to impart legitimacy to Allah's claim, his religion and his revelation! After going through the long episode of the messy mismanagement of the manuscript of the Quran, I could hardly find a grain of trustworthiness as regards to its authenticity that it came down from the "Creator" of the "Earth and the Heaven"! Despite all these misapprehensions, Allah says he sent this Quran in Arabic with clear evidences and proofs for man of understanding! He found no differences between Arabic language and QURAISH dialects? How can a man trust Allah when he broke his promises to his Messenger for mankind? According to a Hadith (BUKHARI Vol. 3, #335) Allah promised that "He will not let the prophet die till he makes straight the "Crooked People" by making them say none has the right to be worshipped but Allah"! When prophet Muhammad died, what was the state of Islamic Monotheism? Could he make the crooked people say, "None has the right to be worshipped but Allah"? Fact of the matter is that he made a prediction before his death that the Muslims would be divided into seventy three factions! Only one of those factions which would remain steadfast to his ideals until resurrection will be led by him to paradise! Lots of doubts and questions were raised by pagans and the people of QURAISH tribe about the authenticity of the Quran! The disbelievers expressed their rejection saying; "THIS QURAN IS NOTHING BUT A LIE THAT MUHAMMAD HAS INVENTED AND OTHERS HAVE HELPED HIM AT IT AND SOME HAVE EVEN DESCRIBED THE QURAN AS THE "TALES OF THE ANCIENTS (V. 25:4&5)"! Then Allah came forward to defend his Book and his messenger saying (V. 69:38-45); "I SWEAR BY WHATEVER YOU SEE AND BY WHATEVER YOU NOT SEE THAT THIS IS VERILY THE WORD OF AN HONOURED MESSENGER (GABRIEL OR MUHAMMAD) WHICH HE HAS BROUGHT FROM ALLAH. IT IS NOT THE WORD OF A POET! NOR IS IT THE WORD OF A SOOTHSAYER! THIS IS THE REVELATION SENT DOWN FROM THE LORD OF THE MANKIND, JINN AND ALL THAT EXISTS! IF MUHAMMAD HAD FORGED A FALSE SAYING CONCERNING US (ALLAH), WE SURELY WOULD HAVE SEIZED HIM BY HIS RIGHT HAND AND CUT OFF HIS LIFE ARTERY"! The Lord of the mankind must have been disappointed to see that only a small number of the mankind believed in his revelation! Allah, as the "Author" of the Quran found no contradiction in his Book! He asks; " DO THEY (DISBELIEVERS) NOT THEN CONSIDER THE QURAN CAREFULLY? HAD IT BEEN FROM OTHER THAN ALLAH, THEY WOULD SURELY HAVE FOUND THEREIN MANY A COTRADICTION" (V. 4:82)! In verse 5 of surah 32, Allah says; "HE REGULATES EVERY AFFAIR OF THE UNIVERSE AND THEN THE AFFAIR GOES TO HIM IN A DAY, THE SPACE WHEREOF IS A THOUSAND YEARS OF WORLD STANDARD TIME"! But the verse 4 of chapter 70 states; "THE ANGELS AND GABRIEL ASCEND TO HIM (ALLAH) IN A DAY THE MEASURE

WHEREOF IS FIFTY THOUSAND YEARS"! Why Allah and the believers do not find contradictions in the Quran? May I now quote few more verses to highlight the inconsistencies of the sayings of Allah: Verse 4 of chapter 32 states; "ALLAH, IT IS HE WHO HAS CREATED THE HEAVENS AND THE EARTH, AND ALL THAT IS BETWEEN THEM IN SIX DAYS "! Verse 9 of chapter 41 states; "HIM IT IS WHO HAS CREATED THE EARTH IN TWO DAYS" and the next verse (#10) says; "HE BLESSED IT AND MEASURED SUSTENANCE FOR ITS DWELLERS IN FOUR EQUAL DAYS"! Verse 12 of the same chapter states; "THEN HE COMPLETED AND FINISHED FROM THEIR CREATION (AS) SEVEN HEAVENS IN TWO DAYS"! In verse 57 of chapter 40, the Lord of the universe unambiguously says; "THE CREATION OF THE HEAVENS AND THE EARTH IS INDEED GREATER THAN THE CREATION OF MANKIND"! Can anyone make something sensible out of these verses quoted above as to the number of "Days" Allah claims to have taken to create the earth and the heaven and everything between them? In verse 109 of chapter 18 Allah asks Muhammad to say to the mankind that "IF THE SEA WERE INK FOR WRITING THE WORDS OF MY LORD, SURELY, THE SEA WOULD BE EXAUSTED BEFOR THE WORDS OF MY LORD WOULD BE FINISHED, EVEN IF WE BROUGHT ANOTHER SEA LIKE IT FOR ITS AID"! On the same subject, Allah changed his stand in verse 27 of chapter 31 saying; "IF ALL THE TREES ON THE EARTH WERE PENS AND SEVEN SEAS WERE INK, YET THE WORDS OF ALLAH WOULD NOT BE EXAUSTED, VERILY, ALLALH IS ALL-MIGHTY, ALL-WISE"! Yet all-wise followers of Allah see no inconsistencies and contradictions in this "Holy Book" of "Divine" words and wisdom!

QURANIC VERSES ON JIHAD

The literary meaning of Jihad is holy fighting in the cause of Allah or any kind of undertaking aimed at establishing Allah's religion (Islam) and making it "Superior" to all other dogmas and doctrines! The most dangerous proposition of Jihad is that it aims at eliminating all faiths and beliefs, if required, through bloodshed and killing showing no respect to humanity! A Hadith of BUKHARI (Vol. 4, #41) defines Al-Jihad in greater details saying; "Holy fighting in Allah's cause, with full force of numbers and weaponry, is given the utmost importance in Islam and is one of the pillars on which it stands! By Jihad Islam is established, Allah's word is made superior and his religion (Islam) is propagated! By abandoning Jihad Islam is destroyed and the Muslims fall into an inferior position, their honor is lost, their lands are stolen, their rule and authority vanish! Jihad is an obligatory duty in Islam on every Muslim, and he who tries to escape from this duty or does not in his innermost heart wish to fulfill this duty, dies with one of the qualities of a hypocrite"!

Verse 190 of chapter 2 is considered to be the first verse revealed in connection with the Jihad and it says; "FIGHT IN THE WAY OF ALLAH THOSE WHO FIGHT YOU, BUT TRANSGRESS NOT THE LIMIT. TRULY, ALLAH LIKES NOT THE TRANSGRESSORS"! This verse needs to be evaluated in the context of inhuman atrocities being carried out across the world by the Islamic terror groups who claim to be fighting in Allah's behest! Where does Allah set the limits? Sky is the limit? If propagation of a divine ideology involves indiscriminate killing of human beings, it sure does lose its pertinence to humanity! In the next verse Allah spells out his war strategy to protect the sanctuary of Mecca which once belonged to the pagans! Verse 191 of the same chapter states; "AND KILL THEM WHEREVER YOU FIND THEM, AND TURN THEM OUT FROM WHERE THEY HAVE TURNED YOU OUT SINCE POLYTHEISM IS WORSE THAN KILLING"! The pagans used this sanctuary at Mecca as their house of worship where they performed various rituals; sometimes even in naked state going round the squire stone-built house filled with statues of deities and that house is now known as "KABAH"! Both Pagans and the Muslims used this sanctuary as the epicenter of their faiths! Pagans were driven away as Allah directed the Muslims in verse 193 of this chapter: "AND FIGHT THEM UNTIL THERE IS NO MORE FITNAH (DISBELIEF AND WORSHIPPING OF OTHERS ALONG WITH ALLAH)! ALL AND EVERY KIND OF WORSHIP IS FOR ALLAH ALONE"!

Allah has put forward his justification for Jihad in verse 216 of chapter 2 stating; "JIHAD IS ORDAINED FOR YOU (MUSLIMS) THOUGH YOU DISLIKE IT, AND IT MAY BE THAT YOU DISLIKE A THING WHICH IS GOOD FOR YOU. ALLAH KNOWS BUT YOU DO NOT KNOW"! Allah reiterates his position on Jihad again in verse 244 of the same chapter saying; "FIGHT IN THE WAY OF ALLAH AND KNOW THAT ALLAH IS ALL-HEARER AND ALL KNOWER"! Allah, as the Commander-in Chief of Jihad offers amnesty to his General: "THEN FIGHT (O MUHAMMAD) IN THE CAUSE OF ALLAH, YOU ARE NOT TASKED AND WILL NOT BE HELD RESPONSIBLE EXCEPT FOR YOURSELF! INCITE THE BELIEVERS TO FIGHT ALONG WITH YOU! ALLAH WILL RESTRAIN THE EVIL MIGHT OF THE DISBELIEVERS AND ALLAH IS STRONGER IN MIGHT AND STRONGER IN PUNISHING"! Beside temptations of a life in paradise, Allah has extensively used threats of severe punishments as a way of subjugation! Verse 24 of chapter 9 states; "IF YOUR FATHERS, YOUR SONS, YOUR BROTHERS, YOUR WIVES, YOUR KINDRED, THE WEALTH THAT YOU HAVE GAINED, THE COMMERCE IN WHICH YOU FEAR A DECLINE AND DWELLINGS IN WHICH YOU DELIGHT ARE DEARER TO YOU THAN ALLAH AND HIS MESSENGER, AND STRIVING HARD AND FIGHTING JIHAD IN ALLAH'S CAUSE, THAN WAIT UNTIL ALLAH BRINGS ABOUT HIS DECISION (TORMENT)"!

Allah has set some principles, in verse 29 of chapter 9, for undertaking Jihad against the infidels who (1) BELIEVE NOT IN ALLAH (2) NOR IN THE LAST DAY (3) NOR FORBID THAT WHICH HAS BEEN FORBDDEN BY ALLAH AND HIS MESSENGER (4) AND THOSE WHO ACKNOLEDGE NOT THE RELIGION OF TRUTH (ISLAM) AMONG THE PEOPLE OF SCRIPTURES (JEWS AND CHRISTIANS) UNTIL THEY PAY THE JIZYAH (TAX IMPOSED BY MUSLIM RULARS ON NON MUSLINS) WITH WILLING SUBMISSION AND FEEL THEMSELVES SUBDUED"! To the Lord, life of this world is a mere enjoyment and as such he asks his believers in verse 38 & 39 of chapter 9; "WHAT IS THE MATTER WITH YOU, THAT WHEN YOU ARE ASKED TO MARCH FORTH IN THE

CAUSE OF ALLAH (i.e. JIHAD) YOU CLING HEAVILY TO THE EARTH? IF YOU MARCH NOT FORTH, HE WILL PUNISH YOU WITH A PAINFUL TORMENT AND WILL REPLACE YOU BY ANOTHER PEOPLE; AND YOU CANNOT HARM HIM AT ALL"! When enemies are beyond reach, it is difficult to fight against them! So, Allah asks his believers; " FIGHT THOSE OF THE DISBELIEVERS (JEWISH, CHRISTIANS etc.) WHO ARE CLOSE TO YOU AND LET THEM FIND HARSHNESS IN YOU"(V. 9:123)! Allah does not believe in the peaceful co-existence of the Muslims, Jews, Christians and others as close neighbors! Though Allah is in possession of 99% of the total mercy, yet his cruelty against disbelievers knows no bound! Allah in verse 4 of chapter 47 instructs his troops; "WHEN YOU MEET DISBELIEVERS WHILE FIGHTING JIHAD IN ALLAH'S CAUSE, SMITE THEIR NECKS TILL WHEN YOU HAVE KILLED AND WOUNDED MANY OF THEM, THEN BIND A BOND ON THEM TO TAKE THEM AS CAPTIVES! EITHER FREE THEM OR TAKE RANSOM FROM THEM ACCORDING TO WHAT BENEFITS ISLAM! THUS YOU ARE ORDERED BY ALLAH TO CONTINUE IN CARRYING OUT JIHAD AGAINST THE DISBELIEVERS TILL THEY EMBRACE ISLAM"! Allah, in verse 39 of chapter 8 says; "FIGHT THEM UNTIL THERE IS NO MORE DISBELIEF AND POLYTHEISM, AND WORSHIPPING WILL BE ONLY FOR ALLAH IN THE WHOLE OF THE WORLD"!

What has been said in the verses above is a difficult proposition! Allah has decided to send Jesus in place of Muhammad who failed to materialize Allah's dream come true! Muhammad in his own words said; "Surely, the 'Son of Mary' will shortly descend amongst you people" (BUKHARI, Vol. 3, #425)! It is also mentioned by some Islamic religious scholars that Jesus is the one who will rule the mankind with Islamic rules and will be able to do away with disbelief and polytheism since he will not accept any other religion except Islam! For the Jihadists, "ALLAH HAS GOT READY GARDENS (PARADISE) UNDER WHICH RIVERSE FLOW, TO DWELL THEREIN FOREVER. THAT IS THE SUPREME SUCCESS" (V 9:89)! Again verse 78 of chapter 22 states; "STRIVE HARD IN ALLAH'S CAUSE AS YOU OUGHT TO STRIVE WITH SINCERITY AND WITH ALL YOUR EFFORTS THAT HIS NAME SHOULD BE SUPERIOR! HE HAS CHOSEN YOU TO CONVEY HIS MESSAGE OF ISLAMIC MONOTHEISM TO MANKIND BY INVITING THEM TO HIS RELIGION OF ISLAM, AND HE HAS NOT LAID UPON YOU IN RELIGION ANY HARDSHIP"! Muhammad says that "The most beloved religion to Allah is Islamic Monotheism! The religion is very easy and whoever overburdens himself in his religion will not be able to continue in that way. So you should not be extremists"! (BUKHARI, Vol. 1 #38). Islamic Monotheism is very easy in the sense that it allows killing as an easy option! Are the Jihadists not extremists who are fighting in the name of Allah and Muhammad all around the globe?

Jihad is a war of fundamentalism that was started by Muhammad in 7th century in the name of Allah against humanity, freedom and liberty! It is not likely to end until the so-called resurrection! Jihad took a stand against humanity by allowing killing and bloodshed in the name of an unseen, divine entity whom Muhammad named as Allah! There are many faiths which have followed similar spiritual concept and ideology but brutal killing of innocent human beings is unique to Islam! All Islamic terror groups operating across the world find the incitement and inspiration in these Jihadi verses of the Quran!

QURANIC VERSES

AGAINST

THE JEWS AND THE CHRISTIANS

The Quran always refer to the Jews and the Christians as the "People of Scriptures"! Besides propagating Muhammad's radical views, the Quran has chosen to demean Judaism and Christianity as redundant and obsolete theology that said to have been written off by Allah after the arrival of prophet Muhammad! The historical rivalry among these three religions has been the cause of heinous hatred and bloodshed worldwide since their emergence from a tiny enclave of the Middle East! They stem from the same roots and later spread out across the globe! The bitter rivalry is basically concentrated in trying to establish supremacy of their respective sponsors, namely Moses, Jesus and Muhammad! Why Muhammad is so vocal against the followers of his predecessors? Because he claims that he is the one sent as the messenger for the whole of mankind, others were not! The Quran contains many verses that are intended to delegitimize Judaism and Christianity giving fictitious and distorted facts that are augmented by misleading arguments manufactured by a group of Islamic scholars!

Addressing the "Children of Israel", Allah brings a severe allegation against them of breaking away from a deal or the so-called "Covenant" they are said have struck with him (V. 2:63)! Some of the Jews are alleged to have transgressed in the matter of the "SABATH" and Allah said to them; "BE YOU MONKEYS, DESPISED AND REJECTED" (V. 2:65)! Allah has used indecent language against his creation, quite unexpected of him as the "Creator" of the earth and the heavens! When Allah speaks against the disbelievers, he uses language like a common, ordinary person! Muhammad, upon being instructed by Allah in verse 139 of chapter 2 says; "DISPUTE NOT WITH US ABOUT ALLAH WHILE HE IS OUR LORD AND YOUR LORD"! The next verse (2:140) states; "ABRAHAM, ISHMAEL, ISAAC, JACOB AND HIS TWELVE OFFSPRING WERE NEITHER JEWS NOR CHRISTIANS; THEY ALL WERE MUSLIMS"! How could they be Muslims when Muhammad and his revelations were yet to come? Because, to be a Muslim one has to recognize Muhammad as the messenger for all mankind and must love him more than their fathers, children and mankind? Author of the Quran has displayed his mistrust on the disbelievers in a number of verses! "O PEOPLE OF THE SCRIPTURE (JEWS AND CHRISTIANS): WHY DO YOU MIX TRUTH WITH FALSEHOOD AND CONCEAL THE TRUTH WHILE YOU KNOW" (V. 3:71)! Conversely the disbelievers bring the same allegation against the Muslims! Who can verify the truth of the matter? Who is right and who is wrong? Allah is totally against the disbelievers! He warns his believers in verse 118 of chapter 3 saying in clear terms that; "O YOU WHO BELIEVE! TAKE NOT AS YOUR ADVISORS, CONSULTANTS, PROTECTORS, HELPERS, FRIENDS THOSE OUTSIDE YOUR RELIGION (PAGANS, JEWS, CHRISTIANS) SINCE THEY WILL NOT FAIL TO DO THEIR BEST TO CORRUPT YOU, THEY DESIRE TO HARM YOU SEVERELY. HATRED HAS ALREADY APPEARED FROM THEIR MOUTHS, BUT WHAT THEIR BREASTS CONCEAL IS FAR WORSE"! Considering the global geopolitical reality, can any Muslim country specially the monarchies in and around the Middle East follow what is said by Allah in the above verse? Allah calls himself the "WALI" or the Protector of the believers, but the reality on the ground suggests otherwise! Those nations seek protection from the non-Muslim countries on both sides of the Atlantic! It also implies that these monarchs themselves are defying the Allah's verses! They have already realized the fact that their protection and survival do not come from heavens as promised! Probably, Palestinians are the ones paying heaviest price for relying on Allah's strategy! Allah heard the Jews saying; "TRULY, ALLAH IS POOR AND WE ARE RICH" (V. 3:181)! He has recorded what the Jews said and their killing of the prophet unjustly! When the time comes, Allah will say to them; "TASTE YOU THE TORMENT OF THE BURNING FIRE"! Allah is displeased with the Jews because they brought a "False" charge against Mary that she had committed illegal sexual intercourse! Also he is annoyed with the Jews for claiming to have killed the "Son of Mary"! So, to dispel all these assertions of the Jews, "ALLAH RAISED JESUS UP UNTO HIMSELF (WITH HIS BODY AND SOUL) AND HE IS IN THE HEAVENS" (V. 4:158)! In verse 159 of chapter 4, the Lord demands that all Jews and Christians must believe in Jesus as the "messenger" of Allah before their death! "ON THE DAY OF RESURRECTION JESUS WILL BE A WITNESS AGAINST THEM"! Allah has accused the people of scripture of hiding the truth saying; "O PEOPLE OF SCRIPTUR! NOW HAS COME TO YOU OUR MESSENGER (MUHAMMAD) EXPLAINING TO YOU MUCH OF THAT WHICH YOU USED TO HIDE (V. 5:15)! A footnote related to this verse explains that the Jews were ordered in the Torah to follow prophet Muhammad when he would come as a messenger for all mankind! What about Jesus? Why he has been ignored? After Moses, it was Jesus who came to the people of Israel! In verse 14 of chapter 5 Allah says; "WE TOOK THEIR COVENANT WHO CALL THEMSELVES CHRISTIANS, BUT THEY ABANDONED A GOOD PART OF THE MESSAGE THAT WAS SENT TO THEM! SO WE PLANTED AMONGST THEM ENMITY AND HATRED TILL THE DAY OF RESURRECTION"! So how can anybody blame the merciful "Creator"? Allah brought another charge against the children of Israel (Jews) in verse 13 of chapter 5 saying; 'BECAUSE OF THEIR BREACH OF THEIR COVENANT, WE (ALLAH) CURSED THEM AND MADE THEIR HEARTS GROW HARD. THEY CHANGED THE WORDS FROM THEIR RIGHT PLACES AND HAVE ABANDONED A GOOD PART OF THE MESSAGE THAT WAS SENT TO THEM"! He has rightly planted enmity and hatred among his adversaries! The defenders of Allah and Islam tried to justify Lord's action in an attached footnote saying; "The Christians were ordered in the Gospel to follow prophet Muhammad when he would come as a messenger of Allah to all mankind"! This sort of reprisal is not expected of a "Creator" who has planted 99% of the mercy in himself! In chapter 51 Allah again reminds his believers not to take Jews and the Christians as AULIYA (friends, protector, helpers) since they take your religion (Islam) as a mockery and fun! Their protector or helper is none other than Allah! Dishonesty on the part of the "author" of the Quran is also evident in the verse 69 of Ch. 5! As per the original text, the verse states; "SURELY THOSE WHO BELIEVE (IN THE ONENESS OF ALLAH, HIS MESSENGER MUHAMMAD AND ALL THAT WAS REVEALED TO HIM FROM ALLAH) AND THOSE WHO ARE THE JEWS AND THE SABIANS AND THE CHRISTIANS-----WHOVER BELIEVED IN THE LORD AND THE LAST DAY, AND WORKED RIGHTOUSNESS, ON THEM SHALL BE NO FEAR NOR SHALL THEY GRIEVE"! The translators, surely with a cunning intent, inserted some words within the brackets in that verse at their own accord! These words are not part of the Arabic text of the Quran! This is not the end of the tempering of the Quran and a related footnote says that this verse (i.e. 5:69) should not be misinterpreted by the readers as provision of this verse has been abrogated by verse 85 of Ch. 3

which says; "WHOEVER SEEKS A RELIGION OTHER THAN ISLAM, IT WILL NOT BE ACCEPTED OF HIM"! This verse sums up the entire purpose of the Quran and why should Allah make a mistake about this? Does it not reinforce the doubt on revelation? How can a provision of the present verse can be annulled or abrogated by a verse of the previous chapter? The abrogation has taken place not by Allah himself but by the authority of an Islamic expert known as IBN ABBAS (TAFSIR AL-TABARI)! In verses 59 and 60 of chapter 5, Allah asks Muhammad to say to the Jews and Christians; "Do you criticize us for no other reason than that we believe in Allah and the revelation"? You are rebellious and disobedient to Allah! He then spells out the recompense for the Jews who incurred Allah's curse and wrath including some Jews whom Allah transformed into monkeys and swine as they worshipped false deities! Those will be worse in rank on the Day of Resurrection in Hellfire"! Darwin said we gradually transformed from monkeys to humans but Allah did the opposite! Science and religion always oppose each other! Allah again in verse 65 of chapter 5 says, if the people of scriptures (Jews and Christians) had believed in Muhammad; "WE WOULD INDEED HAVE EXPIATED FROM THEM THEIR SINS AND ADMITTED THEM TO GARDENS OF PLEASURE IN PARADISE"! In this chapter Allah defines disbelievers as those who think "ALLAH IS THE THIRD OF THE TRINITY"! He claims that the Messiah (Jesus)was no more than a messenger and his mother Mary was a believer in Allah! "THEY BOTH USED TO EAT FOOD LIKE ANY OTHER HUMAN BEING WHEREAS ALLAH DOES NOT EAT"! "Allah does not eat", this assertion does not establish his existence anyway! In the Quran, Allah has always maintained his position that people of scripture (the Jews and Christians) are enemies to his believers! But suddenly he changed his stance once again and said; "THE JEWS ARE THE STRONGEST ENEMY TO THE MUSLIMS AND THOSE WHO ARE CHRISTIANS ARE NEAREST IN LOVE TO THE MUSLIMS"! Why? "BECAUSE AMONGST THEM ARE PRIESTS AND MONKS, AND THEY ARE NOT PROUD" (V. 5:82)! The Monks and Priests are not proud but many of them commit immoral sexual offences with children under their custody inside the holy enclave! Even in the recent past brutal killings of thousands of minors by the church administration have been reported! Yet the "Love" is not lost between Allah and the Christians? Will this love last until the second arrival of Jesus to rule the world by Islamic Sharia Law? Allah's sense of humor is not to be ignored! To punish the Jews, Allah asks them not to eat fat; "WE FORBADE

EVERY ANIMAL WITH DIVIDED HOOF, AND WE FORBADE THEM THE FAT OF THE OX AND THE SHEEP EXCEPT WHAT ADHERES TO THEIR BACKS OR THEIR ENTRAILS, OR IS MIXED UP WITH A BONE. THUS WE RECOMPENSED THEM FOR THEIR REBELLION AND COMMITTING CRIMES LIKE MURDERING OF THE PROPHETS AND EATING OF USURY! AND VERILY WE ARE TRUTHFUL" (Verse 146 of chapter 6)! Are these punishments proportional to the crime committed? The Jews also killed (Crucified) Jesus! For killing the prophets, Allah says he forbade the Jews from eating the fat of the ox and sheep! However, Allah is the "Best of Judges"! Allah claims he alone created the earth and the heavens and as such it is only he who deserves to be worshiped! Verse 31 of chapter 9 states; "THE JEWS AND THE CHRISTIANS TOOK THEIR RABBIS AND THEIR MONKS TO BE THEIR LORDS BESIDES ALLAH AND THEY ALSO TOOK MESSIAH, THE 'SON OF MARRY' AS THEIR LORD WHILE THEY WERE COMMANDED IN THE TORAH AND GOSPEL TO WORSHIP NONE BUT ALLAH "! So, they do not have the right to lead a life in Allah's world unless they all convert to Islam! Some of the Arabian nations have made friendly relations with the Jewish state of Israel despite being warned by Allah in verse 13 of chapter 60; "O YOU WHO BELIEVE! TAKE NOT AS FRIENDS THE PEOPLE (i.e. THE JEWS) WHO INCURRED THE WRATH OF ALLAH"! In verse 197 of chapter 26 Allah questions the Jews (Children of Israel) saying; "IS IT NOT A SIGN TO THEM THAT THEIR LEARNED SCHOLAR ABULLAH BIN SALAM (THE THEN PROMINENT JEWISH LEADER) EMBRACED ISLAM"? There is no other source to verify this claim whether the said Jewish scholar had really embraced Islam or not! However, there is an interesting story narrated in the footnote of V. 66 of chapter 5, related to the story of ABULLAH's conversion! The story says; following the arrival of Muhammad in Medina, Abdullah bin Salam approached Muhammad with an intention to convert to Islam if Muhammad is able to answer three questions to his satisfaction! Q. # 1. What is the first sign of "The Hour" (Dooms day)? Muhammad's reply to this question was; "It will be a fire that will collect or gather the people from the east to the west"! Q.#2. What is the first food which the people of paradise will eat? Answering this question, Muhammad said; "The first food to be served to the people of paradise will be the caudate lobe of the fish lever"! Q.#3. Why does a child attract the similarity to his father or to his mother? In reply to this last question the prophet said; "If the man's discharge precedes the woman's discharge, the child attracts the similarity to the man, and if the woman's discharge precedes the man's, then the child attracts the similarity to the woman"! If this is Islamic science, we have nothing to say as it has come down from none other than Allah! If otherwise, it got to be verified whether the child's similarities have anything to do with the timing of the parents sexual discharge?

How did Muhammad know the answers to all of those question? He knew them through Gabriel! No sooner the questions were asked, Allah immediately sent the answers to Muhammad from heaven! In his own words; "Gabriel has just now informed me of that"! But Abdullah, the Jewish scholar who was to be converted to Islam, expressed his resentment saying; "Gabriel is the enemy of the Jews from amongst the angels"! After being satisfied with the answers he received from Muhammad, Abdullah decided to become a Muslim and said; "I testify that none has the right to be worshipped but Allah and that you (Muhammad) are the messenger of Allah"! But fear of reprisal and backlash from his Jewish friends was going through his mind and then he said; "O Allah's messenger! Jews make such lie as make one astonished, so please ask them about me before they know about my conversion to Islam"! Accordingly Muhammad asked some Jews about Abdullah and all of them characterized him as one of the most superior of their community! Then Muhammad asked them again about their opinion on Abdullah's decision to become a Muslim! The reply from the Jews was that; "May Allah protect him from that"! When Abdullah himself testified that he has converted to Islam then their comment was; "He is the most wicked amongst us"! Abdullah finally said; "O Muhammad, it is this that I was afraid of"! Muslim scholars claim that the religion before Allah is Islam and it means willing submission to the Lord and he has implanted his own religion in innate, with which all humans are equipped! It implies that Mr. Abdullah was born as a Muslim then he converted to Judaism and again reverted to Islam! The humanity, standing on a cross road, is puzzled by the zigzag path to paradise! Had there been a "Creator" of the universe, there would have been a paradise with a straight path leading to it! Even the continuous expansion of the universe, which he claims to have "Created", has gone out of his control and he seems unable to bring that to a halt! How big a universe the Lord needs to cultivate a mankind in line with the so-called "Anthropic Principle"? This natural phenomenon itself negates existence of any "Creator"!

Out of many, the most serious charge Allah brought against the Jews is that they accused Mary of being unchaste! The Jews have been unfairly treated! In fact it was Allah's ambiguous methodology of making Mary conceive Jesus that gave birth to confusion! Why then Allah created a wife (Eve) for Adam if it was possible to create man without mating?

DR. ABDULLAH AL-KAHTANY, an eminent Saudi scholar in Islamic theology, quotes Muhammad as saying; "Every newborn child is born on the innate nature of Islam"! Who then created the Christianity and the Judaism? Quran claims nothing can happen in the "Kingdom" of Allah without his "Will"!

CONCLUSION

How long do we live? As long as the heart continues to beat or as long as we are able to breathe! This is true for every creature on earth! Who controls and determines span of our life? One may die in his mother's womb or may live up to hundred years! From the very inception of civilization people have been nourishing the idea that there is "Someone" living in the heaven who gives life and takes it at his will! With the passage of time this notion has lost its luster! Man's destiny, like all creatures on earth, is unambiguously regulated by the nature; a system that does not seem to be smart or intelligent as human beings! This natural system is unlikely to harbor an intelligent or interactive "Divine Creator"! Though the system itself is not intelligent but it is capable of creating intelligent beings! It is evident from the fact that the nature could not have taken more than four billion years to initiate creation of life at its will at a predetermined time-table on this planet had it been so smart or intelligent! Our ancestors, who had gone through the gradual transformation from four-footed animals to twine-legged homo sapiens, were still not in a position to think of a creation without a "Creator"! Even the Kings and the Popes used to claim that their right to rule over the commons stem from a "King of the Universe"! Some scientists of the modern era also had this notion that their ability to understand laws of nature come from an unseen "Omnipotent" living in the heaven! What is the point scrambling over existence of a "Creator" given the fact that we have not been able to find another planet with an intelligent civilization like ours in this vast universe? Existence of a Creator, whether real or unreal, is not going to impact our way of life in any way nor will it be able to change the course of the Universe! He does not respond to our needs! It seems an absurd thinking that the entire universe was created to incubate only one mankind!

Large or small, every religion revolves around an assumed "Creator"! If the existence of that creator hangs in the balance, than how can we relate our everyday affairs with him? Believing in something must be relevant to reality! We, as humans, cannot forget the fact that there exists a great rift between faith and facts, truth and untruth! In terms of peace and prosperity, religions have done more harm than good to the mankind! Religious acrimonies have divided the humanity into numerous factions that constantly confront each other as enemies! A life hereafter, with lucrative divine dividends, is what motivates a great majority of humans to undertake a race to reach an unspecified destination in the heavens! Which God has ever responded to our needs? Humanity have suffered innumerable debacles; sometimes manmade, sometimes as an "Act of God" since its beginning but it had never seen any divine intervention to alleviate sufferings! His silence speaks a volume and indicates nothing but a vacuum void of substance! A mankind without religion would have lived a better life, leaving aside all worries about an uncertain eternity!

As far as human rights or freedom of speech is concerned, none has the right to stop anyone from saying, believing and practicing any form of faiths he or she likes! At the same time there is no harm to rethink about what we do or what we don't! Nothing deserves to be taken for guaranteed as some of our ancestors did in the past! The religion is not an essential part of life of any other creatures save the humans! Dogmatism is the product of darkness of the past! What does future hold for mankind should not be judged by what happened in the past nor it is to be established on weird hypothesis! We do not have to inherit everything of the past! Intelligence does not grow on the ground nor does it come down from the sky! It is the gradual development of faculty and intellect that should guide the mankind to the end! Revelations from the heavens have no relevance to life both here and hereafter!

THE END

BIBLIOGRAPHY

Translation of the meanings of "THE NOBLE QUR'AN" By Dr. MUHAMMAD TAKI-UD-DIN AL-HILALI and Dr. MUHAMMAD MUHSIN KHAN of Islamic University, Al-Medina. K.S.A.

ISLAMIC RELIEF. Islamic publication, CA, U.S.A.

THE HOLY PROPHET MUHAMMAD By Dr. M.H. DURRANI, Pakistan.

THE TRUTH ABOUT THE ORIGINAL SIN By Dr. ABDULLAH AL-KAHTANY, K.S.A.

THE TRUTH ABOUT JESUS By Dr. MANEH HAMMAD AL-JOHANI, K.S.A.

T.S. ELIOT Edited By Dr. S. P. Sharma, New Delhi, India.

THE MACMILLAN HANDBOOK OF ENGLISH By JOHN M. KIERZEK and WALKER GIBSON". New York, U.S.A.

A HISTORY OF ENGLISH LITERATURE By B.P. CHAWDHURY, NEW DELHI, INDIA.

A BRIEF HISTORY OF TIME by STEPHEN W. HAWKING, Cambridge, England.

THE HISTORY OF THE QURANIC TEXT FROM REVELATION TO COMPILATION By prop. M.M. AZAMI. U.K. Islamic study.

GLOSSARY

1. ABLUTION: Washing different parts of the body with water as part of the preparation for prayers! If water is not available, one may perform what is known as TAYAMMUM i.e. rubbing face and hands with clean earth!

2. AHMAD: According to the Quran this is one of the five names of Muhammad! Jesus is said to have forecasted in his scriptures about arrival of Ahmad (Muhammad) as the last messenger for mankind!

3. AHRUF: The first compilation of the Quran is said to have taken place in seven AHRUF or "Modes" and those were the most common Arabic dialects in which Allah permitted Muhammad to recite the Quran!!

4. AL-BUKHARI: A prominent authority on Hadith literature.

5. AL-BAIT-AL-MA'MUR: This is the name of Allah's house over "Seven Heavens", said to be located exactly parallel to the KABAH at Mecca!

6. AD-DAHR: It means Time but Allah also says; "I am AD-DAHR" meaning I am the Creator of Time, and I manage the affairs of all creation including time!

7. ALIF, LAM, MIM: These are Arabic alphabets used by Allah as "Miracles" of the Quran and none but he alone knows their meanings!

8. ALLAH: This word is the Arabic equivalent of the "Creator" and the "Lord" of the universe. He has ninety nine names and RABB is the frequently used name which, according to the Islamic experts, has no proper equivalent in English language!

9. AL-LAUGH-AL-MAHFUZ: This is the mother book of the Quran also known as the "Book of Decree" held with Allah over Seven Heavens! All affairs and ordainments with regards to the entire universe are recorded in this book!

10. ALLAHU-AKBAR: It means Allah is the most great. It is mandatory for all believers to begin prayers and other Islamic rituals with these words!

11. AR-RA'D: It literally means "Thunder" that glorifies and praises Allah! But it is also the name of an angel in charge of clouds who drives them to different places as ordered by Allah!

12. AR- RUKYAH: Recitation of some verses of the Quran as a means of curing diseases! After the recitation, the reciter blows his breath with saliva over the body parts of the sick persons!

13. ASHRAFUL MUKHLUKAT: The best of creation meaning the human beings.

14. ASTRONOMICAL UNIT (AU): This is the distance between the earth and the sun which is equal to 150 million Km.

15. BIG BANG: A subatomic particle said to have originated the creation of the universe about fourteen billion years ago with an enormous explosion releasing huge amount of energy!

16. BIG CRUNCH: A Singularity condition that is likely to happen if the universe converges back into a tiny dot!

17. BISMILLAH: This is the first word of the Quran which means "In the name of Allah"!

18. BLACK HOLE: An event of Space-Time where gravitational force is so strong that nothing, not even light, can come out of it!

19. BURAQ: An animal bigger than a donkey and smaller than a horse! Riding on this animal Muhammad and Gabriel ascended to the heavens to meet with Allah!

20. DHIKR: This is another name of the Quran! Allah says in verse 9 of Surah 15: Verily, we, it is we, who have sent down the DHIKR!

21. HADITH: Sayings or statements of Prophet Muhammad relating to Islamic ways and acts of worship that are accepted as a model to be followed by the Muslims! Unfortunately these Hadiths are originated from several schools of thoughts that often contradict one another!

22. HIRA: This is a cave in a mountain near Mecca. Muhammad, while meditating in this cave, is said to have received the revelations from Allah through angel Gabriel!

23. HOLY GRAIL: Jesus is said to have taken his last supper on this Grail! This Holy Grail is also famous for the quest undertaken by the heroes in Arthurian romance!

24. HUR: Very fair females created by Allah but not from the offspring of Adam! Their bone marrow will be visible from outside because of excessive beauty! They will have their hymens intact as no man or Jinn ever had sex with them! They will have no menses, urine, stools etc.! These HURS will be married to the male dwellers of the paradise! Each dweller will have two HURS as their wives!

25. IBLIS: Satan's name. He is called SHAITAN in Arabic!

26. INJEEL: It is the Arabic name of Gospel!

27. INSHALLAH: If Allah is willing.

28. ISRAFEEL: He is the angel entrusted with the task of blowing the horn as ordered by Allah when the "Dooms Day" is set to begin!

29. ISHWAR: Hindi name of God!

30. JIHAD: Holy fighting in the name of Allah with full force of numbers and weaponry! It is given the utmost importance in Islam and is one of its pillars! By Jihad Islam is established!

31. JINN: An invisible creation created by Allah from smokeless flame of "Fire"! The verses revealed to Muhammad also apply to the Jinn! After listening to the recitation of the Quran some of the Jinn are said have accepted Islamic monotheism!

32. KABAH: A square, stone-build house inside Mecca mosque complex towards which all Muslims must face while praying! During Hajj, the pilgrims have to go round this House dressed in white which the pagans in pre-Islamic days used to do in naked state! Allah`s palace over Seventh Heaven is said to be located in parallel to this building!

33. KHALIFA: This is an Arabic term used for the Islamic rulers and Caliph is its synonym.

34. KHODA: Most Muslims in the Indian sub-continent use this word to mean Allah, God or the Lord!

35. LAZARUS: Raised by Christ from the dead!

36. LIGHT YEAR: It is the distance travelled by light in one year at a speed of 300 million meters per second.

37. LOTE-TREE: Muhammad was shown this "Tree" when he paid a visit to Allah! It is said to be located at the utmost boundary over the seventh heaven! Four rivers originate at its root: two are hidden and the other two are the Nile and the Euphrates!

38. MAQAM-MAHMUD: The best and the highest place in paradise Allah has built only for Muhammad!

39. MAULA: Lord, or Master or protector. It is widely used in India and its surrounding regions to mean the "Creator" specially in devotional songs and literature.

40. MUTAH: A temporary marriage allowed in Islam to satisfy sexual needs when one is away from home! Though some Islamists claim it to have been abrogated but in effect it is still in practice in many parts of the Middle East!

41. NIGHT OF AL-QADR: The night of decree! Revelation of the Quran is said have taken place at this night! This night is decreed every matter of ordainments including the matter of deaths, births, provisions, calamities for the whole coming year!

42. PROXIMA CENTAURI: Nearest star from the earth. It takes light more than four years to travel from that star to the earth at a speed of 300 million meter per second!

43. QURAISH: A famous tribe in pre-Islamic Arabia. Prophet Muhammad belonged to this tribe. The Quran is said to have been revealed in "QURAISH" dialect!

44. RESTING PLACE: Allah claims to have "Created" this Earth as a Resting Place for mankind!

45. SEVEN HEAVENS: After creating the Earth, Allah rose towards the heaven when it was all smoke! Out of that smoke he created Seven Heavens one over the other! He then built a Palace for himself above the Seventh Heaven! All of the Seven Heavens are currently occupied by prominent prophets starting from Adam to Jesus! Muhammad met them during his visit to "Seven Heavens"!

46. SHIRK: Worshipping any other Gods or deities besides Allah!

47. SPACE-TIME: Present scientific view does not treat Space and Time as independent quantities! What they jointly form is called the "Space-Time"! Time adds itself as the fourth dimension to the commonly known three dimensions of the space. Four dimensional calculation makes it more precise to pin point an event in space.

48. SURAH: Division of verses also known as chapters. The Quran is divided into 114 Surah. The shortest Surah has only 3 verses and while the longest has 286!

49. TALAK: It means Divorce. The Quran has a chapter by this name in which Allah assures Muhammad of providing better wives if he divorces all of his present wives for being disloyal to him! Besides some other formalities, this word has to be uttered loudly three times for divorce to take effect!

50. TAMITH: It means opening of women's hymens with sexual intercourse! Two such chaste wives with intact hymens will be provided to each of the dweller of the paradise!

51. THRONE: In Arabic it is called "ISTAWA". After creating the earth and the heaven, Allah rose over the "Throne"! Before take-off, the "Throne" was on "Water"! Eight angels will bear that "Throne" of the Lord above them on the Dooms Day!

52. UHUD: A mountain near Medina. At its foot took place a battle, between the followers of Muhammad and their enemies, known as the battle of UHUD. Allah initially proposed to help Muslims with three thousand angels and later he increased that to five thousand angels having marks of distinction! Yet forces of Muhammad had to suffer a humiliating defeat as many of his soldiers fled the battle field! Allah then blamed the Satan for the defeat!

53. VAGHWAN: This word is mostly used by the non-Muslims, who follow traditional religions, to mean the "Creator"!

54. VERSE: Verses of the Quran are not like those of the epic poems! First of all they are "Divine" and "Authored" by none other than Allah himself! A single verse may be composed of a single Arabic alphabet! For example NUN, SAD, ALIF, LAM, MIM etc. These Arabic letters make no sense to any one of the mankind including Muhammad! Those alphabets are also known as the "Miracles" of the Quran! Their meanings are known to Allah, the "Author" only!

55. WALI: Arabic word for "Protector". This word has been used a number of times in the Quran to describe Allah as the protector of those who believe in him, his messengers and the Day of Judgment!

56. ZAMZAM: A well inside the grant mosque complex at Mecca believed to have been created as a source of water by divine blessing! Pilgrims drink its water as an antidote against diseases! Many pilgrims coming from distant places carry water of this well back home to use it as medications!